Popular Television in Eastern Europe During and Since Socialism

Routledge Advances in Internationalizing Media Studies

EDITED BY DAYA THUSSU, *University of Westminster*

1 **Media Consumption and Everyday Life in Asia**
Edited by Youna Kim

2 **Internationalizing Internet Studies**
Beyond Anglophone Paradigms
Edited by Gerard Goggin and Mark McLelland

3 **Iranian Media**
The Paradox of Modernity
Gholam Khiabany

4 **Media Globalization and the Discovery Channel Networks**
Ole J. Mjos

5 **Audience Studies**
A Japanese Perspective
Toshie Takahashi

6 **Global Media Ecologies**
Networked Production in Film and Television
Doris Baltruschat

7 **Music, Social Media and Global Mobility**
MySpace, Facebook, YouTube
Ole J. Mjøs

8 **Media Power and Democratization in Brazil**
TV Globo and the Dilemmas of Political Accountability
Mauro P. Porto

9 **Popular Television in Eastern Europe During and Since Socialism**
Edited by Timothy Havens, Anikó Imre, and Katalin Lustyik

Popular Television in Eastern Europe During and Since Socialism

Edited by Timothy Havens, Anikó Imre, and Katalin Lustyik

NEW YORK AND LONDON

First published 2013
by Routledge
711 Third Avenue, New York, NY 10017

Simultaneously published in the UK
by Routledge
2 Park Square, Milton Park, Abingdon, Oxfordshire OX14 4RN

First issued in paperback 2015

Routledge is an imprint of the Taylor & Francis Group,
an informa business

© 2013 Taylor & Francis

The right of the editors to be identified as the author of the editorial
material, and of the authors for their individual chapters, has been asserted
in accordance with sections 77 and 78 of the Copyright, Designs and
Patents Act 1988.

All rights reserved. No part of this book may be reprinted or reproduced or
utilised in any form or by any electronic, mechanical, or other means, now
known or hereafter invented, including photocopying and recording, or in
any information storage or retrieval system, without permission in writing
from the publishers.

Trademark Notice: Product or corporate names may be trademarks or
registered trademarks, and are used only for identification and explanation
without intent to infringe.

Library of Congress Cataloging-in-Publication Data
  Popular television in Eastern Europe during and since socialism / edited
by Timothy Havens, Anikó Imre and Kati Lustyik.
      p. cm. — (Routledge advances in internationalizing media studies)
  Includes bibliographical references and index.
  1. Television broadcasting—Social aspects—Europe, Eastern.
  2. Television broadcasting—Europe, Eastern.—History—20th century.
  3. Television programs—Europe, Eastern. 4. Culture diffusion—
Europe, Eastern. I. Imre, Anikó. II. Havens, Timothy. III. Lustyik,
Kati.
  PN1992.3.E8P67 2012
  791.450947—dc23
  2012013786

ISBN 13: 978-1-138-89156-2 (pbk)
ISBN 13: 978-0-4158-9248-3 (hbk)

Typeset in Sabon
by IBT Global.

Contents

List of Figures and Tables   ix

Introduction   1
TIMOTHY HAVENS, ANIKÓ IMRE, AND KATALIN LUSTYIK

PART I
Popular Television in Socialist Times

1   Television Entertainment in Socialist Eastern Europe:
Between Cold War Politics and Global Developments   13
SABINA MIHELJ

2   Adventures in Early Socialist Television Edutainment   30
ANIKÓ IMRE

3   Television in the Age of (Post-)Communism:
The Case of Romania   47
DANA MUSTATA

4   The Carnival of the Absurd: Stanisław Bareja's
Alternatywy 4 and Polish Television in the 1980s   65
DOROTA OSTROWSKA

5   An Evening with Friends and Enemies:
Political Indoctrination in Popular East German Family Series   81
KATJA KOCHANOWSKI, SASCHA TRÜLTZSCH AND REINHOLD VIEHOFF

vi   *Contents*

PART II
Commercial Globalization and Eastern European TV

6   From a Socialist Endeavor to a Commercial Enterprise:
    Children's Television in East-Central Europe   105
    KATALIN LUSTYIK

7   Intra-European Media Imperialism: Hungarian Program
    Imports and the Television Without Frontiers Directive   123
    TIMOTHY HAVENS, EVELYN BOTTANDO AND MATTHEW S. THATCHER

8   To Be Romanian in Post-Communist Romania:
    Entertainment Television and Patriotism in Popular Discourse   141
    ADINA SCHNEEWEIS

9   Post-Transitional Continuity and Change:
    Polish Broadcasting Flow and American TV Series   159
    SYLWIA SZOSTAK

PART III
Television and National Identity on Europe's Edges

10 Big Brothers and Little Brothers: National Identity in
    Recent Romanian Adaptations of Global Television Formats   177
    ALICE BARDAN

11 The Way We Applauded: How Popular Culture Stimulates
    Collective Memory of the Socialist Past in Czechoslovakia—
    the Case of the Television Serial *Vyprávěj* and its Viewers   199
    IRENA CARPENTIER REIFOVÁ, KATEŘINA GILLÁROVÁ AND RADIM HLADÍK

12 Coy Utopia: Politics in the First Hungarian TV Soap   222
    FERENC HAMMER

13 Why Must Roma Minorities be Always Seen on the Stage and
    Never in the Audience? Children's Opinions of Reality Roma TV   241
    ANNABEL TREMLETT

Contents vii

14 Racing for the Audience: National Identity, Public
TV and the Roma in Post-Socialist Slovenia 259
KSENIJA VIDMAR-HORVAT

Contributors 275
Index 281

Figures and Tables

FIGURES

4.1	Different faces of Anioł the Janitor.	77
4.2	Fandom of *Alternatywy 4*.	78
5.1	The Captain with his white uniform is arguing with the corrupt and suspicious officer of the capitalistic developing country. (Source: Screenshot/German Broadcasting Archive Potsdam/Zur See/ Episode 4/ Timecode 00:20:49.)	89
5.2	The flag of Eastern Germany in Cuba side-by-side with the 'Viva Cuba' Slogan—a visual image of the deep friendship between the two countries. (Source: Screenshot/German Broadcasting Archive Potsdam/Zur See/ Episode 9/ Timecode 00:30:35.)	90
5.3	Among the family pictures of a Cuban working class family there is a portrait of Ernesto Che Guevara. The adored Revolutionist is a universal socialist hero and part of the family. (Source: Screenshot/German Broadcasting Archive Potsdam/Treffpunkt Flughafen/ Episode 2/ Timecode 00:16:55.)	95
7.1	Average minutes of German imports per day.	131
7.2	Percentage change in European import distribution for selected countries, 1980s vs. 2000s	133
7.3	Import percentages by region, 1980s v 2000s.	134
7.4	Breakdown of German imports by genre, 1980s vs. 2000s.	135
7.5	Breakdown of Italian imports by genre, 1980s vs. 2000s.	136
9.1	TVP1 primetime schedule, September 18–24, 1998 (*Tele Tydzień*, 1998).	162
9.2	Polsat primetime schedule, September 18–24, 1998 (*Tele Tydzień*, 1998).	168
10.1	Miss Country Girl promo.	188
10.2	Map of Romania in Miss Country Girl.	188
10.3	Miss Country Girl contest.	189

x   *Figures and Tables*

11.1   208

11.2   The scene from the second sample used in the focus groups. Jarka reads her poem at the International Women's Day meeting to glorify socialist womanhood.   209

11.3   The scene from the third sample used in the focus groups. The Dvořák family and their friends listen with astonishment to the radio announcement about the self-burning act of the student Jan Palach in 1969.   210

11.4   The scene from the first video sample used in the focus groups. Comrade Karpíšek (left) recruits Mr. Dvořák (right) to become a member of the Communist Party.   215

TABLES

1.1   Diffusion of TV Sets: Number of Inhabitants Per TV Set   22

6.1   Television Programs Targeting Minors (Ages: 4–17) on MTV1 (and Total Number of Television Programs) between 1986 and 1998   108

6.2   Television Programs Targeting Minors (Ages: 4–17) between 1986 and 2001 in Hungary on the Five Main Broadcasting Channels: MTV1, MTV2 and Duna TV (Launched in 1993) and Privately-owned RTL Klub and TV2 (Both Launched in 1997) 110

6.3   Percentage of Television Programs Targeting Minors (Ages: 4–17) Between 1986 and 2001 on the Five Main Television Channels in Hungary (MTV1, MTV2, Duna TV, RTL-Klub and TV2)   110

6.4   Television Programs Targeting Minors (Ages: 4–17) by Genre in 2001 (N=399) on the Five Main Television Channels in Hungary (MTV1, MTV2, Duna TV, RTL-Klub and TV2)   111

6.5   The 10 Most Popular Television Programs Among Minors (Ages: 4–17) in October 2000 on the Five Main Hungarian Broadcast Channels (MTV1, MTV2, Duna TV, RTL-Klub and TV2)   112

6.6   Nickelodeon Hungary Program Schedule (June 6, 2011, 4 am–9 pm)   114

6.7   Minimax Hungary Sample Program Schedule Listed by Origin of Production (April 30, 2010, Friday)   115

6.8   Children's Television Channels Available in Hungary (March, 2011)   117

7.1   Comparison of Import Data for 1980s and 2000s   129

7.2	Percentage of Total Hungarian Imports for Selected Countries, 1980s and 2000s	130
7.3	European Import Percentages by Nation, 1980s and 2000s	132
7.4	Percentage of European Imports by Selected Genres and Channels, 2000s	136
7.5	Percentage of Imports by Region at all Broadcasters, 2000s	137
8.1	Frequency and Percentages of Themes at *Garantat 100%*	148
13.1	Children's Reactions to the TV Show Győzike	246

Introduction

Timothy Havens, Anikó Imre and Katalin Lustyik

The three of us met serendipitously at back-to-back academic conferences in Budapest and Amsterdam in the summer of 2009, where the idea for this collection of essays first developed. At "Beyond East and West: Two Decades of Media Transformation After the Fall of Communism" in Budapest, we gathered frequently between sessions, talking excitedly about papers on Eastern European popular television in a conference otherwise largely devoted to journalism, democratic theory and communications policy. A week later, at the "Ends of Television" conference in Amsterdam, we found ourselves equally excited about several papers on Eastern European television, in a conference devoted mainly to Western European and American case studies, theories and concerns.

The quantity and quality of work on popular television in Eastern Europe that we saw at these two conferences convinced us of the need for an anthology such as *Popular Television in Eastern Europe During and Since Socialism*. Not only did we believe that television scholarship in the region had reached a critical mass that warranted its own site for collecting and reflecting upon issues that cut across the former Eastern bloc nations; we also felt that such a volume might spotlight, nurture and reclaim Eastern European television studies from the margins of both television studies and Eastern European media studies. As an intellectual endeavor, Eastern European television studies suffers from the Western nature of most television scholarship and theory, while the field of Eastern European media studies almost exclusively addresses questions of journalism, democracy and civic life.

CENTERING EASTERN EUROPE, CENTERING TELEVISION

The number of conferences, workshops and articles devoted to Soviet and post-Soviet popular culture has exponentially increased in the past 15 years. This attention follows Eastern Europe's transition from state-controlled, relatively isolated national media systems to a progressively integrated European media sphere permeated by processes of globalization

2 Timothy Havens, Anikó Imre and Katalin Lustyik

and media convergence. Such a transition, characterized by geographically uneven processes of democratization, marketization, the transformation of state institutions and civic nation-building within the region, has also been fueled by the staggered enlargement of the European Union. Television's transformation has been especially spectacular, shifting from a state-controlled broadcast system delivering national, regional and heavily filtered Western programming to a deregulated, multiplatform, transnational system delivering predominantly American and Western European entertainment programming. Consequently, the nations of Eastern Europe provide opportunities to examine the complex interactions among economic and funding systems, regulatory policies, globalization, imperialism, popular culture and cultural identity.

At the same time, many of the changes currently sweeping Eastern Europe—the globalization of media industries and programming, the collapse of non-commercial broadcasting, the impact of digitization and channel fragmentation—have also profoundly affected Western European nations. Despite these epochal changes in television, however, books and anthologies about European television continue to identify 'Europe' with Western Europe and contain only a few references to Europe's Eastern peripheries. Even recent volumes such as *Television Across Europe: A Comparative Introduction* (Wieten, Murdock and Dahlgren, 2000), *Worlds in Common? Television Discourses in the Changing Europe* (Meinhof and Richardson, 1999), *Transnational Television In Europe: Reconfiguring Global Communications Networks* (Chalaby, 2009), *Imaginary Dreamscapes: Television Fiction in Europe* (Buonanno, 2005) and *A European Television History* (Bignell and Fickers, 2008) only minimally address Eastern European societies, if at all.

By implication, anthologies and monographs that purport to cover European television and media, while consistently excluding or marginalizing Eastern Europe, perpetuate Western-centric perspectives and generalizations in their approaches, many of which simply do not apply to the very different economic, political and cultural trajectories of socialist and post-socialist television, which we explore below. Similarly, volumes on media globalization tend to bypass Eastern Europe: without meaning to trumpet our own horns, we nevertheless believe it is accurate to say that our own prior work offers some of the only exceptions to this tendency.

As we suggested above, the extant scholarship on Eastern European media that has been published only rarely addresses popular television, preferring instead to focus on journalism and news media that are often associated with more 'serious,' civically-engaged intellectual endeavors. Two pioneering volumes in this vein, *Internationalizing Media Studies* (Thussu 2001) and *Communication, Capitalism, and the Mass Media* (Sparks 1998), neglect even to mention the political potential of popular television and the transitions that popular television underwent after 1989. More recently, *Comparing Media Systems: Three Models of Media and Politics* (Hallin and Mancini 2004), while it does recognize the unique relationship between the press and the state in Central European nations, continues to perpetuate the scholarly silence about popular television, which is arguably as much a part of a nation's 'media system' as the press.

We do not mean to suggest that questions of democracy and the Fourth Estate are unimportant for the formerly communist nations of Eastern Europe, or that theorizing technological and cultural change in the era of digital television is insignificant. Rather, as we hope the following fourteen essays make clear, we intend to show that the traditional questions that have defined popular television studies—questions of identity, representation, cultural power, popular form and the role of institutions in shaping each of these—are crucial to understanding Eastern European culture and the distinct (and similar) roles that both analog and digital television have played in these societies. Specifically, these essays map how national identity, nostalgia, globalization, local production and minority popular culture are articulated in Eastern European television culture in ways that differ significantly from Western European or Anglophone television cultures.

THE CASE FOR AN EASTERN EUROPEAN TELEVISION STUDIES

Eastern Europe's fast pace of media change has attracted considerable interest among communication scholars, and yielded several studies that focus on media regulation, technological and policy changes and the new member states' integration into a European audiovisual sphere. However, television's political and ideological significance has been downplayed or ignored so far in scholarly circles.

Why this scholarly silence surrounding popular television in Eastern Europe? One important reason is the medium's intimate relationship with national languages and cultures, which reduces non-native scholars' access to programs. In addition, Eastern European national critical elites have tended to view the onslaught of foreign entertainment programming, and its impact on local populations, with (sometimes well-founded) suspicion. In the past few years, however, its impact on national cultures and identities has turned television into a crucial site of and window into the region's transformations. The change in the medium's status has also been enhanced by the enduring significance of socialist entertainment programming for post-socialist generations. Television drama and comedy series, animated children's and youth programming, even commercials, many of which circulated within the region during socialism, have re-appeared on local programming since 1989 as an irreplaceable source of national and regional memory and identity and have also inspired serious historical and critical scholarship. This popular register has so far been suppressed both by the exclusive Cold War interest in subversive political cinematic and literary work and by Eastern European intellectuals' investments in European high culture as a repository and model for national cultures. This collection

4 *Timothy Havens, Anikó Imre and Katalin Lustyik*

is the first volume to gather the best writing, by scholars across and outside the region, on socialist and post-socialist entertainment television as a medium, technology and institution.

Scholarship on popular television has always been highly local, rooted in the daily rhythms of domestic life and reception patterns, and structured by often-complex, nationally distinct regulatory and industrial regimes. Hence, the idea that popular television's cultural work would be different in different locales is relatively uncontroversial. At the same time, similar institutional and cultural patterns can be found across supranational regions, as in the long-form telenovelas produced by the commercial television industries of Latin America or the one-off teleplays created by public service broadcasters across Western Europe. The television industries of socialist Eastern Europe also produced recognizable program types, such as cultural variety shows and cabarets, theatrical broadcasts, programs showcasing poetry, a variety of semi-didactic youth programming and highly artistic animated shows for children. Although domestic production has been seriously compromised since the end of socialism, reality shows of various stripes might be good candidates for contemporary signature programming. Throughout the history of television in the region,we find similar cultural concerns, institutional patterns and histories of programming exchange.

In terms of cultural concerns, the relationship between television and national identity takes on a distinct history and inflection in Eastern Europe from that in the West. That is, given the level of program exchange and the ambivalent status of nationalism during socialism, a coherent national identity had difficulty forming on television, as both Sabina Mihelj and Anikó Imre show in their contributions to this volume. Since the collapse of socialism, as Katalin Lustyik and Timothy Havens, et al. chronicle, the region has been swamped by foreign television imports, particularly from the U.S. and Western Europe, again challenging television's capacity to produce strong national narratives, cultures and identities. Meanwhile intraregional trade in Eastern Europe has all but dried up due to the scarcity of Eastern European programming and the tendency among media and government elites to look westward for economic, political and cultural models to replace those that were so badly damaged by the collapse of the Soviet empire.

Questions of national identity and television also take on unique qualities in Eastern Europe because of the sudden and profound changes faced by ethnic minorities since socialism, especially the Roma. While the reconciliation of Roma and other ethnic minorities with dominant national and international populations during socialism posed its own problems, those problems have been exacerbated by the economic hardship that has gripped the region in recent decades—a hardship that has fallen disproportionately on the backs of minorities.[1] At the same time, EU law requires candidate and member states to protect the rights of ethnic minorities, including rights of expression, which often surface in national broadcasting policy and affect the operation of ethnic radio and television stations. As Annabel Tremlett and Ksenija Vidmar-Horvat explore in their contributions to this volume, television continues to be a key site where Eastern European societies wrestle with how to integrate Roma minorities into the popular national imaginary.

Finally, the relationship between the totalitarian past and cultural memory serves as a distinct marker of Eastern European television, particularly the processes of trauma and nostalgia that a number of scholars have observed across the region.[2] In one way or another, the essays by Ferenc Hammer; Anikó Imre; Katja Kochanowski, Sascha Trültzsch and Reinhold Viehoff;and Irena Carpentier Reifová, Kateřina Gillárová and Radim Hladík all engage with cultural memory. Spanning decades and nations, the scholarship here on television and cultural memory in Eastern Europe not only adds to the ongoing theorization of post-communist nostalgia and trauma, but also makes a powerful case for the centrality of popular television in the production, continuation and study of cultural memory. Particularly due to the scarcity of local television production today, the spread of DVDs and other digital distribution and exhibition technologies and the relative cheapness of reproducing and broadcasting old television series, programming from the communist era offers abundant and rich material for the expression and dissemination of nostalgic and traumatic cultural memories. It would seem that old television is, to appropriate Lévi-Strauss' now famous phrase, good to remember with.

The vexed relationship between television and national identity, the role of television in integrating ethnic minorities into the national audience, and its function in the production of cultural memory about socialist times all point to the distinctive and region-wide nature of popular television in Eastern Europe before and since socialism. Still, as several essays in this volume attest, national differences are also important for understanding the cultural politics of television, even as these societies continue to face economic and cultural integration into a global capitalist order. Alice Bardan, Ferenc Hammer, Sylwia Szostak, Adina Schneeweis and Dana Mustata show how program schedules, imported television formats, regulations and program exchanges continue to be marked by national differences, despite how similar these practices may appear at first glance. These essays, in particular, are a testament to the continued ingenuity of television professionals in Eastern Europe to provide relevant popular programming, even under difficult economic and business conditions.

ORGANIZATION OF THE BOOK

The essays that follow provide comprehensive coverage with detailed studies of television systems and programs in 12 Eastern European countries. To do justice to the intricate regional and transnational connections that have

6 *Timothy Havens, Anikó Imre and Katalin Lustyik*

interwoven television cultures of Eastern Europe from the start, we have opted not to follow the traditional national organization that has characterized scholarly approaches to the region in cinema, literary and cultural studies. Nevertheless, while some of the chapters offer regional overviews, others foreground national specificities. The chapters are organized in three parts, which identify the most important areas of and approaches to television in the New Europe:

Part I, "Popular Television in Socialist Times" examines the historical development of socialist television, with a special focus on region-wide generic features and institutional practices. In Chapter 1, "Television Entertainment in Socialist Eastern Europe: Between Cold War Politics and Global Developments," Sabina Mihelj charts the development of television across Eastern Europe, focusing primarily on the pre-1989 era, in order to demonstrate region-wide continuities and similarities, while forcefully arguing that the development of television cultures across the region cannot simply be explained by Cold War political differences. Instead, the development of television in Eastern Europe responded to the same rewards, concerns and beliefs that attended television in the West. In Chapter 2, "Adventures in Early Socialist Television Edutainment," Anikó Imre examines a distinctly Eastern European television genre, the historical adventure series, which struggled to be at once a didactic story about proper citizenship and a popular part of everyday family life. Tracing the national and transnational dimensions of the genre through two representative series, the Polish *Janosik* (1974) and the Hungarian *Captain of the Tenkes* (1964), Imre shows how early socialist TV entertainment conjured up a mythic national solidarity that ultimately consolidated socialist regimes struggling for legitimacy. Although Dana Mustata focuses her analysis on Romanian television in Chapter 3, she nevertheless makes arguments regarding the political nature of television as an object of study that are likely relevant across the region. In particular, she shows how common, Western understandings of Romanian television assume that everything the medium transmitted was subservient to political concerns. By contrast, Mustata demonstrates how the era of strict political control of television was brief-lived in Romania and, moreover, that this era only developed after the medium had gone through changes that were remarkably similar to television throughout the rest of Europe. Chapter 4, "The Carnival of the Absurd: Stanisław Bareja's *Alternatywy 4* and Polish Television in the 1980s" by Dorota Ostrowska picks up on the theme of distinctive Eastern European genres, examining a particular, absurdist instance of the "block of flats" genre, which proliferated across the region during socialist times. Ostrowska goes on to demonstrate how Stanisław Bareja's *Alternatywy 4* enacted an effective critique of the genre and the socialist system, in a manner reminiscent of absurdist Polish literature and film. Finally, Chapter 5 takes us to socialist East Germany, where Katja Kochanowski, Sascha Trültzsch and Reinhold Viehoff trace how East German family series developed generically, focusing in particular on the dichotomy between ideological control and popularity that Imre addressed in Chapter 2. In the East German instance, as the authors demonstrate, the proximity and popularity of West German television had a profound impact on the development of popular television and its predominant textual practices.

Part II focuses on the impact of media globalization on television industries, programs and cultures in Eastern Europe. The section opens with Katalin Lustyik's contribution, "From a Socialist Endeavor to a Commercial Enterprise: Children's Television in East-Central Europe," which examines the changes in children's television since 1989 as an index of broader shifts and concerns in national identity. Ultimately, despite the dominance of Western media conglomerates and imported models of children's television, Lustyik argues that the forms of childhood represented on television are no more (or less) restrictive than those that populated socialist broadcasting in Eastern Europe. Chapter 7, "Intra-European Media Imperialism: Hungarian Program Imports and the Television Without Frontiers Directive" by Timothy Havens, Evelyn Bottando and Matthew S. Thatcher compares import patterns in Hungary in the 1980s and 2000s to argue that, since the collapse of the Soviet Union, Hungarian schedules have been swamped by Western European imports, while Eastern European trade has largely dried up. In part, the authors attribute these changes to European Union media regulations and a broader political and economic effort to re-colonialize Eastern Europe. Chapter 8, "To Be Romanian in Post-Communist Romania: Entertainment Television and Patriotism in Popular Discourse" by Adina Schneeweis explores how the popular Romanian series, *Garantat 100%*, offers discourses of Romanian national identity that differ significantly from dominant national discourses, trying to navigate a path between a wholesale adoption of Western ideals and a retreat into an idealized, local past. Schneeeweis positions this discursive struggle not only in relation to the collapse of totalitarianism and the adoption of democratic institutions in Romania, but also the lure of emigration to the West. The final chapter in this section, Sylwia Szostak's "Post-Transitional Continuity and Change: Polish Broadcasting Flow and American TV Series," traces how Polish television programmers continue to utilize distinctly Polish scheduling practices, even when they air imported television series. The chapter is a good reminder that, even in an era of global television trade, national difference continues to be a relevant category of analysis, though we might need to look creatively in order to find it.

Part III collects essays that examine the continuing importance of national identity in Eastern European television today and the unique ways in which television imagines, activates and perpetuates nationality. Alice Bardan's "Big Brothers and Little Brothers: National Identity in Recent Romanian Adaptations of Global Television Formats" opens this section with an analysis of imported reality TV formats which, she argues,

8 Timothy Havens, Anikó Imre and Katalin Lustyik

tend not to draw substantial audience numbers in Romania. Unlike other Western and Eastern European markets, Romanian television's efforts to reproduce local versions of global reality TV hits have generally failed, due to local discursive and industrial conditions. Chapter 11, "The Way We Applauded: How Popular Culture Stimulates Collective Memory of the Socialist Past in Czechoslovakia—the Case of the Television Serial *Vyprávěj* and Its Viewers" by Irena Carpentier Reifová, Kateřina Gilárová, and Radim Hladík, addresses the Czech television series *Vyprávěj* (*Tell Me How It Was*), a hybrid of comedy, soap opera and documentary that tells the story of an ordinary family whose everyday life is interwoven with the political and social realities of Czechoslovakia's "normalization" period in the 1970s and 1980, a time when numerous political reforms of the 1960s were removed. Employing theories of trauma and comedy, the authors seek to understand the ways in which television comedy might be particularly well-suited to the cultural remembrance of traumatic social events. In Chapter 12, "Coy Utopia: Politics in the First Hungarian TV Soap," Ferenc Hammer traces the representation of electoral politics in *Szomszédok (Neighbors)*, a Hungarian adaptation of the UK soap opera *EastEnders*, which spanned the transitional years of the late 1980s and the 1990s. In Hammer's analysis, *Szomszédok*'s producers struggled to reconcile the populist generic aspects of the soap opera with their own didactic efforts to teach Hungarian audiences how to be good democratic citizens, creating an idealistic portrait of electoral politics for viewers that fell far short of conditions of the ground. Annabel Tremlett's contribution, "Why Must Roma Minorities Be Always Seen on the Stage and Never in the Audience? Children's Opinions of Reality Roma TV" addresses the reception among children of the reality show *Győzike*, which centers on a popular Hungarian Roma musician and his family. While popular criticism has bemoaned the series' use of Roma stereotypes and its depiction of coarse language and behavior, Tremlett finds that Hungarian children read the series merely as a depiction of a conventional Hungarian family, regardless of ethnicity. Consequently, she claims that the series does more to promote a particular vision of the national family in the conditions of post-socialist neoliberalism than it does to promote particular attitudes toward Roma minorities. Chapter 14, "Racing for the Audience: National Identity, Public TV and the Roma in Post-Socialist Slovenia" by Ksenija Vidmar-Horvat also addresses the treatment of Roma minorities in Eastern European television, focusing on a particularly controversial episode of the Slovene talk show *Pyramid*, in which a right-wing member of parliament made numerous offensive comments about the Roma minority. Vidmar-Horvat uses this controversy to examine the complex intersections between discourses of ethnicity, nationality and gender in contemporary Slovenia, as well as the ways in which commercial television frames these issues.

Introduction 9

Together, these essays attest to the vibrancy of scholarship on popular television in Eastern Europe and the importance of such scholarship for renewed theorization in the fields of television and media studies, global studies and Eastern European studies. In particular, we hope that this volume helps contribute to ongoing efforts to bring popular culture into Eastern European studies, to highlight the relevance of Eastern European realities in the study of globalization, and to de-Westernize television and media studies. These were the goals that led us to contemplate such an anthology in the first place, and we trust that its contents go a long way toward achieving those goals, while also providing compelling cases of Eastern European television in their own right.

NOTES

1. Zoltan D. Barany, "Living on the Edge: The East European Roma in Post-communist Politics and Societies," Slavic Review 53 (1994): 321-344
2. Jonathan Bach, "'The Taste Remains': Consumption, (N)ostalgia, and the Production of East Germany," *Public Culture* 14 (2002): 545–556; Svetlana Boym, *The Future of Nostalgia* (New York: Basic Books); Zala Volčič, "Yugo-Nostalgia: Cultural Memory and Media in the Former Yugoslavia," *Critical Studies in Media Communication* 24 (2007): 21–38.

Part I

Popular Television in Socialist Times

1 Television Entertainment in Socialist Eastern Europe
Between Cold War Politics and Global Developments

Sabina Mihelj

Moments of abrupt transformation provide convenient frameworks for interpretation and understanding. They allow us to organize our thinking into neatly separated compartments of 'before' and 'after,' and invite us to identify and explain the patterns that distinguish one from the other. The sudden collapse of socialist regimes in Eastern Europe provided just such a framework. As the bipolar division of the world passed into history, scholars, journalists and casual observers were left grasping for clues that could help make sense of the momentous transformation. The Cold War vocabulary established in the West, often reminiscent of foreign policy slogans promoted by successive American administrations—such as the 'global democratic revolution,' used by Ronald Reagan in his State of the Union address in 1987—provided a vast pool of readymade formulas. The end of the Cold War, went the argument, spelled the demise of communist totalitarianism and cultural isolation, and signalled the triumph of liberal democracy, individual freedom and capitalist economy.

It soon became clear that such formulas provided little insight into the actual processes of transformation occurring in the region. Many of the countries seemed unable to progress beyond the 'transitional' phase, and were plagued by corruption and low levels of political participation and public confidence. Faced with this outcome, several analysts abandoned the initial transition paradigm, and instead acknowledged the existence of multiple transformations, historical legacies and continuities (Stark 1992; Carothers 2002). Debates about post-socialist media followed a similar pattern. Communication scholars approached the changing media landscapes armed with concepts derived from democratization, civil society and public sphere theory, only to find that the reality fell short of established ideals and thresholds (Splichal 1994; Gross 2002; Jakubowicz 2007). Across the region, the news media remained highly politicized and partisan, unable to sustain an independent professional culture and strongly influenced by the ruling political elites. While the accelerated commercialization of the media sector triggered an explosion of new publications, these frequently failed

14   *Sabina Mihelj*

to contribute to a more democratic and diverse public debate, and instead served as vehicles for private gain and personal promotion.

To account for these changes, some media analysts sought to develop alternative interpretive models—based, for instance, on the idea of elite continuity rather than transition (Sparks 2008). Others focused on building a more empirically accurate account of media democratization, one that would be capable of encompassing the diverse outcomes of change in the region (Jakubowicz 2007). Several authors also pointed out that the challenges encountered in post-socialist Eastern Europe are not unique to the region, nor reducible solely to the historical legacies of socialist politics and journalistic culture. The persistent partisanship and politicization of post-socialist media, for instance, is shared by several countries in Southern Europe—most notably Italy, but also Greece, Spain and Portugal—that have never experienced communism, and have long abandoned totalitarian rule (e.g. Splichal 1994). Such similarities with media systems beyond Eastern Europe, as well as the need to account for the diversity of media in the region itself, have prompted several researchers to adopt a comparative approach, and engage in empirical comparisons within and beyond the region (Dobek-Ostrowska et al. 2010; Downey and Mihelj forthcoming).

The body of work surveyed so far has little to say about developments in the realm of popular media and television entertainment. In line with the hierarchy of attention inherited from the Cold War, and guided by the most pressing demands of media reform after 1989, research on post-socialist media has so far been largely concerned with media policies, news genres, journalistic cultures and media ownership. Nonetheless, this literature offers valuable lessons that are worth keeping in mind when examining the transformation of television entertainment. First, it is evident that a simple before-and-after framework will not take us far. While the landscape of popular television in the region changed dramatically over the past two decades, any account of this transformation needs to be mindful not only of discontinuities, but also of continuities with the socialist period. Second, media systems in the region were internally diverse. While some countries entered communism with a well-developed broadcasting infrastructure and entertainment industry, others had to build both virtually from scratch. Local appropriations of the socialist media model differed as well. And third, an adequate interpretation of popular television in Eastern Europe, both before and after 1989, needs to situate regional developments within the broader, international framework of television history.

Building on these points, the following pages set out to chart some of the characteristics of television entertainment in Eastern Europe before 1989. The first part addresses the issue of continuities and discontinuities, focusing on the role of Western imports and entertainment programming. While it is true that the collapse of communism brought significant shifts in both areas, important changes took place long before the end of the Cold War was even remotely in sight. To understand why this was the case, we need

Television Entertainment in Socialist Eastern Europe 15

to set aside the notion of the Cold War as a bi-polar divide, and take into account structural similarities between television cultures on both sides of the Iron Curtain. Some of these structural similarities are outlined in the second part of the chapter. Particular attention is paid to the institutionalization of television as a mass medium with a public service mission, the rift between elite and popular tastes, dilemmas surrounding the relationship between entertainment and education and responses to foreign television programs. Viewed from the perspective of these developments, the history of television entertainment in Eastern Europe was not shaped solely by the ups and downs of Cold War politics, but formed part of broader developments that straddled the East–West divide.

CONTINUITIES AND DISCONTINUITIES

There is little doubt that the availability of Western television programs in Eastern Europe increased after 1989. The fall of socialist regimes removed the remaining ideological obstacles that made Western television politically suspicious. The curiosity about things Western, fuelled by decades of heavily restricted and politically loaded cultural exchanges, made local audiences and broadcasters alike particularly open to cultural imports from the West. At the same time, the proliferation of cable and satellite television originating from the West, and the rise of privately owned television channels domestically—often fuelled by foreign investment—were undermining long-established monopolies in the broadcasting sector. Faced with competition, public broadcasters looked for quick and cheap solutions to their new predicament, and Western television series seemed to provide a perfect fit. Across the region, audiences of public television channels were tuning in for weekly installments of American soap operas and drama series, ranging from *Dallas* and *Dynasty* to *E.R.* and *Beverly Hills 90210* (Štětka forthcoming).

Yet this is not to say that Western television entertainment was unknown in earlier periods, or that its prominence after 1989 can be explained solely by reference to the end of the Cold War. Of course, the situation varied considerably from country to country, as well as from period to period. Soviet television was far more impervious to Western imports—and in fact to any imports—than televisions elsewhere in the region. The first large-scale comparative study of international television flows, conducted in the early 1970s, revealed that Central Television 1—the main national television channel in the Soviet Union at the time—imported a mere 5% of its program (Nordenstreng and Varis 1974, 24). In contrast, the proportion of foreign programs in the rest of Eastern Europe ranged from 17% in Poland to 45% in Bulgaria. A survey conducted a decade later arrived at a similar conclusion: in the Soviet Union, imported programs amounted to a total of 8%, while the figures elsewhere in the region varied from 24% in Czechoslovakia to 30% in the German Democratic Republic (Varis

16 *Sabina Mihelj*

1985, 34). Although a significant part of foreign programming came from the Soviet Union and from other Eastern European countries, the share of Western imports was far from negligible. In the early 1970s, 12% of all imported programming on Hungarian television came from the UK, 10% from France, and 10% from Western Germany. In the case of TV Belgrade in Yugoslavia, as much as 80% of all imported programs came from outside of the socialist bloc and 40% from the U.S. alone (Nordenstreng and Varis 1974, 25). In the early 1980s, an average of 43% of imported programming in Eastern Europe came from Western Europe, and only slightly more—45%—from the Soviet Union and other Eastern European countries (Varis 1985, 35).

Precise figures for individual genres are difficult to collate, but available evidence indicates that much of the material imported from the West consisted of entertainment—principally cartoons and children variety programs, but also television films and series. In 1959, the small but rapidly growing television audience in Yugoslavia could follow the adventures of the female rough collie Lassie—ubiquitous on television screens around Western Europe at the time—as well as a handful of other commercially produced television programs from the U.S.[1] American programming remained a regular feature in the following years. In 1964, for instance, TV Ljubljana treated its young audience to a season of *Dennis the Menace*,[2] while female viewers across the country were purportedly swept off their feet by the charms of Dr. Kildare.[3] A similar craze was sparked by the broadcasting of *Peyton Place* in the late 1960s and the early 1970s. In the Yugoslav Republic of Serbia, the series attracted an estimated 94% of all television viewers.[4]

While Yugoslavia's peculiar geopolitical position and relative independence from the Soviet bloc made its media system particularly open to Western programs, Yugoslav television was not alone in relying on imports from capitalist countries. Across much of Eastern Europe, the easing of censorship and the partial opening to the West following Khrushchev's denunciation of Stalin in 1956 made East–West trade and cultural exchange much easier than they were in the immediate post-World War II years. Over the course of the late 1960s and the early 1970s, Romanian audiences could follow the adventures of the blue dolphin Flipper and his friends in southern Florida, marvel at the ingenuity of the American private investigator Joe Mannix, or tremble for the lives of agents Eliot Ness and Oscar Fraley fighting crime in 1930s Chicago—all characters in American television series distributed worldwide at the time (cf. Paulu 1974, 426). By the early 1970s, even Soviet television became more open to Western entertainment, and broadcast BBC's *Forsythe Saga* and *David Copperfield* (Lapin and Alexandrov 1976, 12). Bulgaria was, in this sense, something of an exception, and remained heavily dependent on Soviet imports throughout. Yet even here, Western popular culture was occasionally allowed into the mainstream—as for instance in the case of the popular song contest

Golden Orpheus, broadcast on TV, which featured performers from the West, including some from the U.S. (Taylor 2006, 125).

Polish openness to television imports from the West—explored in detail in Dorota Ostrowska's chapter—seems particularly remarkable. A study conducted by a Polish sociologist between 1959 and 1962 revealed that local children frequently watched American and British action and adventure series such as *Zorro* and *The Adventures of Sir Lancelot,* and were also rather fond of Walt Disney's cartoons and variety shows, in particular the *Mickey Mouse Club* and *Disneyland* (Komorowska 1964). Adult audiences in Poland also became accustomed to Western popular entertainment. In 1964, a Polish radio and television magazine listed six "most interesting serials appearing on Polish TV," all of which were of American origin.[5] In 1968, a U.S. foreign diplomat working for the consulate in Poznan reported watching the American Western series *Bonanza* and the comic series *Bewitched,* the British musical film *The Beatles and Others* and the American film *Jumbo* starring Doris Day—all broadcast in a single day. In an ironic message sent to the U.S. Department of State, he suggested that Polish authorities were using such "bourgeois Western escapist television fare" to keep the population from attending traditional religious celebrations.[6]

Socialist fondness for Western popular culture may well have been occasionally facilitated by ideological motives of this kind, but ideology and politics alone cannot fully explain this unprecedented openness to Western imports. Another, perhaps more decisive reason, lay in the lack of domestic production. At the time, television was a novelty, experienced technical and creative staff was in short supply and funding was limited. Acquiring a television series or a children's program from abroad was, quite simply, the only feasible solution. By the 1970s, however, the situation had changed. Clumsy experimentation and sudden interruptions of transmission were giving way to more sophisticated, professionally executed and diverse programming, particularly in the area of entertainment (e.g. Vončina 2003, 137–300; Roth-Ey 2011, 273–276; Beutelschmidt and Wrage 2004). Technological advances paved the way for the decline of live television and the growth of recorded programs, as well as for the development of new genres, including made-for-TV films and series (Prokhorova 2003, 10–12).

At the same time, television sets were losing the status of luxury items and came to be treated as household necessities, and television signals were reaching a growing and increasingly diverse audience. Thanks to the constant stream of viewer letters and advances in audience research, it quickly became clear that viewers' preferences were often at odds with the cultural ideals espoused by television professionals and political elites. Rather than seeing television as an instrument of education and information, audiences across Eastern Europe—much as their counterparts elsewhere in the world—were using television primarily as a source of entertainment and relaxation. According to a survey conducted in 1963 in Serbia, programs combining music, humor and other forms of entertainment were achieving

18 Sabina Mihelj

the highest viewing figures, and together with transmissions of football matches regularly rivaled the popularity of primetime news programs.[7] The results obtained by audience researchers in Poland, Czechoslovakia and the GDR brought similar results: serious music consistently scored lowest, while films, quizzes and sports won top marks (Meyen and Nawratil 2004, 359; Paulu 1974, 306–307). The constant stream of letters addressed to Soviet Central Television was equally unambiguous: viewers were complaining about being bored, and demanded more entertainment (Evans 2011). Most worryingly, the desire for light entertainment—rather than solely information-seeking—was also fuelling audience interest in Western radio broadcasts (Bashkirova 2010) and, where available, Western television (Dittmar 2004; Bren 2010, 120–121).

Not everyone was, of course, equally willing to pay attention to audience preferences. Soviet television professionals, for instance, perceived themselves primarily as educators, and fashioned their work based on what they thought the audiences needed rather than on what they actually wanted (Roth-Ey 2011, 270–271). Yet at the same time, popular dissatisfaction with available television programs also signaled that something had to change. If television was to function as an effective tool of mass mobilization and education, and fulfill the socialist promise of bringing culture to the masses, it needed to be sufficiently attractive to all its viewers, not only to the educated elites. The wave of popular unrest that swept through many of the urban centers of Eastern Europe in the late 1960s and the early 1970s provided a further incentive. Arguably, socialist elites had to find a way to reconnect with, or at least pacify, the masses, and popular entertainment offered a suitable tool. At the SED Party conference in 1971, a figure no less prominent than Erich Honecker described East German television as boring, and called on broadcasters to provide their audiences with more entertainment (Steinmetz and Viehoff 2004, 320). In post-invasion Czechoslovakia, television professionals were urged to invest more heavily in light entertainment in an effort to win the hearts and minds of the masses, and prevent them from turning their antennas to television signals from Austria and West Germany (Bren 2010, 121–122). In the Soviet Union, the ability to spend a relaxing evening in front of the TV set came to be viewed as a right—as reflected in the statement "the Soviet person has the right to relax in front of the television after a day's work," attributed to none other than Leonid Brezhnev (Roth-Ey 2011, 201).

Whether prompted by audience demand, lack of popular legitimacy, competition from foreign media or political fiat, television professionals across Eastern Europe were becoming increasingly adept at entertaining their viewers. Television schedules now regularly included not only domestically produced quiz programs and variety shows with celebrity guests, comedy sketches and popular music bands, but also made-for-TV films and mini-series and even a Soviet bloc version of the Eurovision Song Contest (Raykoff and Tobin 2007, xvii–xviii). Domestically produced TV series

Television Entertainment in Socialist Eastern Europe   19

were particularly popular with audiences, and regularly attracted record ratings. In terms of genre conventions, they differed little from their Western counterparts: they frequently depicted the dramas of everyday life in the socialist present, or followed the trials and tribulations of contemporary detectives, police officers, medical doctors and shop assistants. The use of humor was widespread as well. As Katja Kochanowski, Sascha Trültzsch and Reinhold Viehoff show in their chapter, the geopolitical context of East Germany was particularly conducive to the production of domestic television series. It is important to note, however, that similar trends dominated television entertainment elsewhere in the region too. In Czechoslovakia, record numbers of viewers were turning on their sets to watch a never-ending stream of Jaroslav Dietl's serials, including *A Hospital on the Edge of Town* (1977–81), centered on the daily dramas of doctors, nurses and patients at a local hospital, and *The Woman at the Counter* (1977), focusing on the life of a middle-aged, hard-working shop assistant living in a suburb of Prague (Bren 2010). In Yugoslavia, audiences were glued to their screens following the intrigues of *Our Small Town* (1970–71), set in a picturesque Croatian town on the Adriatic coast (Vončina 2003, 241) and laughing at the twists and turns of family life in the *Theater in the House* (1973–84).[8] And the list goes on.

Several of the most popular mini-series managed not only to attract record audience ratings, but also to win praise from socialist authorities. The merger of popular entertainment and state control comes most clearly to the fore in programs that received direct backing from socialist authorities. The production of one of the most celebrated Soviet mini-series from this period, the spy thriller *Seventeen Moments of Spring* (1973), was supervised and generously sponsored by both the KGB and the Communist Party (Prokhorova 2003, 80–81). In Yugoslavia, TV Zagreb's mini-series *The Bonfires of Kapela* (1975) received support from the Yugoslav People's Army, and the screening of its first episode was set to coincide with the official celebration of the anniversary of socialist Yugoslavia.[9] The production of one of the most popular television serials in 1970s Czechoslovakia, *The Thirty Adventures of Major Zeman* (1975) followed a similar template: it was produced in collaboration with the Czechoslovak Army and the Federal Ministry of Interior, and designed to honor the 30th anniversary of the Red Army liberation of Prague (Bren 2010,74).

Not all of the socialist television entertainment, however, was quite so regime-friendly. In Yugoslavia, comic series such as *Theater in the House* (1973–84) and *Hot Wind* (1980) poked fun at the seamy underbelly of Yugoslav affluence, including unemployment and reliance on mass labor migration to the West. Likewise, the Soviet variety show *The Pub of 13 Chairs* regularly included stand-up comedy stints parodying the shortcomings of Soviet society, for instance the scarcity of consumer goods and the mismatch between political visions and everyday life (Paulu 1974, 177). Sergei Lapin, head of Soviet radio and television at the time, found the

20   *Sabina Mihelj*

show rather irritating, yet kept it on air nonetheless—allegedly thanks to Leonid Brezhnev's fondness for the program (Roth-Ey 2011, 279). Such forms of ridicule and criticism of course had their limits, and usually relied on doublespeak and irony, yet they serve as a reminder that socialist popular culture was not ideologically uniform, and that self-congratulatory, mythologized portrayals of socialist reality could coexist with more ambiguous messages.

SIMILARITIES AND DIFFERENCES

To those familiar with trends in Western Europe and elsewhere around the globe, some of the traits of socialist television history outlined so far should have struck familiar chords. The 1950s and the 1960s saw the intensification of international exchanges of television programs globally, not only in Eastern Europe (Havens 2006, 16–24). The growth of television audiences soon outpaced domestic production capabilities, and started generating considerable demand for imported programs. American products, especially entertainment and fiction, were in great demand.[10] By 1964, major U.S. commercial broadcasters had an established presence abroad: CBS was operating in 170 countries and NBC in 80 (Paulu 1967, 215). In the same period, the British BBC also rose as an important player in the international television market (Schlesinger 1986, 275–276). The marked increase in imported entertainment on television screens in Eastern Europe thus formed part of global developments fostered not only by changes in Cold War politics, but also by transnational economic and cultural developments. The same is true of the growth of domestic entertainment and TV fiction in the 1970s. Again, trends noted in Eastern Europe have their counterparts elsewhere: in many countries across Western Europe, but also in Latin America, Japan and Egypt, the decade was characterized by an increase in domestic production capacities (Havens 2006, 24–26).

These similarities should not come as a surprise. In Eastern Europe, international television flows were of course more heavily regulated, the proportion of Western imports smaller, the production of entertainment subjected to tighter political scrutiny, and commercial incentives limited. Yet once we look beyond the realm of state control and funding, and consider the cultural and social aspects of television broadcasting, it quickly becomes apparent that television professionals on both sides of the Iron Curtain were facing many common challenges, and responded to them in remarkably similar ways. To start with, it is worth noting that the rise of television followed a similar schedule in both Eastern and Western Europe. The majority of countries introduced regular television broadcasting in the 1950s, experienced a period of rapid growth of television audiences, and reached the point of saturation in the 1970s. While the exact pace and rhythm of growth varied from country to country, it is impossible to draw a

Television Entertainment in Socialist Eastern Europe   21

sharp contrast between Eastern and Western Europe: the spreading of television receivers in Czechoslovakia, East Germany, Hungary and the Soviet Union proceeded at a rate comparable to that in France, Italy, Norway and West Germany, while patterns in Yugoslavia and Bulgaria resemble those in Portugal or Ireland (Table 1.1).

This expansion of television brought profound changes in the demographic structure of audiences, and turned television into a fully-fledged mass medium. In both Eastern and Western Europe, this shift was greeted with a mixture of apprehension and enthusiasm. On the one hand, it provoked fears of moral degradation, populism and cultural mediocrity. On the other hand, it inspired utopian projections of a better, more educated, refined and politically engaged society. To early television enthusiasts everywhere, broadcasting technology represented a powerful instrument of mass education and cultural refinement. The BBC's founder Lord Reith was notorious for his belief in broadcasting as a means of cultural elevation, as well as for his disdain for popular entertainment and insistence on giving the public what they need rather than what they want (Crisell 1997, 29). Much of early television programming in post-war Italy was inspired by similar ideals. It was unmistakably didactic in tone, and consisted of live transmissions of theater plays, operas and classical music concerts (Monteleone 2006, 302–306). Soviet television professionals were evidently not the only ones who perceived themselves primarily as educators rather than as entertainers. In socialist Eastern Europe and the Soviet Union, didacticism and paternalist attitudes may have been more persistent, and more closely tied to specifically socialist and anti-capitalist attitudes, but at their core, the cultural values that underpinned the work of early television professionals everywhere were similar. Thanks to the institutionalization of broadcasting as a public service across most of Western Europe, such values continued to exert influence throughout the Cold War. As Brants and de Bens (2000, 16) put it, the ethos of public broadcasting in Western Europe was marked by a "cultural-pedagogic logic," and was defined in opposition to private broadcasting. If the responsibility of private broadcasters lied in "providing programs people like" with the aim of, ultimately, attracting "audiences that they can sell to advertisers," the task of public service broadcasting was to provide programs that are "in the public interest," but "not necessarily what the public is interested in." Socialist broadcasters would have found little to disagree with here.

The realities of broadcasting were often far from these ideals. As the reach of television signals expanded and television audiences grew bigger and more diverse, it quickly became apparent that attempts at mass cultural elevation were failing. Much as in Eastern Europe, broadcasters in the West were confronted with a yawning rift between popular and elite tastes, and often reacted to popular pastimes with disdain and fear. Even in the U.S., where commercial broadcasting took root early on and light entertainment proliferated at a fast rate, concerns about its detrimental effects were rife.

Table 1.1 Diffusion of TV Sets: Number of Inhabitants Per TV Set

	U.S.	UK	France	Norway	Ireland	Italy	Portugal	West Germany	East Germany	Czechoslovakia	Hungary	USSR	Yugoslavia	Bulgaria
1960	3.9	4.9	23.9	73.3	23.7	193.2	12.0	16.8	17.1	95.8	44.1	612	1577	
1965	3.6	4.0	7.4	7.6	9.7	8.6	48.8	5.1	5.3	6.6	12.2	14.4	34.3	44.5
1970	3.4	3.4	4.6	4.5	6.8	5.5	22.3	3.6	3.8	4.6	5.8	6.9	12	8.2
1975	3.1	3.0	3.5	3.8	5.6	4.6	12.8	3.4	3.2	4.0	4.4	4.6	7.7	5.8
1980	2.8	2.9	-	3.4	5.3	4.2	7.1	2.6	2.9	3.6	3.9	3.5	5.9	5.3

Note: Calculations based on the total number of television licences (or equivalent) and population estimates based on nearest census figures.
Sources: Brian R. Mitchell, *International Historical Statistics: Europe, 1750–2005*, 6th edition (Basingstoke: Palgrave Macmillan, 2007) and Boris Alekseevich Miasoedov, *Stranachitaet, slushaet, smotrit: statisticheskiĭ obzor* (Moscow: Financi i statistika, 1982).

It was not uncommon for American diplomats and media analysts to look at broadcasting in Europe—including the socialist East—with a measure of admiration, and use the analysis of socialist television to convey their misgivings about television programs at home. A report sent to the U.S. department of State from the American embassy in Moscow described the contrast between two television cultures in a rather telling manner: "U.S. television is entertainment interrupted by commercials, while Soviet television is propaganda interrupted by entertainment" (quoted in Schwoch 2009, 112). The introduction of commercial television and growth of entertainment content in 1950s Britain provoked similar reactions, and helped sustain the value of public broadcasting as the guarantor of quality (cf. Crisell 1997, 108–114).

In spite of these shared misgivings, broadcasters on both sides of the Iron Curtain were becoming increasingly responsive to the diversity of tastes, and opened their waves to variety shows, popular music and comedy. There is no denying that television producers in countries like West Germany, France, Italy and above all Britain and the U.S. led the way and that on average, the growth of television entertainment Eastern Europe lagged behind and was often dependent on copying formats from the West. Apart from that, however, broadcasters both east and west of the Iron Curtain addressed the challenge of entertainment in an analogous manner. Whether it was due to the cultural mission of public service, or due to socialist notions of mass cultural elevation, they were expected to produce programs that were lively and amusing as well as educational and of high artistic and technical quality. In Britain, BBC's *The Forsythe Saga* (1966) was celebrated for turning serious literature into a cultural product of unprecedented popularity, and for prompting a renewed interest in original literary texts (Crisell 1997, 116). In Yugoslavia, a report prepared in 1964 was underpinned by similar ideals. In the realm of culture, television had the task of "providing cultural relaxation and entertainment to the greatest possible number of viewers, without at the same time neglecting the works of special artistic value."[11] The guidelines for television entertainment formulated in 1967 in East Germany were no different in tone. They demanded producers to avoid both "trivialization" and "intellectualism," and advised them to steer away from "aesthetic experiments in form" and "content deemed too intellectually demanding" in order to avoid offending the "the authority and dignity of audiences" (Breitenborn 2004, 392).

What made the dilemmas of television culture both East and West of the Iron Curtain particularly vexing was their link with national culture. Wherever it appeared, television became a national medium par excellence, and functioned as an instrument of national integration domestically as well as a vehicle for national promotion globally. In France, de Gaulle embraced television as means of spreading the knowledge of French culture and inculcating the norms of correct grammar and pronunciation (Smith 1998, 43). In Italy, television was credited with tearing down the barriers of regional

24 *Sabina Mihelj*

dialects and bringing about the linguistic unification of the country (Monteleone 2006, 279). In the socialist East, the nation summoned by television may have been imagined as a nation of workers, but it was a nation nonetheless (Mihelj 2011, 78–80, 86–89). Debates about entertainment and education on television were therefore debates about what constitutes national culture and its distinctiveness, and about who has the authority to define that. Television professionals and policy-makers East and West of course conceived of national distinctiveness and diversity in importantly different ways, but the fundamental dilemmas they engaged with straddled the East–West divide, and stemmed from the growth of mass culture, technological advances and the reshuffling of traditional cultural hierarchies globally. Is the nation best served by a television that provides access to educational materials and highest artistic achievements selected by cultural authorities, or by popular entertainment guided by mass preferences? How to ensure adequate diversity without diluting national distinctiveness, and how to cater for minority tastes without imposing unnecessary burdens on the majority?

In light of the combined burdens of cultural elitism and concerns over national integration, it is of little surprise that cultural anxieties surrounding television often coalesced around foreign imports—and around American television imports in particular. American popular entertainment was doubly suspicious: it embodied the specter of commercialization and the menace of cultural mediocrity, as well as represented an alien force threatening to undermine the authenticity of national culture. Needless to say, the very same reasons also fuelled popular fascination with things American, especially among younger audiences. This applies in equal measure to both sides of the Iron Curtain. Surveys conducted in Italy, France, Britain and West Germany in 1962 revealed that U.S. television programs, and American life more broadly, were associated with violence and crime, superficiality and lack of realism, as well as with vulgarity and immorality.[12] Results obtained in Japan were broadly similar—again, violence and lack of moral standards topped the list of negative impressions.[13] In socialist Yugoslavia, the corrupting influences of popular music, films, dance and television were typically associated with capitalism and described as generically Western rather than American, but the main grievances were almost identical. According to a lengthy report discussed by the members of the Socialist Alliance of the Working People of Croatia in 1958, the "petit-bourgeois popular press" has the function of "diverting the working man from real life and real problems by imposing on him the problems of kings [. . .] film starts, millionaires, speculators, gangsters," but also "by provoking him with sex, crime and cruelty."[14] In a similar vein, authorities in the closed city of Dniepropetrovsk in Soviet Ukraine blamed the growth of violence and 'hooliganism' among local youths in the late 1960s and the early 1970s on French and Japanese films (Zhuk 2010, 143–144). These transnational similarities remind us that reactions to American—or

'Western'—television fare and popular culture were not simply a matter of Cold War tensions, but formed part of broader social and cultural developments that cannot be fitted into East–West dichotomies.

The same is true of the arrival of commercial broadcasting to Eastern Europe after 1989. Much as the reactions to American popular culture and the controversies surrounding entertainment on television, the deregulation of television markets was prompted by pan-European and in fact global developments, and should not be interpreted solely with reference to the fall of communism. Over the course of the 1970s and the 1980s, a host of technological, economic and political developments—including the 1970s economic recession, the rise of transnational corporations, the proliferation of satellite and cable technology and the economic liberalism of Margaret Thatcher and Ronald Reagan—helped bring down the established defences of public broadcasting monopoly globally (Dahlgren 2000). The change in ratios of public and private television in Western Europe speaks for itself. In 1980, television landscapes in the 17 countries of Western Europe comprised some 40 public channels and only five private ones; by 1999, the balance was reversed: while the number of public channels increased to 60, the number of private channels jumped to 70 (Brant and de Bens 2000, 10–11). In Eastern Europe, the explosion of commercial channels started a few years later, but many of its main motivations, as well as the ensuing tensions and concerns, were similar to those in the West.

CONCLUDING NOTES

The overview provided in this chapter is inevitably partial and superficial, and omits several important facets of popular television history in socialist Eastern Europe, including the institutionalization of television as a home appliance, concerns over decency and standards, and the involvement of television entertainment in the changing leisure patterns and shifting relations of gender and generation. These and many other fascinating aspects of socialist television history still await their historian. What should be clear from the brief account provided here is that an adequate understanding of these developments cannot rely on the perception of the Cold War as a black-and-white confrontation between capitalism and communism, nor can it proceed solely from the established interpretive frameworks of post-socialist democratization and economic liberalization. Instead, we should acknowledge that many of the promises and challenges posed by television everywhere were similar, and that both popular and elite reactions to them often defied the logic of the East–West divide. After all, the history of television on both sides of the Iron Curtain, just as the roots of the rival projects of liberalism and communism, stemmed from the same economic, political and social realities: the growth of mass political participation, rising standards of living, urbanization and advances in transport and

26 Sabina Mihelj

communication technologies. Due to that, the history of socialist television forms part and parcel of the longer and more encompassing processes of modernization that were pan-European and global in their reach.

A note of clarification is in order at this point. If this chapter focused primarily on similarities and continuities rather than on differences and discontinuities, it is not because the latter are less important. Nor was this choice of focus meant to suggest that we should discard the Cold War as a frame of reference altogether. Any comprehensive history of television in Europe, or indeed globally, has to pay adequate attention both to what was similar and to what was different, to things that changed and to those that stayed the same. Likewise, there is no doubt that television developments in the 20th century were to an important extent shaped by the Cold War confrontation, which made the policies and ideologies, as well as the day-to-day realities of television cultures in the East importantly different from those in the West. In short, by making a plea for a transnational approach, I do not want to suggest that we should simply collapse the history of popular television in Eastern Europe into a seamless narrative about the global advance of modernity. Rather, we should attempt to write a history that opens up the story of television to the alternative routes and visions of modernity beyond those familiar from Western Europe and Northern America, while keeping in mind their shared roots and common challenges.

NOTES

1. National Archives and Records Administration (NARA), Record Group (RG) 306 U.S. Information Agency, 1900–2003 (USIA), Series P 142 Research Reports, 1960–1999, Box 4, R-26–61 "Foreign reaction to U.S. commercially produced television programs," p. 16.
2. *Delo RTV*, June 21–27, 1964, p. 1.
3. *Delo RTV*, May 3–9, 1964, p. 14.
4. Centar Radiotelevizije Srbije za istraživanje javnog mnenja, programa i auditorijuma—Radio-television of Serbia Centre for Public Opinion, Program and Audience Research (RTS-CIPA), Report 493, Nevenka Perović, "Igrane emisije radija i televizije," in *Rezultati istraživanja programa* 13, p. 12.
5. NARA, RG 306 USIA, Series P142 Research Reports, 1960–1999, Box 25, R-51–1965 "Overseas television developments in 1964."
6. NARA, RG 59 General Records of the Department of State, 1763–2002 (DoS), Central Foreign Policy Files, 1966–1969, Box 409, Airgram from the American Consulate Poznan to Department of State, "TV Schedules and Religious Observances," May 25, 1969.
7. Arhiv Jugoslavije—Archives of Yugoslavia (AJ), Fond 142 Socijalistički savez radnog naroda Jugoslavije—Socialist Alliance of the Working People of Yugoslavia (SSRNJ), Box 207, "Dokumentacija uz teze o mestu, ulozi i zadacima štampe, radija i televizije o daljem razvoju društveno-ekonomskih odnosa," Jugoslovenski institut za novinarstvo, 1965, p. 8.
8. RTS-CIPA, Report 645, *Odnos gledalaca prema TV seriji 'Pozorište u kući'*, 1974, p. 1.

Television Entertainment in Socialist Eastern Europe 27

9. Arhiv Hrvatske Radiotelevizije—Archives of Croatian Radio-television (ACRT), "Kapelski kresovi," *List Radiotelevizije Zagreb*, 35, December 10, 1975, p. 7.
10. NARA, RG 306 USIA, P142, Box 4, R-26–61 "Foreign reaction [. . .]," p. 2.
11. AJ, Fond 130 Savezno izvršno veće—Federal Executive Council (SIV), Box 566–942, "Stanje i problemi razvitka televizije u Jugoslaviji," Beograd: Jugoslovenska radio-televizija, 1964, p. 26.
12. NARA, RG 306 USIA, P142, Box 12, R-163–62 "The Impact of American Commercial Television in Western Europe," 1962, pp. 7–8.
13. NARA, RG 306 USIA, P142, Box 11, R-152–62, "The Impact of American Commercial Television in Japan," 1962.
14. Hrvatski državni arhiv—Croatian State Archives (HDA), Fond 1228-Socialistički savez radnog naroda Hrvatske—Socialist Alliance of the Working People of Croatia (SSRNH), Box 933, "Pregled i analiza zabavne štampe," 1958, p. 1.

REFERENCES

Bashkirova, Elena I. 2010. "The Foreign Radio Audience in the USSR during the Cold War: An Internal Perspective." In *Cold War Broadcasting: Impact on the Soviet Union and Eastern Europe. A Collection of Studies and Documents*, edited by A. Ross Johnson and R Eugene Parta, 102–120. Budapest: Central European University Press.

Beutelschmidt, Thomas, and Henning Wrage. 2004. "'Range and Diversity' in the GDR? Television Drama in the Early 1970s." *Historical Journal of Film, Radio and Television* 24(3): 441–454.

Brants, Kees, and Els De Bens. 2000. "The Status of TV Broadcasting in Europe." In *Television across Europe*, edited by Jan Wieten, Graham Murdock and Peter Dahlgren, 7–22. London: Sage.

Breitenborn, Uwe. 2004. "'Memphis Tennessee' in Borstendorf: Boundaries Set and Transcended in East German Television Entertainment." *Historical Journal of Film, Radio and Television* 24(3): 391–402.

Bren, Paulina. 2010. *The Greengrocer and His TV: The Culture of Communism after the 1968 Prague Spring*. Ithaca, NY: Cornell University Press.

Carothers, Thomas. 2002. "The End of the Transition Paradigm." *Journal of Democracy* 13(1): 5–21

Crisell, Andrew. 1997. *An Introductory History of British Broadcasting*. London and New York: Routledge.

Dahlgren, Peter. 2000. "Key Trends in European Television." In *Television Across Europe*, edited by Jan Wieten, Graham Murdock and Peter Dahlgren, 23–34. London: Sage.

Dittmar, Claudia. 2004. "GDR Television in Competition with West German Programming." *Historical Journal of Film, Radio and Television* 24(3): 327–343.

Dobek-Ostrowska, Bogusłava, Michał Głovacki, Karol Jakubowicz and Miklós Sükösd, eds. 2010. *Comparative Media Systems: European and Global Perspectives*. Budapest: Central European University Press.

Downey, John, and Sabina Mihelj, eds. Forthcoming. *Comparing Media Systems in Central and Eastern Europe: Politics, Economy and Culture*. Aldershot: Ashgate.

Evans, Christine. 2011. "Song of the Year and Soviet Mass Culture in the 1970s." *Kritika: Explorations in Russian and Eurasian History* 12 (3): 617–45.

28   *Sabina Mihelj*

Gross, Peter. 2002. *Entangled Revolutions: Media and Democratization in Eastern Europe*. Washington, D.C.: Woodrow Wilson Center Press.

Hanson, Philip. 1974. *Advertising and Socialism: The Nature and Extent of Consumer Advertising in the Soviet Union, Poland, Hungary and Yugoslavia*. White Plains, NY: International Arts and Sciences Press.

Havens, Timothy. 2006. *Global Television Maketplace*. London: British Film Institute.

Jakubowicz, Karol. 2007. *Rude Awakening: Social and Media Change in Central and Eastern Europe*. Cresskill, NJ: Hampton Press.

Komorowska, Jadwiga. 1964. *La television dans la vie des enfants, Enface* 17(2–3): 83–240. Translated by M. C. Unrug.

Lapin, Sergei G., and V. Aleksandrov. 1976. "Television in the Age of Détente." *Current Digest of the Soviet Press* 28(39): 12–13.

Meyen, Michael, and Ute Nawratil. 2004. "The Viewers: Television and Everyday Life in East Germany." *Historical Journal of Film, Radio and Television* 24(3): 355–364.

Miasoedov, Boris Alekseevich. 1982. *Strana chitaet, slushaet, smotrit: statisticheskiĭ obzor*. Moscow: Financi i statistika.

Mihelj, Sabina. 2011. *Media Nations: Communicating Belonging and Exclusion in the Modern World*. Basingstoke: Palgrave Macmillan. Mitchell, Brian R. 2007. *International Historical Statistics: Europe, 1750–2005*, 6th edition. Basingstoke: Palgrave Macmillan.

Monteleone, Franco. 2006. *Storia della radio e della television in Italia*. Venezia: Tascabili Marsilio.

Nordenstreng, Kaarle, and Tapio Varis. 1974. *Television Traffic—A One-way Street? A Survey and Analysis of the International Flow of Television Material*. Paris: UNESCO.

Paulu, Burton. 1967. *Radio and Broadcasting on the European Continent*. Minneapolis, MN: University of Minnesota Press.

Paulu, Burton. 1974. *Radio and Television Broadcasting in Eastern Europe*. Minneapolis, MN: University of Minnesota press.

Prokhorova, Elena. 2003. "Fragmented Mythologies: Soviet TV Mini-series of the 1970s." Ph.D. Diss., University of Pittsburgh.

Raykoff, Ivan and Robert Deam Tobin 2007. "Introduction." In *A Song For Europe: Popular Music and Politics in the Eurovision Song Contest* edited by Ivan Raykoff and Robert Deam Tobin, xvii–xxi. Aldershot: Ashgate.

Roth-Ey, Kristin. 2011. *Moscow Prime Time: How the Soviet Union Built a Media Empire and Lost the Cultural Cold War*. Ithaca, NY: Cornell University Press.

Schlesinger, Philip. 1986. "Trading in Fictions: What Do We Know about British Television Imports and Exports?" *European Journal of Communication* 1(3): 263–287.

Schwoch, James. 2009. *Global Television: New Media and the Cold War, 1946–69*. Urbana and Chicago, IL: University of Illinois Press.

Smith, Anthony. 1998. "Television as a Public Service Medium." In *Television: An International History*, 2nd ed., edited by Anthony Smith, 38–54. Oxford: Oxford University Press.

Sparks, Colin. 2008. "After Transition: The Media in Poland, Russia and China." In *Finding the Right Place on the Map: Central and Eastern European Media Change in a Global Perspective*, edited by Karol Jakubowicz and Miklós Sükösd, 43–72. Bristol: Intellect Press.

Splichal, Slavko. 1994. *Media beyond Socialism: Theory and Practice in East-Central Europe*. Boulder, CO: Westview Press.

Stark, David. 1992. "From System Identity to Organizational Diversity: Analyzing Social Change in Eastern Europe." *Contemporary Sociology* 21(3): 299–304.

Television Entertainment in Socialist Eastern Europe 29

Steinmetz, Rüdiger, and Reinhold Viehoff. 2004. "The Program History of Genres of Entertainment on GDR Television." *Historical Journal of Film, Radio and Television* 24(3): 317–325.

Štětka, Václav. Forthcoming. "Back to the local? Transnational media flows and audience consumption patterns in the CEE region." In *Comparing Media Systems in Central and Eastern Europe: Politics, Economy and Culture*, edited by John Downey and Sabina Mihelj. Aldershot: Ashgate.

Taylor, Karin. 2006. *Let's Twist Again: Youth and Leisure in Socialist Bulgaria.* Vienna and Berlin: Lit Verlag.

Varis, Tapio. 1985. *International Flow of Television Programmes.* Paris: UNESCO.

Vončina, Nikola. 2003. *Najgledanije emisije, 1964–1971: Prilozi za povijest radija i televizije u Hrvatskoj V.* Zagreb: Hrvatska radiotelevizija.

Zhuk, Sergei I. 2010. *Rock and Roll in the Rocket City: The West, Identity, and Ideology in Soviet Dniepropetrovsk, 1960–1985.* Washington, D.C.: Woodrow Wilson Center Press.

2 Adventures in Early Socialist Television Edutainment

Anikó Imre

SOCIALIST TELEVISION AND ENTERTAINMENT

'Socialism'[1] and 'entertainment' sit uneasily together. At the very minimum, entertainment implies the luxury of having some degree of freedom over how to spend one's leisure time. Throughout the 1960s and 1970s, however, when television became a national medium in the Soviet-controlled region, viewers' freedom came down to a choice between turning their black-and-white television sets on or off, if they could even afford one. Moreover, under totalitarian state control, program imports, production and schedules were centrally monitored to conform to ideological directives that prescribed how socialist citizens should spend their leisure time in the ultimate service of the collective good. By virtue of being a home-based medium whose appeal is affective and intimate, television's emergence into a mass medium presented state party authorities with both a challenge and an opportunity. It posed a danger as an instrument of quiet subversion in the domestic sphere, which slipped past the surveillance of other public institutions. At the same time, its attraction as a mass medium of entertainment could be harnessed to forge a unity within the larger national family around shared identifications and pleasures, which could in turn fortify the frayed bond between state authorities and the broader population.

Most state socialist regimes recognized early on that, in order to benefit from the propaganda potential of television, they had to do more than prohibit and censor foreign program flows. To retain some control over the medium that John Ellis called "the private life of the nation state" (Ellis 1982, 5), they had to get in on the game and provide their populations with indigenous, party-approved entertainment. Nationalism became the cornerstone and mediating terrain of socialist governments' media policies across the region; and television was the key instrument of nationalistic edutainment. By the 1960s, Stalinist principles of forced Marxist-Leninist internationalism had lost their credibility along with the communist utopia of a classless, egalitarian international brotherhood. This created an opening for national regimes to adjust the central Soviet rhetoric in order to consolidate their own domestic powers. The dispersion of television broadcasting allowed for the subtle and measured deployment of entertainment in the domestic sphere of leisure. This would alleviate widespread disappointment with the realities of socialism and strengthen patriotic identification with the cause of the nation. Patriotic television edutainment helped to create a common ground between citizens and state governments in an unstated opposition to the Soviet occupier.

During the Cold War, writers, filmmakers and other intellectuals were regarded as flagship figures of anti-communist resistance. Dissident literature and film were charged with sending political messages in allegorical double language to 'the people,' who retreated into their homes away from politics, drawing a clear contrast between the public and private spheres. However, it has become increasingly clear that the sharp division between oppressor and oppressed, along with the opposition between the public sphere of resistance and the domestic sphere of escapism conceals a much more dispersed field of negotiations over power, characterized by compromise and cooptation rather than conflict and opposition. The evidence is not simply in the secret police files that have revealed since 1989 that some of the most respected intellectuals themselves were spies for the secret police. Rather, a closer look at television edutainment shows a vast field of power legitimation practices at the party's disposal—along with potential minefields that threatened to expose these practices—which existed below the international radar of high cultural products.

Research in the messy field of the affective politics of socialist television is in its infancy. My current contribution to such research discusses what we may consider the quintessential genre of popular fictional television edutainment in its first two formative decades: the historical adventure series. Sitcoms, soap operas and dramatic series produced in the U.S. and, to some extent, in Western Europe in the post-war years became synonymous with commercial scripted television entertainment worldwide. In comparison, when television became a household fixture in socialist countries in the 1960s, national broadcasters modeled their first domestically produced series after a narrow selection of foreign entertainment fictions focused on the past and turned sharply away from the present.

This generic preference had several advantages. Importing historical drama series reduced the likelihood that Western products and lifestyles and with them the contagious ideology of consumer capitalism would seep in. Furthermore, from the late 1960s through the 1970s, during their heyday, domestically produced historical adventure series allowed socialist regimes to teach selective history lessons and foster national identifications that also appeared to conform to ideological prescriptions demanded by the Soviet occupiers. These series contained ostentatious demonstrations of adherence to Soviet dogma, such as the glorification of folk culture or plotlines that rewarded peasant characters at the expense of the wealthy and powerful classes. Although such elements appear comically tendentious today, they were subtle enough not to undermine the shows' power

32 Anikó Imre

of identification with the nationalistic spectacle. In the most liberal socialist countries, the programs' propagandistic excess was released in another register of entertainment, political cabaret, inspiring hilarious ironic sendoffs.[2] The real lessons of these programs were borne out of the powerful convergence between folk mythology and high cultural legitimation. Historical adventure series glorified masculine national heroism in the face of a general notion of oppression, a traveling metaphor that could be applied to any threat to national sovereignty, with little regard to the historical accuracy of such depictions. While the shows situated these heroic struggles in the national past and made allusions to the international communist class struggle against capitalism, such allusions were canceled out by the undertones of national resistance against Soviet domination.

The offerings of socialist television broadened considerably in the 1980s with the introduction of color sets and the addition of second and, in some cases, third state broadcast channels, followed by the arrival of cable and satellite programming. However, the emotional impact of the early series, grounded as it was in the well-timed confluence of nationalistic identification and entertainment affect, has left a profound nostalgic residue that has endured into post-socialist times. As I discuss at the end, viewer nostalgia has also turned these series into platforms for political legitimation and touristic self-branding.

I elicit my argument about fostering state-directed nationalism through television edutainment from a closer look at two popular series: *The Captain of the Tenkes* (*A Tenkes kapitánya*, Hungarian Television, 1964) and *Janosik* (Polish Television, 1974). These two programs are exemplary of broader aesthetic, social and media policy trends of the 1960s and 1970s. Their success with audiences and the effectiveness of the political messages they communicated are rooted in three interrelated factors, all of which identify television entertainment as a key terrain for sustaining Eastern European nationalisms and for visualizing the contradictions at the core of these nationalisms at the same time. The first aspect is the socialist historical adventure series' loose treatment of historical facts, places and people. Paradoxically, this looseness proves essential to consolidating a spatio-temporally bound, linear national history around prominent historical actors. Both shows feature semi-fictional characters against a vague historical backdrop. As I show through my analysis of the genealogy of the Janosik story that informed the TV series, the national heroes on whom the protagonists are based actually operated across multilingual and multicultural territories well before the 19th-century struggles for national sovereignty began and before 20th-century national borders were drawn.

Second, the nationalistic projects at the heart of these adventure series are supported by a contradictory double cultural legitimation. They borrow from the alleged authenticity of folk culture, also fulfilling Marxist-Leninist expectations. However, this folk authenticity is invariably established through the mediation of national poets and writers, who have assumed

Adventures in Early Socialist Television Edutainment   33

ideological leadership roles in the cause of national independence since the late 18th century. Third, the historical figures after whom the protagonists are modeled were far from heroic. They were social bandits, local Robin Hoods, who embody a wish-fulfilling, contradictory collective belonging to a European cultural sphere and a voluntary submission to exoticizing Western European images of the periphery. The prevalence of such outlaw heroes conveys a regional specificity to the development of nationalisms and nation-states in Eastern and Southern Europe.

TELEVISION BROADCASTING AND
THE SOCIALIST ADVENTURE SERIES

Television was first introduced in some countries of the region in the pre-war period, in step with the U.S. and Western Europe. Small-scale state television broadcasting began as early as 1936 in Hungary and 1937 in Poland. World War II and its aftermath, involving the political and economic restructuring of the Soviet sphere of influence, interrupted the development of television infrastructures. State broadcasting did not start up again until the late 1950s. It began, for the most part, with sporadic broadcasts received by a few thousand subscribers in each country. Regional cooperation began almost immediately. The first program exchange, a 1957 Hungarian initiative, was titled Intervision, and included Czechoslovakia, Poland, the German Democratic Republic and Hungary ("A magyar televízió").

It was not until the 1960s, however, that the proliferation of television sets in the homes and the quality and quantity of programming transformed television into a truly national form of entertainment. In Hungary, where regular communist broadcasting began in 1957, the number of programming hours a week jumped from 22 to 40 between 1960 and 1965 ("A magyar televízió"). The Slovene broadcaster, Television Ljubljana, started transmitting its own television programming in 1958, with 700–800 television sets in Slovenia and about 4,000 in all of Yugoslavia, compared to 90% of all homes in the U.S. at the same time (Pusnik and Starc 2008, 779). In Czechoslovakia, where the war interrupted pre-war experimental broadcasts, trial public broadcasts began in 1953. The rapid increase in television access in the 1960s played a central role in the liberalization of the country's political climate. This liberalization was frozen following the Prague Spring of 1968, which was brutally crushed by the Soviet Union, turning television back into being the mouthpiece of the communist puppet regime (Newcomb 2004, 640). Television Romania was established in 1956 and added a second channel in 1968. This was then suspended in 1985 due to dictator Ceausescu's energy saving program until after 1989 according to Mustata's account in chapter 3 of this volume. In most countries, however, the mid-1960s saw the launch of a second channel and the extension of broadcast time to five, then six, and eventually seven days a week.

34   *Anikó Imre*

By the mid-1960s, all Soviet satellite governments faced a pressure to revise their ideological positions and programming policies to adjust to the opportunities and challenges presented by the new home-based mass medium. The launch of communication satellites, beginning with Sputnik-1 in 1957, the first Earth-orbiting artificial satellite and a crucial part of the Soviet space and communication strategy, increased fears of access to Western programming even in countries that did not share broadcast signals with the West. This challenge could only be minimized by rechanneling desires for capitalist lifestyles towards fostering national cohesion on the party leadership's terms. Communist governments therefore embarked on a careful import policy and a strategic domestic production of scripted programming in the 1960s. The first post-war broadcasts produced in communist Eastern Europe were of live theatrical and sports events, as well as news programming, feature films and a range of educational cultural programming. Television's shift to the center of public culture in the 1960s allowed communist governments to expand and solidify their educational-propaganda mandate through entertainment.

The greatest political risk involved in the expansion of television broadcasting was that, unlike feature films or print publications, broadcast signals could not simply be confined to state borders. Inhabitants of large regions in Yugoslavia, East Germany, Czechoslovakia, Hungary and Albania received either Austrian, Italian or West German programming. As Dana Mustata explains in Chapter 3 in this volume, even Romanian viewers suffering from the information lockdown and scarcity of programming imposed by the Ceausescu's dictatorship were able to access relatively more liberal Hungarian, Serbian, Bulgarian and Russian television. The risk of unpredictable social and cultural influences that state authorities were willing to take varied within the region. At the most liberal extreme, Slovenian TV Ljubljana and Croatian TV Zagreb established an official cooperation with the Italian RAI (Radiotelevisione Italiana) in the early 1960s. This happened despite protests from Communist Party authorities, who were anxious about the influx of Western news programs and the consumerist values transmitted by fictional programming (Pusnik and Starc 2008, 782–783). Significantly, such unprecedented openness towards Western-type entertainment was finally approved because it strengthened the national leadership's own strategy of championing Slovenian values and the cause of national independence in opposition to the top-down encroachment of Yugoslavian federalism, which was pushed by the government authorities who controlled the Yugoslav state broadcaster RTV (Pusnik and Starc 2008, 786).

However, especially in countries where access to capitalist broadcasting offered constant comparison, the ideological directives behind the new programming policy had to be carefully formulated lest they undermine a regionally coordinated vision of socialist utopia. Media and communication reforms in the 1960s therefore focused on television as the main institution

Adventures in Early Socialist Television Edutainment 35

for implanting socialist democratic values within entertainment. Television had to provide carefully selected information. It also had to shape the tastes of citizens to understand and appreciate Eurocentric art and culture and resist what were widely perceived as the detrimental effects of television: reducing faculties of appreciation for cultural quality as well as general mental and physical laziness.[3]

Socialist entertainment thus occupied a precarious place, carefully navigated by party authorities: it had to be democratic, addressing all citizens of the state; but it also had to adhere to the standards and values of Eurocentric taste and education. In both imported and domestically produced programs, it had to avoid genres that would create too much excitement about the West or were perceived as in low taste. Nationalistic historical adventure series were an ideal genre to cater to these contradictory demands. They seamlessly transferred to the new medium the project of an already established nationalistic literary culture focused on battles between good and evil, where the good side was embodied by masculine allegorical figures who defended the nation and resisted the evil intruder or oppressor. Such depictions stretched from 19th-century epic poetry inspired by earlier nationalistic movements and anti-establishment rebellions to the tales of partisan resistance and World War II heroism particularly favored by Moscow.

The allegorical structures and gender schemes of these narratives were also easily mapped onto a number of existing literary and film genres: popular boys' adventure stories by valued national and regional authors (e.g. Ferenc Molnár's *Pál Street Boys*, first published in 1907, an international favorite among boy-bonding stories); adolescent adventure tales about boys conquering nature; overtly propagandistic novels and films about heroic boy groups, often in wartime contexts (e.g. Arkady Gaidar's *Timur i evo komanda/Timur and his Platoon*, 1940); an abundance of war films and partisan films (e.g. the Yugoslav epic *Walter Defends Sarajevo*, dir. Hajrudin Krvavac, 1972); male-bonding TV series set in wartime (e.g. the Polish favorite *Czterej Pancerni I Pies/The Tank Crew of Four and a Dog*, 1966); and historical novels and film epics that evoked selected and glorified events from the national and European past. Feature films such as the Polish *Colonel Wolodyjowski* (dir. Jerzy Hoffman, 1969), the Bulgarian *Measure For Measure* (dir. Georgi Dyulgerov, 1981), the Romanian *Mihai Viteazul* (dir. Sergiu Nicolaescu, 1970), the Albanian *The Great Warrior Sandberg* (dir. Sergei Yutkevich, 1953), the Yugoslav *Battle of Kosovo* (dir. Zdravko Sotra, 1989) and the Hungarian *The Stars of Eger* (Dir. Zoltán Várkonyi, 1968), for instance, are all set during the region's Ottoman occupation and provide memorable lessons in patriotic male heroism. American Western films were also seamlessly incorporated into this loose genre of historical family edutainment (see Imre, 2011).

An entire subset of literary works, films and television programs about larger-than-life men fighting enemies of the nation revolve around outlaws. The television series of the 1960s and 1970s about outlaws often drew on

36   *Anikó Imre*

national writers' reworking of the unruly, often scant sources, which were at times embellished by folk songs and stories and often almost entirely reinvented in subsequent literary treatments. The seven-part Hungarian series *Sándor Rózsa* (1971), about the eponymous 19th-century outlaw, was adapted from early-20th-century writer Zsigmond Móricz's novels. The Lithuanian *Tadas Blinda* series (1972), featuring popular actor Vytautas Tomkus, was named after an outlaw hero whose story had been central to the national literature. In Bulgaria, the TV series *Kapetan Petko Voyvoda* (1974) celebrated 19th-century insurgent Petko Kiryakov Kaloyanov, who had joined forces with Garibaldi around 1866 to fight Ottoman Turks in Crete. The Romanian state commissioned a number of adventure films and television series, including the feature film *Haiducii/The Outlaws* (1966), followed by six other films about outlaws including *Iancu Jianu, the Tax Collector* (1980) and *Iancu Jianu, the Haiduc* (1981). They were directed by Diny Cocea and scripted by party-favored writer Eugen Barbuthe (Neubauer et al, 2010).

The early 18th century yielded an especially rich and ideologically profitable historical background against which to develop domestic historical adventures series about mythical outlaws-turned-national-heroes. In East-Central Europe, roughly the territory of the Habsburg Empire stretching across present-day Hungary, the Czech Republic, Slovakia, Poland, the Ukraine, Romania, Serbia, Croatia and Slovenia, the late 17th and early 18th century was a time of peasant uprisings against the Habsburgs. The most memorable and successful of these was led by Hungarian magnate Ferencz Rákóczi II, Prince of Transylvania, the richest landlord in the Kingdom of Hungary. His military operations were mostly conducted in the borderland area between the Habsburg and the Ottoman Empires. Rakóczi, also funded by the French crown looking to overthrow Habsburg domination in Europe, recruited the emancipated peasant soldiers of northeastern Hungary called *hajdus* or *haiducs* to join him. With their help, he seized control of much of Hungary by 1703. After several battles and much negotiation, the uprising failed and the prince was forced into exile first in Poland and then, for the last 18 years of his life, in Turkey. The subsequent return of Habsburg domination turned him and his fighters almost instantly into folk heroes. Some of his men went into hiding in inscrutable border areas and sustained themselves by highway robbery. Although these outlaws were not discriminating as to whom they robbed—or murdered, in many cases—folk stories, songs and later nationalist writers elevated them to the status of justice warriors who carried the legacy of the uprising by protecting the poor against the rich, many of whom were German-speaking foreigners.

Rákóczi and his outlaw followers were further revived and embraced in the region during the national revolutions of the 1840s. They were also appropriated by socialist party authorities by the 1960s, when nationalism made its way back into the official rhetoric. For the socialist regimes of the 1960s, the Rákóczi uprising and the outlaw resistance in its aftermath was appropriately heroic, safely removed from the present in history, and not associated with bloody revolts, unlike 19th-century national revolutions, which were feared to carry the risk of igniting street demonstrations. The uprising's benefits also included a narrative of unity and cooperation between peasants and the highest nobility. It was ideal for fortifying national consciousness, unimaginable under the earlier, forced internationalism of Stalinist crackdowns in the 1950s. At the same time, it provided a contained affective outlet through television entertainment, restricted to a kind of national fandom and intimacy that fused the national and the nuclear family.[4]

Not the least important, unlike feature films or literature, the historical adventure series often slipped under the radar of censorship because it qualified as family or youth entertainment, aligning such series with a flourishing animation and children's film production. By contrast, art films of the time that took up the resistant hero/outlaw theme fell into two different categories, both under heavy censorship: some were produced as propaganda material by official party culture, such as *Mihai Viteazul* (*Michael The Brave*, Sergiu Nicolaescu, 1971), the spectacular national epic production ordered and controlled by Ceausescu to boost national pride. Others expressed subtle allegorical opposition to the regime. Miklós Jancsó's stark black-and-white feature *Szegénylegények* (*Round-Up*, 1966) depicts the Austro-Hungarian Monarchy's revenge on outlaws who had gone into hiding in the aftermath of the 1848 revolutions through blatant historical anachronisms and a modernist aesthetic, which invited reflection on the ideological purges conducted by communist governments in the 1950s.

What the edutainment series have in common is that they were instrumental in fostering national unity through television entertainment not despite but because of the fact that they were mostly made up. In other words, their affective power and longevity within national memory derives precisely from folk culture's and high literature's mutual validation of nationalism's loose treatment of historical fact. These series are, for the most part, also trans-regional and often trans-European in their construction. The nationalism they weave around improper, outlaw heroes implies an unacknowledged embrace of colonial, Western European constructions of the Eastern peripheries as rebellious and wild, a kind of permanent Wild East where the laws of civil nation-states are subordinated to popular justice.

NATIONALISM AND ENTERTAINMENT: *TENKES* AND *JANOSIK*

A Tenkes kapitánya (*Captain of the Tenkes*, 1964) was the very first drama series produced by the Hungarian state broadcaster Magyar Televízió, running in 13 25-minute parts in 1964. It is also one of the most memorable series of all time. It is set in the early 1800s, during the Rákóczi uprising.

38   *Anikó Imre*

Peasant *kuruc*[5] leader Máté Eke, in charge of a handful of freedom fighters, hides out in wine cellars in the hills of Western Hungary to protect the poor against the occupying Habsburg army, who conduct their operations from the castle of Siklós. In each episode, the outlaws circumvent or overcome the well-armed Habsburg soldiers with cunning, an intimate knowledge of the local environment and the help and collaboration of local villagers.

The series began broadcasting in January 1964, on a Saturday. The episodes were repeated in the course of the next day. The entire series was broadcast again in the second half of 1964, followed by over 10 subsequent reruns so far. The episodes were molded together into a feature film almost immediately, released in 1965 (Deák-Sárosi 2006). Writer Ferenc Örsi turned his script into a juvenile adventure novel in 1967, to be reprinted six more times just during the Kádár period. Thanks to a large extent to regular reruns, the theme song is recognized by everyone in Hungary to this day. The show even inspired a popular song, which topped the Hungarian charts shortly after the series was launched. Even a stage musical adaptation has been produced recently, performed annually against the backdrop of Siklós Castle, the location for both the series and the actual historical events on which it is loosely based.

The Polish *Janosik* (1974), directed by Jerzy Passendorfer, has also enjoyed uninterrupted, cult popularity since its release. It is about a Slovak outlaw with a Hungarian name, who operated across several fluid borders during his short life in the 18th century. Poems and novels written of Janosik's life are required reading in Slovak and Polish schools. His story inspired 10 films and TV series altogether in the Czech, Slovak and Polish territories between 1929 and 2009. Similar to *Tenkes*, it has been released on DVD recently.

Janosik and *Tenkes* are remarkably similar in their aesthetic and narrative dimensions, their educational mission to reinforce a Marxist-socialist version of national histories, and their post-socialist cult endurance. Their construction is virtually identical: a memorable title sequence shows the heroes, in folk period costumes, riding on horseback in a wide shot that evokes Westerns, to an inspiring 'adventure' tune. In both cases, the theme music took on a life of its own by mobilizing affective associations with freedom and social justice. The music itself generated a kind of socialist television fandom at the interface of folk motifs and state-sanctioned high culture. In *Janosik*'s case, it was composed by Jerzy Matuszkiewicz, a widely celebrated jazz musician and composer, who had also established himself in the Polish film industry, something that lent instant prestige to the production. At the same time, the theme evokes Polish highland folk songs, with flutes, trumpet and guitar sounds, infusing the folk tunes with the sense of adventure and romance. *Tenkes*'s theme was composed by venerable composer (of Serbian origin) Tihamér Vujicsics. The instrumental melody resonates with the 'Rákóczi March,' which is considered an unofficial Hungarian anthem. It is likely that the March itself was actually written in the aftermath of the uprising, in the 1730s, and existed in several versions. But the popular tune had also been lifted into classical music by Hector Berlioz in his 'La Damnation De Faust' (1846) and by Franz Liszt, who drew on the theme when writing his Hungarian Rhapsody no. 15. The music thus instantly carried a subtle set of connotations in which folk culture, national history and national art were validated by the music's previous career in European high culture.

Both series adopt a mixed procedural-serial format. Most episodes are self-contained adventures with predictable outcomes, with plots that have the heroes get out of a hopelessly tight spot, set against the larger collective story arc of historical events. The adventures take place in a dialectically conceived nationalistic universe where the honest underdog fights the good fight against the evil but not too smart oppressor. The episodes often introduce a humorous tone, mostly due to the failed intrigues of the ridiculous Count Horvath in *Janosik* and the bumbling Baron Eberstein in *Tenkes*, as well as comic sidekick characters such as the scheming innkeeper Dudva in *Tenkes*. Both shows obey the rules of tame socialist representational decorum and stay away from depictions of sex and blood—often cited by fans as the main positive distinction of this native entertainment format over most of American film and television. Sword fights, chases and modest battle sequences provide low budget but effective spectacle. The shows' heteronormative gender regime is fundamental to the central socialist regulation of nationalistic pleasures. The inevitable romantic element is concentrated on broadly drawn female characters whose main contribution is to pine after the heroes. The latter then appropriately resist these temptations and demonstrate loyalty to a single special, clean and handsome peasant girl (Maryna and Veronika, respectively). The romance is already established at the beginning of *Tenkes* and develops only slightly across the episodes, mostly due to outside intrigue, which only serves to reinforce socialist family values.

Although the series is unwatchable by today's standards of nimble cinematography, special effects, fast-paced, clever dialogue and naturalistic acting, they delighted socialist audiences at the time. By the 1960s, the historical adventure genre had been well-recognized by Polish and Hungarian audiences, who were familiar with Zorro movies, Douglas Fairbanks films and other Western costume adventure dramas, such as the French-Italian production *Fanfan la tulip* (1952, dir. Christian-Jacque). The nationalistic fandom that the series ignited was also anchored in the actors who played the leads. Peperezcko, widely considered a 'hunk,' delivered many viewers in Poland as well as the GDR to the series. His role was similar to those of other television and movie actors who established a limited transnational fandom within the socialist bloc. The best known of these is probably Gojko Mitic, the Serbian-born movie and television star, who played the lead Indian characters in the famed GDR Westerns, or *Indianerfilme*. Gyula Szabó, who played Eke Máté, the Captain of the Tenkes, was less

40 *Anikó Imre*

young, less tall and less dashing but well-liked and credible as the heroic paternal protector and freedom fighter. Both series enlisted the best and most popular acting talent of the time.

The oddest aspect of these series to the contemporary viewer is the ethnographic sequences that interrupt the narrative's unfolding to feature folk dance and music. These apparently unmotivated inserts were paradoxically meant to authenticate the historical events and characters on which the programs are loosely based, showcasing 'organic' elements of national culture. The folk elements often clash with the other educational purpose of the series, which requires teaching and modeling European erudition. The two purposes cross most jarringly in the series' use of language: while the Eurocentric education of the masses necessitates using the most normative, literary register of language, the desire to create folk authenticity produces an inevitably forced provincial dialect. The dialect used in *Tenkes* is a geographically unspecific mix of rural accents as it is imagined by actors trained in prestigious drama schools. Janosik and his band use the Polish Gorale highlander dialect. What is missing from both series is precisely the daily language that most viewers would speak. This schizophrenic situation, in which catering to the regular viewer was undermined by efforts to educate the ideal viewer, characterized the entire period of socialist media cultures.

Tenkes's scriptwriter Ferenc Örsi said in his memoir that he had written the series at his children's request, who were disappointed when imported series such as *Robin Hood* and *Zorro* ended in the early 1960s (in Deák-Sárosi, 2006). This is a charming anecdote that covers up what was no doubt a range of political considerations behind launching the first dramatic series. It also inadvertently reveals the place and intention for such a series: to address what was perceived as a child-like populace's legitimate yearning for innocent entertainment that is in step with European trends but also reinforces nationalism as a glue between party-led government and anti-communist viewers in their homes, while flashing its Soviet-approved educational intention. The series was recognizable to viewers for its folk tale resonances familiar from youth and children's fiction, most notably 'Ludas Matyi,' ('Matt the Goose Boy'), an epic poem written by Mihály Fazekas in 1804, first published in 1817. The story has its origins in folk tales that reach back to the 16th century, about a poor boy who takes cunning revenge on a greedy feudal overlord for stealing his goose. The story, embraced by the socialist regimes as a parable about peasant intelligence versus capitalist greed, inspired a number of filmic adaptations, most famously Attila Dargay's 1977 animated tale of the same title. *Ludas Matyi* was also the name of the Hungarian socialist government's own satirical newspaper (1945–92), which published officially approved humor that also allowed some pokes at socialism.

Apart from the evidence of lower production values, there is nothing particularly televisual about either series. The historical adventure cycle

Adventures in Early Socialist Television Edutainment   41

encompassed and easily crossed between film and television at this experimental time when socialist regimes were trying to figure out what to do with an emerging entertainment mass medium, and when—in the absence of commercial television—film, TV and radio were under the same state control and budget. This is why both series were easily condensed into features films, which elevated the prestige of the series as essential parts of national culture.

FROM CROSS-BORDER SOCIAL BANDIT
TO SOCIALIST NATIONAL HERO

Both series solicited nationalistic identification right from the credit sequence by the joint effects of music, heroic action and spectacular landscape. The introductory themes evoked and encapsulated the oppressed poor's rightful fight against the rich, and, in case of *Tenkes*, foreign overlords. The backdrops were different: in case of *Tenkes*, it was the rolling hills of Western Hungary near Siklós Castle; in the case of *Janosik*, the high mountains of the Tatras. However, both are open outdoor landscapes that provide the perfect hiding and battle places for manly men, much like in Westerns. Neither were historically accurate sites of the Rákóczi uprising and its aftermath. Siklós Castle simply provided an appropriately scenic location, irrespective of the fact that most of the actual military operations and brigand activities took place in northeastern Hungary and present-day Ukraine and Slovakia. Such inaccuracy was minimized by referencing some of the historical figures and events of the uprising in selected episodes, including Rákóczi himself.

In a similar vein, the Polish series moves the historical Janosik from his actual place of birth and life in the Slovak-Hungarian lower Tatras to the Polish highlands. This area had been previously embraced by Polish intellectuals of the 1830s and then again after the crushing of the anti-Russian Polish uprising in 1864 as the mythical birthplace of ancestral Polish culture. Nationalist writers were fascinated by the ethnic group called Gorale who lived in this border area, a shepherd community who spoke their own Polish-Slovak dialect and originally migrated there from the Romanian region of the Carpathians. The Gorale were 'discovered' and romanticized in nationalistic accounts as a group unspoiled by civilization and foreign influence. Literary accounts of outlaw heroes, including Janosik, were associated with the Gorale long before the TV series, which gives its protagonist a highland accent that instantly evokes a long history of popular nationalism located in the Gorale highlands (Rassloff 2010).

The same vague historiography applies to the main characters in both series. Although the protagonist of *Tenkes*, Máté Eke, is not based on a single historical persona, the character and the plots are familiar from the large folk and literary web gradually woven around the Rákóczi uprising,

42   *Anikó Imre*

the majority of it generated in the 19th century. The actual life of the outlaw Juraj Janosik is dwarfed by the richness and complexity of the mythic afterlife in which he became a national legend in Slovak, Polish and Czech cultures alike. Even his name has multiplied in the course of its various appearances, oscillating among Johannes, Georg, Janko, Janik, Janicek, Jasiek, Janosz, Janos, Juro and Durko (Rassloff 2010). 'Janosik' is a derivation of the Hungarian 'János' with the Czech/Slovak -ik suffix attached (Vortruba 2006). A Slovak-Hungarian borderland figure, his legend only entered Czech culture in the late 19th century, after being established as a Slovak folk hero. In his work on social bandits, Eric Hobsbawm saw him as a noble robber, while Milichericik considered him a rebel against feudal exploitation. A marker of historical transformation in the ethnically and religiously complex Carpathian region, Janosik's story was shaped by market songs, fairy tales, brigand stories, shepherd myth, nativity plays, the literatures of national revival and across various media in socialism and thereafter (Rassloff 2010).

It is significant that, similar to other 17th- and 18th-century outlaws, Janosik became nationalized during the 19th-century national revivals only once Western European literary Romantics became interested in the lawless and exotic peripheries. His legend fit the European outlaw model, which was greatly influenced by Friedrich Schiller's *The Robbers*. Schiller was a professor of history at the University of Jena in Saxony, where many Slovak intellectuals took his courses and absorbed a fervent German ethnic activism. Cultural nationalism was thus first channeled back to Central and Eastern Europe through German high cultural mediation. On a European scale, Janosik's nationalistic-romantic appropriation was further facilitated by authors such as Lord Byron and Alexander Pushkin. Byron became available in Polish in 1830s and in Hungarian in the 1840s (Vortruba 2006). From Schiller to Dumas, from Scott to Mérimée, from Pushkin to Verga, Europe-wide high Romanticism rendered the old outlaw-bandit figure palatable, honorable and at times misanthropic in stories set in the European peripheries, which were associated with passion, desire, pride, revenge and lack of concern for the rule of law and convention. At the same time, this Western European projection created a wider exposure for Eastern European literatures and cultures. Eastern European folk poetry collected by writers was translated into French and German and was then plagiarized and pastiched, embellished by colorful inventions of *haiducs* and vampires (Neubauer et al, 2010).[6] Such high cultural works about Janosik depart from folk songs, which rarely celebrate the brigand; rather, they paint the image of an ethnic rebel against Hungarian oppression. Jan Botto's poem *The Death of Janosik* is one of the most memorable records of the legend's high literary nationalization, which is included in the Czech and Slovak national educational curriculum at all levels (Vortruba 2006).

Under 20th-century authoritarian regimes, two kinds of Janosik myths were taken up: in the pro-Nazi Slovak Republic and post-war

Adventures in Early Socialist Television Edutainment 43

Czechoslovakia, Janosik was deployed variously as both representative and subversive of the ruling regime. During the war years, communist artists evoked Janosik subversively. In 1941, the illegal Slovak Communist Party initiated 'Janosik Combat Units' to carry out anti-governmental agitation. Underground agit-prop literature of the time reactivated Janosik's rebellious Hungarian *kuruc* imagery. After the communist takeover of 1948, the new rulers decided to convert the subversive Carpathian highwayman into a patriotic icon of the socialist state. The national opera embarked on a giant production of Jan Botto's *Death of Janosik*; and the state sponsored several patriotic films about him. The most successful of these was the two-part *Janosik* (1962–63), directed by Paľo Bielik, featuring battle scenes with thousands of extras in brilliant color. The film fuses the myth of a noble robber with a socialist-realist interpretation of class struggle. It is comparable in its parameters and effort to build a shared socialist national ground to Passendorfer's 1974 Polish film version of *Janosik*, which followed the 1973 TV series. The film and the series established Janosik as a Polish national hero, subtly repositioning him in Polish history through the location, costumes and set design, which were suggestive of the late 18th and early 19th century as much as the early 18th century. The new ethnic contours of the noble robber in the Polish versions are evident in the choice of his antagonist Bartos, a sneaky killer who is identified as a Slovak-Hungarian (Rassloff 2006).

Socialist governments eagerly capitalized on the accumulated cultural appeal of outlaw historical figures when they deployed television as a nationalistic edutainment platform. Early historical adventure series were successful in solidifying popular nationalism not simply because audiences naively gobbled up the nationalism presented in depoliticized entertainment formats. In fact, the underlying political propaganda intent of these shows was almost certainly not lost on viewers. However, the shared recognition of such intent did not necessarily undermine the affective bonding within national fandom. On the contrary, it created yet another layer of identification, which only rendered more complex the experience of budding national television spectatorship. The added aspect of ironic awareness was articulated in cautious jokes and political parodies of the time. For instance, while the Janosik myth was embraced by the Czechoslovak state, it was also often parodied or rendered fantastic, as in *Zbojnik Jurko* (*Robber Jurko*) 1976, Viktor Kubal's famous animated feature. From the 1970s on, political cabaret provided an outlet for a growing number of satires. The film *Paco, The Brigand of Hybe* (1975, dir. Martin Tapak, based on a novel by Peter Jaros) is a parody of Bielik's sweeping nationalistic movie *Janosik*. Stanislav Stepka's Radosina Naïve Theater performed in the 1970s the parodic play *Jaáánosíík* in student bars and other places of alternative culture, connecting political cabaret with the avant-garde as well as jazz, rock, beat and amateur theater. Such performances demystified not only the Janosik tradition but also the

44 *Anikó Imre*

institution of academic theater, along with official socialist state culture and its fabricated national identity, conveyed through the convoluted language of socialist newsspeak (Rassloff 2006). Political cabaret thrived in Hungary as well. The fandom around *Tenkes* and the historical outlaw adventure genre was no doubt boosted by Géza Hofi's legendary parody of the tendentious acting and contrived speech in the series *Sándor Rózsa*. Such parodies only fermented a kind of oppositional nationalist unity over the shared skill to engage in double talk and laughter.

CONCLUSIONS

The contradictory nature of national intimacy that the historical adventure genre built around the outlaw figure has become even more evident in post-socialism. On the one hand, right-wing nationalist factions have drawn on the early 18th century for validation, as is indicated in the very name of the most prominent Hungarian ultranationalist website, 'kurucinfo.hu.' On the other hand, the popular nationalism associated with the early adventure series has been mobilized by various corporate and state players as a consumer enticement and branding strategy. In 2008, on the 15th anniversary of Slovakia's founding, Prime Minister Robert Fico called Janosik "the greatest role model for my government" (Rassloff 2006). *Tenkes* has been embraced for destination branding purposes by the city of Siklós, where the series was shot. The local government, eagerly supported by citizens nostalgic for the memories of the early 1960s when TV cameras and stars swirled around, built a wax museum that features the main characters. In addition, since 2009, the Year of Cultural Tourism in Europe, Siklós has been home to a folk festival that evokes a vague historical tableau based on the TV show, complete with women in folk costumes baking bread, an equestrian show, wine tasting, crafts and a musical based on the TV show set against Siklós Castle.

The transition from national mobilization to touristic city-branding has been rendered fairly seamless by the blatant inauthenticity and constructedness of the TV-generated national myth. As I have argued, through providing carefully measured nationalistic fictional programming, socialist regimes were able to co-opt and redirect against a Moscow-based, distant communist regime the oppositional potential of nationalism's affective charge. They surreptitiously consolidated anti-Soviet resistance on an emotional ground that disguised propaganda as innocent entertainment. This was so not despite but because of the fictionalization at the heart of these series: the bandits in the center were lifted from historical periods of pre-national state formations and operated across shifting borders and linguistically hybrid territories. For the most part, they were robbers and murderers, who had to be retroactively nationalized and elevated as heroes in tendentious encounters between folk and high culture.

Adventures in Early Socialist Television Edutainment   45

Besides calling attention to the importance of television in studies of socialist national cultures, these shows, considered together, also produce unintended accounts of a historical regional culture arching over the singular national histories. This cross-border relevance, due primarily to television's international distribution during socialism, itself building on the common trajectories of nationalism emerging from common imperial cultures, outlines a regional experience, way of expression and identification. This regional vision contests the national fragmentation to which academic research in the social sciences and Slavic studies often subject these cultures, and to which they subject themselves for economic or political reasons. This has thus been the beginning of a larger argument for considering popular socialist television an indispensable resource with which to complement and connect social scientific accounts of East European nationalisms and cultural approaches so far focused on East European literature and cinema.

NOTES

1. I privilege the term 'socialism' over 'communism' here as it is the way most of the Soviet satellite regimes themselves increasingly preferred to designate themselves following the Stalinist 1950s.
2. See Géza Hofi's memorable parody of the series *Rózsa Sándor* (1971, dir. Miklós Szinetár), inspired by the mythical adventures of the eponymous 19th-century Hungarian outlaw.
3. For instance, to conform to these directives, in 1968 Hungarian Television (MTV) divided its programming among different departments this way: art films and programs that promoted cultural appreciation made up 30% of all programs; 9% of broadcast time went to literary and dramatic programming; news programs, responsible for political agitation, consisted of 29%; youth and children's programming made up 11.5%; and informational programming such as nature documentaries took up 2.5%. In addition, a daily morning program called "School Television," where experts gave lectures on a broad range of academic subjects to viewers invested in supplementary education, made up 11% (Horváth). With the addition of Friday, a sixth day of weekly programming, that year (Monday remained a non-broadcast day devoted to work), programs were reorganized so that each weekday had a distinct educational profile. Entertainment programs were concentrated on the weekend.
4. Rákóczi's portrait is currently on the 500-Forint banknote in Hungary, his statues pepper the landscape and there is no town that would not have streets and schools named after him.
5. A term used to denote armed anti-Habsburg rebels in the Kingdom of Hungary between 1671–1711.
6. "It may be said then that the theme of the haiduc-outlaw was a powerful influence over the emergence of the vernacular literatures of South-Eastern (and Eastern) Europe, involving an intense back-and-forth of literary activities and influences—from country to country, from East to West and vice versa, and from metropolitan, printed 'high' literature to performative balladry" (Neubauer et al, 2010).

46   *Anikó Imre*

REFERENCES

Dawidziak, Mark. 2010. "'Mad Men' Phenomenon Made AMC a Big-Name Brand." *The TV Blog with Mark Dawidziak.* July 25, 2010. http://www.cleveland.com/tv-blog/index.ssf/2010/07/mad_men_phenomenon_made_amc_a_big-name_brand.html.

Deák-Sárosi, László. 2006. "Nemzeti kalandfilm-sorozatunk." *Filmkultúra* http://www.filmkultura.hu/regi/2006/articles/essays/tenkes.hu.html.

Ellis, John. 1982. *Visible Fictions.* London: Routledge.

Horváth, Edina. "A magyar televízió müsorpolitikája—1968." Hungarian Television (MTV) Archives. http://www.tvarchivum.hu/?id=279930.

Imre, Anikó. 2011. "Eastern Westerns: Socialist Edutainment or National Transvestism." *New Review of Film and Television Studies* 9(2): 152–169.

Lavery, David. "*Breaking Bad* as Basic Cable Quality TV." *Critical Studies in Television.* http://www.criticalstudiesintelevision.com/index.php?siid=13805.

"A magyar televízió története." ("The History of Hungarian Television"). Hungarian Television Archives. http://mek.niif.hu/02100/02185/html/516.html.

Mustata, Dana. 2012. "Bordering Romania: Transmitting and Receiving Television." *Journal of Popular Film and Television* (forthcoming).

Neubauer, Joep Leerssen, Marcel Cornis-Pope, Biljana Markovic, Dragan Klaic. 2010. "The Rural Outlaws of East-Central Europe." In *History of the Literary Cultures of East-Central Europe: Junctures and Disjuncture in the 19ᵗʰ and 20ᵗʰ Centuries. Volume 4: Types and Stereotypes,* edited by Marcel Cornis-Pope and John Neubauer, 407–440. Amsterdam: John Benjamins Publishing.

Newcombe, Horace, ed. 2004. *Encyclopedia of Television.* London: Routledge.

Pusnik, Marusa and Gregor Starc. 2008. "An Entertaining (R)evolution: The Rise of Television in Socialist Slovenia." *Media Culture and Society* 30(6): 777–793.

Rassloff, Jutta. 2010. "Juraj Janosik." In *History of the Literary Cultures of East-Central Europe: Junctures and Disjuncture in the 19ᵗʰ and 20ᵗʰ Centuries. Volume 4: Types and Stereotypes,* edited by Marcel Cornis-Pope and John Neubauer, 441–456. Amsterdam: John Benjamins Publishing.

Ungár, Tamás. 2002. "A Tenkes kapitánya és a panoptikum." *Népszabadság Online,* June 8. http://nol.hu/archivum/archiv-65713.

Vortruba, Martin. 2006. "Hang Him High: The Elevation of Janosik to an Ethnic Icon." *Slavic Review* 65(1): 24–44.

3 Television in the Age of (Post-)Communism
The Case Of Romania

Dana Mustata

Studies on television in Eastern Europe so far have been consistent in understanding television through notions of political control that have reiterated the East–West opposition of the Cold War. Whether political control has been acknowledged, denied or complicated, television in this European geopolitical space has been limited to conceptual structures that have prioritized politics at the expense of attention to the medium itself. This is not to deny that politics have played an important role in Eastern European television, nor to deny that politics do form an important contextual situatedness for understanding television. However, limiting television to political understandings loses sight of the very object of study: the medium of television. Even though scarce, scholarship on television in Eastern Europe has so far fit into a politically reductionist trend that has produced political stories of television, rather than television histories. Emerging scholarship in this area needs therefore to initiate such television histories by attempting to first understand the medium before discussing its relations to politics.

Previous scholarship on television in communist regimes persistently followed the politically reductionist trend, in which television has been invariably described from the premise of political submissiveness. Noam in his book *Television in Europe* (1991) introduced broadcasting in the former Easter European regimes as "subordinated to the pursuit of state control over society" and "rigorously nonindependent" (Noam 1991, 274). Burton Paulu wrote in 1974 in *Radio and Television Broadcasting in Eastern Europe* that transmission and programming contents were subject to Party control. Paul Flenley (1997) in the edited book *Television in the Russian Federation* talked about a "centralised state-controlled system serving the ideological and political needs of the Soviet Communist Party" and wrote that "the fundamental role of television and radio in Soviet society still remained the same, i.e. to mobilize support for government and Party policy" (Flenley 1997, 111). Writing about the (former) Soviet Union, Mickiewicz (1988; 1997) wrote about factual television programs in the former Soviet Union from the same political perspective. This politically reductionist trend of scholarship on Eastern European television has taken political and historical factors as *a priori* determinants for conceptualizing

48 *Dana Mustata*

television in these European spaces. Upcoming scholarship on Eastern European television needs to start with understanding the medium itself before making arguments on the relations between the medium and its political context.

The discussion included in this chapter is not as ambitious as setting up a new framework for conceptualizing television in Eastern Europe. However, it is meant to point out to the fact that television should be looked at through looser political filters, at times even abandoning presumptions of relevant East–West differences. Looking at the case of Romania, I will argue that television has only been a national medium at a specific stage in its development and has been defined by political control for a transient period in its communist history. Starting from what John Ellis (2000) described within the British context as fundamental periods in television's development ('the era of scarcity' and the 'era of availability'), I will show that Romanian television has undergone the same steps of development; and it was the specifics of the availability era that enabled political control of the broadcast institution in the late 1970s and throughout the 1980s. Local political and historical differences among television broadcasters in different European countries are inherent to this specific stage of development; and it is at this stage that politics had a leading role in the local paths that the medium took. Once again, this is not meant to deny politics when it comes to the history of television in Eastern European countries. Rather, it is meant to deny the central role of politics in the study of television history in this area. Besides national politics, other factors played the main role in the development of Romanian television: from technological, professional, institutional factors specific to the medium to European broadcast relations.

THE MEDIUM WITHOUT BORDERS

Transnational broadcast relations were central to the incipient phase of Romanian television. They played out despite and to the detriment of the state's socialist politics and marked a period in the history of Romanian television when it resembled television in other European countries. This period was characterized by what John Ellis (2000) referred to as 'the era of scarcity': limited television channels, partial broadcasting time, discontinuous television schedules and an emergent penetration of television into domestic private spaces and daily routines. In the age of scarcity, television had yet to claim its identity, form and social role. The unsettled character of the medium also characterized the early phase of Romanian television. The following discussion will illustrate how this early phase of scarcity allowed Romanian television to avoid political control. The pursuit of know-how became the main driving motor behind early Romanian television. This empowered television professionals who took charge of the medium and

Television in the Age of (Post-)Communism   49

undermined political control. Relations with other media as well as relations with foreign broadcasters became the channels through which the first expertise was acquired in early Romanian television.

Romanian television's age of scarcity lasted until roughly the late 1960s. From the first broadcasts in 1956 until the late 1960s, television in Romania lacked a clear aesthetic, professional and institutional identity. Just like in other countries, this status of uncertainty allowed first of all for experimentation with other art and media forms. Early Romanian programs that were highly valued, also among international juries, were in fact musical films presented as televised compilations of choreography and sound. *Omul din umbra la soare* (*The Shadow Man in the Sun*) directed by Valeriu Lazarov in 1964 won a special mention of the jury at the Monte-Carlo International Television Festival (Pasca 2001, 5). Another musical film *Omul si Camera* (*The Man and the Camera*) also directed by Valeriu Lazarov won three international prizes: first prize at the Cairo International Festival of Television Films, the award for best directing act and most original work at the Prague International Television Festival and the award of international critics together with a special mention of the jury at the Monte-Carlo International Television Festival (Pasca 2001, 6). The film showed a choreographed synchronization of the sound with the camerawork, while the camera focused in a reflexive way on presenting to the viewer the new television environment: the studio, the lighting, the mise-en-scene.[1] TV directors such as Lazarov were the first acknowledged professionals of Romanian television. The role of directors as the first professionals of television was justified by the lack of an aesthetic identity of the early medium. This emphasizes that television was tributary to other art forms in its incipient stage and this was not only characteristic of Romanian television, but of television in most countries.

Like anywhere else in the world, Romanian television was also indebted to the radio in its early stage. The first television content consisted of genres taken over from the radio: current affairs programs, theater plays, children's programs, music recitals, interviews and the weather bulletin. The migration of radio programs to television took place through the end of the 1960s. *Mai aveti o intrebare?* (*Do You Still Have a Question?*) was a science program that first became popular on the radio before it gained popularity on television. "There was a time when everything that was the best on the radio—both people and programs—were taken, no questions asked, and transplanted into television" said Dionisie Sincan, the creator of *Mai aveti o intrebare*. (Sincan 1996, 215). The pioneers of Romanian television were in fact radio professionals.

> In 1960, just like the rest of my colleagues, I was brought from the radio—where I was a presenter—to the 'news' department of television. Those were the crazy years of pioneering, when television was submissive to radio from all points of view. Everything was live, the

50 Dana Mustata

16 mm film was still a dream and the only illustrative materials used were photographs. [. . .] Back then, television news was searching for its ideal form, being still indebted to radio. Cross-cuts were also used in television, alternating from one news presenter to another (Florin Bratescu qtd. in Munteanu 1972, 40)

While early television was searching for its identity, its institutionalization also remained up to negotiation. This is something that Elsner, Muller and Spangenberg (1990) also described in the case of early German television, arguing that the lack of a medial identity created a space of negotiation between different social and political actors. In Romania, the uncertain status of the new medium followed a loose political regulation and enabled the rise of television professionals able to negotiate and undermine political power. From the beginning, Romanian television was envisioned by the Communist Party as an institution in the service of the country's ideology. Since its founding in 1956, it was placed under the supervision of the Radio and Television Committee responding to the Council of Ministers. This political body was meant to ensure the ideological and political role of the broadcast institution in society. However, what television was and what it could be was still to be discovered at that time.

In that uncertain period of television, interpersonal relations played a central role in the organization and managing of the broadcasting institution. In 1962, the General Secretary of the Romanian Communist Party Gheorghe Gheorghiu-Dej appointed Silviu Brucan to be Vice President of television, with whom he had a relation of trust and friendship.

There used to be between us a personal relation unusual for someone who was ruling the country and the Party with a strong hand and who was used to everybody responding to his decisions as if to a military command. We started working together as early as 23 August 1944 (that is, the day Romania entered the sphere of Soviet influence), when his rule within the party was still uncertain. The fact that he had asked me to help him write his speeches on the basis of his honest appreciation of me created this 'special bond' between us. [. . .] In 1962, when I returned to Romania after almost seven years as Romanian ambassador to the United States, Gheorghiu-Dej called me in and offered me the position of state minister, the second-in-command at the Ministry of Foreign Affairs. I refused vehemently, arguing I was not a good diplomat and I did not like an executive position, which didn't allow me to make personal contribution. [. . .] After a month, he called me in again and told me that in Romania we had to create a television that ought to educate the people, but also entertain them. After my years spent in America, I was the best person to spearhead this. He told me that what we called television did not please him and every time he watched programs in the evening, he did not find them interesting. (Brucan 1996, 41)

Television in the Age of (Post-)Communism   51

As Vice President of television, Silviu Brucan became inspired by British television in his vision of what Romanian television could be. His management challenged the political supervision of the Party over the new broadcast institution.

> I liked the idea of organizing the institution of television. I thought of some policies that needed to be instituted. I warned [Gheorghiu-Dej], however, that I would only accept his offer if I were given the freedom to do what I thought was best and if other high officials wouldn't interfere. He agreed and at the first meeting that we analyzed the activity of Radiotelevision, I reported that I had received five phone calls from members of the political party, who were also present there at the meeting. Two of them thought the programs were informative and entertaining, while three protested that I was showing naked women on television or that I was allowing [. . .] satire programs that mocked the Party, or that the series the 'Saint' perverted the youth and incited them to crimes. I asked then: "Who should I listen to, comrade Gheorghiu?" He replied immediately: "To yourself. It's your responsibility." And then he warned everybody to let me be as "Tache (that is, Silviu Brucan) knows what he's doing." (Brucan 1996, 41–42)

Brucan brought on Romanian television entertainment, such as political satires and British series. He developed close relations with the BBC, which became a source for the transfer of know-how to the television center in Bucharest. "Ever since I was appointed to run our Radio and Television system, the visit to the BBC became an important objective of mine," wrote Silviu Brucan to the managing director of BBC Radio, Frank Gillard in 1964.[2]

To M.B. Latey, head of BBC Eastern European Service, Brucan confessed: "Knowing the way TV programs are done in England is a must these days. For the time being, I ordered some British equipment at Marconi."[3] In December 1964, Brucan went on a three-week visit to the BBC to learn about aspects of organization at a television production center, from architectural design to administrative issues.[4] At the BBC, Brucan was very much appreciated for his genuine interest in learning television.

> He is their equivalent of our Director-General. [. . .] He is a most engaging and amusing person and his English is fluent. I found him an excellent company and very ready to talk freely, even dangerously. [. . .] He professes a life-long admiration for the BBC and wants to spend his time with producers and in studios, seeing how programmes are prepared and directed, not in a round of official lunches, dinners and receptions. What a relief to have a visiting potentate with that kind of purpose in mind![5]

52   *Dana Mustata*

A letter signed by A.S.W. Skempton, Senior Assistant at BBC's Television Liaison, spoke of the relations that Silviu Brucan envisioned between BBC and Romanian Radio and Television, which were not to abide by Party control:

> Mr. Brucan, as you know, is in sole charge of television in Romania, although he only carries the title of Vice President and he made it quite clear during his visit that he would be only too glad to help the BBC quoting specifically that we could send our cameramen freely throughout Romania and they could return with undeveloped film. There would be no restrictions of any sort and no censorship.[6]

On December 9, 1964, the first agreement between the BBC and the Romanian Committee for Radio and Television was signed.[7] The agreement facilitated mutual assistance, consisting of special television facilities to be granted to visiting production teams. Both parties were to make available television programs at reasonable prices upon request. Moreover, Romanian radio and television could send to Britain an agreed number of television employees to visit the BBC in order to become familiar with its production methods.

Silviu Brucan resigned from his position at Romanian television upon Ceausescu's ascension to power in 1965. However, Romania's relations with the BBC continued after his resignation. In 1966, the new management team of Romanian television visited the BBC with the purpose of studying its general system of organization, its editorial offices and production work, being particularly interested in the making of science programs, school TV, variety shows, current affairs and live broadcasts, but also in methods of doing public research.[8] In 1968, the new vice president of Romanian television, Bujor Ionita, visited the BBC's engineering division to discuss the introduction of color TV in Romania. The BBC noted at the time: "This visit provides a golden opportunity to build up a PAL system in Eastern Europe."[9] In March the same year, another Romanian team made up of Catinca Ralea Petrut (TV producer and editor) and Virgil Cojocaru (TV cameramen) visited the BBC with the aim of exchanging experience, this time on matters related to audience research. The visit was also aimed at acquiring materials and organizational experience for the second channel of Romanian television that was being planned at the time: "The Rumanians [sic] plan to open a second television channel largely devoted to cultural and educational programs and they are also on the lookout for serial stories and feature films," recorded the BBC.[10]

Relations with the BBC driven by the pursuit of know-how were central to the development of early Romanian television. They were the accomplishment of the first professionals of Romanian television and undermined political visions about the medium. These circumstances were enabled by the status of scarcity of early Romanian television. They promoted a

Television in the Age of (Post-)Communism 53

medium in which foreign transfers and exchanges, as well as relations with other media played the determining role.

THE NATIONAL MEDIUM

From the 1970s onwards, Romanian television embarked upon a phase of consolidation. The new medium had earned its place within domestic households, the number of viewers increased and several programs became highly popular, while television schedules became diverse and integrated within the patterns of everyday life. Starting out with 571 broadcast hours in 1957, Romanian television increased its broadcast offer to 1,369 hours in 1961, 3,161 hours in 1971, up to 4,642 hours in 1975, reaching the peak of 5,377 hours in 1980.[11] The number of TV subscriptions also increased dramatically in this period: from 28,000 subscriptions in 1957 to 2,692,000 in 1975 and to 3,713,000 by 1985.[12] From the 1970s Romanian television offered a wide variety of genres. Children's and youth programs were the most numerous on the schedule. Other genres on offer were factual and current affairs, cultural programs, sports, social investigation programs, science programs, 'how-to' instructional programs, interactive programs with viewers and a wide range of other entertaining forms: from varieties to weekend magazines to films and series. There were also programs targeted at specific audiences, such as those for ethnic minorities, broadcast in German and Hungarian, respectively. Occasionally, international programs such as *Varieties Programme* by Polish Television, *Seara televiziunii finlandeze (The evening of Finnish Television)*, *Canzonissima* (selections of the newest varieties by Radiotelevisione Italiana) were broadcast as part of mutual agreements with other countries.[13] In 1968, the second public channel started broadcasting and local TV stations were set up. The children's series *Aventurile lui Val Vartej (The Adventures of the Val Vartej Crew)*, the daily social investigation program *Reflector*, or the weekly programs *Telecinemateca* and *Teleenciclopedia* became popular among audiences. All this marked the transition of Romanian television towards what John Ellis (2000) defined as an 'era of availability.' This stage in television's development was characterized by the diversity of content, the differentiation of audience categories, by broadcast output guided by demand-led strategies, by the increasing power of scheduling and the consolidation of television as a social institution. According to Ellis, diversification and differentiation were the central markers of the availability era. Programming and scheduling strategies ensured the diversification of content and the differentiation between audience categories, between time slots and rhythms of daily lives. Differentiation and diversification occupied also the central roles in the consolidation phase of Romanian television and introduced the Romanian broadcaster to an era of availability. I will argue that this logic of differentiation turned Romanian television into a ground for power struggles at

54   Dana Mustata

this stage of its development. Scheduling became the platform where power struggles over television took place. "Scheduling is 'powerful' in the management of television and [. . .] it defines the nature of broadcast output in the era of availability" (Ellis 2000, 138). In Romania, television professionals and political leaders disputed the output of television throughout the 1970s by means of scheduling strategies. Upon the institutional and artistic consolidation of Romanian television by the end of the 1960s, it became clearer what television could do and how it could be used. This increased political claims over the broadcasting institution which was to result in a strict dictatorial control by the 1980s.

Two strands of scheduling marked the transition of Romanian television from the era of scarcity to the era of availability: *generic scheduling* and *frequent scheduling*. *Generic scheduling* implied the prioritizing of specific genres on the television schedules, while program titles within the broader generic umbrella often changed. Children's and youth programs took up the most programming time on Romanian television throughout the 1970s. Despite the fact that these had to comply with the Party's provisions on the educational role of television in society, within this generic prioritization, program-makers accommodated different modes of address: from the directly instructional and educational to the entertaining or even hybrid formats such as children's magazines. Scheduled daily, specific titles within this generic umbrella did not have a stable and recurrent timeslot. This diversity of modes of address also made it possible to integrate an entertaining dimension to these programs, alongside the political-educational direction envisioned by the Party. Often programming alternated between the two different functions of this genre. Educational and instructional programs were followed by more entertaining broadcasts, such as children's series, cartoons or children's magazines at the weekends. Instructional programs included *Teleschool*, but also programs with themes that presented greater interest to viewers such as hobbies or children's competitions.

Frequent scheduling was another strategy that successfully accommodated the interests of the three power actors who negotiated over the output of television in Romania: political leaders, program-makers and audiences. This type of scheduling referred to the (few) programs on Romanian television that had a secure daily and weekly slot in an otherwise shifting schedule. Frequent scheduling is a historically contingent term, as it refers specifically to the transition period of Romanian television from a phase of scarcity to the era of availability. A program such as *Reflector* was a constant presence on the Romanian TV schedules of the 1970s. It was a social investigation program that became very popular between 1970 and 1977 and aimed at solving concrete cases of social injustice (usually reported by viewers themselves): from thefts, misdemeanors to political corruption. It was scheduled every weekday except for Wednesdays from 8 to 8:10 pm. *Reflector* is a great example of a program that guaranteed its position on the schedules by attending to the Party's political vision, but also to the interest of the viewers and the ambitions of program-makers. It became a showcase for the best journalistic work inside Romanian television, assembling an outstanding team of Romanian television professionals: Alexandru Stark, Florin Bratescu, Carmen Dumitrescu, Anca Arion, Stefan Dimitriu and others. By the end of the 1960s and in the early 1970s, *Reflector* was a politically desirable program as Stefan Dimitriu, former *Reflector* program-maker and reporter, remarked:

> In 1967, there was the 9th Congress's re-launching of the Communist Party. Ceausescu wanted then to create his own cult and to this purpose he wanted to compromise everything related to his predecessor, Gheorghiu-Dej. We took advantage of this situation. It was then a period when Ceausescu found it convenient to criticize many existing conditions, including the Party organization, and the behavior of some ministers or Party officials. And we inside the television center [. . .] took advantage of this situation, knowing we were backed up by Ceausescu himself.[14]

Last but not least, the program was greatly popular, reaching an audience share of 63%.[15]

> The audiences saw themselves absolved from bureaucracy, incompetence or everything that was going wrong in society and that's why they liked it. [. . .] Initially, we would get inspiration on our cases from letters or phone calls we received from viewers. We would be approached on the bus by people, who pitched us ideas for cases to investigate. If a case was crazy enough for us to investigate, we would take it on.[16]

Interestingly, the fate of *Reflector* at the end of the 1970s marked a shift in the power balance inside Romanian television and signaled the rise of political domination within the broadcast institution. In 1977, the program was suspended shortly and then resumed as a political investigation program. The propaganda secretary, Dumitru Popescu, also nicknamed 'God' because of his political influence, was appointed to take charge of the political renovation of *Reflector*.

> 'God' Popescu indoctrinated us on how to make these social investigation programs. As he was not happy with the way the new political enquetes came out, [. . .] he brought in politicized people from the written press to make these programs. The programs had to be 'ceausist' and as politically biased as possible. They brought in people from Scanteia, from Romania Libera, from other Party publications. [. . .] We had become a second-hand working force.[17]

56   Dana Mustata

The program underwent great transformation to the extent that "only the name remained of the original *Reflector*,"[18] while the rest was plain propaganda. In the 1980s, the memory of *Reflector* as a social investigation program was being erased and many archived records of the program were destroyed. "We are now left without some of the most important documents of that era, because indeed some of them were professional masterpieces, but also valuable documents about things that would happen in a society pretending to be perfect," confessed Dimitriu.[19]

The death of *Reflector* at the end of the 1970s marked the beginning of an extraordinary period in Romanian television history: the totalitarian period. It is a period unique to the context of Ceausescu's dictatorship, one characterized by exhaustive political control. It put an end to the diversification of broadcast output, the very essence of television in the age of availability. By the mid-1980s, Romanian television broadcasting was reduced to two hours on weekdays and four to five hours on the weekends. The diversity of genres in the television schedule was replaced by content that was predominantly politicized. A report on programming inside Romanian television in the 1980s stated:

> From the point of view of diversity, three main categories can be distinguished: a) politicized economic programs, b) political programs and c) other programs [. . .] The economic programs are without content, without sense, without aim. [. . .] Point b): *Telejurnalul* [the news bulletin] [. . .] should get some inspiration from the Bulgarians. It offers first of all a luxury of details about domestic political events, and presents only secondarily foreign news that only talk about the 'diseases' of capitalism: unemployment, poverty, economic crisis. [. . .] c) In the category of the 'other', programs are not really diverse.[20]

On the new schedules, news was the main TV output, complemented by political and economic programs and coverage of Ceausescu's work visits. Other genres on offer were heavily politicized to the extent of losing their defining generic characteristics. Music programs promoted political songs dedicated to dictator Ceausescu and his wife Elena; cultural programs talked about the political loyalties of cultural personalities, scientific programs presented the superiority of Romania's technical advancements, while children's and youth programs offered propagandistic education for youth. This political harmonizing of broadcast output made propaganda the dominant mode of address on Romanian television, promoting the Party ideology and building upon Ceausescu's personality cult.

While broadcast output became uniform and politicized, modes of address were no longer targeted at different audience groups, but rather at the viewing pleasures of the Ceausescu family. Radio Free Europe called Romanian television at the time a "private state institution" that attended to the viewing taste of one family.[21] A similar statement was made at an

Television in the Age of (Post-)Communism 57

OIRT meeting in Prague where the moderator said: "I salute the large delegation of the Socialist Republic of Romania, consisting of one person. It is a one-person delegation, because Romania makes television programs for one man."[22] In this period of imposed scarcity, local channels together with the second national channel were also closed, the main channel only offering politicized programming for the dictatorial family. Professionalism inside Romanian television was also stifled, as the example of *Reflector* showed.

The totalitarian period of Romanian television derailed the development of Romanian television from an era of availability to a phase of politicized scarcity. This stage, which spanned from the end of the 1970s throughout the 1980s, was marked by the supremacy of politics in Romanian television history. This was the outcome of power struggles between television professionals and political leaders by means of scheduling and programming strategies in the 1970s. This claim of national politics over Romanian television was enabled by the logic of differentiation and diversification which was central to the era of availability. When television proved its maturity by generating a wide variety of broadcast content and addressing a wide range of audience groups throughout daily rhythms of life, the need for political control over television became evident in Ceausescu's Romania.

THE MEDIUM OF EUROPEAN INTEGRATION

With the fall of Ceausescu's regime in December 1989, the politics of Romanian television were bound to change. In the days of the Revolution, staff meetings took place inside Romanian television and discussed the (non-)independent status of the public broadcaster, the dangers of television's relations with political power, the new post-communist scheduling and the communist legacy of the institution.[23] Without bringing any solutions to these problems, these meetings made it clear that a redefinition of Romanian television had to take place in terms of broadcast output, editorial professionalism and the broadcaster's role in a democratic society. It was a redefinition in search for diversification of broadcast output and differentiation from the communist past.

In the aftermath of the fall of the Berlin Wall, there was great interest among Western broadcasters in the former communist territories. Cooperation between the West and the East was at its peak in the early post-communist years. In Romania, French broadcasters went to Bucharest in 1990 to exhibit their broadcast technology. Other broadcasters donated antennae to the Romanian television center, which allowed the receiving and rebroadcasting of foreign television programs on the Romanian channels. Romanian news was included at that time in the global flows of information, becoming part of the World Report, for instance.[24] However, the most concentrated effort to enable the European integration of

58   Dana Mustata

former communist television centers came from the European Broadcasting Union (EBU), the Western European organization in charge of broadcast exchange and cooperation in the area. In 1993, the EBU assimilated the former Organisation Internationale de Radiodiffusion et de Télévision (OIRT), which had been responsible for broadcast infrastructures in the socialist bloc. The countries formerly isolated by the Iron Curtain were gradually included in the Eurovision satellite operations by installing earth stations in these countries. Loan agreements for this were arranged with the European Bank for Reconstruction and Development. The first station was set up in Prague in March 1993, followed by Bucharest, Sofia, Warsaw and Budapest and in 1994 by Slovenia, Moldova, Ukraine and Slovakia (Potter 1994, 11). Most of the countries in the former Soviet Union and former Republic of Yugoslavia were only integrated in the EBU infrastructures in a later phase.

While at the international level efforts were made for the European integration of former communist broadcasters, locally, Romanian television was eager for cooperation with the West.

> The foreign [television] teams who came here saw our work conditions and they were very generous in offering their competence to help us. There were teams who came over and spent time here to instruct us. There were foreign universities and TV broadcasters who offered apprenticeships to our young employees. Some went to CNN, some to the Thomson Foundation, others went to Canadian or Dutch broadcasters. There was a great opening coming from them, but also from us.[25]

Foreign transfers of content were much needed in the early post-communist years. The most urgent necessity that Romanian television faced at the time was the increase in broadcast hours from a few hours daily to full broadcast days, from a one-channel model to a two-channel one. With this, there also came the challenge to redefine the form of broadcast output from a communist to a democratic model. An immediate solution to this was the (re) broadcasting of foreign content. Channel Two retransmitted programs of foreign TV stations for the most part:

> On the second channel, we would broadcast the news bulletins from Spanish, French television [. . .], Deutsche Welle [. . .], we also broadcast the BBC news. [. . .] People received a much diversified range of information. This continued in the first two-three years after the Revolution until we managed to rehabilitate ourselves.[26]

Foreign films were also integrated into the TV schedules. After being interrupted in 1981, *Dallas* came back to the Romanian TV screens. The TV guide wrote at the time:

Television in the Age of (Post-)Communism 59

Among the mysteries the dictatorship left unsolved, there is also the crime inside the Ewings' swimming pool, which marked the sudden end to the broadcast of the series [in Romania]. If after 11 years you're still interested in what happened, perhaps you will get a chance to find out. But for the time being, you will have to watch the first series of conflicts within the odious clan Ewing, which will be broadcast starting with Thursday, 21 February.[27]

Simultaneously, the TV Guide attempted to repopularize programs and genres from the communist regime. It presented for instance, articles on the tradition of TV theater on Romanian television, on the ideal Romanian TV announcer,[28] or on valued professionals of the broadcast institution.[29] These efforts were not successful, however; forms and programs associated with Ceausescu's regime could no longer be revived. Former professionals were also downgraded on a political, rather than a professional basis, while others left the broadcast institution. This was also due to the fact that a proper public television criticism was missing at the time:

The only thing I can now truly hope for is for you to be able to ask for (can I say for the continuation) of a radio-television criticism that will prioritize the highest professional standards and the respect for value. [A criticism] that will analyze your profession competently, but subtly, generally, but also specifically in terms of programs, critically but not unconstructively, attentively but not vindictively. Before many other rights, which I am sure you deserve and you will ask for, I humbly believe it is important and necessary for you to have a critical objective and pertinent assessment of what you are doing, so as to avoid the confusion of values and the anarchy of criteria.[30]

Under these circumstances, Romanian television produced new forms and modes of address that were absent from the communist TV schedules, such as advertisements, the daily horoscope, religious programs, talk shows and quiz-shows. Advertisements introduced to Romanian audiences Western products for the first time. The daily horoscope was a 10-minute segment at the beginning of the schedule, while religious programs broadcast church masses and issues of religious interest on Sunday morning.[31] The programs extended the broadcast output to audience groups that were previously not recognized by Ceausescu's regime.

However, the most popular post-communist genres were the talk show and the quiz show. The advent of talk shows was timely on Romanian television. A television viewer wrote to the editorial board of the TV guide *Panoramic Radio TV* in February 1990: "I would like to ask you to include in the schedule in the near future a series of programs discussing the alphabet of democracy. You should invite to these programs competent people, political scientists, jurists, specialists in constitutional law."[32] At

60 *Dana Mustata*

the beginning of 1990, the talk show was used as a platform for introducing new political actors. The format took the form of a televised debate or a roundtable. The programs were often moderated by new television president Razvan Theodorescu and vice director Emanuel Valeriu. By June 1990, the talk show fell victim to public criticism. The new television management, Theodorescu and Valeriu, who were in the center of these broadcasts, were criticized for favoring the new political regime and not allowing a voice for the opposition.

The quiz show had a similar fate. The first quiz show on Romanian television was *Robingo*, broadcast for the first time in August 1993. It was a primetime program, under an UK license. The program was moderated by a newcomer at the television center in Bucharest, a young entertaining presence on the screen. Soon after its first broadcast, *Robingo* was involved in a political scandal. As Diana Lazar noted in an article in *Cotidianul* on May 7, 2007, the new president of television at the time, Paul Everac, organized that year the first live New Year's program broadcast simultaneously from three different studios. He himself participated in the show without going through the usual pre-selection and competed for the high prizes that the show advertised. This generated a lot of public criticism. While quiz shows have been associated with public scandals already in the 1950s in America (Mittel 2004, xv), the scandal generated by *Robingo* had a political character revealing that politics was still central to the new post-communist, Western-inspired new television forms.

In the aftermath of the Revolution, Romania was compensating for its need for diversification and differentiation by means of Western transfers (rebroadcasting Western content), exchanges (cooperation with the West) and adaptations (as was the case of the new post-communist genres). While all the other European broadcasters were at the peak of the availability era in the early 1990s, Romanian television was coming out of a national regime that had derailed its course from an era of availability to an era of imposed scarcity. Under these circumstances, the Romanian broadcaster found itself in need of diversification of its broadcast output. Integration with the West became a priority and this took attention away from national broadcast politics. While efforts were made for Romanian television to be welcomed back to Europe, the national legacy of television remained in crisis. Issues of political interferences and a lack of a proper local public criticism maintained the Romanian broadcaster within the political discourse of the communist regime. The collapse of communism seemed to offer a hastened integration within the Western infrastructures, but this integration appeared to deny the very national differences that a former communist broadcaster was bringing to Europe. In June 1990, the live broadcasting of the bloody attacks against opposition voices to the newly elected government in Romania shocked the world and alerted it to the country's democratic handicaps. The State Department of the U.S. issued at the time the following official statement:

Television in the Age of (Post-)Communism 61

Attacks organized against the headquarters of oppositional political parties and independent newspapers and attacks against the politicians who were democratically elected through peaceful means, by workers personally summoned to Bucharest by president Iliescu are threatening to bring totalitarianism back to Romania. We are asking President Iliescu and his government to immediately stop any action against the incipient process of democracy in Romania. Particularly, he must call back from the streets all those workers organized into violent groups ('vigilantes') and publicly pledge that these people will never be encouraged to come back. (Berry 2004, 49)

The efforts at integration within the Western audiovisual landscape concealed the political handicaps of the Romanian broadcaster just freed from dictatorial practices of control. Cooperation with Western broadcasters and adoption of Western program forms did not resolve the political differences of Romanian television, which remained subject to political power. These failed attempts at integration marked what John Ellis referred to as a "pseudo-triumph" of West versus East, which denied the return of "history and difference" to Europe (Ellis 2000, 62). The new opportunity created by the political reconfiguration of Europe engaged communist television in a political process of European assimilation and a neglect of television as a national medium. Upon the fall of communism in Romania in 1989, European broadcast politics appeared to be at the center of the post-communist rehabilitation of Romanian television, while national politics maintained their control over the institution. The post-dictatorial search for diversification and differentiation of Romanian television maintained the national political interest in the broadcast institution. At the same time it justified the entrance of Romanian television into the space of European politics.

CONCLUSIONS

Political control has not been the defining characteristic of communist television in Romania, nor has the development of the Romanian broadcasting institution differed completely from Western broadcasters. In fact, Romanian television has undergone the same stages of development which John Ellis singled out in the British context up until the 1990s: the era of scarcity and the era of availability. In the early phase of its development, which coincided with Ellis' era of scarcity, Romanian television was predominantly guided by relations with foreign broadcasters and connections with other media (radio or film). Such a context characterized early television across Europe. In this early stage, politics of control were not representative of Romanian television. It was upon the initiation of Romanian television into the era of availability when television proved to have become a means of differentiation and diversification under the communist regime, that political

62 *Dana Mustata*

interest in the broadcasting institution gained traction. This transformed Romanian television into a platform of power struggles between television professionals and Ceausescu's politics, with the exclusive victory of the latter in the 1980s. This brought Romanian television to an exceptional stage: the dictatorial stage characterized by scarcity and politicized content. After the fall of communism in 1989, Romanian television's search for diversification and differentiation introduced it to the sphere of European broadcast politics, while the broadcaster maintained its former submissive relation to national political power.

Romanian television testifies to the same model of development that John Ellis designed for British television. Understanding the dynamics of television in each era provides useful insights into when and how television lent itself to political control. The era of scarcity shows television as a predominantly transnational medium, in which cross-border exchanges and resemblances between broadcasters across Europe undermined national politics. It was only in the era of availability, when television consolidated its aesthetic forms and social role, that national politics played an increasing role in the workings of the medium. It was at this stage that television fulfilled its status as a national medium and its relations to national politics became tighter. Under former communist regimes, such as Romania, these relations took the form of political control. Nevertheless, the dynamics of Romanian television in the availability era provide also insights into alternative factors that played a relevant role in the development of the medium despite political control: television professionals in the 1970s and European broadcast politics in the post-communist period.

Television in the former communist Eastern Europe is in need of approaches that produce television histories, rather than political histories of television. That means emerging studies on Eastern European television need to look first and foremost at the medium itself, before understanding how it related to its political context. The scarce scholarship available on Eastern European television so far has told primarily a political story, looking into the political context of television and reproducing the Cold War history of divisions between the East and the West. However, television in this geopolitical part of Europe has its own story to tell, a story that may reshape the map of Cold War Europe, a story that may tell about similarities and exchanges of television across Europe in the 1950s and 1960s and a story that may explicate how television lost its power struggle to political regimes of control later in its development. This article attempted to tell such a television story.

NOTES

1. Tape 41678, Bucharest: Arhiva Multimedia, Televiziunea Romana.
2. E 1/2, 309/1 "Romania. Brucan Silviu," October 1964, BBC Written Archives Centre, Caversham, UK.

Television in the Age of (Post-)Communism   63

3. Letter from Brucan to Latey in E 1/2, 309/1 "Romania. Brucan Silviu," November 1964, BBC Written Archives Centre, Caversham, UK.
4. E 1/2, 309/1 "Romania. Brucan Silviu," December 4, 1964, BBC Written Archives Centre, Caversham, UK.
5. E 1/2, 309/1 "Romania. Brucan Silviu," November 13, 1964, BBC Written Archives Centre, Caversham, UK.
6. Idem.
7. "Relations between the C.R.T and the BBC" in E 1/2, 309/1 "Romania. Brucan Silviu," 9 December 1964, BBC Written Archives Centre, Caversham, UK.
8. "Visit of Romanian TV Officials, 17th May" in E 1/2, 310/1 "Romania. Brucan Silviu," November 13, 1964, BBC Written Archives Centre, Caversham, UK.
9. Letter by L.E. Pauley dated January 26, 1968 in E 1/2, 311/1 Romania, Ionitza, B., BBC Written Archives Centre, Caversham, UK.
10. Letter to Stephenson from J.A. Birch dated October, 4 1967, E 1/2, 313/1, BBC Written Archives Centre, Caversham, UK.
11. *Evolutia unor indicatori economico-financiari (The Evolution of Economic and Financial Indicators)* in Radiotelevision File D135, Vol. 37, p. 93: Bucharest: Council for the Study of the Securitate Archives.
12. Idem.
13. International exchange programs were a strategy of reciprocal programming between countries. Reciprocity agreements constituted in fact a practice within OIRT and even within EBU to institutionalize control over the reception of foreign programs as well as to ensure distribution of national television content abroad (Eugster, 1983: 1–19).
14. Personal interview with Stefan Dimitriu, Bucharest, 17 January 2008.
15. Pavel Campeanu, "500 de emisiuni fata in fata cu publicul" *Cinema*, 3, Year X (111), Bucharest, March 7, 1971.
16. Personal interview with Stefan Dimitriu, Bucharest, January 17, 2008.
17. Idem.
18. Idem.
19. Idem.
20. Nota (Material despre TV), Nr. 152/V.C./F.N/ 14.06.1984 in Radiotelevision File D 135, Vol. 37, p. 115: Bucharest: Council for the Study of the Securitate Archives.
21. Nota nr. 334 din 3.05.1985 in Radiotelevision Files, D 135, Vol. 81, p. 84: Bucharest: Council for the Study of the Securitate Archives.
22. Informare, 29.05.1986, in Radiotelevision Files D 135, Vol. 81, p. 26: Bucharest: Council for the Study of the Securitate Archives.
23. Tape RRD 9–3128, Arhiva Multimedia, Televiziunea Romana, Bucharest: TVR.
24. Personal interview with Nicolae Melinescu, Bucharest: August 27, 2009.
25. Idem.
26. Idem.
27. "Ewing Redivivus", *Panoramic Radio-TV*, II, 4, January 28—February 3, 1991.
28. Iosif Sava, "Crainicul Ideal," *Panoramic Radio-TV*, I, 36, September 10–16, 1990.
29. "Carmen Dumitrecu si Alexandru Stark . . . sau dupa 20 de ani," (photo by Vasile Blendea) *Panoramic Radio-TV*, 1, 36, September 10–16, 1990.
30. Cleopatra Lorintiu, "In loc de cronica. Stimati redactori ai Radioteleviziunii Romane Libere," *Panoramic Radio-TV*, I, 7, February 19–25, 1990.
31. *Panoramic Radio-TV*, I, July 6–16, 1990.
32. *Radio Televiziunea Romana Libera*, I, 7, February 19–25, 1990.

64 *Dana Mustata*

REFERENCES

Berry, David. 2006. *The Romanian Mass Media and Cultural Development.* Hampshire: Ashgate.

Brucan, Silviu. 1996. "Idila mea cu televiziunea." In *Viziune Tele. 40 de ani de televiziune*, edited by TVR, 41–42. Bucharest: TVR Directia de Logistica si Memorie.

Ellis, John. 2000. *Seeing Things. Television in the Age of Uncertainty.* London: I.B. Tauris

Elsner Monika, Thomas Muller and Peter M. Spangenberg. 1990. "The Early History of German Television: The Slow Development of a Fast Medium." In *Materialities of Communication*, edited by Hans Ulrich. Gumbrecht and Karl Ludwig Pfeiffer. Stanford: Stanford University Press.

Flenley, Paul. 1997. "Television in the Russian Federation." In *Television in Europe*, edited by James A. Coleman and Brigitte Rollet, 111–121. Exeter: Intellect Books.

Lorintiu, Cleopatra. 1990. "In loc de cronica. Stimati redactori ai Radiotelevizionunii Romane Libere." *Panoramic Radio TV* 19–25 (February).

Mickiewicz, Ellen P. 1997. *Changing Channels: Television and the Struggle for Power in Russia.* New York: Oxford University Press.

Mickiewicz, Ellen P. 1998. *Split Signals Television and Politics in the Soviet Union.* New York: Oxford University Press.

Mittel, Jason. 2004. *Genres and Television: From Cop Shows to Cartoons in American Culture.* New York and London: Routledge.

Munteanu, Nicolae C. 1972. "Cu Florin Bratescu despre Reflector." *Cinema* (August).

Noam, Eli. 1991. *Television in Europe.* Oxford: Oxford University Press.

Pasca, T. 2001. *TVR in competitii nationale si internationale (1962–2001).* Bucuresti: Societatea Romana de Televiziune.

Paulu, Burton. 1974. *Radio and Television Broadcasting in Eastern Europe.* Minneapolis, MN: University of Minnesota Press.

Potter W. 1994. "The Implementation of Satellite Technology in the Eurovision Network." *EBU Technical Review* (Winter).

4 The Carnival of the Absurd
Stanisław Bareja's *Alternatywy 4* and Polish Television in the 1980s

Dorota Ostrowska

Alternatywy 4 (*4 Alternative St*) is a Polish comedy television series made by Stanisław Bareja in the winter of 1981–82, and broadcast for the first time only in 1986–87 due to problems with censorship. It consists of nine episodes of about an hour long each: 1 *Przydział/Tenancy Agreement*, 2.*Przeprowadzka* (*Moving Flats*), 3 *Pierwsza noc* (*The First Night*), 4 *Profesjonaliści* (*Professionals*), 5 20-ty stopień zasilania (*Power Supply of the 20th Degree*), 6 *Gołębie* (*Pigeons*), 7 *Spisek* (*The Plot*), 8 *Wesele* (*The Wedding*) 9 *Upadek* (*The Fall*). The series shows the life of the inhabitants of a newly erected block of flats in one of a large Warsaw estates located at 4 Alternative Street in the early 1980s. The inhabitants of the block of flats and the problems they have with one another and with the representatives of the state administration present a true microcosm of Polish life then as far as the relationships between different social groups as well as the interactions between the people and the socialist state are concerned.

The series is an important document of 1980s Poland in at least two different ways. On the one hand, the series refers directly to the housing shortages that were chronic in Poland, as well as to role which housing played in engineering a new socialist society. The aim of the socialist state was to make Warsaw, the capital, in the words of the 1950s political slogan, "the socialist capital for every citizen: worker, peasant and intellectual" (Crowley 2003, 33). On the other hand, the satirical and at times absurdist tone of the series makes it a unique and unusual production for Polish television. It was only in the context of the Solidarity movement that television was able to absorb and present in the form of the comedy series a very strong cabaret and satirical culture, which had been thriving throughout the postwar period, and to which Bareja and the series scriptwriters, Jan Płoński and Maciej Rybiński, were important contributors.

My overall argument in this article is that *Alternatywy 4* was a result of a very interesting and unique set of cultural influences including the impact of cabaret and the culture of satirical theater, the student culture of street protests, which resembled an art happening labelled 'surrealist socialism,' and a critique of the 'block of flats' genre developed by Polish TV in the 1970s and reflecting the socialist state's 'propaganda of success.'

66 *Dorota Ostrowska*

The confluence of these elements contributed to the series' overtly political character and raised issues about the relationship between the series and the culture of contestation associated with Solidarity, which shaped it. This relationship could be best described by drawing on the idea of the 'carnivalesque' defined by Mikhail Bakhtin in *Rabelais and his World* as "the boundless world of humorous forms and manifestations [which] opposed the official and serious tone of medieval ecclesiastical and feudal culture" (1984, 4). The common denominator of various carnival activities is that "they belong to one culture of folk carnival humour" (Bakhtin 1984, 1).

In the first part of the article, I will briefly introduce the series and its importance for the television culture of the 1980s. Secondly, I will discuss the relevance of Bakhtin's concept of the carnivalesque for Bareja's series. Thirdly, I will provide an overview of the cabaret and satirical subculture which was flourishing in Poland in the post-war period and present the ways in which *Alternatywy 4* grew out of these kinds of cultural practices. Next, I will demonstrate the relationship between *Alternatywy 4* and an avant-garde student-led current within the Solidarity movement, Pomarańczowa Alternatywa/Orange Alternative. Finally, I will show how *Alternatywy 4* was contesting and challenging an established genre on Polish television in the 1970s, the block of flats genre.

ALTERNATYWY 4

Alternatywy 4 is most easily classified as a television series rather than a television serial. The series was produced by Poltel, which was a production arm of Polish Television. Unlike numerous television serials produced by film units for television broadcasts with a more concise version shot for a cinematic release, the television series was characterized by simpler and more schematic narratives, lower production values and quicker shooting time. The location of the narrative in the block of flats also naturally limited the number of actors and locations used. Compared to other programmes shown on Polish television in the 1980s, *Alternatywy 4* perhaps came closest to a soap opera (Polish: *telenowela*). According to Violetta Buhl, Bareja's first assistant director on *Alternatywy 4*, the director insisted that "we are not going to go for polished shots. A good joke is more important." He put his ideas to work by shooting each scene starting with "one long take and then a series of medium close ups." This is how "all soap operas are shot today," concludes Buhl (Gazeta).

In *Alternatywy 4* the new flat occupants include a surgeon and a crane operator (who, due an administrative error, find themselves assigned to the same flat), a provincial apparatchik, a petty thief with a heart of gold, a university professor who is also a dissident, a high-ranking party official, a disabled elderly man who is cared for by a family repatriated from Eastern Poland ("Kresy") after the change of the Polish borders in 1945, an opera

The Carnival of the Absurd   67

singer, a primary school teacher, an opportunist academic, a foreman in a factory who is a representative of the working class, and the manager of the block cooperative. The series portrays the events that lead to the block inhabitants obtaining the flats, moving in, and starting their lives together as a community.

The distinctive characteristic of the series is the presence of countless gags, anecdotes and jokes and constant allusions to events in Polish history and political life, which were not allowed to be discussed openly in public. As a result, *Alternatywy 4* is a series of vignettes from everyday life in the final decade of socialism, which includes stark portraits of the members of Polish society. For instance, one of the characters recounts different periods in his life and mentions the dates (1968, December 1970, a trip to Radom in 1976 and finally 1980), which are the dates and, in the case of Radom, locations, of strikes and protests that led to the foundation of the Solidarity movement. The series satirizes the working of the secret police by showing them installing an elaborate surveillance system in the new flat of the pro-fessor-dissident, whom they want to pin down for his illegal activities. His frequent travels to Gdańsk—the epicentre of the Solidarity movement—are mentioned in passing by his neighbours with a twinkle of an eye. The fact that the TV series was broadcast despite including numerous political illusions and innuendos was a sign of more lax censorship regulations in the final years of socialism in Poland. These also contributed hugely to the series' popularity.

Critics of Bareja's work noted that he was always acutely aware of political and social changes in Poland; and that his films and TV work changed and became sharper and more critical as time went by, culminat-ing in *Alternatywy 4* (Pawlicki 1988, 3).[1] While his comedies in the 1960s focused on the marital problem of a couple (*Mąż swojej żony* (*Husband of his Wife*; 1961) and *Żona dla Australijczyka* (*A Wife for an Austra-lian*; 1964)), in the 1970s, with *Poszukiwany-poszukiwana* (*Man-woman Wanted*; 1973), *Nie ma róży bez ognia* (*A Jungle Book of Regulations*; 1974), *Brunet wieczorową porą* (*Brunet Will Call*; 1976) and *Co mi zro-bisz, jak mnie złapiesz* (*What Will You Do When You Catch Me?*; 1978) the tone of the comedies darkened, becoming more ironic and with a sharper satire aimed at various aspects of life in socialist Poland such as bureau-cracy, official and party hierarchies, lack of manners and the careerism of party apparatchiks.

Arguably, what made *Alternatywy 4* unique not only within Bareja's work but also among Polish TV productions was the moment when the series was conceived, filmed and broadcast. Work on the series began in 1981 in the climate following the triumph of the Solidarity move-ment, which was founded in August 1980. The series was authorized for production in 1981. This was the year when the censorship regulations were relaxed due to the advent of the Solidarity movement. In the period between the legalization of Solidarity in August 1980 and the introduction

68　*Dorota Ostrowska*

of Martial Law in December 1981 "almost anything could be approved by production apart from the works which openly criticized the Soviet Union" (Gazeta). *Alternatywy 4* was the only TV series whose filming progressed during Martial Law, which began in December 1981 and lasted until July 1983, and in spite of the boycott of TV by many artists, who protested in this way against the introduction of Martial Law. Connected with the Solidarity movement, Bareja was able to exempt his team from the boycott of television, theater and cinema imposed by Solidarity as a response to Martial Law when the television management was militarized and TV anchors in military uniforms reported on evening news programs. As this was the only production made in Poland at this period the TV bosses were eager not to disrupt it in order to maintain some vestiges of normality during these very unusual times (Gazeta). For this reason they did not interfere while *Alternatywy 4* was shot, which made the shoot "a real enclave of freedom" during the dark days of Martial Law according to Violetta Buhl (Gazeta). The series then experienced many problems with the censors and it did not get broadcast until 1986–87, nearly six years after it was finished. In fact Bareja managed to make another TV series, *Zmiennicy* (*Substitues*; 1986) in the meantime about a pair of taxi drivers in Warsaw, and the first episodes of both series were broadcast at the same time (Replewicz 2009; Łuczak 2002). In a way then the history of the series' production and broadcast did not just coincide with but was a result of a complicated and contradictory set of historical circumstances at one of the most important and volatile moments in post-war Polish history.

The series contained a devastating critique of the ways in which television had been indiscriminately used as a tool of the state propaganda. The 1970s was the period of growth of Polish television, when it began to broadcast on two channels and in color. Importantly, it also acquired its own production base and did not have to rely so heavily on the film units.[2] Much of the television programming was devoted to various kinds of reportage and documentary programming, which depicted Poland as a fast-developing and rapidly modernizing country. In *Alternatywy 4* Bareja decided to deconstruct one of the most eagerly and most frequently portrayed issues, that of social housing, where the vast majority of Poles lived.

THE CARNIVALESQUE

Bareja was always associated with entertainment for the masses, who were seen as indifferent towards more sophisticated types of cinema and television proposed by various art house directors in Poland. Yet, the social engineering in Poland did lead, not least because of the housing policy of which Bareja was deeply critical, to turning everybody into a working mass contributing to socialist society. Paradoxically, the Solidarity movement, being the broadest possible movement with its roots in the working classes but

The Carnival of the Absurd   69

cutting across and encompassing all social, economic and political groups, turned the socialist masses into a civil society. This empowered civil society informed the reaction of the television audiences, who enjoyed the blasphemous nature of Bareja's humor displayed in his series. The orthodoxy that was the object of the jest was represented not only by the socialist party and its social projects but also by the television this party sanctioned and enabled to exist. In other words, *Alternatywy 4* was the moment when television, the apparatus of state propaganda, was subverted on television and through one of the most important formats of socialist TV—the series set in the block of flats.

Bakhtin remarked that folk humor "offered a completely different, non-official, extraecclesiastical, and extrapolitical aspect of the world, of man, and of human relations; they [forms of protocol and ritual based on laughter and consecrated by tradition] built a second world, and a second life outside the officialdom, a world in which all medieval people participated more or less, in which they lived during a given time of the year" (1984, 6). This 'two-world condition' was palpable in Poland at the time of the making of *Alternatywy 4*. The impact of what was called the 'carnival of Solidarity' was such that this other non-official form of culture could enter the mainstream and be broadcast. This concerned various examples of cabaret and satirical theater, which could reach a broader audience thanks to television broadcasts. It also encompassed the performance-based street happenings organised by students involved in a movement called Pomarańczowa Alternatywa (Orange Alternative). *Alternatywy 4* exploited the format of the 'blocks of flats' genre, which was known to the Polish audiences from earlier TV productions made throughout the 1970s, in particular *Czterdziestolatek* (*A Forty-Year-Old Man*; 1973) and *Rodzina Leśniewskich* (*The Leśniewskis*; 1978). It is because of its familiar TV format on the one hand and irreverent and iconoclastic humor, on the other, that *Alternatywy 4* was able to bridge the official cultural forms endorsed by the bosses of Polish television, and those cultural practices which were associated with the subcultures flourishing on the margins of the mainstream.

Much of the celebration of the socialist state's successes with the housing policy as well as the coverage of countless stiff and staged party functions and ceremonies are presented in all seriousness and then ridiculed in *Aternatywy 4* much in the same way in which "in the folklore of primitive peoples, couple with the cults which were serious in tone and organisation were other, comic cults which laughed and scoffed at the deity ('ritual laughter'); coupled with serious myths were comic and abusive ones; coupled with heroes were their parodies and doublets" (Bakhtin 1984, 6). In the final episode of the series the block of flats at Alternatywy 4 Street is chosen as an example of the social housing to be visited by an international delegation of the city mayors. The janitor is in his element coercing the inhabitants to present a picture-perfect life in the block of flats decorated for the occasion with flowers, flags and slogans. The inhabitants appear

70   Dorota Ostrowska

to collaborate in staging the performative orthodoxy of the socialist state underpinned by prescribed set of rituals and behaviors, but in fact they decide to use the visit to completely undermine the all-powerful janitor and the power system he represents. When the foreign mayors finally arrive they are shown ruined and soiled flats whose inhabitants are all degenerates, drunkards, violent and jobless. Thus in Bareja's series all forms of the state rituals are treated with the same derisive and flippant humor which eventually ends up laying bare the spectacle of the state propaganda which is void of any power to persuade or inspire.

The power and popularity of *Alternatywy 4* was linked to its ability to both mirror and deform the everyday reality of Poland in the 1980s. The audiences were well familiar with the situations and characters portrayed on screen that formed part and parcel of life in the socialist system. With the exaggerated and at times grotesque humor the series was bending the realist frame, thus forming "the basic carnival nucleus" which "belongs to the borderline between art and life. In reality, it is life itself but shaped according to a certain pattern of a play" (Bakhtin 1984, 7). The challenge of the carnivalesque effect of Bareja's series was that it was not comforting but unsettling and destibilizing, much like the carnivalesque laughter described by Bakhtin as "ambivalent; it is gay, triumphant and at the same mocking, deriding. It asserts and denies, it buries and revives" (11). *Alternatywy 4* exposed the vestiges of the corrupted socialist everyday, it challenged them with sharp satire; but being itself a product of and broadcast on state socialist television, the series also had to assert the enduring power of socialism. In the end it was only the comic frame which made the series acceptable for both the audiences and the television bosses. Bareja himself admitted that without jokes and gags his films would be very dark, and that without humor his vision of Polish reality would be very difficult to accept.[3]

There were three different cultural elements which contributed to why *Alternatywy 4* became an exposition of the Bahktinian carnivalesque. The first was the context of the cabaret culture with which Bareja and his various script collaborators were closely linked. The second one was the student movement the Orange Alternative, and the third one was the block of flats genre, which was a format that provided a basis for the critique of Polish propaganda-driven television, at the heart of which was the failed miracle of social housing, a flag project of post-war Polish governments.

CABARET AND SATIRE

Stanisław Bareja was an established and experienced, although not very well-respected, director by the time he embarked on the project that resulted in *Alternatywy 4*. His profile was that of a director who was interested in making popular and genre films and TV series. Polish cinema, and

The Carnival of the Absurd   71

later television under late socialism was supposed to produce genre films such as comedies or crime films. Tadeusz Lubelski quotes a party directive that states that "along with films that are ideologically engaged, there is a need to develop the production of entertainment films, comedies and social dramas, which are aimed at the mass audiences, but free of primitivism and bad taste" (Lubelski 2009, 268). How to reconcile good taste with broad appeal was something that the critics found very difficult to do. They often associated popularity with bad taste, which had an impact on the way in which Bareja's films were received. His was the kind of auteurism that did not sit comfortably with the dominant idea of an auteur filmmaker in socialist Poland mostly because in the socialist system box office success and genre filmmaking were of secondary importance. For instance, Bareja had problems getting into a film unit in the system where every director had to be a part of one. Krzysztof Zanussi said he was interested in having him in TOR, a legendary unit linked to such directors as Krzysztof Kieślowski, because he said he understood that the art house is always somehow dependent on popular and genre film production (Hollender and Turowska 2000). It seems that Zanussi's view of Bareja was quite unique in Polish film circles. In time a term was coined to describe the type of humor that Bareja cultivated in his films, 'bareizm,' a neologism in the form of an adjective derived from the surname of the director. 'Bareizm' referred to kitsch entertainment filmmaking, which only more recently gained more positive connotations and came to mean creative engagement with the absurd aspects of reality (Lubelski 2009, 270).

Perhaps it was this partial isolation of Bareja from his film colleagues as well as his interest in comedy and satire that led to his connections to a very different part of Polish culture—that of student theater and the cabaret of comic artists and stand-up comedians. The cabaret created a kind of subculture that was accessible through student clubs and theater festivals, as well as limited satirical programmes on television, such as cabaret marathons and cabaret nights, which were broadcast late in an often censored format, radio programs and finally satirical columns in official newspapers. In the late sixties Bareja participated in a comedy-based game show, *Małżeństwo doskonałe (Perfect marriage*; 1967–69) developed by satirist Jacek Fedorowicz and comedy film and TV director Jerzy Gruza. This collaboration was followed by another one between Jacek Fedorowicz[4] and Stanisław Bareja, which consisted of a series of short films for television, a version of a candid camera show (Lubelski 2009, 358). In one episode a 'talking mailbox' instructs people about the proper way to drop mail in the mailbox, and encourages them to tap or gently caress the mailbox in order to insure speedy service. The bemused clients of the national mail service follow all the instructions while the mailbox thanks them and salutes them for their cooperation with what it calls "a modernising initiative of the national mail service."[5] These short films had a strong documentary aspect, which also informed Bareja's subsequent film and TV projects, including *Alternatywy*

72   *Dorota Ostrowska*

4, which has a very rough, cheap look and naturalistic performances, and none of the glossiness and color of Bareja's films from the 1960s.

Małżeństwo doskonałe was broadcast live for the Studencki Teatr Satyrykow (Student Satirical Theater in Warsaw; STS), which was a student cabaret theater operating between 1945 and 1975. It gathered an impressive group of artists and musicians who were interested in cabaret and satire. The theater was run by Stanisław Tym—another one of Bareja's collaborators on the film he made before *Alternatywy 4*, *Miś* (*Teddy-Bear*; 1981) and in which Tym played the main character. Stanisław Tym was not only an actor but also a writer of satirical editorials for broadsheets. *Miś* is often seen as a high point in Bareja's career but it was also a prelude to *Alternatywy 4*. The film is about a manager of a state company who needs to get to London before his wife does in order to get money deposited in a foreign account. The premise of the film is absurd in the Polish reality of the late 1970s because of the restrictions imposed by the state on foreign travel and possession of Western currencies by Polish nationals. The real purpose of the film was to present such paradoxes of life in socialist Poland. The film became famous for various gags and jokes and is remembered for its sharp satire and anecdotes. One of its critics wrote that "never before in cinema had anybody included so many critical remarks about the functioning of the socialist system in Poland" (Skotarczak quoted in Lubelski 2009, 411). One of the most memorable gags shows the lunch bar Apis, where the cutlery and the metal plates are fixed to the tables with metal chains and screws (Lubelski 2009, 411). Depending on one's point of view the customers of the lunch bar look like inmates served by a very rude and obnoxious waitress, or potential thieves of the bar's cutlery and tableware, which has to be protected from them with chains and screws. The film was also seen by contemporaneous audiences as an alternative to the Cinema of Moral Disquiet, of which Krzysztof Kieślowski and Krzysztof Zanussi were among the main representatives. In both cases, the films revealed some morally unacceptable or questionable aspects of the social and political system in Poland but used different filmic and generic tools to engage with them.[6]

For the purposes of writing a script for *Alternatywy 4*, Bareja teamed up with two young journalists from an official student weekly, *ITD* (*And So On*). Janusz Płoński was an editor of the weekly in the 1970s, who mostly reported on various student theater festivals. Płoński had a very extensive exposure and good insight into the talent and creativity of his generation, and the kind of uncensored humor that flourished at such festivals. Maciej Rybiński was a regular columnist for the weekly, writing on a range of topics, which became less veiled and more explicit as the impact of August 1980 and the Solidarity movement became more pronounced.

Rybiński's column was entitled "Jestem, więc myślę" ("I am, therefore I think"), an inversion of the Socrates's "Cogito ergo sum." This inversion was telling because it pointed out to how living calls for thinking logically

The Carnival of the Absurd 73

and critically but that the reality on which the journalist was reporting often defied logic and reason. Rybiński and Płoński might have come to Bareja's attention through their writings not just in the weekly but also because of the crime novel they published about the world of car racing in 1970s Poland, *Góralskie tango*. The novel, along with Płoński's and Rybiński's journalism work, showed that the two were critically minded and very much aware of the various cultural trends of their times. Judging from the profile of his previous collaborators, Fedorowicz and Tym, these qualities were highly attractive to Bareja.

In the magazine *ITD*, there was an interest in American youth culture. There was also a sex column; and the front of the weekly often featured an attractive young woman, while on the last page there was photo of a topless or completely nude woman, sometimes of non-white ethnic origin. The weekly also contained advertisement for different brands of products including clothes and cosmetics produced by Polish state-owned companies. But these images of real and pseudo prosperity were subverted by a reportage that showed some of the absurdities of life in socialist Poland. A good example of it was the photo reportage about window displays in Poland. A complete subversion was presented on the final page, which consisted of satirical drawings by Andrzej Mleczko and an anonymous satirical column. The satire pointed out some absurd, nonsensical and humorous aspects of contemporary life. It included slogans inspired by the official ones that populated Polish cities and villages. This type of 'graphic' humor found its way into *Alternatywy 4*, where one could spot the following slogans: 'Enthusiasm + Planning = A Flat,' 'Work-Effort-Success,' 'A Flat—A Gain for the Working Masses of Cities and Villages' and 'Fewer Errors—More Flats.'

Overall *ITD* was very much an example of the student culture, whose representation was tightly controlled and had to be aligned with the propaganda needs of the socialist state. There was potential in it for subversion and there was a sense that a different way of life was possible. But this could only come to the surface with the explosion of the Solidarity movement and strikes in the Gdańsk shipyard. The script of *Alternatywy 4* was written in this period.

ALTERNATIVE THEATER AND STREET HAPPENINGS

An interesting aspect of Janusz Płoński's very constrained writing in *ITD* were his reports from attending various student festivals.[7] It is very likely that much of the humor which inspired *Alternatywy 4* emerged from Płoński's exposure to and participation in these live performances. These cabaret festivals were often quite close to an artistic happening and had elements of the avant-garde. In the 1970s and 1980s Wrocław (Ger. Breslau), a university city in Southwest Poland, was one of the centers of Polish student and theater

74   *Dorota Ostrowska*

life, where some of the most successful Polish experimental theater performances happened associated with Jerzy Grotowski, Henryk Tomaszewski,
Jerzy Grzegorzewski, Kazimierz Braun and Tadeusz Różewicz (Romanienko
2007). The culture of cabaret and experimental theater was seen as a source
for one of the most unusual student movements in Poland in Wrocław, called
Pomarańczowa Alternatywa (Orange Alternative), which was described by
Misztal as "a cabaret movement" (1990, 83).

Pomarańczowa Alternatywa came to life in 1980 under the tutelage of
art history student Waldemar Fydrych. The movement published a manifesto[8] and staged an event "which proclaimed freedom of the imagination
and condemned 'symmetry' as too predictable an order in society" in 1981
(Misztal 1990, 80). It then was inactive during the Martial Law period and
re-emerged in 1987 with another series of events and street happenings.
The historical trajectory of the Pomarańczowa Alternatywa overlapped
with that of *Alternatywy 4*. Both were the result of the same set of historical circumstances and grew out of related sources of cultural and personal
influences. Both identified their origins in the theater of the absurd but
also in that of provocation by opening reality into a sphere of imagination,
play and subversion—thus creating a new cultural and aesthetic sphere—
'socialist surrealism.'

Pomarańczowa Alternatywa emerged at the time of the 'Festival of Solidarity' and was enabled by the Solidarity movement. However, unlike Solidarity itself, Pomarańczowa Alternatywa did not have any specific political
or social aims and objectives. Rather, it wanted to disclose the inconsistencies, paradoxes and absurdities of life under socialism through a series of
live street events. It proclaimed its aims in 1981 in the form of a Manifesto,
which was organized around three broad aims:

> Firstly, it proposed that imagination is the key to individual freedom.
> Secondly, it suggested that politics and politicians have, albeit unwill-
> ingly, contributed to the survival and rebirth of free imagination and
> surrealism. This survival came about despite the temporarily successful
> ideology of rationalism. Thirdly, it stated that the entire world is an
> object of art and that surrealism makes it possible to treat the world as
> play. (Misztal 1990, 81)

The rebirth of Pomarańczowa Alternatywa in 1987 included a series of
15 joyful, careful and subversive events they called 'carnivals,' named for
instance 'Who is Afraid of Toilet Paper' and 'Toilet Paper-Part Two' (at
the time of chronic shortages of toilet paper in Poland), 'The Day of the
Army Maneuvers' and 'The Day of Militiamen' (in the country that has
just survived Martial Law, when power was in the hands of a group of
army generals) (Misztal 1990, 81–82). This is a description of one of the
Pomarańczowa Alternatywa events, which happened in Warsaw in 1988:

The Orange Alternative came out on the day traditionally celebrated as the anniversary of the creation of the secret police. Scores of young people gathered around the statue of Feliks Dzierżyński, the founding father of the Soviet Secret police, laying wreaths and chanting their love of policemen. The protest scenario had undergone a surrealist reversion; it was simply awkward to arrest demonstrators who were declaring their friendship with the police forces. (Misztal 1990, 82)

What was interesting about Pomarańczowa Alternatywa is that its objectives and the sphere of its activity were not different from the subversive humor contained in Bareja's films and TV series. Slogans were a pervasive and constant element of life under socialism, and one of the most common and visible sources of humor. They were exploited by Pomarańczowa Alternatywa, cabarets and also by the makers of *Alternatywy 4*.

Romanienko observes that low levels of state activity actually allow for subversive actions. She argues that "communist officials did indeed have low or no state capacity in dealing with the complex socioeconomic and cultural problems that led to the Solidarity uprisings, and this declining state capacity was further paralysed through the theatrical device of street-level demonstrations involving humour" (2007, 136). She sees the situation as one that allowed for the emergence of Pomarańczowa Alternatywa. But we could also argue that the same happened in Polish television, which was changing after the departure of the TV tsar of the 1970s, Maciej Szczepański, and the wave of criticism directed at television and enabled by the emergence of Solidarity 1980. During Szczepański's reign over Polish television in the 1970s, "making a series which did not contribute to the rhetoric of the 'propaganda of success' was virtually impossible" (Replewitz 2009, 252). In the 1970s, television was a powerful tool for the Polish socialist party to promote its political goals and develop a rhetoric referred to as 'propaganda of success.' Poland was shown as a modern European country, which was growing and developing very rapidly and successfully. Although some degree of economic growth and social change did indeed take place, mostly thanks to the loans taken by the Polish government from Western banks, from the mid-seventies the economic conditions of the majority of the population began to worsen, which was a reason for the waves of strikes and finally the emergence of Solidarity. The TV series *Czterdziestolatek* is a good companion piece to *Alternatywy 4* because it portrays Polish reality according to the propaganda of success and at the same time makes Bareja's series an important part of a quasi-cinema and TV genre, whose shared characteristic is that it is set in the block of flats. It was "during a few months of the [Solidarity] 'carnival' that the social satire gained in value [and] television became interested in the project [*Alternatywy 4*]" (Replewitz 2009, 252).

76 Dorota Ostrowska

"BLOCK OF FLATS" GENRE

The "block of flats" TV series genre was very popular because it addressed a central problem for Poles—that of housing. *Czterdziestolatek*, like all other series of this kind, was set in Warsaw—the city which epitomized the Polish post-war reconstruction effort but also a new type of city, and country, that socialist Poland and its capital were to become. *Czterdziestolatek* was a story of a model Pole under socialism: a 40-year-old engineer, "a father of two children, an owner of a Fiat 126p, and a 3-room flat on a Warsaw estate"[9] (Lubelski 2009, 359). The family had "strong principles, favours education and professionalism over material goods but can be quite snobbish and easily taken by different fashions," which may take them off the course in their realisation of the successful and peaceful life (359). A number of characters, including neighbors and friends, set them straight; and it is their interactions with them that offer the model family a strong sense of community. Bareja drew a far less palatable picture of the life of the Polish middle and working classes on the Warsaw housing development. He managed to really uncover the reality and show the failure of the social project in place since the end of World War II.

His take on this genre was almost a reaction to and subversion of the norms of the genre. Whilst in other series the focus is specifically on the problems of a modern Polish family in the 1970s, Bareja concentrates on the context in which a set of families lives, thus creating a social microcosm that is determined by the material conditions of their lives. What was ingenious in Bareja's series was the focus on the material failure of the construction project, which adversely affected social and communal ties, thus making this material failure an allegory for socialist Poland *tout court*. His other innovation and his greatest dare was to use the comedy framework to show the problems of living in the Polish estate. What was new on screen and unseen previously (but familiar from real life) were wobbly stairs, uneven walls, failed plumbing, two families forced to live in one flat because of an administrative error, the janitor who is terrorizing the inhabitants of the block, drunken workers and perpetual housing shortages.

Alternatywy 4 shows that the country never managed to surmount the housing problems it began to face after the World War II. The absurdity of the situation had to do with the fact that the place was falling apart even before it was completed and lived in. The message was that there is something wrong with the very idea at the origins of this construction effort and could be read more broadly as a critique of the whole project of building socialism in Poland. This is the message that the series relentlessly conveyed in each of the episodes. The workers were not heroic; worse, they were not even conscientious. They were corrupt, incompetent, lazy and drunk most of the time. Each episode of the series tellingly begins with a group of builders on a top of a building having a drink with one of them falling down by

The Carnival of the Absurd 77

Figure 4.1 Different faces of Anioł the Janitor.

accident—a reference to numerous unreported and covered-up accidents at the Polish building sites at the time. The buildings were not built on time and not according to the plan (in one of the episodes a future inhabitant is not able to establish in which block of flats under construction his flat is because the plans have changed so many times).

Perhaps the most comical but also most disturbing character of the series is that of the building's janitor, Anioł (Angel). He is a small-town apparatchik who gets a new post in Warsaw as a janitor. This post constitutes a de facto demotion rather than promotion but as Anioł explains to his sobbing wife—"we have to get really down in order to be able to jump really high." He is putting his words into action by controlling tightly the life of the inhabitants of the block by opening their mail and constantly snooping around. He even forces them to join the tenants' club, which he sets up in the basement of the building. The tenants end up revolting against Anioł, whose presence and actions serve as an allegory for the role of the secret police in socialist Poland. This kind of a character and the rebellion of the inhabitants would not have been allowed to be shown on Polish TV before 1980, when Solidarity was founded in an act of defiance against the Polish government.

CONCLUSION

Bareja's carnival of the absurd still continues. The following that the director enjoys through his fan base is quite phenomenal. The films and the TV series, in particular *Alternatywy 4*, are frequently broadcast on state television. There are two big fan websites and at least one that deals specifically

78 Dorota Ostrowska

with *Alternatywy 4*.[10] The series' appeal cuts across the generational divide. Teenagers see the series as a convincing document of the past, "an attractive document of the times which is part of the history curriculum at schools today. Importantly, the series shows that past world in a very logical way: this dinosaur of a country had to die" (Gazeta). Those who are middle-aged today view the series through a more nostalgic lens, as a snapshot of the times when they were children. This is how an active member of the online forum dedicated to *Alternatywy 4* explains the appeal of the series: "In short, [this series is such an phenomenon for us] because it is our childhood. In the 1980s most of us [those active on this forum] were children and it is only natural that we have a positive attitude towards that time. [. . .] *Alternatywy 4* is a social drama but it is also a comedy which deals with the everyday of our childhood" (Snofru 2011). For an older age group the appeal of Bareja changes as the nostalgia for socialism grows. A member of another online forum explains: "for a long time I had been put off by a certain 'primitivism' of Bareja's works. For some time, however, my attitude has been changing as I discover many valuable elements in his works. Bareja's films are for me a journey into the past, to the reality which is linked to the period of my childhood, and my youth, which were at times difficult, but today I remember them with great melancholy" (Jakobian 2011). It is this nostalgia for the socialist past which grows even more mythical as the time passes that contributes to the final and currently the most enduring element of the carnivalesque of *Alternatywy 4*. Thus bridging the Poland of today with that of the socialist era *Alternatywy 4* is not just the carnival of the absurd but the carnival of nostalgia as well.

Figure 4.2 Fandom of *Alternatywy 4*.

The Carnival of the Absurd 79

NOTES

1. *Alternatywy 4* was not the only television series which Bareja made for television. He was also involved in the making of the very first Polish TV series *Barbara i Jan* (*Barbara and Jan*; 1965). Also in 1965 he directed a very successful first Polish crime series, *Kapitan Sowa na tropie* (*Captain Sowa investigates*), and he concluded his career with another TV series *Zmiennicy* (*Substitues*; 1986) before his untimely death in 1987.
2. I discuss this period in the history of Polish television in Dorota Ostrowska and Małgorzata Radkiewicz, "POLAND: costume dramas: cine-televisual alliances in the socialist and post-socialist Poland" in *European Cinemas in the TV Age*, ed. Dorota Ostrowska and Graham Roberts, 107–124 (Edinburgh: Edinburgh University Press, 2007).
3. *Bareizm*, dir. by Agnieszka Arnold (1997; Warszawa: Wytwórnia Filmów Dokumentalnych i Fabularnych Telewizja Polska—II Program).
4. Fedorowicz became a scriptwriter for two of Bareja's films in the 1970s *Poszukiwany-poszukiwana* (*Man-woman Wanted*; 1973), *Nie ma róży bez ognia* (*A Jungle Book of Regulations*; 1974), where he also played the main role.
5. This episode is available at http://www.youtube.com/watch?v=_crv9wTpfH (accessed August 12, 2011).
6. I wrote briefly about the *Dekalog* as a companion piece to *Alternatywy 4* in Dorota Ostrowska, "Cinema in Ten TV Episodes: Dekalog by Krzysztof Kieślowski," *Critical Studies in Television* 4, 2 (2009): 90–98.
7. Janusz Płoński, "Próba porozumienia," *ITD* 15, April 11, 1976 (an article about START-Festiwal Studenckich Teatrów Debiutujących/Festival of Debutant Student Theaters); "Chleba i teatru powszedniego," *ITD* 19, May 9, 1976 (an article about contemporary avant-garde theater); "Dała jej mamusia słodkiego cycusia . . . ," *ITD* 20, May 16, 1976 (an article about Ogólnopolski Festiwal Piosenki i Piosenkarzy Studenckich w Krakowie/Polish Festival of Student Song and Singers in Cracow).
8. "Manifest surrealizmu socjalistycznego" ("Manifesto of the Socialist Surrealism") is available at http://www.pomaranczowa-alternatywa.org/images/manifest_web.jpg (accessed August 13, 2011).a
9. A three-bedroom flat usually measured about 50 square meters or about 538 square feet.
10. http://www.bareja.republika.pl/, http://www.bareja.neostrada.pl/glowna.htm and http://www.alternatywy4.net/ (accessed August 13, 2011).

REFERENCES

Arnold, Agnieszka, dir. 1997. *Bareizm*. Wytwórnia Filmów Dokumentalnych i Fabularnych (Warszawa), Telewizja Polska—II Program.
Bakhtin, Mikhail. 1984. *Rabelais and His World*. Translated by Hélène Iswolsky. Bloomington, IN: Indiana University Press.
Crowley, David. 2003. *Warsaw*. London: Reaktion Books LTD.
Fydrych, Waldemar. "Manifest surrealizmu socjalistycznego" ("Manifesto of the Socialist Surrealism"). http://www.pomaranczowa-alternatywa.org/images/manifest_web.jpg.
Gazeta Wyborcza. "'Alternatywy 4.' Antysocjalistyczny pamflet za pieniądze władzy ludowej." http://www.alternatywy4.net/forum-post,73.html.

80   *Dorota Ostrowska*

Hollender, Barbara and Z. Turowska. 2000. *Zespół "TOR"*. Warszawa: Prószyński i S-ka.

Jakobian. August 7, 2011 (14:32), comment in "Księga Gości," http://net3.pl/uslugi/ksiega.php?p_user=bareja&p_nrksiegi=0&p_nrstrony=4&p_cod=.

Lubelski, Tadeusz. 2009. *Historia kina polskiego. Twórcy, filmy, konteksty*. Warszawa: Videograf II.

Łuczak, Maciej. 2002. *Miś czyli rzecz o Stanisławie Barei*. Warszawa: Prószyński i S-ka SA.

Misztal, Bronisław. 1990. "Alternative Social Movements in Contemporary Poland." In *Research in Social Movements, Conflicts and Change Vol. 12*, edited by Louis Kriesberg, 67–88. London: Jai Press INC.

Ostrowska, Dorota. 2009. "Cinema in Ten TV Episodes: Dekalog by Krzysztof Kieślowski." *Critical Studies in Television* 4(2): 90–98.

Ostrowska, Dorota and Małgorzata Radkiewicz. 2007. "POLAND: Costume Dramas: Cine-televisual Alliances in the Socialist and Post-Socialist Poland." In *European Cinemas in the TV Age*, edited by Dorota Ostrowska and Graham Roberts, 107–124. Edinburgh: Edinburgh University Press.

Pawlicki, Maciej. 1988. "Niespotykanie spokojny człowiek." *Film* 15: 3–5.

Płoński, Janusz. May 9, 1976. "Chleba i teatru powszedniego." *ITD* 19.

Płoński, Janusz. May 16, 1976. "Dała jej mamusia słodkiego cycusia . . ." *ITD*, 20.

Płoński, Janusz. April 11, 1976. "Próba porozumienia." *ITD*, 15.

Płoński, Janusz and Maciej Rybiński. 1978. *Góralskie tango*. Warszawa: KAW.

Replewicz, Maciej. 2009. *Stanisław Bareja. Król krzywego zwierciadła*. Poznań: Zysk i S-ka Wydawnictwo.

Romanienko, Lisiunia. 2007. "Antagonism, Absurdity, and the Avant-Garde: Dismantling Soviet Oppression through the Use of Theatrical Devices in Poland's 'Orange' Solidarity Movement." *International Review of Social History* 52: 133–151.

Snofru. May 9, 2011 (13:59), comment on "Dlaczego Alternatywy 4 to fenomen?", http://www.alternatywy4.net/forum-post,1432.html.

5 An Evening with Friends and Enemies
Political Indoctrination In Popular East German Family Series

Katja Kochanowski, Sascha Trültzsch and Reinhold Viehoff

Germany was divided into two states with different ideologies but with a shared cultural heritage and language from 1949 until 1989. State-owned television production in East Germany (German Democratic Republic; GDR), like the entire political and social system of the GDR, was indissolubly tied to this division of Germany after World War II. The two-state solution also affected TV productions in West Germany although for different reasons. TV programs in the GDR were faced with a double bind. On the one hand, they were obliged to fulfill the Eastern bloc's expectations to spread the socialist ideology and program. On the other hand, the GDR found itself in constant rivalry with the West German economic and political system and its TV programming, which presented a permanent temptation for East German viewers. This dilemma set the frame for the establishing and performance of the GDR's TV system from the very beginning. The GDR responded to this problem by waging "class warfare on the air" by developing programs fiercely hostile and diametrically opposed to any outcomes and innovation in Western TV programs (Dittmar 2010).

Unfortunately, from the point of view of the viewers living in the GDR, West German TV programs were, in a certain sense, more attractive than those of the socialist system itself. It was common knowledge in the GDR, including the political leaders, that the majority of the GDR's citizens watched West German TV programs, despite this being officially prohibited (Meyen 2003). The politically desired monopoly of party-controlled television actually never came into existence. It was especially the case that East German non-fictional content—news, documentaries, live reports etc.—were judged very critically by the audience in the GDR since they could easily be compared with their West German equivalents. As a result, viewers in Eastern Germany lost trust in non-fictional formats such as the socialist news. The more the credibility of news and current affairs content diminished, the more attractive fictional and entertainment programs became to the audience. Since fictional programs are not directly related to reality and current affairs, they could not directly be judged by criteria like truth and therefore ideologically motivated deviations from reality could

82   Katja Kochanowski, Sascha Trültzsch and Reinhold Viehoff

not easily be uncovered. They could not 'lie,' at least not in the sense that informational and documentary programs were suspected to do. Therefore, in this field of entertainment, the regime managed to propagate ideological messages more excessively than in non-fictional telecast. The transmission of ideological images via fictional programs turned out to be of great significance, resulting in a unique mixture of ideological and entertaining elements, which became symptomatic of East German TV series.

Television family series throughout the 1960s and 1990s and their reflection of the relationship between the two German states, as well as between the GDR and the Eastern and Western bloc, will be discussed. Following Mikos (1994, 139) we define family series in a wider sense: First, the family is the most relevant and most targeted audience of television from the very beginning, and second, not even the simplest story can be told about someone without mentioning their family, without—as is the core of the dramatic family series—portraying the protagonist in a certain family context. Indeed the family frame is a central element for most of the East German TV series and therefore an analysis of such series can be seen as paradigmatic for this genre in general.

An analysis of series from three decades outlines six stages of genre development within which the increasing desire for entertainment—also demanded by head of state and party leader Erich Honecker in 1971—was met (Pfau 2009; Pfau and Trültzsch 2010). Moreover, it is possible to trace the political agenda behind GDR TV productions. Political changes at the national and international levels were reflected in the series via the use of different countries as backdrops and via the representation of different countries either as friends (socialist countries), foes (capitalist countries) or 'foreigners' (most developing countries). Since there was a wide range of foreign countries depicted in several series over the years, even small changes, as, for instance, the improving relations with Western Germany after the 1972 treaty or the declining importance of the Soviet Union after the political developments of Glasnost and Perestroika can be detected. Following these political changes the viewer can also recognize the increasing self-confidence of the GDR as it developed from a country feeling isolated from everyone except their Eastern allies and feeling threatened by the Western world to a self-confident, internationally accepted partner.

RESEARCH ON EAST GERMAN TELEVISION

As television transmissions in East and West Germany both started in 1952, they were in constant rivalry. This intra-German competition and the fact that East German television was used as a form of political agitation and propaganda made it indispensable that TV series portrayed and judged other countries (Steinmetz and Viehoff 2008, 22–40). The unique political and broadcasting conditions led to a unique program, which has been a topic of research especially in the last 10 years. Starting in 2001 the German Research Foundation funded the research project Program History of East German Television located at four universities (Berlin, Potsdam, Halle, Leipzig) with 10 thematically focused subdivisions (see *www. deutsches-fernsehen-ost.de*). Since then a number of books and papers have been published mostly by members of the project (see the German book series MAZ), the main outlet being Steinmetz and Viehoff (2008). The collaboration project made East German Television a topic of academic research, while earlier, especially before 1990, it was reduced to pure ideology by Western scholars (for example Hartmut-Laugs and Goss 1982) or, after 1990, as an aside to (West) German TV history (as in Hickethier and Hoff 1998). Regarding family series, Pfau (2010) presented a complete history of the genre and its development over the time, showing the change from a direct and offensive propaganda to a more humorous and entertaining propaganda. Also, Trültzsch (2009a) discussed these changes and argued that special methodological approaches are needed to analyze GDR entertaining programs (see Trültzsch 2009b). An overview of the development of the genre under the special political and institutional conditions was published by Pfau and Trültzsch (2010) and in a short English version by Trültzsch and Viehoff (2011).

Satjukow and Gries (2003, 2004a, b) focused on enemies and friends in East German propaganda and media in a more general way, while Brademann-Fenkl (2007); Köbbert (2007) and Kochanowski and Trültzsch (2009) discussed such images in selected TV series. A more general overview on this specific topic was recently published by Kochanowski (2011) and is a basis for this paper.

CHANGES OF DEVELOPMENT IN THE EAST GERMAN FAMILY SERIES—AN OVERVIEW

Similar to most East European socialist and communist countries, East German television was tightly connected to the political system from the very beginning. Different bodies that were supposed to observe and control media production were integrated into high political offices such as the Cabinet. According to the Marxist press theory, media ought to be propagandist, rabble-rousing and organizational. Thus, East German viewers were to be educated according to the communist ideology. Even though the government put an emphasis on media from the start, it was not until the Prague Spring in 1968 that they really understood the power of television. Czech TV producers supported the reform efforts of the people and, therefore, reported about it. This had a tremendous impact on public opinion. People were in favor of these political changes. The socialist neighboring states intervened. However, since the TV stations were spread all over the city of Prague, it was impossible for them to take them over in one day.

84 *Katja Kochanowski, Sascha Trültzsch and Reinhold Viehoff*

Information about the desired reforms was broadcast until the last station was put under control. As a result, the SED (socialist unity party) integrated different bodies to control the media in September of the same year. (Pfau 2009, 95–99; Hoff quoted in Hicketier 1998; Herbst, Ranke and Winkler 1994). Producers worked in a highly observed atmosphere in which they had to justify their series continuously. Before a series' production was granted, the authors had to ensure the ideological correctness of their work. Productions were supported by special political partners who observed the process and suggested changes. Moreover, social partners were informed about the series' specific social or professional background. It was their job to make a production more realistic. In addition to this, series were under review by leading members of the government and the media at different times of the process. Thus, media output was controlled from the very start of the production to the very end (Kochanowski 2011).

The general development was from series conveying a rather simplistic ideology towards series that tried to be entertaining, whilst subliminally and obliquely transmitting an ideological agenda. Only a few series referred to foreign countries directly. Only in *Zur See* (*At Sea*; 1977) und *Treffpunkt Flughafen* (*Meeting Place Airport*; 1986) were there explicit references. Other than that, internationalism and foreign affairs were mentioned only briefly, usually in tangential subplots. Certain examples will be analyzed in particular, without claiming completeness. At the same time, we are not claiming that the propaganda was successful. While the series did propagandize certain images, it has not yet been analyzed what success these had in influencing people's minds.

EXPERIMENTAL STAGE 1960–67: *HEUTE BEI KRÜGERS* (*TODAY AT THE KRÜGERS*, 1960–63)

Heute bei Krügers[1] can be seen as the first real family TV series.[2] Twenty-five episodes[3] were broadcast between 1960 and 1963. It was on the air irregularly, mostly in the afternoon on Saturday or Sunday. Dramaturgical deficits as well as changing broadcasting times and variation in the length of each episode demonstrated that the typical characteristics of the genre were not yet fully developed. The main characters are the Krüger family and their immediate environment: coworkers, neighbors, etc. Even though the plot deals with a range of topics, the recurring themes are the establishment of socialism in the GDR and the government's fight against Cold War crises.[4] One example of this specific thematic connection is the 10th episode; one person's lapse and its social consequences are tied together with international political incidents in order to convey the 'bogeyman' image of the West. The Krügers talk about the negative impact of listening to Western radio and watching Western television to their next-door neighbor Mrs. Schmidt, who enjoys West German entertainment and

An Evening with Friends and Enemies   85

news programs. Discussing the issue, Mrs. Krüger draws a parallel to the Olympic Games of 1936. Like the Nazi regime, Western governments intentionally use entertainment to cover up problems that exist in people's everyday life; Mr. Krüger puts West Germany (FRG) on the same level as the Third Reich. This sequence[5] uses strong propagandistic arguments against watching West German TV. The harsh tone was considered normal for this period of the Cold War and has to be seen as a response to the West German Hallstein Doctrine. In general, West Germany was openly presented as the direct successor to the Third Reich: not only threatening the 'peaceful' GDR and planning another (Third) World War, but also as a political system that, being brutally capitalist, suppressed working classes. The GDR propaganda justified this to be a true and objective observation with, firstly, the "anti-socialist and warmongering" West German demand for exclusive representation of all Germans (Hallstein Doctrine). Secondly, the establishment of a new West German Army, and the joining of NATO were said to be proof that the West German Army was effectively an 'offensive army' comparable with the Wehrmacht of the Third Reich. Using the Krüger family as an exemplary microcosm, the episode, thus, aims to demonstrate that decent socialist people, prototypically the whole Krüger family, understand the deceitful strategies of the enemies and, thus, avoid their television programs.

In the episode mentioned above, West German media report about a potential military conflict following the dispute between the U.S. and the Soviet Union over nuclear weapons[6] and inform about the confrontation of Soviet and American troops at the Berlin Wall in October 1961.[7] The program warned of food shortages as a consequence of these crises, which, thus, leads Mrs. Schmidt to hoarding goods. However, the episode shows that it is actually Mrs. Schmidt and others like her that cause the shortage of goods (the famous 'deficit'). At the end of the episode, Mr. Krüger points out that the coverage in West German news is destructive propaganda, and (it is said quite literally) only East German news can be trusted. These blatant ideological statements are only thinly veiled by a rather flimsy dramatic set-up lacking almost any entertainment value. From today's point of view this propagandistic presentation seems not to have had a good chance to influence viewers practically, since it can easily be identified as propaganda.

This episode tries to stigmatize the reality as presented in West German news programs as factually untrue, negative and dangerous anti-GDR propaganda. The presentation of Cold War confrontations is strongly biased against West Germany and the U.S. West German TV is demonized for intentionally spreading lies and West Germany and the U.S. are also accused of systematic deception. The ideological message is stated bluntly: due to its weakness the U.S. could not stop the building of the Berlin Wall. The GDR, and, thus, also the Soviet Union, had proven to be stronger. The most prominent foes of the GDR at the time, West Germany and the U.S., are presented as the roots of all evil. West German media

86   *Katja Kochanowski, Sascha Trültzsch and Reinhold Viehoff*

are accused of offering their service to U.S. propaganda in order to lead GDR citizens astray.

INSTITUTIONALIZATION 1968–77: *DIE LIEBEN MITMENSCHEN (THE LOVELY FELLOW NEIGHBORS,* 1972)

The fact that in June 1968, under the direction of Manfred Seidowsky, a department specifically dedicated to the production of TV series was founded, emphasizes the importance attached of TV series from that point on. At the same time one could assume that this new organizational background was also a reaction to the events in Prague earlier the same year, and part of the reorganization of GDR television towards more political control. But indeed plans to establish the new department had existed since June 1967 but were realized according to larger reorganizations of the institutional control one year later. (Cf. Pfau 2009, 95–99) The main topic of the series in this stage was still the establishment of the GDR as an independent state. In the years of the Hallstein Doctrine,[8] East German television programs expressed a strict anti-West alignment (Cf. Kannapin 2005, 143) in which West Germany, portrayed as 'the other Germany,' and the U.S., representing the 'bad boys' and antagonists of the Soviet Union, bore the brunt of the criticism.

For the political leaders Cold War antagonists were in general divided into 'outer' and 'inner' enemies. In the outer group were the so-called capitalists. In the 1950s and 1960s West German politicians, leading personalities in the military and the economy as well as American and British 'enemy figures' were variously branded as nationalists, imperialists, militarists, fascists and capitalists—all 'class enemies.' 'Inner enemies' were citizens of the GDR who worked as Western agents or spies.

Friends, in contrast, were united in their aim to spread socialism throughout the world. Together they fought to ostracize capitalism and 'aggressive imperialism.' Socialist values and characteristics such as peacefulness, solidarity and happiness (Gries and Satjukow 2003, 25) were to serve as moral guidelines and demonstrate socialist responsibility. The East German people were supposed to achieve a homogenous socialist awareness so that they could work together towards a better future in a socialist state (Viehoff 2004, 10ff.). The propagated dichotomy clearly was friends (especially the Soviet Union) versus foes (militarists, capitalists and saboteurs) (Gries and Satjukow 2003, 27). As we want to show for the family series, these categories were not rigid but more fluid, since it was differentiated depending on the social status or class of the protagonists. So the rigid propagandistic scheme was adapted to a more pragmatic and dramaturgically more useful one.

The 10 episodes of *Die lieben Mitmenschen*[9] (seven in 1972, three in 1974) had a formative influence on TV series production in East Germany. In 1972 this series was on the air Fridays at 8 pm; in 1974 it was broadcast

An Evening with Friends and Enemies   87

on Sundays. It did target families as audiences and was very popular: The three new episodes in 1974 were produced because of the many requests by viewers (Pfau 2009, 114). The main characters of the series are the widow Carola Bärenburg with her outdated bourgeois attitudes and her great-nephew Hans, who is a student and lives in lodgings at her home. Hans is presented as a modern, committed socialist. In the few episodes that reference foreign countries, quite a sophisticated image of him is drawn.

In episode five, Mrs. Bärenburg is visited by her old friend Liliane and her son Jochen from Frankfurt am Main in West Germany. Liliane openly calls the GDR a dictatorship. Even though Mrs. Bärenburg obviously does not suffer hardship, her friend asks her to move to Frankfurt am Main. Jochen disagrees with his mother's attitude of questioning the GDR in general. Jochen, who is portrayed as being interested in the socialist country without his mother's "ideological bias," opposes Liliane's provocative statements. He even discusses the pros and cons of both political systems with Hans and his friends.[10] Jochen acknowledges the advantages of the GDR's education system and explains that the conditions for students in Frankfurt am Main are much more difficult due to financial pressures.[11] Moreover, Jochen is impressed by the students' political commitment and their (fictional) right to influence political decisions.[12]

Two stereotypes are being juxtaposed in this episode. Firstly, there is the old lady Liliane disapproving of GDR dictatorship, perceiving the country as a politically dependent socialist satellite state, and demanding the prompt reunification of Germany; and secondly, her son Jochen, who is presented as being open-minded about the GDR. Advantages of the socialist state are illustrated with the help of the character of Jochen. His political views are plausible in the context of the student movements in West Germany in 1967–68, when students increasingly read communist papers and got involved with socialist projects. In the East German TV series the superiority of socialism[13] is thus being confirmed by West German socialists.

Less delicately portrayed is a western country to which the relations were neutral. In episode eight Mrs. Bärenburg is visited by a friend who is a high ranking officer in the French Ministry of Foreign Trade. Carola Bärenburg tries to impress him with old-fashioned status symbols like a butler. This, however, reflects badly on her rather than on her French guest, who is described as being a moderate bourgeois. He shows himself open towards the country and tolerates its political and economic situation, not mentioning differences from his home country. He even criticizes France for its liberal and capital-friendly constitution.[14] Again, the quality of and equality in the GDR education system is praised.[15] Moreover, this shows that the French had an early interest in trading with East Germany. France, however, was influenced by the West German Hallstein Doctrine[16] and never realized its plans of economic cooperation with East Germany. The description of France is benevolently neutral; there are even traces of French hostility towards West Germany with its rigid Hallstein Doctrine

88   *Katja Kochanowski, Sascha Trültzsch and Reinhold Viehoff*

that has also harmed French economic interests. The GDR is presented as very self-confident—on equal terms with France. More than once it seems that France would have benefited more from closer trade relations with East Germany than vice versa.[17]

The Soviet Union was the most important ally of the GDR and it had supremacy over the Eastern bloc; but the description of the USSR follows different patterns. The close relationship between the two countries is highlighted even though the fateful and negative entanglements in their shared past are always taken into consideration. Since the only son of Carola Bärenburg was killed during the war at the Eastern front in Russia, she is very critical towards the Soviet Union and its inhabitants. The third episode deals with this problem. Tanja, a student from Leningrad (now St. Petersburg), takes care of the widow after an accident. The young woman talks about her horrible experiences during the siege of Leningrad by the German Wehrmacht. However, she came into contact with German communists and now feels solidarity towards the GDR; she even found German friends.[18] This report helps Mrs. Bärenburg to overcome her disapproving and biased attitude towards the Soviet Union. The connection between the two through German communists is made plausible with the help of Tanja's personal story. At the same time, the reconciliation and fraternization after Word War II is symbolically fulfilled on an individual level by Carola Bärenburg and Tanja. The German gratitude for liberation from the Nazi regime by the Soviet army is the fundamental and leading motive of this reconciliation. The fateful entanglement of the GDR with the 'big brother' is worked out emotionally and it shows that parallel to a strong friendship, a mutual dependency developed between the two countries.

TV SERIES AS FORMS OF EDUCATION TOWARDS A SOCIALIST PERSONALITY 1973–78: *ZUR SEE* (*AT SEA*; 1977)

After the German treaty[19] in 1972 it became more difficult to refer to stereotypical enemy images. The SED wanted to support this new policy of *rapprochement*, but still felt the need to shield their people from Western influences. This conflict of interests was resolved by objectivizing the confrontation of ideologies; depersonalizing the discussion being the most obvious consequence (Schütte 1997, 1). Accordingly, the development of socialist society as well as the formation of socialist personalities (Pfau and Trültzsch 2006) became the central topics in TV series after 1973. Even though the entertaining elements gained more importance, ideological propaganda could still be widely found.

The nine episodes of *Zur See*[20] were first aired in 1977. It was broadcast in primetime at 8 pm on Fridays. Some episodes reached up to 70% of the viewers (Pfau 2009, 138f.). By viewer ratings it was the most successful series produced for GDR television.[21] The plot centers on the life of a ship crew on board the trading vessel *Fichte* traveling to exotic and mostly capitalist countries.[22] This choice of setting not only satisfied the wanderlust of East German viewers but also allowed negative attributes to be ascribed to a range of Western countries while repeating positive images of socialist countries (Stein 1976, 2).

The dramatic constellation reflects the state's self-image: being in difficult conditions in international politics can only be met by solidarity, friendship, clear and hierarchical guidance, a well-structured routine within the collective, plus very careful contacts with foreigners who differ from friends just the way the friend-enemy scheme of international politics suggests.

The presence of the two ideologies in the series differs. While socialist friends are met throughout the world, in capitalist and socialist harbors, as well as at sea, the East German ship comes across Western ideologies in capitalist harbors only. Partners are introduced explicitly, namely: Soviet, Polish and Cuban friends (always referred to as 'comrades'). Yet, there is a certain ranking amongst these friends. The dominance of the Soviet Union is the same as in real politics. The East German ship gets into trouble three

Figure 5.1 The Captain with his white uniform is arguing with the corrupt and suspicious officer of the capitalistic developing country. (Source: Screenshot/German Broadcasting Archive Potsdam/Zur See/ Episode 4/ Timecode 00:20:49.)

times due to capitalist intrigues. In episode three a fire breaks out on board caused by carelessly discarded cigarette stubs. The East German sailor, who was supposed to supervise the loading of the ship, had left his station in order to allow the local workers a break and get them some water—just what the ideal of socialist solidarity would require of him. The workers from the capitalist country, however, ignore the possible consequences of their actions. Thanks to up-to-date nautical engineering the crew is able to quickly extinguish the fire.

In episodes four and seven the GDR crew has even bigger problems to face. In the anti-imperialistic conflict they are dependent on help from the Soviet Union's superpower. Episode four features the crew of the *Fichte* trying to prevail against the administrative machinery of a capitalist country that accuses the crew of having caused a collision with a Liberian freighter. The local police do not investigate impartially and even leak false information to the press.

Neither the crew nor the GDR government can react adequately to this organized harassment on an institutional level since the GDR did not concurrently have an embassy in the state in question due to the Hallstein

Figure 5.2 The flag of Eastern Germany in Cuba side-by-side with the 'Viva Cuba' Slogan—a visual image of the deep friendship between the two countries. (Source: Screenshot/German Broadcasting Archive Potsdam/Zur See/ Episode 9/ Timecode 00:30:35.)

An Evening with Friends and Enemies 91

Doctrine.[23] This problem takes on a very delicate significance when the West German ambassador offers his help to the captain if he agrees to become a West German citizen. Yet, the Soviet embassy proves to be a true socialist friend, offering help without asking for a favor in return.

In episode seven the ship receives a profitable shipment in a harbor of a South or Latin American country. The presumed inferior local shipping company subsequently tries to get the contract back using criminal methods. First, they try to hide a mysterious box on board the ship. Later a bribed pilot allows the towline to slip into the propeller and the *Fichte* is badly damaged. Thanks to the help of Soviet divers the damage is repaired. Thus, there are strong parallels between events in the TV series and those in real life politics at the time. In both cases the Soviet Union repeatedly had to secure the existence of East Germany. The GDR is portrayed as relatively weak and in need of help from the 'big brother' Soviet Union.

Ships and crews from Poland and Cuba also help the East German ship; however, their support is not as explicitly anti-imperialist but more humane in nature. Episode five tells the story of a young crew member who needs surgery at sea. Working as a team, a Polish physician and a Cuban physician, assisted by the East German captain, save the sailor's life. In this specific context the East German crew relies on their helpful friends from Poland and Cuba, represented by their naval doctors. However, with regard to the countries' roles in international politics Poland, Cuba and the GDR are equals.

Contrary to the GDR's friends, its foes are not named explicitly. Therefore, it is not specific countries but capitalism in general that is the enemy. The fact that all capitalist harbors are situated in Latin America is due to the limited possibilities of filming abroad: Cuba was used as the filming location for all exotic settings. The official policy was that, if both blocs during the Cold War could live in peaceful coexistence then this would be to their mutual advantage. This complex political background, however, was lacking important ideological messages to be presented on screen. Instead, class struggles dominate the relationships between the East German crew and other naval workers. Instead of receiving support from other crews, the East German crew has to endure harassment and falls victim to acts of sabotage.

Two countries form an exception to the overall 'faceless enemy' that is capitalism: West Germany and Liberia. In episode four, it was due to the West German Hallstein Doctrine that the crew of the *Fichte* was unable to receive help from an East German embassy and was thus left without any representative (i.e. ambassador) to help and defend them. Moreover, the West German ambassador tried to convince a well-educated East German to emigrate to the West. Those were the two major fears of the GDR government: international isolation and a brain-drain of highly-educated GDR citizens headhunted by the West. The second country explicitly named

92   *Katja Kochanowski, Sascha Trültzsch and Reinhold Viehoff*

is Liberia. It is a capitalist developing country and well connected to the U.S. Liberia is supposed to represent the U.S., which itself is not explicitly named. Thus, it is West Germany and the U.S.—the two arch-enemies—that get extracted out of capitalist anonymity.

Both ideologies are characterized as being diametrically opposed to each other. Socialists are only ascribed positive attributes; they are focused on people and have an altruistic nature. Capitalists, by contrast, are egoistic and self-centered. For their personal gain they are willing to ignore moral rules or even break the law. Throughout the series, capitalist people of all social classes are portrayed according to these stereotypes: the ship owner as a big businessman in episode seven, the bartender as an entrepreneur in episode three, the administrative machinery in episode four and the laborers as the loader in episode three. The laborers are exploited by the capitalist system and are, therefore, forced to commit petty offences out of need.

The overall impression created by this TV series is one of an aggressive international fight against socialism in general. Despite being the repeated target of anti-socialist attacks the crew of the *Fichte* remains neutral and they even help capitalist ships and their crews when in trouble. Yet, this support is mainly limited to crew members who can be classified as representatives of the working class such as sailors and longshoremen. The crew's behavior can thus be interpreted as conforming to the ideology of the working classes overcoming national differences in their pursuit of victory in the international class struggle.

TV SERIES WITH MAINLY ENTERTAINING CHARACTER: 1978–84: *BÜHNE FREI* (*STAGE FREE*, 1983)

It was not until 1978 that with *Rentner haben niemals Zeit* (*Pensioners Never Have Time*) humorous entertainment became the main focus with the amount of direct ideological propaganda declining. Ideological views were now more subtly embedded in the plot in order to convince the viewers that everyday life in the GDR was worth living. This also included critique on a certain level: minor discontentment, mostly regarding deficits in supply with goods and services were criticized as fads—mostly regarded with favor. Yet, this critique never turned into criticism of the system in general.

Bühne Frei[24] (seven episodes in 1983) makes use of the new subgenre by placing family stories within the artistic background of a revue theater—for the GDR a new combination. The series, aired Fridays at 7 pm, was not very popular with the audiences. First it reached only about 20% of the viewers (compared to 47% for *Rentner haben niemals Zeit*) and was secondly it was rated very low (satisfying, 3.29 on a scale from 1=very good to 5=unsatisfying) (Pfau 2009, 160). The series is set at the vaudeville theater Odeon[25] but focused on family stories of the artists and the staff.

An Evening with Friends and Enemies 93

International contacts and relations are only mentioned in passing, but surprisingly as common and natural. The series suggests that there seem to be no travelling restrictions, as if the Wall did not exist at all. On the one hand, theatrical shows of specific foreign artists are made a topic; on the other hand, the engagement of East German artists abroad is described, without naming the countries. The episodes combine artistic scenes like musical performances, dancing and artistic elements with more dramatic elements such as problems in relationships, health problems related to the artistic work, etc. Regarding the international relations, two general tendencies mark this series. First, capitalist countries are not mentioned as desired destinations for GDR artists although the series evokes the impression that it was quite common for East German artists to travel to non-socialist countries. The protagonists only speak explicitly about their engagements and journeys to countries of the Eastern bloc. Even language problems disappear. Interestingly, they use German, rather than Russian, as the dominant language of the socialist bloc.[26] The political change through the strike of Solidarność in Gdańsk[27] and the connected upheaval are probably the reasons why the neighboring state of Poland is not mentioned anymore. Second, it is clearly pointed out that working in the GDR is attractive to many European artists and performers, no matter whether they come from socialist or capitalist countries. Moreover, the opposed political ideologies do not seem to have any influence on the artistic work at the *Odeon;* there are very few differences in the depiction of Eastern and Western characters. In addition, there are no conversations or discussions about the social or political conditions in the GDR. Both facts indicate the increased international self-confidence of the GDR and emphasize that East German culture productions were of the highest quality. The special artistic environment and the new self-confidence make it possible to almost entirely renounce the previous polarization of friends and foes.

EXPERIMENTS WITH NEW FORMATS 1985–90: *TREFFPUNKT FLUGHAFEN (MEETING PLACE AIRPORT, 1986)*

The appealing character of the preceding period became even more predominant in the years between 1985 and 1990. Ideological aspects decreased further; however, they never disappeared completely. During this period TV productions followed international trends in television program production (long-running series, modern dramaturgical techniques such as multiplot stories and cliff-hangers[28] or visual effects[29]).

The eight episodes of *Treffpunkt Flughafen*[30] (coproduced by Cuban TV) were first broadcast in 1986—on Sundays at 8 pm, during primetime. Due to the choice of actors and the use of a similar subject, the series was considered to be a sequel to the earlier TV series *Zur See*, especially as it continued with the same semantic model as the earlier series. The key

94   *Katja Kochanowski, Sascha Trültzsch and Reinhold Viehoff*

difference is that in *Treffpunkt Flughafen* the GDR was represented by an air crew instead of a naval crew.[31] At the center of all episodes are the lives and adventures of the air crew of the state-owned company Interflug. The cast included a noticeable number of foreign actors, who helped create an international and multicultural atmosphere.

The Cold War is explicitly addressed in this TV series, reflecting the new-found role of the GDR as a strong and reliable partner within the international community of socialist countries. A clear differentiation is being made between friends and foes. Interestingly, European countries, whether friends or foes, were completely dropped as subjects or locations from this series. One reason for this omission could have been the dissonance amongst East European countries at that time caused by the democratizing process in Poland.

The key focus of the series is on the GDR's international relations to socialist developing countries, especially Vietnam, Cuba, Nicaragua and Angola. These friends depended on help from the GDR. In the course of the series the crew undertakes numerous solidarity missions. They take medical goods to Angola in episode three; in episode seven they do the same in Nicaragua and, additionally, take injured Sandinista rebels back to East Germany for medical treatment. Other acts of solidarity are only hinted at, but not explicitly highlighted. For instance, the Vietnamese stewardess Li had received her job training in the GDR. Such educational training was clearly considered a part of socialist solidarity. Moreover, members of the air crew help with the harvest in Vietnam and Cuba. In such situations the GDR took over the role of the 'big brother' previously held by the Soviet Union.

Focusing on problems of developing countries (like neocolonialism) and trouble spots (like socialist revolutions), the TV series attributes certain characteristics to the foes of these developing countries, mostly the U.S., that were monotonously propagated. Yet, there is only one episode in which the crew actually meets people from capitalist countries. In episode three the crew is on a 'solidarity mission' to Angola when they suddenly need to make an emergency landing at an airport in the Democratic Republic of Congo. Not only is the Congo one of the developing countries in Africa which had chosen the capitalist route, but there are also two stereotypical capitalists at the airport to reinforce the point. The UK is represented by Mr. Jackson and the U.S. by Major Morris. The belligerent and imperialistic alignment of capitalism is strongly emphasized. Major Morris, obviously a Vietnam veteran, is described as aggressive, especially towards the Vietnamese stewardess Li. Li remembers her painful childhood during the war. Her memories explain her wish for lasting peace. Dramaturgically, both figures are diametrically opposed; Major Morris symbolizing capitalism and imperialism, Li socialism.

The Vietnam War becomes a subject of the series again in episode six. The crew flies to Vietnam and visits Li's family. The viewers learn that the horrendous living conditions in Vietnam were directly caused by the war. The U.S., however, is not explicitly named as the aggressor. It was rather expected that the viewer would know about the American involvement in this (last) Vietnam War at the time of the first broadcasting of this series.

Jackson and Major Morris fulfill another stereotype in episode three. The U.S. was said to use the Democratic Republic of Congo as a bridgehead to secretly supply rebels with arms so they could fight against the nascent socialist government. Peaceable governments keep coming under attack because their antagonists are supplied with military equipment by the U.S. and the UK. This underhand aggression is repeatedly named as a typical characteristic of capitalism.

In episode seven the East German pilot witnesses an air strike on a Nicaraguan (military) hospital, which is in breach of international law. For the Nicaraguans and their supporters these imperialistic aggressions were everyday occurrences. Since the Nicaraguan people are depicted as friendly, the viewer gets the impression that the imperialists attack the working class of that country without any reason; the GDR supports its socialist friends within the global anti-imperialistic conflict. This line of reasoning can be found in all contacts with developing countries. After the crew visits capitalist Congo in episode three, they travel to socialist Angola in episode five. The advancement of the two developing countries can, therefore, be easily compared. Both suffered from colonial exploitation in their past. Again this is said to be the reason for their underdevelopment. After their liberation, however, both progressed very differently. Angola finally seems to really be

Figure 5.3 Among the family pictures of a Cuban working class family there is a portrait of Ernesto Che Guevara. The adored Revolutionist is a universal socialist hero and part of the family. (Source: Screenshot/German Broadcasting Archive Potsdam/Treffpunkt Flughafen/ Episode 2/ Timecode 00:16:55.)

96   Katja Kochanowski, Sascha Trültzsch and Reinhold Viehoff

independent. The people are able to choose their way of living and use their countries' resources as they like. Congo, in contrast, has traded the former suppression for neocolonialism. This is similar to the unadulterated friend-versus-foe-propaganda of the GDR, which blamed the capitalist industrial countries of exploiting the developing countries.

Although the images of friends and foes used in this TV series are multilayered, they can still be easily decoded. Therefore, the viewers had no problem understanding the ideological message. It is striking how explicitly the judgments are expressed in this production, leaving almost no room for other interpretations. Stereotypes of friends and foes are tightly linked to certain political systems and even particular nations. Throughout the series the GDR is portrayed as an active friend who is able to improve the situation in friendly socialist countries concertedly and selflessly.

EPILOGUE: SERIES AFTER THE OPENING OF THE WALL

The fall of the Berlin Wall was, of course, a pivotal point in the history of East German TV productions. Productions after 1990 were strongly influenced by this new situation. Many series were still being broadcast, which had been planned or even produced by the former television producing body of the GDR. The producers tried to react dramaturgically to the changes in the political landscape. But as a consequence of the changing geopolitical situation issues of foreign policy were rarely mentioned. The focus of attention in TV productions from 1990 was more set to the problems connected with the many transformations within the GDR. The series *Agentur Herz* (*Agency Heart*), broadcast Monday and Thursday at primetime in 1991, focused on unemployment. The agency tries to find jobs mostly for former popular artists. People are confronted with widespread social and financial problems. They only get paid for few jobs and most of them are relegated to social isolation caused by the 'Wende.' The series *Luv und Lee* (*Windward and Leeward*), which aired in 1991, focuses on economical changes and centers on the strategies of a married couple, where both husband and wife get unemployed at the same time. They have to rethink their occupational perspectives, since the state-owned ship company closed down and they work hard to get along with the new Western service style and techniques within the Western companies. Depression and problems within the family are discussed. Finally the last episode makes sure to have a fairytale ending, since both start working on a new ship and leave East Germany for a better place. There are several examples of series that consequently focus on contacts and problems between the people from the two former German countries. The key themes of the 1991 series are the steep rise in unemployment, the bleak prospects for the future, the feeling of suddenly being useless, as well as the one-sided transfer of Western economical and institutional systems.

Another new subject in East German TV series was the worries of East Germans about West Germans rightly or falsely reclaiming properties. Yet, the earlier prejudices were not confirmed; within the series the reunion of their families was the only thing that visitors from the Western part had in mind, not any material interests. Real life experiences of East Germans were often quite different, since a lot of property moved to Western German hands and also dubious businessmen used the chance of making deals in Eastern Germany in the months of the transformation process. In the fictional television series it was easy to overcome enemy images by focusing on family reunion stories and highlighting family connections in the sense of Willy Brandt's words—"what belongs together now comes together." The new distinction was drawn between family coming as friends from the Western to the Eastern part of Germany on the one hand and suspect persons or enemies coming to make money and gain property at the expense of East German citizens on the other hand.

Other 'former enemies'—mostly the U.S.—were described, too. It seemed as if the often used stereotypes of friends and foes had now become meaningless. Series produced after the opening of the Wall seemed relatively neutral with regards to questions of international relations with a noticeable lack of the previously so predominantly employed stereotypes of friends and foes. In the seventh episode of *Spreewaldfamilie* (*Family from the Spreewald*), which was broadcast on Friday, January 16, 1991 at 8 pm, one family member who moved to the U.S. after World War II comes back to the Eastern river forest region Spreewald. It is irritating that the producers did not choose the more credible option to have a relative in Western Germany. According to the disappearance of the old stereotypes in the series, even the brother-in-law from the U.S. does not have any attribute of the former enemy image. He is integrated into the family as if he never left Spreewald—the former problematic relations between the GDR and the U.S. are not worth mentioning. Also the differences of everyday life in the two systems are not discussed or mentioned at all. Thus, the series does not explicitly refer to any former image typical for the series before 1990.

RESULTS: PARALLELS AND ANALOGIES OF IMAGES OF FRIENDS AND FOES IN TV SERIES AND IN POLITICAL SITUATIONS

The analyzed TV series show clear parallels and analogies between friends and foes in real politics and their representation in media productions. Throughout the analyzed TV series capitalism as the GDR's major foe is mostly portrayed as a vague scheme. When enemies are named explicitly producers generally use the two countries which appeared the most threatening to the GDR: firstly, the U.S. as the nuclear superpower of

98 Katja Kochanowski, Sascha Trültzsch and Reinhold Viehoff

the opposing political bloc and the antagonist of the GDR's partner and friend the Soviet Union, and secondly, West Germany as the neighbor and political opponent who refused political recognition to the GDR while also holding on to the ideal of a united German nation. This West German position made a truly independent East German state more difficult or even impossible for quite a few years. The few other Western European countries that appear in the series are less clearly stigmatized. There is a favorable view of France, whereas the UK is described as being very similar to the U.S. Moreover, in the early East German TV series, people of different generations are represented as having different political views, e.g. older West Germans seem to be more prejudiced and more critical of the GDR than younger ones (e.g. in *Die lieben Mitmenschen*).

The description of friends also shows parallels between the political reality and the media pictures. The Soviet Union had to continuously secure the existence of the GDR and is portrayed as the country's best friend and protective 'big brother.' The remaining socialist 'friends' were ranked according to their power and their geographical distance from the GDR. Following this logic, European socialist countries were considered to be of greater importance. Just as the influence of the Soviet Union decreases over the course of time, so does the role of the other European socialist countries. On the one hand, this might be due to the easing of political tensions and the changes within these countries in the 1980s. On the other hand, it is all too easy to stage the GDR as a self-confident country supporting developing countries in Africa, Asia and Latin America. Countries that had to fight for their choice of socialism are particularly widely used in the series, namely Vietnam, Cuba and Nicaragua as well as certain African socialist developing countries. They are described as victims and heroes at the same time and, therefore, have a stronger dramaturgical value for ideological elements than countries which might be shining examples of socialism (like the USSR), but whose fight for their political ideals happened about 40 years ago. The powerful image of a current anti-imperialistic conflict is missing. The anti-imperialistic fights of the developing countries were supported by the GDR—in reality as well as in the TV series—since the East Germans connected them ideologically with the German Labor movement.

During the political changes of 1989–90 the clearly defined images of friends and foes disappear almost completely; only in very few episodes and sequences are these images subsequently questioned or refuted. The clear connection between political changes and their staging in the TV series make the tight links between television and the political system in the GDR obvious. The demonstrated patterns of production served not only to legitimatize but also to enhance the influence of the GDR in the world. It was supposed to transmit the image of a self-confident country to the audience; a country on the right track in matters of domestic and foreign policy that needed not only to demarcate itself from the capitalist countries, but also to protect itself against them.

NOTES

1. Authors: Marianne Reinke/ Gerhard Weise, script editors: Ilse Langosch/ Reimar Dänhardt (17, 19), production: Rolf Figelius (17, 18).
2. After the two-parted, not preserved series *Die Vormanns und ihre Freunde* (*Vormann Family and Friends*).
3. There are only five episodes preserved completely and two partly in the German broadcasting archives (DRA).
4. For a detailed analysis of the series see Trültzsch 2007.
5. Cf. episode 10 [00:23:30].
6. This finally was settled in the Vienna Summit on June 4, 1961.
7. On October 27, 1961 Soviet and American tanks stood face-to-face at Checkpoint Charlie, Berlin.
8. This doctrine was supposed to ensure that West Germany was seen as the only Germany. Governments that would start diplomatic relations with (economically weak) East Germany were threatened to lose those with (economically strong) West Germany. As a result, the GDR was isolated—except from countries of the socialist bloc.
9. Authors: Gert Billing (1–8), Helmut Grosz (9), script editors: Horst Enders (1–8), Rita Müller (1–8), Birgit Mehler (9–10), production: Wolfgang Luderer.
10. Cf. episode 5 [00:19:00].
11. Cf. episode 5 [00:30:00].
12. Cf. episode 5 [00:30:00].
13. Marx' developmental law of the society is meant here.
14. Cf. episode 8 [00:44:00].
15. Cf. idem.
16. Cf. episode 8 [00:43:00].
17. Cf. episode 8 [01:08:00].
18. Cf. episode 3 [00:49:00].
19. In the German treaty (Grundlagenvertrag) of 1972 both countries agreed to aim for better relations and they accepted the independence of each German state.
20. Author: Eva Stein, script editors: Heide Hess, Rudi Thurau, production: Wolfgang Luderer.
21. Cf. Pfau 2004, p. 360. Moreover, *Zur See* had the second best audience critic of all family series; also cf. Hoff in Hicketier 1998, p. 402.
22. For a more detailed analysis of friend and foe images in the series see Kochanowski 2011.
23. This one episode is situated in the past.
24. Author: Thomas Jacob, Script editor: Birgit Mehler, Director: Thomas Jacob.
25. For an analysis of this series see Raue 2004.
26. Mostly because of the German audience.
27. The crisis in Poland started in the summer of 1980.
28. Both were still experimental and, therefore, not always logical.
29. Especially *Tiere machen Leute* uses effects such as fading in stars, etc.
30. Authors: Gert Billing, Manfred Mosblech, script editors: Dr. Manfred Seidowsky, production: Manfred Mosblech.
31. For a more detailed analysis of friend and foe images in the series see Kochanowski 2011.

REFERENCES

Brademann-Fenkl, Judith. 2007. "Zwischen 'Resonanzboden' und 'Gegenbild': Zur identifikatorischen Inszenierung von Fremdheit in ausgewählten Beispielen

100 *Katja Kochanowski, Sascha Trültzsch and Reinhold Viehoff*

der DDR-Reiseliteratur der 1970er Jahre und der Fernsehserie Zur See von 1977." In *Abbild—Vorbild—Alltagsbild: Thematische Einzelanalysen zu ausgewählten Familienserien des DDR-Fernsehens*, edited by Sascha Trültzsch, 181–232. Leipzig: Leipziger Universitätsverlag.

Dittmar, Claudia. 2010. *Feindliches Fernsehen: Das DDR-Fernsehen und seine Strategien im Umgang mit dem westdeutschen Fernsehen.* Bielefeld: transcript Verlag.

Feldmann, Klaus. 1996. *Nachrichten aus Adlershof: ein Insider des DDR-Fernsehens erinnert sich.* Berlin: Edition Ost. Gries, Rainer and Silke Satjukow. 2003. "Von Feinden und Helden. Inszenierte Politik im realen Sozialismus." In *Aus Politik und Zeitgeschichte. Beilage zur Wochenzeitung 'Das Parlament'*, Jahrgang 2003, Heft B53, 20–29. Bonn: Bundeszentrale für Politische Bildung.

Hartmut-Laugs, Petra and John A. Goss. 1982. *Unterhaltung und Politik im Abendprogramm des DDR-Fernsehens.* Köln: Verlag Wissenschaft und Politik.

Herbst, Andreas, Ranke, Winfried, and Winkler, Jürgen. 1994. *So funktionierte die DDR. Lexikon der Organisationen und Institutionen.* Reinbek: Rowohlt Verlage.

Hickethier, Knut (with Mitarbeit von Peter Hoff). 1998. *Geschichte des deutschen Fernsehens.* Stuttgart: Verlag J.B. Metzler,.

Kannapin, Detlef 2005: "'DDR-Identität' oder DDR-Bewusstsein im DEFA-Spielfilm?" In *Politische Identität—visuell*, edited by Wilhelm Hofmann and Franz Lesske, 133–152. Münster: Lit Verlag.

Köbbert (Kochanowski), Katja. 2007. "Der Kalte Krieg im Wohnzimmer. Eine Untersuchung außenploitischer Freund- und Feindstereotype in unterhaltenden Fernsehserien der siebziger und achtziger Jahre." In *Abbild—Vorbild—Alltagsbild: Thematische Einzelanalysen zu ausgewählten Familienserien des DDR-Fernsehens* edited by Sascha Trültzsch, 233–269. Leipzig: Leipziger Universitätsverlag.

Kochanowski, Katja. 2011. *Fakt ist, wir sind hier nicht bei Freunden … Politische Freund- und Feindbilder in Unterhaltungsserien der DDR.* Marburg: Tectum.

Kochanowski, Katja and Sascha Trültzsch, Sascha. 2009. "Der Kalte Krieg hautnah: Eine Analyse der Serie Treffpunkt Flughafen mit besonderem Fokus auf die propagandistische Einflussnahme auf Unterhaltungssendungen des DDR-Fernsehens durch staat-liche Institutionen." In *Heimat und Fremde: Selbst-, Fremd- und Leitbilder in Film und Fernsehen*, edited by Claudi Böttcher, Judith Kretschmar and Markus Schubert, 111–130. München: Meidenbauer.

Meyen, Michael. 2003. *Einschalten, Umschalten, Ausschalten? Das Fernsehen im DDR-Alltag.* Leipzig: Leipziger Universitätsverlag.

Mikos, Lothar. 1994. *Es ist dein Leben! Familienserien im Fernsehen und im Alltag der Zuschauer.* Münster: MAkS Publikationen.

Pfau, Sebastian. 2009. *Vom Seriellen zur Serie—Wandlungen im DDR-Fernsehen. Die Entwicklung von fiktionalen Serien im DDR-Fernsehen mit dem Schwerpunkt auf Familienserien.* Leipzig: Leipziger Universitätsverlag.

Pfau, Sebastian and Sascha Trültzsch. 2006. "Sozialisation in Familie und Betrieb: Familienleitbilder und Verflechtung der Lebenswelten Beruf und Familie in der DDR." In *Handbuch zur Kinder- und Jugendliteratur in der DDR,* edited by Rüdiger Steinlein, Heidi Strobel and Thomas Kramer, 64–73. Stuttgart, Weimar: J.B. Metzler.

Pfau, Sebastian and Sascha Trültzsch (with Mitarbeit von Katja Kochanowski and Tanja Rüdinger). 2010. *Von den Krügers bis zur Feuerwache. Vademekum der Familienserien des DDR-Fernsehens.* Mit Datenbank CD-ROM. Leipzig: Leipziger Universitätsverlag.

Raue, Burkhard. 2004. "Bühne frei. Ein Blick hinter die Kulissen einer Varieté-Serie des Fernsehens der DDR." In *Alternativen im DDR-Fernsehen? Die*

An Evening with Friends and Enemies 101

Programmentwicklung 1981 bis 1985, edited by *Vollberg* Dittmar, 387–412. Leipzig: Leipziger Universitätsverlag.

Satjukow, Silke and Rainer Gries. 2004a. *Unsere Feinde. Konstruktion des Anderen im Sozialismus.* Leipzig: Leipziger Universitätsverlag.

Satjukow, Silke and Rainer Gries. 2004b. "Seid wachsam! Feindbilder in sozialistischen Gesellschaften," 845–854. In *Deutschland Archiv. Zeitschrift für das vereinigte Deutschland,* Jahrgang 37, Heft 5. Bonn: Bundeszentrale für Politische Bildung.

Scholtyseck, Joachim. 2003. *Die Außenpolitik der DDR.* München: R. Oldenbourg.

Schütte, Georg. 1997. "An vorderster Front zum Klassenfeind. Fernsehjournalismus in der DDR." In *Leit- und Feindbilder in DDR-Medien,* edited by R. Waterkamp, 66–73. Bonn: Bundeszentrale für Politische Bildung

Stein, Eva. 1976. "Geschichten vom besonderen Alltag der Seeleute." In *Film d. Fernsehens d. DDR,* edited by Helmut Sakowski, Daniel Druskat. Berlin: Fernsehen d. DDR, Programmdirektion, Abt. Öffentlichkeitsarbeit.

Steinmetz, Rüdiger and Reinhold Viehoff, ed. 2008. *Deutsches Fernsehen Ost: Eine Programmgeschichte des DDR-Fernsehens.* Berlin: VBB, Verlag für Berlin-Brandenburg.

Trültzsch, Sascha. 2007. "Mehr Kontext in die Analyse—kontextualisierte Medieninhaltsanalyse: Erläutert an einigen Familienserien des DDR-Fernsehens." In *Medienkulturanalysen: Neuere Forschungskonzepte in den Medienwissenschaften,* edited by Florian Hartling and Sascha Trültzsch, 189–208.. Frankfurt a. M.: Lang.

Trültzsch, Sascha. 2009a. "Changing Family Values from Straight Socialist to Bourgeois on East German TV." In *Popular Culture and Fiction in four decades of East German Television,* edited by Uwe Breitenborn and Sascha Trültzsch, 225–234. Frankfurt a. M.: Lang.

Trültzsch, Sascha. 2009b. *Kontextualisierte Medieninhaltsanalyse. Mit einem Beispiel zum Frauenbild in DDR-Familienserien.* Wiesbaden: VS-Verlag.

Trültzsch, Sascha and Viehoff, Reinhold. In press. "Undercover: How the East German System Represented Itself in TV series." In *Uncertain Entertainment: Popular Television in Totalitarian Europe* edited by Peter Goddard and Rob Turnock: Manchester University Press.

Viehoff, Reinhold, ed. 2004. '*Die Liebenswürdigkeit des Alltags.' Die Familienserie Rentner haben niemals Zeit. Mit einem Beitrag zum Familienleitbild in der DDR.* Leipzig Leipziger Universitätsverlag.

Part II

Commercial Globalization and Eastern European TV

6 From a Socialist Endeavor to a Commercial Enterprise
Children's Television in East-Central Europe

Katalin Lustyik

INTRODUCTION

The collapse of communism in Eastern Europe and the introduction of global capitalism gave rise to a "total reorganization of life, ending up in a privatized, globalised, de-monopolized economy" (Haraszti 1987, 34). Commenting on the importance of research into the transformation of media systems in the region, Sparks argued that "the scope and magnitude of the changes are so great, and the challenge they pose to some of the established ways of thinking about the media so serious, that this kind of work is of pressing importance" (1998, 7). The academic research initially carried out, however, had several limitations in its scope and subject: the press and television were often singled out as key institutions in the process of transformation with the predominance of news and policy-related analysis[1] (Downing, 1996).

Eastern European children's mediated culture, if mentioned at all, constituted little more than anecdotal evidence and was discussed mainly in publication footnotes (e.g. Szekfű 1996). Children's television, however, can provide a useful lens to investigate a variety of broad social, political and economic issues related to the transformation of media systems in the region. Children, suggests Scheper-Hughes and Sargent, are "central figures—and actors—in contemporary contests over definition of culture, its boundaries and significance" (1998, 2). As the political, cultural and economic aspects and roles of the media change in a society, and society itself undergoes profound transformations, so does children's media and many of the characteristics of children's programming. Television in particular can be thought of as a battleground on which anxieties about the future of a nation (especially those in transition) are debated. The status and structure of children's television can be perceived as an index of changes within the broadcasting system such as the diminishing of its public service roles and commercialization of its content (Buckingham et al. 1999a). In this chapter, the term "children's television program" refers to "any program produced or commissioned by a children's department and/or one placed in scheduling periods set aside for children, identified in the television schedule as 'for

106 Katalin Lustyik

children,' or is shown on a dedicated children's channel" (Buckingham et al. 1999a, 80).

Historical period labels such as "communist era," "socialist era" or "Soviet era" as well as geographical labels such as "Eastern Europe," "East-Central Europe" and "Central and Eastern Europe" are often used interchangeably in the literature with reference to some or all parts of the former Soviet Union, Poland, Hungary, East Germany, Czechoslovakia, Bulgaria, Romania and Yugoslavia. Although there are fundamental differences among these countries, such "labels still describe a genuine unit of analysis for global system purposes" (Sklair 2002, 223). The term "East-Central Europe" is used in this chapter, referring primarily to Hungary, Poland, the Czech Republic (Visegrád countries) and secondarily to Slovakia and Romania. The time period from post-World War II until 1989 will be labeled as "socialist" and since the turn of the 1990s as "post-socialist."

While Hungarian children's television is selected as a case study to provide concrete examples, even the countries within East-Central Europe differ considerably from one another, although in general, the overall stuctural changes within children's media culture show many similarities. Undertaking this project has involved the collection and analysis of different types of data. In-depth interviews were conducted between 2000 and 2002 with representatives of children's television networks, Hungarian Television (MTV), the Hungarian National Radio and Television Commission (ORTT), Nickelodeon Hungary and media research groups such as AGB Hungary (AGB Nielsen Media Research), with the aim of gathering valuable insight from those whose work is connected to children's media in the region. Data compiled from a longitudinal study of Hungarian television programming in Hungary was examined to detect changes in children's programming since the mid-1980s.[2] The websites of the most prominent Hungarian television networks, dedicated children's channels targeting East-Central European viewers as well as regional media watch groups and media regulatory bodies were monitored on a regular basis.

Projects embarking on the mission to examine the transformation of children's television and compare the "old" television with the "new" one might end up being accused of using such debates as a "convenient vehicle for laments about cultural decline that are based on little more than nostalgic fantasies about an illusory bygone age" (Buckingham et al. 1999a, 183). The socialist broadcasting system educating and "looking after" children in comparison to new commercial channels bombarding them with cheap violent Japanese anime, as some parents lamented, needs to be examined in a broader context (e.g. Rosdy 1999; Lázár 2003).

The first part of the chapter focuses on the transformation of children's television from a state-controlled broadcasting system in monopoly position to an emerging privatized, deregulated and increasingly competitive national media landscape. The second part of the chapter examines the process of children's television becoming fully integrated into the global

From a Socialist Endeavor to a Commercial Enterprise   107

entertainment industry. This period includes the expansion and growing influence of both regional and global media conglomerations targeting specifically young media consumers. I argue in the conclusion that although children's television and more broadly children's media today differ greatly from what existed during the socialist era, both are based on an equally narrow conceptualization of childhood and the child media user.

CHILDREN'S TELEVISION UNTIL THE 1990S

Digitization, convergence, increased commercialism and competition with the arrival of cable and satellite providers, the deregulation of state-controlled broadcasting systems and the decline of public service principles are some of the processes that describe the massive changes that occurred within the media industries of Eastern Europe during the last decades (e.g. Splichal et al. 1990; Downing 1996; Havens 2006). The significance of the changes that occurred within children's television cannot be understood without the acknowledgement of the overall changes that had taken place at various levels of media operation, such as at the level of political direction, the character of the material presented, broadcasters' relationship to their audiences and the economic basis of the media activity (Sparks 1998; Lustyik 2003).

During the socialist era, children's television existed within the confinements of the state-controlled media system, received continuous financial support and operated by principles far removed from the market but under the guidance of the ruling party. One of the purposes of communication, even in the case of young viewers, was "to transit the instructions, ideas and attitudes of the ruling party" (Williams 1961, 54). György Aczél, a high-ranking Hungarian party official who directed cultural life in Hungary between 1956 and 1988, wrote in *Socialism and the Freedom of Culture* that the mission was "to make sure that the genuine, socialist-oriented endeavours of most young people are not hindered or discouraged, but supported and developed" (1984, 20). Broadcasters and program-makers had to share the party's responsibility to nurture loyal citizens. Children's programming constituted a regular and stable part of the television schedules in the region since the early 1960s. Most important was the five- to ten-minute long evening programming block sometimes referred to as the "good-night tale" scheduled before the main evening news, an essential part of the bedtime family rituals. Daytime programs ranging from puppet shows and studio competitions to television series based on required school readings aired on weekends and during school holidays. Many of these educational and entertaining programs were produced domestically, while others were acquired through Intervision, a highly politicized organization established in 1961 among Eastern European television broadcasters to facilitate information and program exchanged within the region (MTV, personal communication 2002).

108   *Katalin Lustyik*

In the case of Hungary, children's television operated between the late 1950s and late 1980s under the supervision of The Children and Youth Department of the state-controlled Hungarian Television (Magyar Televízió, MTV). During the 1960s and 1970s, later referred to as the "golden era" of children's television, the Department employed 25 people, operated its own puppet studio and commissioned some of the most popular children's shows of the socialist era such as *Mi újság a Futrinka utcában?* (*What's up in Futrinka Street?*; 1962), *Mekk mester* (*Baa, the Handyman*; 1974), *Frakk, a macskák réme* (Frakk, the Cats' Nightmare; 1971), *Kukori és Kotkoda* (*Kukori and Kotkoda* 1971) and *Magyar népmesék* (*Hungarian Folktales*; 1977) (MTV, personal communication 2002).

By the mid-1980s, children's television departments in the region found themselves in an increasingly unstable political and financial situation as their institutions, in order to achieve more political and economic independence, tried to appeal to wider adult segments of their slowly shrinking audiences. Under these circumstances, children's departments became an "endangered species" bullied by more powerful departments serving economically and politically important audience groups (MTV, personal communication 2000). Normative principles such as "providing children with a diversity of programming designed specifically for their age, which encouraged their physical, mental and social development to the fullest potential without the intention of exploiting them" had been thrown out of the window according to Eszter Farkas who lead the Children and Youth Department for years (Farkas 1998; MTV, personal communication 2002). The traditional and paternalistic type of service for the child audience had gradually disappeared from the realm of Hungarian Television by the late 1990s. Breaking down the figures presented in Table 6.1, it becomes clear that MTV1 gradually decreased the amount of programs dedicated to children and youth audiences between 1986 and 1998, while the total number of programs increased. By 2000, only 2.5 percent of the total airtime (440,720 minutes) was devoted to children and youth programming (Farkas 2000).

In the turbulent political times of the late 1980s and early 1990s, children's departments faced severe budget cuts, many employees lost their jobs, puppet and animation studios shut down and the international exchange programs ended—all without being noticed or debated beyond the institutional walls.

Table 6.1   Television Programs Targeting Minors (Ages: 4–17) on MTV1 (and Total Number of Television Programs) between 1986 and 1998

1986:	135	(total 691)
1992:	82	(total 874)
1998:	121	(total 832)

Source: Terestyén, 1999

From a Socialist Endeavor to a Commercial Enterprise 109

The public only became aware of the downsizing and dismantling of the children's television department when the daily routines of millions of families with young children were affected by the disappearance of the traditional evening children's programming block offered for decades.

The new, often viciously debated national media laws of the early 1990s restructured the media landscape of the region allowing an increasing number of stations to compete. In the race for viewers, political support and advertisers, primetime was becoming a crucial and very valuable broadcasting time that could not be "wasted" on children. Hungarian Television, in competition with new national and regional private broadcasters launched after the passing of the Media Law of 1996, after shifting its schedule several times finally ended up dropping its children's evening block *Esti Mese* (*Evening Tale*) in 1997. The national papers reported the event as a whole nation "mourning" the symbolic "execution" of *Tévé Maci*, the little teddy bear character. As the host of the block, he welcomed and then wished good night to children encouraging them to brush their teeth, put on their pyjamas and head to bed. He served as a key symbol for children's television and was labelled by the press as "the most loyal employee" of Hungarian Television working there for more than 30 years[3] (e.g. Lőcsei 1999; "Eltünt" 1999).

While Hungarian Television lulled children to sleep with lively game shows and romantic Latin American telenovelas, Russian children found news bulletins instead of their traditional evening block, *Spokoinoi nochi, malishi* (*Good Night, Little Children*). The press reported the change with a string of nostalgia and disbelief:

> The programme, featuring the unsophisticated yet charming puppets [. . .] had been on the air for some 40 years, from de-Stalinization to de-Sovietization. Several generations of Soviet and Russian kids, including myself, and my son (now 18), had been brought up on it. I knew many children who would refuse to go to bed until the programme's gentle concluding song, *All the merry toys are now asleep*, sounded in their crammed communal flats. (Vitaliev 1998)

Those working within the industry described the overall transformations that occurred in children's television in the region during the 1980s and 1990s as "drastic and dramatic" (Farkas 1998). As state broadcasters were 'abandoning' their children audiences, bidders for new broadcasting licenses pledged to revitalize children's television and invest in domestically produced programming for young viewers as part of their public service commitments.

With the launch of two nation-wide commercial broadcasters in 1997, TV2 (ProsiebenSat1) and RTL-Klub (RTL Group), the number of children's programs increased greatly by 1998 but dropped considerably by 2000 as shown in Table 6.2.

110   *Katalin Lustyik*

Table 6.2   Television Programs Targeting Minors (Ages: 4–17) between 1986 and 2001 in Hungary on the Five Main Broadcasting Channels: MTV1, MTV2 and Duna TV (Launched in 1993) and Privately-owned RTL Klub and TV2 (Both Launched in 1997)

1986:	153
1992:	140
1998:	580
1999:	571
2000:	368
2001:	396

Source: Terestyén 1999, 2000, 2002.

During their first years of operation, both TV2 and RTL-Klub offered a variety of programs, especially on weekends, as laid out in their license agreements (ORTT, personal communication 2002). Their initial "enthusiasm" and level of commitment, however, drastically plummeted once they realized that inexpensive U.S. and Japanese cartoons were often just as popular as their more expensive in-house productions (Hirsch 2002). They also found it easier to obtain imported rather than domestically produced shows, most of which were safely guarded in the archive of Hungarian Television, which was reluctant to license them at a "reasonable" price to its new competitors (ORTT, personal communication 2002; Minimax, personal communication 2002).

If we look at the *ratio* of broadcast time dedicated to children to total broadcasting time on the five main broadcast channels between 1986 and 2001, it actually decreased by close to 50% as indicated in Table 6.3 (Terestyén 2002).

An increase in the portion of children's programs imported from a small number of countries, particularly from Japan and the U.S., was another tangible change throughout the region. Animation constituted the majority

Table 6.3   Percentage of Television Programs Targeting Minors (Ages: 4–17) Between 1986 and 2001 on the Five Main Television Channels in Hungary (MTV1, MTV2, Duna TV, RTL-Klub and TV2)

1986:	15.3%
1992:	9.9%
1998:	14.1%
1999:	12.3%
2000:	8.3%
2001:	8.5%

Source: Terestyén 1999, 2000, 2002.

From a Socialist Endeavor to a Commercial Enterprise 111

Table 6.4 Television Programs Targeting Minors (Ages: 4–17) by Genre in 2001 (N=399) on the Five Main Television Channels in Hungary (MTV1, MTV2, Duna TV, RTL-Klub and TV2)

Genre	RTL Klub	TV2	MTV1 & MTV2	Duna TV
Animation	73 (number of programs) 79.3% (percentage on that channel)	149 98%	27 44.3%	12 35.3%
Clay animation	0	0	3 4.9%	3 8.8%
Puppet show	0	0	10 16.4	0
Play	1 1.1%	0	3 4.9%	0
Feature film	0	1 0.7%	4 6.6%	6 17.7%
Documentary film	9 9.8%	0	3 4.9%	5 14.7%
Entertainment show	9 9.8%	2 1.3%	6 9.8%	8 23.5%
Sport show	0	0	2 3.3%	0
Music show	0	0	3 4.9%	0

Source: Terestyén 1999, 2000, 2002.

of the imports that, in general, tend to cross cultural borders easily and have a long shelf life (e.g. Thussu 2006). In addition to their broad appeal, animation is a relatively "difficult genre for national competition" because of its high production cost and ease to dub into local languages (Straubhaar and Duarte 2005, 246).

Specifically in Hungary, between 1986 and 2001, broadcast time devoted to animation (for all ages) increased nine times on national channels (Terestyén 2002). As imported cartoons came to constitute the lion's share of children's programming, less popular and more expensive genres quickly receded from the schedules (Farkas 1998). As shown in Table 6.4, animation constituted between 80–100% of programs offered to children between April and July 2001 on RTL Klub and TV2.

The once-again shrinking budgets allocated for children's programming forced commercial broadcasters to rely on inexpensive imports and state

112 Katalin Lustyik

broadcasters, obligated more strictly to include some domestic shows, to continuously recycle their archived programs rather than to invest in new productions. In general, one minute of a domestically produced children's program, on average, cost as much as an entire U.S. program around 2000 in Hungary (MTV, personal communication, 2002). Out of the 399 children's programs collected and coded between April and July 2001 from five broadcasters (see Table 6.4), close to 200 originated from the U.S. Hungarian shows made up only 10% of the 261 programs offered on the two commercial channels ("Az országos" 2002).

The inability or disinclination of broadcasters to invest in diverse local production meant that Hungarian children rarely had the chance to see themselves on television after the end of the 1980s. Instead, they followed the lives of American teenagers on the screen or watched locally produced content that targeted primarily adults. Four out of the 10 most popular programs among children in October 2001 were domestic productions: two primetime fictional programs, and a music show that consisted of Hungarian wedding and folklore inspired music (see Table 6.5).

Dáridó, launched in 1998 on TV2, soon became one of the most popular programs with millions of predominantly rural viewers tuning in each week. While both locally and regionally produced children's programs completely vanished during this transitional period, some of them were brought back to fame in 1999 by a new generation of entrepreneurial parents filled with nostalgia and disdaining imported violent cartoons.

Table 6.5 The 10 Most Popular Television Programs Among Minors (Ages: 4–17) in October 2000 on the Five Main Hungarian Broadcast Channels (MTV1, MTV2, Duna TV, RTL-Klub and TV2)

1. *Dáridó a világ körül* (*Dáridó' around the World*)—Hungarian music magazine for adults

2. *Pokemon*—Japanese anime

3. *Wild Angel*—Argentinean telenovela

4. *Jurassic Park*—U.S. feature film

5. *Tom and Jerry*—U.S. animation

6. *Barátok Között* ("Among Friends")—Hungarian primetime soap opera

7. *Naked Gun and a Half* (U.S. film)

8. *Pasik!* (*Those Men!*)—Hungarian sitcom

9. *Születésnapi Dáridó* (*Birthday Dáridó*)—Hungarian music magazine for adults

10. *The Adventures of Foxi Maxi*—U.S. animation

Source: "AGB Hungary," 2001.

From a Socialist Endeavor to a Commercial Enterprise 113

CHILDREN'S TELEVISION SINCE 2000

By the second half of the 1990s, the emerging media markets in East-Central Europe became a high priority for global children's media networks already available in North and South America, Western Europe and parts of Asia and the South Pacific region, leaving fewer and fewer unclaimed territories on the globe. Nickelodeon, along with Disney and the Cartoon Network, are often referred to as the "masters of the children's television universe" (Westcott 2008). Owned by the largest transnational media corporations, Viacom, the Walt Disney Corporation and Time Warner, respectively, "the accumulation of enormous capital, marketing experience and the control of the global market have given them a tremendous competitive edge" to expand globally (Wu & Chan 2008, 198). These companies owned and operated children's television channels, participated in joint ventures or licensed third parties to operate their programming services.

Disney has been one of the most recognized and popular media brands among children in the region, especially in the forms of animated films, comic books and well-known Disney characters. In Hungary, Mickey Mouse was among the first official "Western" visitors to children. In late May of 1989 Disney promoted the very first performance of *Disney's World on Ice* in the region. Mickey's and Donald Duck's busy and well-publicized schedule included a visit to the U.S. Embassy in Budapest and to a traditional Hungarian restaurant, where they learned to make Hungarian goulash and dance the csárdás, a Hungarian folk dance ("Mickey" 1989). In the early 1990s, Disney was the only U.S. distributor offering a regular weekly series in Russia, Hungary, Poland, Bulgaria, Slovenia and the Czech Republic. By the mid-1990s, 750 hours of the 3,500 hours of Walt Disney's licensed programming worldwide were broadcast throughout Eastern Europe dubbed into local languages ("Robert" 1996). Weekend afternoon Disney programming blocks such as *Walt Disney Presents Duck Tales* or *Chip'N'Dales' Rescue Rangers,* a two-hour block broadcast on Hungarian Television sponsored by Johnson and Johnson, were not-to-be-missed shows on television for young viewers ("Johnson" 1990). Disney programs became an even more stable feature of children's television throughout the 2000s, although they gravitated from state (later public) broadcast television to national commercial stations and also to dedicated children's television channels owned by the Walt Disney Company such as Jetix Europe (today Disney XD), Playhouse Disney and The Disney Channel.

Cartoon Network was the first among the three global children's television networks to make its dedicated channel available via cable subscription. The network had a strong recognition among viewers, especially with cartoon classics from the Hanna-Barbara studio such as *Tom and Jerry* or *The Flintstones,* which were broadcast in East-Central Europe in the 1980s and even earlier. Cartoon Network became available in Hungary in 1994 and by the end of the decade, it reached approximately 1.2 million cable

114   *Katalin Lustyik*

Table 6.6   Nickelodeon Hungary Program Schedule (June 6, 2011, 4 am–9 pm)

List of programs (origin, genre, production date):
SpongeBob SquarePants (U.S., animation, 1999)—5 episodes/day
Ben and Holly's Little Kingdom (UK, animation, 2009)—3 episodes/day
Dora, the Explorer (U.S., animation, 2000)—3 episodes/day
Go, Diego! Go! (U.S., animation, 2005)—2 episodes/day
Back at the Barnyard (U.S., animation, 2007)
Penguins of Madagascar (U.S., animation 2008)—3 episodes/day
Cat Dog (U.S., animation 1998)—2 episodes/day
Ni Hao Kai-lan (U.S., animation, 2008)
The Wonder Pets (U.S., animation, 2006)
The Adventures of Jimmy Neutron (U.S., animation, 2002)
My Life as a Teenage Robot (U.S., animation, 2003)
Avatar: The Last Airbender (U.S., animation, 2005)—2 episodes/day
Drake and Josh (U.S., sitcom, 2004)—4 episodes/day
iCarly (U.S., sitcom, 2007)—4 episodes/day
Unfabulous (U.S., sitcom, 2004)
The Fairly OddParents (U.S., animation, 2001)—2 episodes/day
Fanboy and Chum Chum (U.S., animation, 2009)
The Troop (U.S.-Canada, live action series, 2009)

households in the country with a population of about 10 million ("AGB Hungry Tables" 2000; AGB Hungary, personal communication, 2002).

Nickelodeon television programs made their debut on commercial broadcast television in 1997 in Hungary and the Nickelodeon Hungary channel was launched in 1999 as part of the company's expansion into Eastern Europe and the Baltic Republics (Nickelodeon Hungary, personal communication, 2002). The majority of children's channels operating in Hungary today provide a local language feed and a website but no locally produced content. As the sample schedule of Nickelodeon Hungary reveals, the channel primarily relies on relatively old U.S. Nickelodeon cartoons scheduled in endless rotation (see Table 6.6).

The biggest competition in the region for the U.S.-based channels was Minimax, a children's television network formed in the late 1990s in Poland then in Hungary. Within a few years Minimax rapidly gained recognition and became one of the highest rated children's television channels in Hungary (AGB Hungary, personal communication, 2002). The idea of the network was conceived by four people in a Budapest apartment and backed by regional private investors who also strongly believed in the revitalization of children's programming originating from the region. The

From a Socialist Endeavor to a Commercial Enterprise   115

core mission of the network at the time was to offer mainly European content for children between the age of 4 and 14, with the inclusion of shows produced and exchanged during the socialist era (Lori 2000). Minimax soon became an influential cultural entity and was proudly celebrated even in political circles as an Eastern European media success story in the early 2000s. Beyond being a trusted television channel, fans could soon purchase the monthly Minimax magazine, visit its popular website www. minimax.hu, attend local cultural and charity events, and even embark on the weekend Mimimax river cruise on the Danube. Books, videos,

Table 6.7   Minimax Hungary Sample Program Schedule Listed by Origin of Production (April 30, 2010, Friday)

Local and regional content (origin, length):

Minimax News (Hungary, 5 min.)

Have you read it? (Hungary, 5 min.)

Hungarian Folk Tales (Hungary, 5 min.)

Bob and Bobek (Bob a Bobek, králíci z klobouku, 1979, Czechoslovakia, 8 min.)

Non-local content dubbed in Hungarian (origin, length):

My Little Pony (U.S., 20 min.)

Martha Speaks (U.S., 25 min.)

Elmo's World (U.S., 15 min.)

Global Grover (U.S., 5 min.)

Adventures of Bert and Ernie (U.S., 10 min.)

Mary-Kate and Ashley in Action (U.S., 30 min.)

Viva Pinata (Canada/U.S., 15 min.)

Busytown Mysteries (Canada, 25 min.)

Chuggington (UK, 10 min.)

Mr. Bean (UK, 10 min.)

Timmy Time (UK, 15 min.)

Roary the Racing Car (UK, 10 min.)

Fifi and the Flowertots (UK, 10 min.)

Lenny and Tweek (Germany, 5 min.)

Leo and Fred (Germany, 5 min.)

Once Upon a Time . . . Man (France, 25 min.)

Pat & Stan (France, 5 min.)

Geronimo Stilton (Italy, 25 min.)

Bindi, the Jungle Girl (Australia, 25 min.)

Source: Minimax Hungary program schedule.

116   *Katalin Lustyik*

DVDs, toys, clothing and food products displaying the Minimax logo soon made their way into supermarkets and department stores. The brand also expanded within the region by establishing a Minimax channel in Romania in the summer of 2001, followed by one in the Czech Republic and Slovakia in the winter of 2003.

While Minimax's programming once consisted of over 80% of European shows, with 20–25% from Eastern Europe (Minimax, personal communication 2002), today it relies heavily on global hits from the U.S., the UK, France, Canada and Australia, such as *Postman Pat, Global Grover, Elmo's World, My Little Pony, Franklin* and the *Magic School Bus*. In the sample schedule of Minimax Hungary from April 30, 2010 (see Table 6.7), only three five-minute programs, *Minimax News, Have You Read It?* and *Hungarian Folk Tales* represent Hungarian content with one old Czechoslovakian cartoon *Bob and Bobek* adding regional flavor.

Minimax went through several owners during the past decade; it was proudly but briefly owned "100%" by the Hungarian company Mediatech ("Száz" 2003). Since 2007, it belongs to Chello Central Europe, the Central Europe-based content division of Liberty Global, a transnational media company registered in the U.S. Minimax is now branded as "Central Europe's leading children's channel with a target audience of 2–12," with local language feeds and dedicated websites in Hungary, Romania, the Czech Republic, Slovakia, Moldova and the former Yugoslavian countries with the exception of Slovenia (Chellomedia 2011). In Croatia, Serbia, Montenegro, Bosnia and Herzegovina, Minimax debuted in early 2007.

Children's television has become one of the fastest growing and most lucrative sectors of the media entertainment industry in Europe (Papathanassopoulos 2002). A pan-European study conducted in the mid-1990s with the involvement of 22 public television stations in 17 countries concluded that even public service broadcasters, traditionally committed to children by providing diverse programming that addresses their special interests, were increasingly operating under a "market logic" (Biltereyst 1997). "Now more than ever familiar in children's programming," observed Biltereyst are "programming strategies or processes such as standardization, routinization, competition, internationalization, the emphasis on entertainment, [and] the decline of local production" (1997, 101). While the UK is often described as the most competitive children's media market in Europe, East-Central Europe has been following in the UK's footsteps at an accelerated speed (Mavise 2011). Polish households with cable and satellite subscription can access 38 children's channels, some targeting Polish children specifically such as Cartoon Network Poland, Disney Channel Polska and Cbeebies Poland. Others, such as Cartoon Network Europe, Al Jazeera Children's Channel or Baby TV (several versions available besides the Polish version) cater for pan-regional audiences (Mavice 2011). Even in Hungary, despite its much smaller media market, 12 children's channels are present in 2011 (see Table 6.8).

From a Socialist Endeavor to a Commercial Enterprise 117

Table 6.8   Children's Television Channels Available in Hungary (March, 2011)

Name	Broadcasting company	Genre	Main targeted country
Baby TV (Version in English)	BABY NETWORK LIMITED	Children's channel	United Kingdom
Boomerang (version in Hungarian)	TURNER BROAD-CASTING INTER-NATIONAL LIMITED	Children's channel	Hungary
Cartoon Network (version in Hungarian)	TURNER BROAD-CASTING INTER-NATIONAL LIMITED	Children's channel	Hungary
Disney Channel	WALT DISNEY COMPANY LIM-ITED (THE)	Children's channel	United Kingdom
Disney Channel (version in Hungarian)	JETIX EUROPE CHANNELS B.V.	Children's channel	Hungary
Duck TV	MEGA MAX MEDIA, S.R.O.	Children's channel	Slovakia
Duck TV HD	MEGA MAX MEDIA, S.R.O.	Children's channel	Slovakia
JimJam (Version in Hungarian)	JIMJAM TELEVI-SION Ltd	Children's channel	Hungary
KidsCo (version in Hungarian)	KIDSCO Ltd	Children's channel	Hungary
KIKA	GERMANY	Children's channel	Germany
Minimax (Version in Hungarian)	CHELLO CEN-TRAL EUROPE, S.R.O.	Children's channel	Hungary
Nickelodeon (version in Hungarian)	NICKELODEON U.K. LIMITED	Children's channel	Hungary

Source: MAVISE database of TV companies and TV channels in the European Union (2011)

Children's contemporary media environment has been increasingly shaped by transnational media conglomerations and commercial interests throughout Eastern Europe as well. The continuous cross-promotion and cross-selling of media products, with every cartoon selling another toy, every toy getting someone else interested in a forthcoming book, magazine, film and video game (e.g. Kinder 1991; Pecora 2002; Steemers 2010) has become prevelant in the region as well. In today's multiplatform and

118   *Katalin Lustyik*

predominantly profit-driven media systems throughout Europe, even the Hungarian *Tévé Maci*, the teddy bear character discussed earlier, has been "revived" and available to be purchased in the form of books and DVDs. Children can play with him online and befriend him on Facebook where he had already over 19,000 fans by 2010. A Hungarian online store specializing in stuffed cuddly bears offers a dedicated page to *Tévé Maci* fans within its "Famous Hungarian Bears" section (Maci 2011), and many other television characters of the socialist era have been rediscovered and rebranded for new generations of children.

CONCLUSION

This chapter provided a brief overview of the transformations that occurred in the arena of children's television in the region of East-Central Europe, focusing on the period between the mid-1980s and 2011. While television programs made specifically for children comprised an important core broadcasting service during the socialist era, since the 1980s, they have increasingly been exposed to the pressures and regulations of a globally interconnected media environment, in which the survival of television practices aimed at children stem primarily from market principles closely following trends observed in Western countries for decades.

In today's media landscape, commercial media organizations promote the conceptualization of the child as an active and competent "media consumer," who is more influential than ever before, but whose power is given, expressed and experienced primarily through consumption. Institutions primarily serving and defining children as consumers rather than citizens have been accepted as an inevitable consequence of East-Central Europe's integration into the global media market. When a handful of Hungarian parents called Minimax to complain about the existence and frequency of advertising in 2000, the management assured them that it was a "small and inevitable price" for the operation of the only network offering regional and high quality educational content (Minimax, personal communication, 2002).

According to Buckingham et al., "the market can provide quality and diversity" and "it can foster children's social, cultural and intellectual development; it might even 'empower' them in certain ways. It is simply that these are not its primary aims" (1999b, 65). Like McChesney (1993), who questions our common assumptions about the 'absolute naturalness' of a commercial-based media system of the U.S., we should critically examine the extensive commercialization of children's media cultures in post-socialist East-Central Europe that is perceived to be a "natural" development. The rapid and substantial expansion in commercial media directed at children and young people in the region has not received nearly as much public attention and deliberation as some other aspects of contemporary children's mediated culture such as media violence (e.g. *Dragon Ball Z*) or children's online safety (e.g. Haszán 1999).

From a Socialist Endeavor to a Commercial Enterprise 119

It is essential, however, to be cautious against conceptualizing children's culture during the socialist era as "better" or less problematic. How different are television programs created primarily to support the "socialist-oriented endeavors" of young people—to use the Aczél-quote (1984, 20) again—from those primarily created to encourage the "market-oriented" endeavors of toddlers and teens today? The media during the socialist era heavily guarded the traditional borders of childhood by serving, representing and conceptualizing children as vulnerable, passive, helpless and impressionable, who need ed continuous education, moral as well as political guidance.

Children in the region today, like children in so many other parts of the world, are addressed more informally, entertained even when educated with often more innovative, extensively researched, creative and interactive programs than they were ever before (Wasko 2001; Hendershot 2004; Banet-Weiser 2007). As part of the continuous "dialogue" with programmers, children are encouraged to write letters, draw pictures, participate in focus groups, and cast their votes on various issues (e.g. Nickelodeon's *Kids' Choice Award*), although their voices can easily get lost when they try to communicate with pan-regional networks covering several time zones and languages (e.g. Lustyik 2010). After generations of East-Central European viewers growing up in a paternalistic media system in which their voices, opinions and preferences mattered little, today there might be more ways for some young consumers to shape their media environment. Such possibilities, often described by media professionals as giving children "power" to create their own media environment and "freedom" to cast their votes and express themselves, however, can be rather limited. As Williams put it, "anything can be said, provided that you can afford to say it and that you say it profitably" (1989, 133).

The consequences of the profound transformation of children's media culture in East-Central Europe are proving to be more complex and contradictory than either critics or enthusiasts expected. Since Mickey Mouse and Donald Duck's first official visit of to the region in 1989, children's television, once shielded behind the Iron Curtain, has become shaped by and fully incorporated into the global entertainment industry with rather limited real input from the public ("Mickey" 1989). The constructions of the child television viewer during the socialist and post-socialist eras in many ways seem equally narrow and ideologically charged. The difference is that today this narrow and limiting construction is obscured by the endless appeals to consumer "choice" and "freedom" offered to younger and younger media users.

NOTES

1. Slavko Splichal, John Hochheimer, and Karol Jakubowicz (eds.), *Democratization and the Media: An East-West Dialogue* (Ljubljana: Communication and Culture Colloquia, 1990); Slacvo Splichal, *Media Beyond Socialism: Theory and Practice in East-Central Europe* (Boulder, CO: Westview,

120   Katalin Lustyik

1994); David L. Paletz, K. Jakubowicz and Pavao Novosel (eds.), *Glasnost and After: Media and Change in Central and Eastern Europe* (1995); Liana Giogri, *The Post-Socialist Media: What Power the West?* (Aldershot: Avebury, 1995); John Downing, *Internationalizing Media Theory: Transition, Power, Culture: Reflections on Media in Russia, Poland and Hungary, 1980–95* (London: Sage, 1996); Colin Sparks (with Anna Reading), *Communism, Capitalism and the Mass Media* (London: Sage, 1998).

2. A longitudinal study of television programming has been conducted by the MTA-ELTE Kommunikációelméleti Kutatócsoport (Hungarian Academy of Science and Eötvös University Communication Research Group) since 1985. The primary purpose of the project was to assess the overall changes within television programming during a period of profound socio-political transitions in Hungary. The research team collected data about programs offered on five terrestrial television channels: Hungarian Television (MTV), Duna Televízió (after 1993) and RTL-Klub and TV2 (after 1997). The program schedule published in the weekly *Rádió and Televízió Újság* in the month of March every year was used for data collection, each program that appeared in the schedule from the opening hour until the last program was coded. Results of the projects were published regularly (see Terestyén 1999, 2000 and 2002).

3. MTV's second channel, MTV2 (also referred to as m2 today), which has minimum viewership, ended up hosting *Esti Mese,* scheduling it between 6 pm and 7 pm in response to public pressure.

REFERENCES

Aczél, György. 1984. *Socialism and the Freedom of Culture.* Budapest: Corvina.

"AGB Hungary Tables." 2000. In *Médiakönyv* edited by Gabriella Cseh, Mihály Enyedi Nagy & Tibor Soltészky, 523–587. Budapest: Enamike.

Banet-Weiser, Sarah. 2007. *Kids Rule!: Nickelodeon and Consumer Citizenship.* Durham: Duke University Press.

Biltereyst, David. 1997. "European Public Service Television and the Cultural-educational Logic." *Asian Journal of Communication* 72: 86–104.

Buckingham, David, Hannah Davies, Ken Jones and Peter Kelley. 1999a. *Children's Television in Britain: History, Discourse and Policy.* London: British Film Institute.

Buckingham, David, Hannah Davies and Ken Jones. 1999b. "Public Service goes to Market: British Children's Television in Transition." *Media International Australia* 93: 65–76.

Chellomedia. 2011. Minimax. http://www.chellomedia.com. Accessed March 31, 2011.

Downing, John D. 1996. *Internationalizing Media Theory: Transition, Power, Culture: Reflections on Media in Russia, Poland and Hungary, 1980–95.* London: Sage.

"Eltűnt a tévémaci az MTV raktárából." 1999. *Blikk Online*, October 14. Accessed December 10, 2000, http://www.blikk.hu.

Farkas, Eszter. 1998, March. "Dilemma of production and broadcasting of Hungarian children's programs." Unpublished paper presented at the *Second World Summit on Television for Children*, United Kingdom.

Farkas, Eszter. 2000. "A dobogókői beszámoló." Unpublished paper presented at the *Media Conference*, Dobogókő, Hungary.

From a Socialist Endeavor to a Commercial Enterprise   121

Giogri, Liana. 1995. *The Post-Socialist Media: What Power the West?* Aldershot: Avebury.

Haraszti, Miklós. 1987. *The Velvet Prison: Artists under State Socialism.* New York: Basic Books.

Haszán, Zoltán. 1999. "Az ORTT letiltott egy rajzfilmsorozatot." *Magyar Hirlap Online,* April 24. Accessed December 10, 2000, http://www.mno.hu.

Havens, Timothy. 2006. *Global Television Marketplace.* London: British Film Institute.

Hendershot, Heather. 2004. "Introduction: Nickelodeon and the Business of Fun." In *Nickelodeon Nation: The History, Politics and Economics of America's only TV Channel for Kids,* edited by Heather Hendershot, 1–14. New York: New York University Press.

Hirsch, Tamás. 2002. "Új nézők, új csapdák." *Médiamix,* April 20–23. Accessed December 10, 2002, http://www.mediamix.hu.

"Johnson and Johnson to Sponsor Disney Programming in Soviet Union and Eastern Europe." 1990. *PR Newswire,* December 13.

Kinder, Marsha. 1991. *Playing with Power in Movies, Television, and Video Games: From Muppet Babies to Teenage Mutant Ninja Turtles.* Berkeley, CA.: University of California Press.

Lázár, Fruzsina. 2003. "Mese és valóság a képernyőn." Magyar Nemzet Online, October 23. Accessed December 10, 2003, http://www.mno.hu.

Lőcsei, Gabriella. 2002. "Mese, mese, meskete a tévé műsoráról." *Magyar Nemzet Online,* September 27. Accessed December 10, 2002, http://www.mno.hu.

Lori. 2000. "Minimax: Új csatorna indul." *Kreatív Online,* March 1. Accessed December 10, 2001, http://www.kreativ.hu.

Lustyik, Katalin. 2003. "The Transformation of children's television from communism to global capitalism in Hungary." Ph.D. Diss., University of Colorado at Boulder.

Lustyik, Katalin. 2010. "Transnational children's television. The case of Nickelodeon in the South Pacific." *International Communication Gazette* 72(2): 171–190.

Maci Bolt. 2011. "TV Maci." http://www.macibolt.hu/pag/tvmaci.php. Accessed March 31, 2011.

Mavise. 2011. MAVISE database of TV companies and TV channels in the European Union. http://mavise.obs.coe.int. Accessed March 3, 2011.

McChesney, Robert. 1993. *Telecommunications, Mass Media, and Democracy: The Battle for the Control of U.S. Broadcasting, 1928–1935.* New York: Oxford University Press.

McChesney, Robert. 2003. "Children, Globalization, and Media Policy." In *Children, Young People and Media Globalisation,* edited by Cecil von Feilitzen and Ulla Carlsson, 23–32. Göteborg: NORDICOM.

"Mickey Mouse/Donald Duck." 1989. Business Wire, May 23.

"Az országos csatornákon műsorra tűzött gyermekműsorok főbb jellemzői." 2002. ORTT. www.ortt.hu/elemzesek/20/1149623521gyerek_20020308.pdf.

Papathanassopoulos, Stylianos. 2002. *European Television in the Digital Age.* Cambridge: Polity.

Pecora, Norma. 2002. *The Business of Children's Entertainment.* New York: Guilford Press.

"Robert A. Iger, President, Capital Cities, ABC, Inc. announces a consolidation of the international operations of Capital Cities/ABC Inc." 1996. *PR Newswire,* June 25.

Rosdy. 1999. "A gyermekbarát televízióért." *Magyar Nemzet Online,* April 22. Accessed December 10, 2000, http://www.mno.hu.

122   Katalin Lustyik

Scheper-Hughes, Nancy and Carolyn Sargent. 1998. "Introduction: The Cultural politics of chilhood." In *Small Wars. The Cultural Politics of Childhood*, edited by Nancy Scheper-Hughes & Carolyn Sargent, 2–21. Berkeley, CA: University of California.

Sklair, Leslie. 2002. *Globalization: Capitalism & its Alternatives.* Oxford: Oxford University Press.

Sparks, Colin (with Anna Reading). 1998. *Communism, Capitalism and the Mass Media.* London: Sage.

Splichal, Slavco, John Hochheimer and Karol Jakubowicz. 1990. *Democratization and the Media: An East–West Dialogue.* Ljubljana: Communication and Culture Colloquia.

Splichal, Slavco. 1994. *Media Beyond Socialism: Theory and Practice in Central and Eastern Europe.* Boulder, CO: Westview.

Steemers, Janette. 2010. *Creating Preschool Television: A Story of Commerce, Creativity and Curriculum.* London: Palgrave MacMillan.

Straubhaar, Joseph D. and Luiz G. Duarte. 2005. "Adapting US Transnational Television Channels to a Complex World: From Cultural Imperialism to Localization and Hybridization." In *Transnational Television Worldwide* edited by J. K. Chalaby, 216–253. New York: I.B. Tauris.

"Száz százalékig magyar kézben a Minimax." 2003. *Magyar Nemzet Online,* April 6.

Szekfű, Antal. 1996. "Intruders welcome? The Beginning of satellite television in Hungary." *European Journal of Communication* 20(5): 15–35.

Terestyén, Tamás. 1999. "A magyarországi televíziós műsorkínálat változása a nyolcvanas évek közepétől a kilencvenes évek végéig." *Jel-Kép* 1: 41–62.

Terestyén, Tamás. 2000. "A magyarországi televíziós műsorkínálat 1999-ben." *Jel-Kép* 1: 43–67.

Terestyén, Tamás. 2002. "A magyarországi televíziós műsorkínálat alakulása 2001-ben." In *ORTT Beszámoló az Országos Rádió és Televízió Testület 2001. évi tevékenységéről,* 188–215. Budapest:ORTT.

Thussu, Daya K. 2006. *International Communication: Continuity and Change,* 2nd ed. London: Hodder Arnold.

Vitaliev, Vasil. 1998. "Projections." Transitions, April. http://www.ijt.cz/transitions. Accessed August 10, 1999.

Wasko, Janet. 2001. Understanding Disney: The Manufacturing of Fantasy. Cambridge: Polity.

Westcott, Tim. 2008. "Masters of the Children's Television Universe." *Screen Digest* report, January 31.

Williams, Raymond. 1961. *The Long Revolution.* New York: Columbia University Press.

Williams, Raymond. 1989. *Resources of Hope: Culture, Democracy and Socialism,* edited by Gale, Robin. London: Verso.

Wu, Huating and Joseph Man Chan. 2008. "Globalizing Chinese Martial Art Cinema: The Global-Local Alliance and the Production of Crouching Tiger, Hidden Dragon." *Media, Culture and Society,* 29 (2): 195–217.

7 Intra-European Media Imperialism

Hungarian Program Imports and the Television Without Frontiers Directive

Timothy Havens, Evelyn Bottando and Matthew S. Thatcher

The predominance of American television programming on the international markets and on the schedules of broadcasters everywhere has become a commonplace observation in global media studies. Although American influence has diminished and regional and local production centers have grown in the past 30 years (Tunstall 2007), American product continues to account for nearly 70% of all worldwide trade in television programs, and the trade deficit between the EU and the U.S. in audiovisual products continues to hover above $7 billion per year.

The Television Without Frontiers (TVWF) Directive, recently renamed the Audiovisual Media Services Directive, was initially designed to redress this trade imbalance by requiring EU member states to reserve a majority of their broadcast time for works of European origin. The relevant section of the Directive, Chapter III, Article 4 states that, "Member States shall ensure where practicable and by appropriate means, that broadcasters reserve for European works, within the meaning of Article 6, a majority proportion of their transmission time, excluding the time appointed to news, sports events, games, advertising, teletext services and teleshopping" (European Union, 1989)

Despite the measured success of TVWF, representatives of smaller nations, particularly those formerly socialist nations that were admitted to the EU in 2004, have worried about the impact of imported Western European programming on the viability of their domestic audiovisual industries and the integrity of their national cultures. Is the Directive primarily an opportunity to craft a transnational European identity that is inclusive of both Eastern and Western cultures (Aiello 2005), or is it the cultural wedge of a neocolonialist Western project (Böröcz 2001)?

While we cannot answer this question directly in this paper, we do demonstrate through empirical analyses of television import data that, since the harmonization of media laws with the Directive in Hungary in 1996, there has been a marked increase in the volume and variety of program imports from highly commercialized Western European nations. In conventional analyses of television flows, these increases are often masked by

124 *Timothy Havens, Evelyn Bottando and Matthew S. Thatcher*

the predominance of American imports, which this study also documents. However, we go beyond documenting American dominance to explore the ways in which program imports from other nations have and have not been affected by the TVWF Directive.

The increase in Western European imports do not seem to be determined by foreign direct investment in Hungarian television broadcasters; rather, a thorough analysis of import data reveals an increase in imports from highly commercialized television markets everywhere. The conclusion of this analysis is that TVWF has fostered one-way cultural dialogs between Hungary and other European nations with large commercial television industries. Beyond this tendency, the Directive has also served to bolster the bottom lines of commercial television industries around the world. Moreover, an important consequence of the Directive has been a significant decrease in program imports from other nations in the Central and Eastern European region, and, quite likely a weakening of Central European regional identity.

We wish to make clear from the outset that we do not view the Directive as *the* primary force explaining the sad state of domestic television production and regional trade in Hungary and across the region; nor do we see the Directive as *a* primary force. However, as the preeminent cultural policy regarding television in the EU, the Directive was quite clearly designed to protect the television culture of member states: our argument is that, in the case of Hungary and probably several other nations in Central and Eastern Europe, the Directive has failed to achieve this goal. Moreover, the Directive has worked *with* commercial forces across the EU to stifle, rather than protect, European cultural diversity.

THE TELEVISION WITHOUT FRONTIERS DIRECTIVE AND/AS NEOIMPERIALISM

The history of the TVWF Directive is interwoven with the history of European integration, the collapse of socialism in Central and Eastern European nations in the late 1980s and early 1990s, and prevalent academic and policy discourses about American media imperialism. Just two years after the "Single European Act" created a unified European economic market, in 1989 the TVWF Directive was established to provide a framework for 'capital mobility' within audiovisual industries throughout Europe. While television and radio signals were previously under the auspices of national markets, the TVWF defined television and radio broadcast signals as "services entitled to free movement within the internal market," (Harcourt 2005, 9).

According to Aubry (2000), TVWF represented "an important step towards the liberalization of the broadcasting sector in Europe" (18). Aimed at "strengthening the broadcast industry," (Auby, 18) the new Directive hoped to stimulate the growth of European-based media businesses and promote European cultural production. The main focus of the TVWF

Directive was to invoke the logics of free trade as a means to encourage "exploitation of new technologies (initially cable and satellite)" by opening up member states' broadcast markets to competition (Harcourt 2005, 9).

Considered more than just an economic measure, the TVWF Directive has been interpreted as a means for Europe to 'talk back' to the dominance of U.S.-based cultural exports and construct a "collective European identity," (Aiello 2005, 5). According to Aiello, the TVWF Directive is a means for Europe to "use its existing (audio)visual heritage (so far fragmented and nation-specific) to define and crystallize its own symbolic capital" (13). Referencing the increase in the dominance of U.S. television exports in the European marketplace, Aiello claims that the TVWF Directive represents not only an economic venture, but a political strategy of "talking back" to "US economic dominance over the European audiovisual space [that] has resulted in the colonization of European (audio)visual imagery" (7).

Although the validity of the 'media imperialism' thesis has been roundly and rightly criticized (Tomlinson 1991), no one debates the predominance of U.S. imports on European television screens, or the success of TVWF in decreasing U.S. imports on a continent-wide scale. Particularly with the development of private, commercial broadcasting—and later cable and satellite channels—many of which relied heavily on U.S. imports, politicians and academics throughout Europe began to be concerned about the viability of their domestic audiovisual industries and the integrity of their national cultural identities. While numerous audience studies began to question the power of imported television in initiating cultural change (Ang 1985; Liebes and Katz, 1993), there was no doubt that the economic viability of domestic television production was threatened by 'wall-to-wall *Dallas*,' particularly given the growing fiscal challenges among commercial and public broadcasters, and the fact that imported programming is almost always cheaper than domestically produced programming (Hoskins, McFadyen and Finn 1997; Morley and Robins 1995).

Two primary measures exist for determining the degree of U.S. domination of European television, specifically, and global television more generally. The first relies on trade deficits between the U.S. and other trading blocs, while the second measures deficits in terms of total hours of programming exchanged. Most observers place the current audiovisual trade deficit between the EU and the U.S. at between $7 billion and $10 billion per year, but these numbers can fluctuate significantly depending on the overall global economic situation and consequent pricing of programming, such that yearly changes in revenue do not necessarily reflect changes in the amount of programming traded. As a result, measuring the amount of programming hours traded is a better indicator of audiovisual deficits between the EU and the U.S. Unfortunately, such measures are rarely made for EU exports to the U.S., which are instead almost always measured in revenues. Nevertheless, EU statistics frequently track both the value and the volume of imported U.S. television.

126   *Timothy Havens, Evelyn Bottando and Matthew S. Thatcher*

According to the most recent figures, the U.S. continues to dominate European television schedules, accounting for 59.5% of imported fiction series and 55.7% of televised films in 2008. However, the amount of European produced programming has risen in recent years, to 39.1% from 36.1% in 2005, suggesting the success of EU audiovisual regulations, especially the TVWF Directive and the MEDIA Programme, which facilitates the continental circulation of European television programs (European Audiovisual Observatory 2008).

We see then a split regulatory logic that underlies the TVWF Directive. On one hand, the Directive is designed to protect the viability of the audiovisual industries in European nations, especially against the economic power of global Hollywood. On the other hand, the Directive is part of a larger project of sustaining and increasing a sense of Europeanness among citizens in an effort to strengthen the EU and diminish divisive nationalism. A related, but less frequently stated, goal is to facilitate the global expansion of European television industries.

Although TVWF has been pitched as a way to strengthen the European market, new member states have suggested that the policy weakens their developing media industries. As the TVWF Directive calls for the removal of trade barriers among member states in order to protect "European" cultural products, new member states may be faced with a deluge of media productions from other European nations (Wheeler 2004). In addition, as post-socialist member states enter the EU, they bring with them their own unique concerns regarding media development and the need to assimilate to EU trade rules. As one form of dominance over the media system has fallen, new member states are left to question this new version of control.

While the TVWF Directive calls for a liberalization of the European broadcast market, many of the new member states are still in the process of reconceptualizing their national media industries following the end of state-run media control. As media industries are still in their naissance in these post-socialist states, the imperatives of economic liberalization through the TVWF Directive are especially straining to national media development. Coman (2004) remarks,

> this process of integration within European regulations on mass media appears, for many actors of the post communist press, as a loss of development freedoms gained with the fall of communism and of its rules regarding the functioning of mass media. (212)

While the TVWF Directive intends to 'harmonize' trade among EU members, the focus on television and film productions as commodities has troubled many new members, who see their accession into the EU as a chance for other member states to flood their markets with their film and television productions. In an address to the 1998 Birmingham European Audiovisual Conference, Jabukowicz (2004) stated,

Intra-European Media Imperialism   127

on very old maps unexplored areas of which little was known used to be marked with the words "Here be dragons." That, before 1989, was how many in Western Europe viewed maps of Central and Eastern Europe. Later, as they looked at maps of the region, what they often saw was words: "Here be markets" (158).

Early research done by Burgelman and Powels (1992) verified the concerns expressed by Jabukowicz. Though they acknowledge that the TVWF Directive is intent on resisting "Americanization" (170), the free market view of EU audiovisual policy is inauspicious for small states "[. . .] since they risk losing in the medium term an audiovisual sector which has been the very basis of their communication system," (174). The pair also noted that the "possibilities of exploitation to be [. . .] profitable," (174) for nations within the EU with a more developed media system was distinctly possible within a unified market.

While facing the challenge of reconfiguring their media systems, these new member states are required to assimilate EU standards that encourage media liberalization. Under the strain of competition from neighboring EU countries, national production and diversity of programming in these nation-states may be strained (Shein 2004). This has been a difficult move for post-socialist nation-states. As Shein (2004) notes, "The move towards economic and media policy liberalization has created a situation in which it is rather difficult to increase the amount and variety of national TV production and support the development of the independent producers" (190).

These debates over the impact and desirability of adopting EU media regulations, including the TVWF, form part of a larger discussion about the consequences of the EU's 'Eastern enlargement' from the perspective of peripheral European nations. Böröcz (2001), for instance, argues for thinking of EU expansion as a distinct form of neoimperialism. He identifies four main forms of imperial control—funneling capital from the periphery to the metropole, creating a 'cognitive mapping' of national or ethnic superiority and inferiority, exporting the governmental controls and institutions of the imperial state, and utilizing these other forms of control to advance the core state's interests in the global arena—and identifies how each of these practices characterize the relationship between the EU and the nations on its Eastern borders.

The post-socialist television industries of Central and Eastern Europe provide a centralized node where each of these forms of neoimperialism operates. Foreign direct investment by Western European media firms such as Bertelsmann, ProsiebenSat1 and Canal Plus help repatriate advertising revenues from Central and Eastern Europe, while the large amount of Western European content on television screens across the region might be seen as an effort to promote the superiority of Western European cultural practices. At minimum, the heavy reliance on imported versus domestic programming among broadcasters in Central and Eastern Europe suggest

128 *Timothy Havens, Evelyn Bottando and Matthew S. Thatcher*

that Western European culture is more powerful, better quality, more modern and more successful than media culture from Central and Eastern Europe. Finally, as regards the use of these forms of control to advance the global interests of the core imperial nations, the current study demonstrates empirically how the large, affluent nations of the West have capitalized on the TVWF Directive to subsidize their own global media expansion.

CHANGING IMPORT PROFILES IN THE 1980S AND 2000S

To examine the impact of commercialization and EU accession on Hungarian television broadcasting, to which the TVWF Directive is a major contributor, the present study compared television imports in the 1980s and 2000s across all Hungarian broadcast channels. These channels included MTV1 and MTV2 in the 1980s, both of which were state-run broadcasters, and Duna Televízio, MTV (both public broadcasters), RTL Klub and TV2 in the 2000s.[1] Information about the nation-of-origin, channel, genre, duration and daypart (primetime, early morning, overnight, etc.) were collected for each imported program. These data were collected from published television schedules, rather than from taping actual broadcasts, as is the custom in these types of program flow analyses. While the latter method undoubtedly provides more valid data, the method we employ here has the benefit of providing access to a much larger amount of time and data, including historical comparisons, which would be impossible with the conventional method. In essence, then, we have traded validity for comparative breadth.

Program schedules were collected from two time periods, ranging from 1983–88 and from 2001–04. The 1980s time frame was selected because this period was one of general liberalization of Hungarian television schedules, with community cable systems legally available beginning in 1984 and the right of reception of foreign broadcasts affirmed in the 1984 media laws (Szekfü 1989). Consequently, although political considerations certainly influenced import decisions, we can assume that those decisions also included some consideration of the perceived cultural fit between programming and audience preferences. By contrast, the 2000s were chosen for comparison with the 1980s, because commercial broadcasting had fully come into its own by this time, having begun only in 1997. In addition, during this period, programmers and regulators were looking to harmonize with EU media regulations in anticipation of accession in 2004, as evidenced most strongly by the 1996 Act on Radio and Television Broadcasting, which, like the TVWF Directive, required broadcasters to "devote over half of their annual transmission time for European works" (European Union, 1989). Comparing these periods, then, permits us to compare television imports prior to the introduction of commercialism and EU media laws with a period afterwards. The resulting comparison allows us to speculate about the potential impact of TVWF on Hungarian television imports.

Import data for the 1983–89 period totaled 74 days worth of programming, including 483 distinct imports totaling 395.5 hours. Between 2001 and 2004, we collected data for 168 days, during which 4,499 programs were imported, totaling 4,844.25 hours. These collection procedures also differ from conventional programming flow analyses, which typically sample two weeks per year. To some degree, decisions about how many days per year and what specific dates to sample were determined by the information we had. However, we also purposely selected dates from throughout the year to account for any seasonal bias in our data, such as the heavier reliance on imports at commercial broadcasters in summer months when ratings decline and advertising revenues drop. In addition, the lopsided number of days analyzed in each time period is less than ideal. Again, this is a function of what was available to us for analysis, but we quite consciously decided to use all of the data from the 2000s that we had, rather than restrict it to 74 days to make it consistent with the 1980s data. Given the longer broadcasting hours, larger number of channels and greater amount of imported programming in the 2000s period, as compared with the 1980s, we felt that the largest possible sample size would yield a more thorough snapshot. Finally, in neither period were the number of days analyzed consistent across years, as Table 7.1 makes clear. Practically speaking, this means that the import landscape of certain years is overrepresented in our sample. To some extent, we make up for this inconsistency by comparing across time periods, rather than within them. Despite these concerns about the reliability of our data, however, we believe that the comparative analyses we make below do capture a rough sketch of the main changes that have occurred in Hungarian television landscape between 1983 and 2004.

Table 7.1 Comparison of Import Data for 1980s and 2000s

1980s		2000s	
Year Analyzed	# of Days	Year Analyzed	# of Days
1983	6	2001	14
1984	6	2002	111
1985	24	2003	14
1986	18	2004	29
1987	12	Total # Days	168
1988	12		
Total # Days	74		

130   *Timothy Havens, Evelyn Bottando and Matthew S. Thatcher*

Table 7.2   Percentage of Total Hungarian Imports for Selected Countries, 1980s and 2000s

Source	1980s	2000s
UK	19.2%	5.2%
France	14.5%	4.7%
U.S.	11.5%	57.3%
(West) Germany	11.2%	5.7%
Soviet Union/Russia	8.7%	.2%
Czech/Slovak	8.3%	.5%
EU Coproduction	6.4%	4.1%
Poland	4.6%	1.0%
Italy	2.7%	4.9%
Australia	.9%	1.7%
Canada	.9%	1.1%
(Former) Yugoslavia	.8%	.7%
Peru	.1%	.6%
Argentina	—	5.1%
Hong Kong	—	.5%
Mexico	—	4.6%
Venezuela	—	.6%

Comparing the two time periods, U.S. programming experienced by far the greatest increase in the overall percentage of imports, jumping from 11.5% in the 1980s to 57.3% in the 2000s (see Table 7.2). All other major importers in the 1980s experienced steep declines in terms of overall percentages between the two time periods. However, a handful of smaller importers, including several Latin American countries, Hong Kong, Australia, Canada and Italy, experienced overall increases in the percentage of imports between the 1980s and the 2000s. Although the total percentage of imports from these nations remains small, especially when compared with the complete domination of American imports, the fact that producers from these nations not only held their own against the massive American increase, but actually improved their percentages, is noteworthy.

These later observations suggest the dangers of concentrating exclusively on the spike in American imports, which may mask other important developments in the programming practices of Hungarian broadcasters. To take an extreme example, for instance, despite the fact that the total *percentage* of German imports decreased from 11.2% in the 1980s to 5.7% in the 2000s (Table 7.2), the average number of minutes of German imports per day during the sample periods jumped from 34 minutes to 93 minutes

Intra-European Media Imperialism 131

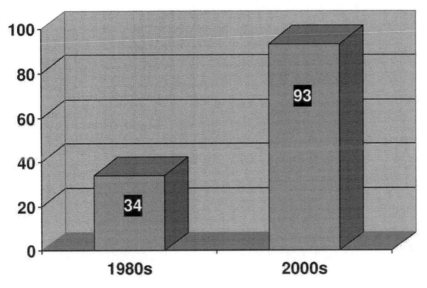

Figure 7.1 Average minutes of German imports per day.

per day (Figure 7.1). Of course, during this same period, the amount of broadcast time nearly quadrupled due to longer programming days and the increase from two to four broadcast channels. Nevertheless, German programming seems to have done quite well holding its own against the onslaught of American programs

The fact that the amount of German programming remained relatively stable between the two time periods raises the question of how other nations have fared between the two time periods, and how we might best characterize the empirical changes we see in Hungarian import data. To better answer these questions, we concentrate in this next section on comparing European imports across time periods to discover the fate of different national programming imports. Such an analysis then helps us better characterize the underlying roots of the programming changes we note.

Growth in Commercial, Decline of Regional European Imports

The clearest trend in European imports has been a steep decline in Eastern European and a comparative rise in Western European programming in Hungary (Figure 7.2). Compared to all imported programming, Western European imports declined by nearly 60% in the 2000s, while Eastern European programming declined 90% (Table 7.3). Relative to one another, however, Western European imports grew to nearly 92% of all European imports in the 2000s. Across the board, the percentage of Eastern European imports fell dozens of points, while many Western European imports grew

132   *Timothy Havens, Evelyn Bottando and Matthew S. Thatcher*

Table 7.3 European Import Percentages by Nation, 1980s and 2000s

Source	1980s	2000s
UK	22.7%	18.6%
France	17.0%	16.8%
(West) Germany	13.2%	20.1%
EU Coproduction	7.6%	14.5%
Spain	3.8%	1.2%
Italy	3.2%	17.3%
Netherlands	2.5%	.2%
Austria	.9%	.7%
Sweden	.9%	1.2%
Denmark	.6%	.4%
Switzerland	.6%	.4%
Portugal	.3%	—
Ireland	—	.2%
Iceland	—	.2%
Norway	—	.3%
Total Western Europe	73.3%	92.1%
Soviet Union/Russia	10.4%	.7%
Czechoslovakia (Czech Republic, Slovakia)	9.7%	1.7%
Poland	5.4%	3.5%
Yugoslavia (Croatia, Serbia)	.9%	2.1%
Total Eastern Europe	26.4%	8.0%

by similar numbers, and the percentage of European programs imported from Italy soared more than 400% from 3.2% in the 1980s to 17.3% in the 2000s (see Figure 7.2). Of course, one might argue that this change is merely a readjustment of an overly Eastward looking programming market during the 1980s, which had been encouraged by Soviet coercion and the Intervision program exchange network. Without those artificial restrictions, we might expect Western European programming to return to a more natural level, given the historical and cultural similarities among European nations. While such an argument might account for some of the change in the distribution of European imports, it surely cannot account for the fact that the total number of hours of Italian imports in the 2000s exceeded those of the Czech Republic by more than 1500%. Rather, given that both nations could arguably be said to be equally culturally proximate (or distant) to Hungary, something more than a simple cultural readjustment must be the cause of the import discrepancy.

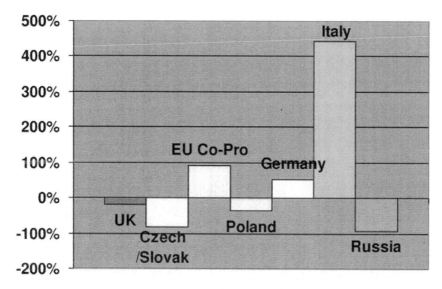

Figure 7.2 Percentage change in European import distribution for selected countries, 1980s vs. 2000s

The notable exception to the growth in the percentage of programming from Western European nations is the UK, which underwent an 18% drop between the 1980s and the 2000s. These data are anomalous and difficult to speculate about given the limitations of our information. However, it should be pointed out that the UK still accounts for nearly one-fifth of all European imports in Hungary. Moreover, given the high opinion that many broadcasters worldwide held of the BBC in the 1980s, along with the relative lack of other sources for cultural program imports, it is likely that MTV1 was heavily reliant on BBC programming to help fill outs its broadcast schedules and its remit as a public broadcaster at the time.

In almost every instance, however, Western European nations significantly increased their import percentages over their Eastern neighbors. Of course, Latin American exporters had far more dramatic increases, which along with U.S. imports, cut into Western European import percentages (Figure 7.3). Nevertheless, it seems unquestionable that the benefits of the TVWF Directive have only accrued to Western European imports, not Eastern European ones. In short, the Directive has only protected certain Western European nations' export revenues, while Eastern European television production has shriveled.

The benefactors of the TVWF Directive have not only been Western European nations, but commercial television producers in particular. Certainly, with regard to non-European imports, this development seems clear enough: the nations in Table 7.1 that increased their import percentages in the 2000s are all major players in the global commercial television trade. A closer look at how the programming makeup of German and Italian

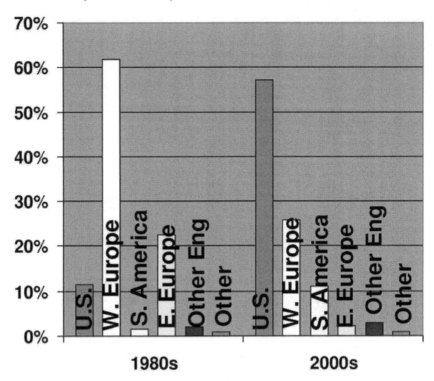

Figure 7.3 Import percentages by region, 1980s v 2000s.

imports has changed since the 1980s underscores the fact that this observation holds true for European programming as well, as the proportion of popular genres has grown significantly in relation to cultural genres.[2]

Germany and Italy are two of the most highly developed and highly commercialized television markets in Europe, and both markets rely heavily on international revenues to subsidize domestic production. In both cases, the percentage of cultural programming imports to Hungary from these nations has declined since the 1980s, while the proportion of popular programming has increased. Figures 7.4 and 7.5 show the changing fortunes of various imported programming genres from Germany and Italy. In the 1980s, films accounted for the majority of imports from both nations. Of course, not all films are classifiable as cultural programming, as the category is broad enough to include both popular and cultural films. Nevertheless, the category certainly does include cultural programming, and films in general tend to have more cultural legitimacy than television serials.

The next largest category in German imports in the 1980s was series. In both Germany and Italy, the ratio of series to other import genres spiked in the 2000s, growing more than 10% in Germany and from 0% in Italy in the 1980s to nearly one-fifth of all Italian imports by the 2000s. In many

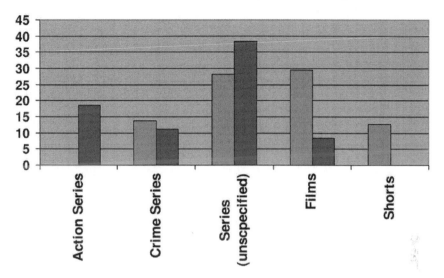

Figure 7.4 Breakdown of German imports by genre, 1980s vs. 2000s.

ways, series are the cultural antithesis of films; that is, while films tend to have cultural legitimacy because of their generic traits, including their non-serial nature and their identifiable authorship, television series tend to lack legitimacy because the genre does not possess those attributes (Ellis 1982). Again, this category is too large to make indisputable generalizations about, but it does seem reasonable to suggest that most series are perceived as popular, rather than cultural programs.

The decline in cultural programming and rise in popular programming becomes even clearer when we look at more narrowly-defined genres. In Germany, the action series, a highly popularized genre, grew from 0% of imports in the 1980s to 18.5% in the 2000s, while the crime genre, a staple of German television for decades, held nearly steady (see Figure 7.4). By contrast, films shorts, which we can reasonably identify as cultural programming because they deviate from the standard format of commercial films and television programs, accounted for 12.6% of German imports in the 2000s, but did not appear at all in the data collected from the 2000s. In a similar vein, biography series accounted for 20% of Italian imports in the 1980s, but none of the imports in the 2000s, while crime series were not imported in the 1980s, but accounted for 11.7% of imports in the 2000s.

The importation of popular Western European programming has especially been facilitated by commercial broadcasters, but the public service broadcasters are not immune to these developments, even as they facilitate Central European program exchanges more readily than their commercial counterparts. Returning to our earlier classification of popular and cultural programming, 100% of imports labeled as 'action series' appeared on the

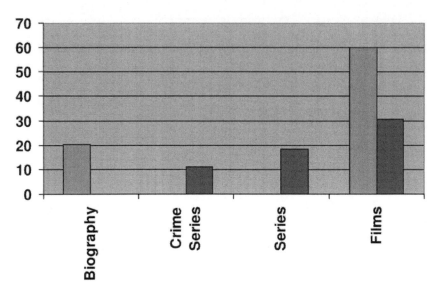

Figure 7.5 Breakdown of Italian imports by genre, 1980s vs. 2000s.

commercial broadcasters, while almost 90% of imported European films were broadcast by the public service broadcasters (Table 7.4). Similarly, the public broadcasters accounted for 93.3% of Central and Eastern European imports (Table 7.5).

In interviews, program acquisitions official at both MTV and Duna TV were aware of this tendency to buy programming from Central and Eastern Europe, as well as European films. While they saw this acquisition strategy as part of what distinguished them from the commercial broadcasters, they also lamented the fact that they were unable to compete with the commercial broadcasters for the newest Hollywood movie releases and popular series. In fact, the acquisitions executive at MTV was quite proud of the fact that she had acquired rights to the U.S. actions series *24* (personal interview, anonymous MTV acquisitions executive; personal interview, anonymous Duna TV acquisitions executive). In other words, the

Table 7.4 Percentage of European Imports by Selected Genres and Channels, 2000s

Genre	MTV	RTL	Klub	TV2
Action series	—	22.9%	77.1%	—
Crime series	58.1%	—	30.2%	11.7%
Series	53.9%	6.2%	21.9%	18.0%
Films	30.8%	1.3%	9.2%	58.6%

Intra-European Media Imperialism 137

Table 7.5 Percentage of Imports by Region at all Broadcasters, 2000s

Region	MTV	RTL Klub	TV2	Duna TV
U.S.	35.4%	74.8%	63.3%	32.7%
Western Europe	44.1%	11.3%	18.2%	25.8%
Latin America	4.3%	11.7%	17.3%	11.1%
Eastern Europe	7.2%	.5%	0%	2.3%
Other English-speaking	8.9%	.3%	.9%	2.8%
Other	.2%	1.4%	.2%	.9%

programming professionals at the public broadcasters compete in the same programming markets as their commercial counterparts, and their perceptions of what kinds of programming are appropriate for their audience differ only in some respects. A clear example of these more commercialized tendencies at the public broadcasters is the fact that MTV accounted for a majority of imported European television series in Hungary and 58% of imported European crime series, which we might reasonably define as predominantly commercial programming.

CONCLUSION

Without a doubt, the TVWF Directive has helped maintain the presence of European programming on Hungarian television schedules into the 2000s against a deluge of programming from North and South America, Canada and Australia. It might plausibly be argued that the Directive has therefore served its main purpose, which is the protection of European television programming in an era of global commercialization. However, the cost of such protection, at least in Hungary, has been the near complete disappearance of imports from Central and Eastern European nations, especially when it comes to contemporary programming. If we believe that the purpose of TVWF is merely a way to guarantee the commercial viability of television industries in select European nations, then it has succeeded. If, however, we take seriously the ideal that the Directive should to some degree promote intra-European dialogue and protect Europe's cultural diversity, then its success has been far more measured. In fact, along with Western European foreign direct investment in Central and Eastern European television industries, the domination of Hungarian television by Western European powers is remarkably similar to the domination of European television markets by the U.S. prior to TVWF.

The cultural argument of TVWF is based on the idea that it is possible to foster European unity alongside national diversity. However, such

138 *Timothy Havens, Evelyn Bottando and Matthew S. Thatcher*

a process requires dialogue among participants. What we have in Central and Eastern European television today is, instead, more like a monologue dominated by Western European powers. The dialogues that existed prior to the collapse of socialism between Central and Eastern European nations was shattered with the introduction of commercial broadcasting, which depressed television production across the region and led to heavy dependence on cheap, imported programming. EU regulations have done nothing to repair such dialogues. Of course, it can be argued that these nations have little in common, and all of them would prefer to look West, but given the recent social changes they have in common, their longer historical experiences as targets of Western European imperialism, and their similar current economic challenges, it seems likely that a basis for significant cultural dialogue does exist among Central and Eastern European nations. However, a concentration on protecting European audiovisual culture writ large prevents consideration of these important subregional cultural exchanges. If their intent is truly the protection of European cultural diversity, then EU regulators would do well to consider such subregional differences and explore ways to protect their cultural integrity as robustly as they now protect powerful Western European nations.

NOTES

1. MTV1 was the main state broadcaster in Hungary in the 1980s, while MTV2 was similar to a 'second' public service channel in Western Europe, programming mostly cultural programming; MTV2 was sold off to private broadcasters in the 1990s. Meanwhile, Duna TV is a publicly-funded channel that began broadcasting in 1992 and aims at Hungarian speakers in neighboring countries. The commercial channels RTL Klub and TV2 are both majority-owned by foreign media conglomerates, with approximately 25% domestic ownership. The ownership partners and percentages of these channels has changed frequently since they began broadcasting in 1997. In 2004, when this study was conducted, Luxembourgeois media powerhouse CLT-UFA, itself a subsidiary of Bertelsmann, AG, was the majority owner of RTL Klub, while Scandinavian SBS Broadcasting, controlled 49% of the voting stock of TV2. In addition, Disney held part ownership in TV2 through German television producer Tele-München Fernseh, while UK production firm Pearson owned more than 20% of RTL Klub. Local owners included the production house MTM Communications, which controlled 28% of TV2's voting stock, and the state monopoly telephone company MATÁV (Gálik 2004).

2. The distinction between commercial and popular programming that we invoke throughout this section is, in many ways, arbitrary, and not necessarily a distinction that we are wont to endorse. Nevertheless, it is undoubtedly a distinction that held significance in both time periods, which is why we find the distinction useful. Ader (2006) defines cultural programming as "consists of ambitious performances of high artistic merit" (2), notably opera, theater, symphonies and experimental films. See also Rowland and Tracey (1990) for a discussion of the importance of cultural programming among public broadcasters in the 1980s.

Intra-European Media Imperialism 139

REFERENCES

Ader, Thorston. 2006. *Cultural and Regional Remits in Broadcasting*. Strasbourg, France: European Audiovisual Observatory.

Aiello, Giorgia, 2005. "'Talking back' as a Strategy in Identity Formation: The European Union vs. the US on Issues of (Audio)visual Representation." Paper presented at the annual meeting of the International Communication Association, New York, May 26–30.

Ang, Ien. 1985. *Watching Dallas*. New York: Methuen.

Aubry, Patrice. 2000. *The Television Without Frontiers Directive: Cornerstone of the European Broadcasting Policy*. Strasbourg, France: European Audiovisual Observatory.

Böröcz, Jozsef. 2001. "Introduction: Empire and Coloniality in the 'Eastern Enlargement' of the European Union." In *Empire's New Clothes: Unveiling EU Enlargement*, edited by Jozzef Böröcz and Melina Kovács, 4–50. Telford, UK: Central European Review, Ltd.

Burgelman, Jean-Claude and Caroline Pauwels. 1992. "Audiovisual Policy and Cultural Identity in Small European States: The Challenge of a Unified Market." *Media, Culture and Society* 14: 169–183.

Coman, Mihai. 2004. "Romanian Television and the Challenges of European Integration." *Trends in Communication* 12: 211–222.

Ellis, John. 1982. *Visible Fictions: Cinema, Television, Video*. London and New York: Routledge.

European Audiovisual Observatory. 2008. *Yearbook 2008—Film, Television and Video in Europe, Vol. 2, Trends in European Television*. Strasbourg, France.

European Union. 1989. *Television Without Frontiers Directive*. http://europa.eu/legislation_summaries/audiovisual_and_media/l24101_en.htm (Accessed April 2, 2012).

Gálik, Mihály. 2004. "Hungary." In *Media Ownership and its Impact on Media Independence and Pluralism*, edited by Brankica Petkovič, 191–218. Ljubljana: Peace Institute.

Harcourt, Alison. 2005. *The European Union and the Regulation of Media Markets*. Manchester and New York: Manchester University Press

Hoskins, Colin, Stuart McFadyen and Adam Finn. 1997. *Global Television and Film: An Introduction to the Economics of the Business*. New York and Oxford: Oxford University Press.

Jabukowicz, Karol. 2004. "We need an EU with a Heart, a Social Conscience, and Courage." *Trends in Communication* 12: 157–161.

Liebes, Tamar and Elihu Katz. 1993. *The Export of Meaning: Cross-Cultural Readings of Dallas*. Oxford: Polity Press, 1993.

Morley, David and Robins, Kevin. 1995. *Spaces of Identity: Global Media, Electronic Landscapes and Cultural Boundaries*. London and New York: Routledge.

Papathanassopoulos, Styliannos. 2002. *European Television in the Digital Age*. Oxford, UK: Polity.

Rowland, Willard D. Jr. and Michael Tracey. 1990. "Worldwide Challenges to Public Service Broadcasting." *Journal of Communication* 40 (2): 8–27.

Shein, Hagi. 2004. "Specification of the Notions of National and Own Production as a Broadcasting Policy Concern in New Member states." *Trends in Communication* 12: 181–191.

Szefkü, András. 1989. "Intruders Welcome? The Beginnings of Satellite Television in Hungary." *European Journal of Communication* 4: 161–171.

140   *Timothy Havens, Evelyn Bottando and Matthew S. Thatcher*

Tomlinson, John. 1991. *Cultural Imperialism: A Critical Introduction.* Baltimore: Johns Hopkins University Press.

Tunstall, Jeremy. 2007. *The Media Were American: US Mass Media in Decline.* Oxford, UK: Oxford University Press.

Wheeler, Mark. 2004. "Supranational Regulation: Television and the European Union." *European Journal of Communication* 19: 349–369.

8 To be Romanian in Post-Communist Romania

Entertainment Television and Patriotism in Popular Discourse

Adina Schneeweis

INTRODUCTION

> I've been nagging you about [. . .] having to do something about national cohesion [. . .] Because we must do something [. . .] Because you don't earn dignity and honor by bemoaning or cursing others, but by proving that we are better and more honest; and only by being able to see ourselves, as we are.[1]

With these words, the host Cătălin Ştefănescu closed the 2001 season of *Garantat 100%*—the longest entertainment television program still broadcasting on Romanian public television. Including host monologues, live music, short documentaries telling stories of local talent and passionate living and on-set politico-artistic celebrity guests, the show has celebrated localism via exemplars of inventive and creative living in an age of transition to democracy. For almost the entire time it has been broadcast, the program has not had direct competitors—format- and message-wise—on either public or commercial stations. Its structure has changed from emphasizing local stories and uniqueness (in the short films) to highlighting culture and the arts, after the show's move to the capital eight years ago. In its 12 years of broadcast, *Garantat 100%* has always been committed to a local agenda, and has talked about Romania—about socio-political and cultural issues, about Romanianness, Romanian identity, diaspora, immigration and emigration—about what I call here 'the Romanian.' Despite its self-identified label to be a cultural program today, my interest in *Garantat 100%* lays with its entertainment function, with its message of (a special sort of) patriotism, as it was formulated in its 2001 season—a significant moment for the show, as I explain shortly. As a self-proclaimed program "about and for Romanians," I ask what type of Romanianness it has promoted, proclaimed, sold and constructed. What type of "national cohesion"[2] has *Garantat 100%* been representing?

The program stands as a signifier of the Romanian post-communist media landscape. Its mission and content are positioned between Western

142 *Adina Schneeweis*

orientation and efforts towards democratization on the one hand, and the call of the local and the specifically Romanian on the other hand. At the same time, *Garantat 100%* has to grapple with the pressures to maintain a steady audience, to entertain and satisfy local viewers used to sensationalized television content. The show has balanced such (often) competing forces by pushing an educational and moralizing agenda that seeks to make Romanians feel better about being Romanian—perhaps a contributing factor to its decade-long, consistent success.

My aims here are two-fold. The first is to discuss the program for its contribution to public discourses in post-1989 Romania—how does entertainment television talk about Romania, Romanians, nationalism, patriotism, and how do these issues relate to talk of democratization and the country's socio-economic development? How has the talk of *Garantat 100%* fit into the landscape of popular discourses of the time? Second, I position my observations in the wider context of the Romanian media market, where the show must succeed. I use critical discourse analysis (CDA)[3]—as a method and theoretical positioning—to analyze the case study of *Garantat 100%* and to explore the framing of such volatile concepts as democratization, nationalism, patriotism and Romanianness as a means to build national cohesion, in the midst of tumultuous socio-political changes. I treat the language and content of *Garantat 100%* as discursive practices reproducing and creating a fabric of knowledge[4] about what it means to be a 'guaranteed' Romanian. Analyzing the different texts of the program, I view linguistic choices to be not accidental, but informed and meaningful.[5] CDA is useful to help make evident the possible links between texts and social hierarchies,[6] as reflected in the mediated practice of talking about what it means to be Romanian. I draw here from almost three years of experience working for the program and from personal communication with the host, producer and staff working for *Garantat 100%*.[7] I also use audience ratings to offer observations about the program's impact.

'Garantat' in Romanian means 'guaranteed,' 'fail-safe,' and 'authentic'— and, as such, the program has stood for local talent, local meaning and local passion in difficult and changing times for democratizing Romania, challenged by high emigration rates to Western Europe and the U.S. What is most significant about *Garantat 100%* is the attention it has received, not only from notable award granting institutions,[8] but also in popular discourse, where it is common to hear about news, events or people that are 'guaranteed 100 percent.'

As an opinion leader, whose Facebook page is run by a fan and has gathered 4,877 people that 'like' it (by the date of this publication), Ştefănescu is an interesting case himself,[9] given the longevity of his success and appeal, and the niche offering of his program. He has been writing his own monologues and prompts (in collaboration with his producers); in many ways, he runs the show. And so I ask what *Garantat 100%* contributes to the media discourses of the 2000s. This study adds to the thin research on

To be Romanian in Post-Communist Romania   143

entertainment programs in Eastern Europe and to the even thinner body of research on Romanian media in postcommunism.

Since the Romanian Revolution in December 1989 that overthrew the communist regime, new governments have made substantial efforts to adjust to democratic and capitalist systems, largely attempting to emulate Western models. The Romanian media have gone through a series of transformations, towards increased professionalism and higher quality standards. Following the explosion of freedoms in the early 1990s, new print publications and private radio and television stations have invaded the media market. Content-wise, television production in particular has shifted to a focus on entertainment and sensationalism, on both public and private stations,[10] having to cope with new market demands and competition from imported content. The bulk of the programming in the last 22 years (films, dramas, situation comedies, and soap operas, as well as successful formats for television talk shows, game shows, reality and news shows) has been imported mostly from Western countries, mainly from the U.S.; and yet local production is certainly on the rise. Radio and television outlets are protected by law, as are author rights; still, there is no updated, postcommunism law of the press.[11] Despite legislative efforts to transform the state television into a public service institution, commercial channels have taken over, while public service channels[12] have encountered "growing deficits and crises of legitimacy."[13] Scholars have also cautioned against a state control of the media system, still evident in Romania. Henry Carey, for instance, wrote in 1996 about public television that it "preaches traditional, ethnocentric loyalty to Romania," and supports "elite" efforts to "mislead public loyalties from the truth."[14]

It is in this context that the texts of *Garantat 100%* must be judged. The program more than anything else must survive in a market of public vs. commercial competition, of local vs. Western content struggle for airtime domination. And so I first read the texts about Romanians in light of the show's strategy and intentionality. But the messages and representations of "the Romanian" constructed are marks of more than just a bottom-line orientation. They must be seen in a larger national context of popular discourses, of ideological battles for legitimacy and truth about Romania and Romanianness—in a context when nationalism and patriotism talk is both rising and being challenged, as I turn to show now.

PATRIOTISM AND NATIONALISM POST-1989

The moment of 2001 when I explore popular discourses of patriotism and nationalism is not devoid of historical context. In other words, patriotism and nationalism do not start afresh after the fall of communism in December 1989. Over a century of traditions, discourses and doctrines[15] have constructed a strong, yet contradictory, body of knowledge on what

144   *Adina Schneeweis*

Romanian and Romanianness mean. For the purpose of this discussion, I define patriotism to mean love, devotion and pride for one's country, nation, culture and people, and to include a range of expressions from celebrating tradition to advocating for one's patria. The term 'nationalism' today is divorced of its original meaning established with the nationalist movements of the 19th century that sought nation-building. More often, it is viewed now with scepticism and slight hostility, as it connotes a negative or extremist sort of patriotism, a xenophobic, intolerant and exaggerated national pride.[16] As others have shown, however, overly emphasizing the difference and distinction between (good) patriotism and (bad) nationalism can be misleading; they are ambivalent, polymorphous, flexible concepts, with different connotations and resonances, with overlapping meanings.[17] Here, I distinguish between them to the degree that in the discourse framed on *Garantat 100%* they appear distinct.

On the Romanian scene of popular and political discourses, talk of nationalism and patriotism post-1989 has been uncertain, following an era when communism had overused the nationalist discourse and had made citizens uncertain about their identity as Romanians[18] and about using patriotism as a positive characteristic. A first reaction was to emphasize the positive and 'traditional' aspects of Romanianness, such as the foods, the landscape, the literature and the folklore that were old enough to be stripped of recent communist influences. Earlier seasons of *Garantat 100%* took this route as well, including a section on recipes, usually filmed in traditional restaurants and 'culture'-filled locations; this reportage was always framed in tones that celebrated cultural uniqueness and specialness. A subsequent development, Romanian politics shifted towards embracing pro-European discourses and towards rejecting tradition-driven patriotism. Patriotism has also become a reaction to xenophobic and extremist nationalism (primarily led by the discourse of the nationalist party România Mare[19] and its outspoken public figure of Corneliu Vadim Tudor). In the midst of economic struggles, disillusionment with the challenges of the democratizing 1990s, and discourses downgrading anything Romanian, many Romanians started working abroad and many youth have been immigrating to Western countries. Some have proclaimed, in this context, a diminishing of the strength of national identity. And yet another discursive direction has been to formulate the Romanian culture in its own right, in a European context, and striving to shed inferiority and superiority complexes alike.[20]

To which such trend in talking about Romanianness does *Garantat 100%* subscribe? It is precisely at this conjuncture of different popular discourses of patriotism and nationalism that the work of the entertainment program must be seen. Returning to moderator Ştefănescu's words cited at the outset of this chapter, his call for doing "something about national cohesion, and especially about the fact that patriotism doesn't necessarily mean laying it on real thick" is in fact an effort against the extremist nationalistic approach. And as he calls for his public to be "able to see ourselves as we are,"[21] he fights against an inferiority complex—a decrease in national confidence accentuated by the rush to become more Westernlike, to fit in, to Europeanize (and, ultimately, to join North-Atlantic Treaty Organization and the European Union[22]). In a climate of instability and political controversy, *Garantat 100%* brings in celebratory patriotism to introduce fresh excitement about being Romanian.

THE CASE OF GARANTAT 100%

Garantat 100% has been broadcasting without interruption since March 1999, securing a faithful audience[23] and consistently higher national audience ratings than programming on competing commercial channels, as I show shortly. It proclaims itself to be a program about and for the everyday Romanian, the only program where Romanians themselves are in the center of attention—this is a show about "Romanians who are worth being known by their compatriots."[24] Although originally produced regionally, in Cluj-Napoca, the program has been broadcast on the national station *TVR1*, as well as on the international *TVRi*, the regional *TVR Cluj*, and more recently on *TVR Cultural* and *TVR Info*.

Hosted by Cătălin Ştefănescu since the beginning, the hour-long show's format included short documentary films for its first four years.[25] The characters presented in the documentaries included inventors, musicians and musicologists, unusual athletes and talented imitators, crafts enthusiasts, self-made astronomers, impromptu village physicians, peculiar artists or merely genius folk, with their out-of-the-ordinary stories, remarkable pasts, young and old, from across Romania, all given as examples of (entertaining and) inspirational living. After its move to Bucharest in 2003, the program changed its format to a talk show structure and is now described as a cultural show.[26] It has always included on-set guests, renowned local or foreign figures, as well as some less known to the public, from the worlds of film, theater, music, art and politics. Conversations with the guests have centered on living one's passion and inspiring viewers to do the same,[27] on Romanian cultural richness discussed in connection to the country's high emigration rates, and, most relevant for my interest in this analysis, on the country's image locally and internationally.

The program's structure to include, at first, three-to-four short films, averaging five minutes in length, and later two documentaries, 10–12 minutes long, is unique in the Romanian entertainment media landscape, especially at the time of analysis. Most other weeklies on the market focused on emotional issues, struggling couples, and reunited families.[28] In that sense, *Garantat 100%* did not have a direct competitor—and especially not during its broadcast hour. The only other programs with similar entertainment and socio-moralizing purpose were *Impact*, broadcast on the commercial station *Prima TV* on a weekday afternoon,[29] and *Ştirile de Sâmbăta Asta*,[30]

146 *Adina Schneeweis*

also on *TVR1*, which offered humorous political commentary and skits. For the analyzed time period, the 2001 season, *Garantat 100%* was broadcast Saturdays at 7 pm, a most desired time slot, which almost guarantees a sizeable audience—especially since the competing commercial stations *Pro TV*, *Antena 1* and *Prima TV*, showed news during this time slot.

I used two audience measurement ratings, obtained from *TVR1*, to assess the program's audience: AMR (absolute numbers reflecting the percentage of viewers watching *Garantat 100%* when compared to all monitored subjects that could be watching it) and SHARE (relative number of viewers that watch *Garantat 100%* when compared to the total number of people that are watching TV at the same time). In a sense, SHARE represents the program's capacity to attract an audience in its time slot. I compared AMR and SHARE figures, taken for two audience groups, labeled 'national' (2,434 cases observed) and 'large urban' (895 cases observed in cities with more than 200,000 people).

According to both audience measurement tools, *Garantat 100%* recorded a higher national audience than competing stations for the entirety of its 2001 season (with the exception of two shows in April and May). The audience size differed for urban areas, where *TVR1*'s audience size dropped below that of viewers watching news on private stations. *TVR1* was surpassed a few times by *Acasă*, a commercial channel broadcasting almost exclusively soap operas and telenovelas. Overall, this data suggests that the bulk of the program's viewers at the time of analysis lived in rural and small urban areas—and were often discussed as such in editorial and staff meetings. Ştefănescu counted on this type of viewership, engaged his audience with direct messages and by responding to letters, made himself available by talking quite informally about himself, his experiences and acquaintances, and he especially tailored his moralizing, educational or humanitarian comments for this type of vision of his audience.

THE ROMANIAN ON *GARANTAT 100%*

Method. CDA offers useful tools to assess a text's multiple commitments and aims. The concept of *recontextualization* draws attention to how texts may incorporate other texts, or how social practices employ other social practices.[31] As an example, on *Garantat 100%* the moderator frequently pulls from Western discourses of modernization and of the Protestant work ethic to suggest the need for his public to do something with their lives. As such, it is important methodologically to consider the program in its socio-political context, as it attempts to educate its audience in the spirit of both capitalist and patriotic values—and as it seeks to draw and maintain an audience. For these purposes, analyzing *Garantat 100%* means taking its *strategy* into account. I therefore assume content to be intentional in its message, direction, packaging and technical aspects, in order to achieve

To be Romanian in Post-Communist Romania   147

intended goals—whether chosen or imposed upon in the show's institutional and organizational context. I start here from the critical premise that the media hold the power to contribute to knowledge-creation, to ascertain specific versions of truths in the public sphere.[32] In that sense, I treat televised talk and texts to mean not only linguistic and formal structures, but to also denote systems of rules and practices.[33]

The 2001 season presented particular interest, as it was characterized by an increase in the prestige of the guests appearing on the show, and it was also the last year before the program's move to the capital. In other words, during this time, *Garantat 100%* attracted sufficient public and media attention that it presented appeal at a national level for the *TVR* headquarters. The program also received two significant awards for its 2001 season.[34] Twenty-three episodes made up this season, broadcast weekly on Saturday evenings before the news, between January 13 and June 30 (with two breaks on February 10 and March 10).

To answer the main question asked in this chapter—that is, what definition of 'the Romanian' the entertainment program *Garantat 100%* has constructed and sold, given the program's slogan to be a show about Romanians and for Romanians—I conducted a CDA in several steps, beginning with an analysis of content and theme frequency. The program's topics and themes were generated inductively. Then, beginning with a reading of the texts (introductory speeches) and careful watching of the 23 episodes, I examined both object positions (unusual, humorous, cultural or traditional practices referenced) and subject positions (the people talked about). I categorized these positions thematically, around subject positions, paying specific attention to the object positions associated with each. I weighed linguistic choices (vocabulary, metaphors, descriptions, images) alongside editorial practices of organizing and prioritizing information, by highlighting some key elements, generalizing others and leaving others out. I also paid specific attention to key terms, such as Romania, nation, democracy, patriotism and its derivatives. I used the host's entire communicative language to aid in the interpretation, from his vocal habits (intonation, rhythm, word emphasis) to his nonverbal behavior (body and face movement and gestures).[35] All quoted text is my translation.

Guiding questions in the analysis included: What does being "100 percent guaranteed," "100 percent fail-safe" mean? What does being Romanian mean? How are Romanians talked about? And how is Romania as a country/nation/culture talked about? How are patriotism and nationalism connected with being Romanian? How are patriotism and nationalism connected with the country's process of democratization? How are key words used in the program?

Moderation as Strategy. Ştefănescu's art of moderation is particularly well suited for the nature of the entertainment program. And he certainly entertains through his language and body expressions, which are informal, relaxed and engaging. He often slapped his forehead or his knees,

Table 8.1 Frequency and Percentages of Themes at *Garantat 100%*

Themes	The Romanian	Stories and storytelling	Current conditions	Other nations	Audience	Solution for Romania	Global issues	Culture, literature, arts	Holidays
Frequency	20	17	11	9	8	7	6	5	5
Percentage	86.95	73.91	47.82	39.13	34.78	30.43	26.08	21.75	21.75

To be Romanian in Post-Communist Romania 149

scratched his head, and looked for confirmation from the audience on set when he found himself particularly entertained by a guest. He often chuckled and mocked. And his questioning approach was unceremonious: "Where've you been?,"[36] "What do you read? *Do* you read? What's your favorite story?,"[37] "What do you like to eat?,"[38] "Can you cook?," "Do you dance? Let's dance,"[39] "How did they take a guy wearing tennis shoes, jeans and long hair to be a radio director?,"[40] "How's it with the ladies?"[41] As an accomplished public speaker, he only ridiculed his own experiences, and never those of others; he was more critical, however, of current conditions in Romania and frequently qualified his statements by identifying his personal opinion. Still, his focus was not to denigrate or criticize, but instead to offer learning and positive modeling, consistent with the program's mission.

In the host's quest to attain simplicity and ease in his speech, to win the public and easily convey his views across—expected qualities of a good public speaker[42]—little was left to chance. Spontaneity in his talk and manners, his reactions and facial expressions were planned and practiced beforehand. His choice—that is, his strategy, as I laid out the concept here to mean a systematic pursuit of a goal—to be "friendly" and approachable was consistent between the interviews and the documentary voice-over, in Ştefănescu's voice. Jargon and colloquialisms, humor, cynicism and satire—all strategies helped create a sense of intimacy and closeness, necessary in order to nurture viewers and encourage them to return to the show, week after week. The host posed to be 'one of us' and as such asked himself questions out loud about the hot topics of the moment. And once he connected to the audience—and made them laugh—Ştefănescu introduced the more serious topics, centered on Romanians and the country's struggles.

The Romanian: The Exceptional Survivor. Nearly every edition of the 2001 season discussed the state of Romania, of Romanians, how foreigners may be viewing Romania, what it means to be Romanian or the issue of Romanian emigration (82.6%).[43] The moderator most often framed all such key issues in conversations about a host of issues, ranging from the weather and holidays to political and social events. Yet consistently, the program returned to talking about the specialness of Romanians, at home and abroad, in their own eyes and in the views of others, with what they think and what they do. On *Garantat 100%*, Romanian means exceptional—and to construct such knowledge, the texts compared and contrasted anything and everything to the Romanian who always has something to contribute. To be Romanian is worthwhile, the show claimed. Ştefănescu offered a very clearly-defined patriotism—one that moved away from blind love and stood apart from intolerant manifestations at the same time. The patriotism at *Garantat 100%* celebrated a Romanian citizen that succeeds and mends his/her own fence.

Table 8.1 displays the most frequent topics of *Garantat 100%*. What is most significant about this assortment of issues discussed is that most

150 *Adina Schneeweis*

of the themes gravitated around and supported that of 'the Romanian.' In other words, the topic of the day, be it current events or the Easter holidays, always served as atmosphere setters and strategic pathways to the chief aim and topic of the program, which is talking about exceptional Romanians.

'The Romanian' as a theme roughly referred to descriptions and depictions of Romanians, of the country as a nation and culture. The theme of 'stories and storytelling' encompassed anecdotes, personal stories or friends' experiences and comments[44]—backdrops for moralizing commentary. Current conditions in Romania, tackled either mockingly, with cynicism (a "normal life for an industrialized society, solid in its democratic workings, as Romanian society is at this time"[45]), or with complete seriousness were most often another springboard for an analysis of Romania, Romanians, and their image in the world. Often, Ştefănescu asked his guests, "Where do you think Romania is at these days?"[46] And never did the conversation end there: "What can we do?"[47]—and so the program dedicated considerable attention to forward-looking and finding a solution for Romania's struggles. Anecdotes about other nations provide useful comparisons, to either offer encouragement and a model for Romanians, or to discourage an overemphasis on what others can do—we can do it, too, claimed *Garantat 100%*. Culture, the arts, literature, theater and acting and holidays were more infrequent themes—as were history and historic personalities, the weather, or the communist past (which all appeared in fewer than a quarter of the episodes).

In every third phrase, Ştefănescu's monologues invoked one of the key terms explored here (for instance, the host commented on 'this nation,' 'this people,' and 'our compatriots'), and in every fifth, 'Romanian' or 'Romania' appeared (to illustrate, "Are you German or are you Romanian?,"[48] "Are you ever ashamed to be Romanian?,"[49] "Given your artistic, political, and media experience, have you reached an understanding about our nation?"[50]). Regardless of the type of guest—be they from the political, artistic, media, sports or musical arena—questions about Romanians were never absent. Significantly, Ştefănescu talked of nation but not of *nationalism*, sensitive perhaps to critiques to the perceived aggressiveness associated with the concept.[51] He may have likely sought disassociation from the radical discourses of the extremist political party România Mare.

'Romanian' on *Garantat 100%* means *being 100 percent guaranteed—100 percent fail-safe*. But this is a very qualified definition, with a threefold meaning. It means first the one living a passion, the out-of-the-norm; second, it covers the 'normal' people; and third, the Romanian on this program is the one who has not given up in a time of struggle. This last element of the definition is quite significant here, and I turn to it momentarily. The first two aspects are necessarily related and they feed off each other: The program claimed to be both about everyone—the 'simple man,' the 'anonymous' *and* about the 'famous in their village, in their building, in their neighborhood';[52] both about the everyday sort of person *and* about the out-of-the-ordinary. The definition of the Romanian shifted between

To be Romanian in Post-Communist Romania   151

"people that are not on the front pages of newspapers and magazines"[53] and those who are not banal.

At first glance, Romanian seemed to mean not 'the superlative.' In a March edition, for instance, the moderator addressed at length a concerned viewer's question about laughing at and ridiculing *Garantat 100%*. In his answer, Ştefănescu explained the Romanian that makes it into the program—the Romanian subject that is worthy of (media) attention. He said:

> We laugh at some Romanians, because that's how they are—amusing. We take our hats off to others, some intrigue us, we envy others. That's how this nation that we are part of looks like, for the most part. This is who we are. I hope you wouldn't enjoy a program where we only talk about how great Romanians are, about our famous athletes, our scientists, about how Romanians are such a first-rate nation. That would be hypocritical. Just as much as it would be to say that we're the scum of the scum. But the bad part is that we've gotten used to talking about ourselves only in the superlative. It's tough to get used to seeing ourselves as we are.[54]

Here, Ştefănescu made a claim away from devotional and proud patriotism that celebrates the patria no matter what. The Romanian worth talking about (in this program) is not "the superlative." Instead, he is the "anonymous" he or she, living "all over this country":

> Everywhere, in every film we've presented, in every story we've had the joy to tell you, we have had the simple man in mind. Anonymous Romanians, from all over this country, who are celebrities in their own village, in their apartment building, in their neighborhood, because people know them to have a special habit, or just because they do amazing things in complete anonymity; they don't care about being famous, and go about their business, because [. . .] they are crazy about something, because they honestly believe in their passions.
> [. . .] See, on *Garantat 100%* we've decided to show you the people that are not on the front pages of newspapers and magazines. So that you see what sorts of people live in Romania.[55]

Ştefănescu's—and the program's—strategy is evident here. In describing (and addressing) "all sorts of Romanians," he covered any and every audience member, he spoke to every variant of the watching citizen, in an effort to allow them to relate to the Romanian represented on the show. As I mentioned early on, the show must be competitive, must attract and maintain a steady audience, particularly in rural and small urban areas; and the everyday Romanian lives in those homes.

But the more prevalent—the most frequent, most emphasized and most celebrated (in interviews and monologues alike)—subject was that of the

152 *Adina Schneeweis*

exceptional Romanian. The examples abounded—this program is "about Romanians who do special things"[56]:

[A]ny citizen with a pursuit, who does something special, anything, as long as it's not illegal, as long as it's not violent.[57]

[C]razy about something, because they honestly believe in their passions.[58]

[People who] don't conceive of life outside of their passion.[59]

[People who] take responsibility for what they want to do. People who are worth knowing. [. . .] You can do as they do. Or not.[60]

The exceptional (and the ordinary) Romanian was never packaged alone. The partner to this patriotic talk was a forward-looking orientation, necessary in the socio-economic and political context of the early 2000s in Romania. Frequently, and in no equivocal terms, Ştefănescu made moralizing statements—that Romania needs "fixing," in a very particular kind of way. The theme that I have here called "solution for Romania" supports the definition of the Romanian that does not give up in difficult times. The January 20 edition stated most explicitly: "Welcome back to *Garantat 100%*, the program that shows you that there are *Romanians who are not resigned*."[61] When Ştefănescu said, "So that you see what sorts of people live in Romania," he worked to convey one of the program's main points—to educate audiences on genuine Romanianness and help the country progress. Remarks such as these maintain the attention of a viewer hungry for inspiration in the real-life context of challenging politico-economic transition.

Some other examples from Ştefănescu's texts:

[. . .] this nation still has a chance, [. . .] we can't put our weapons down, [. . .] eventually we'll catch the train. [. . .] One of my friends [. . .] mumbled [. . .] "It's all over, mate! This country is all over and done with. The battery's dead!" It's like he hit me over the head with a two-by-four. And then I got even more worked up, and said: "I have to shout even louder on this program that Romanians still have a chance."[62]

No matter how hard it is for some of us now, we must learn to look towards the future and to think differently. Otherwise, we stand no chance. We'll be stumbling in the dark.[63]

We hope with all our hearts that you receive this program as [. . .] a fight against the frost that sometimes threatens the mind of the Romanian. And if not the mind, the courage to overcome harder moments,

To be Romanian in Post-Communist Romania 153

troubles, inertia, [. . .] dragging along, living in exaggerated memories, insecurities, frustrations [. . .][64]

This last passage is particularly relevant for discussion—"inertia" and "dragging along" are explicit references to public voices that regretted the fall of communism. At the same time as most of the host's remarks and demeanor were humorous and casual, Ştefănescu was always firm that we must not regret the communist past. He fervently spoke against resigned voices that stopped believing in democratization and mourned the old regime—in a sense, all of *Garantat 100%* is a cry of support for the Romanian that can. A repeated question asked on-set guests, "What do you think is stalling us?"[65] The majority of invited celebrities also regarded Romania to have favorable chances, in the efforts to join NATO and in general—to adapt to a European, democratic system, to make necessary changes for a more just (and less corrupt) infrastructure, and so forth. Many were optimistic about Romania's future; but not all, and Ştefănescu pressed the latter for arguments and explanations. Again, the goal was to change people's mentality (to mend their own fence), and so the conversations must necessarily be constructive.

Finally, a comment on authenticity bears note. It can be seen perhaps as slightly paradoxical that *Garantat 100%* promoted local values, stories and people and proclaimed itself to be 100% local, Romanian and yet it borrowed a Western format and sometimes recontextualized ideological content (such as the Protestant work ethic or North American talk show models). Moreover, in Ştefănescu's words at the end of the 2001 season, the show has promoted an alternative to the "sea of Western and Eastern garbage that has invaded us lately!"[66] The fact that the host only alluded on this one and only occasion to the wave of occidental content that his program has been competing with fits with the positive and non-competitive tone of the show, but also may be seen as diplomatic in not drawing attention to its not quite 100% autochthonous packaging. Instead, his emphasis is on calls to action and to boldness in his advocacy for transitioning Romania.

CONCLUSION

Patriotic discourse at *Garantat 100%* is a sum of strategies that shapes and defines a Romanian to be celebrated, promoted and aspired to. The strategies include a strong emphasis on exceptional examples—be they documentary subjects or on-set guests—coupled with an elevation of the ordinary Romanian to the status of the out-of-the-ordinary, as well as a forward-looking orientation towards improving living in the country. This celebratory discourse is unique in the landscape of popular discourses in the early 2000s Romania. It is neither embracing tradition for the sake of tradition, nor is it advocating for all things Western. It is neither nationalistic nor

154 *Adina Schneeweis*

extremist, nor is it a demoralized manifestation of being Romanian in transition. The patriotism that Ştefănescu sells with enthusiasm and great stage performance is rooted in local, rural and urban, stories, people, and outstanding or quirky living. It is genuine. It is 100% guaranteed.

I asked at the outset what story of the Romanian *Garantat 100%* sold and I extensively described the Romanian citizen that the patriotic discourse of *Garantat 100%* constructed and endorsed: the extraordinary Romanian who moves forward, who is ready for democracy, who sheds nostalgia for the past and who takes responsibility for his/her life and future. This celebrated version of the Romanian constitutes an important (and often unheard) element on the public stage—it is the Romanian that neither fails in competition to European neighbors, historical figures or American artistic and athletic celebrities, nor is this Romanian always superior in such comparisons. *Garantat 100%* neither criticized unnecessarily, nor did it ignore the country's struggles[67]—especially in the context of the politico-economic efforts towards joining NATO and the EU.

I also suggested that the show must include attention to the everyday audience member. To garner large audiences and stand out among its competitors within the public and commercial entertainment field, the program must therefore sell its story to a national, predominantly rural and small urban audience. I showed the moderator's strategy in order to both entertain, by offering uniqueness, novelty and peculiarity, and educate, by advocating for a rigorous, responsible living. The talk at *Garantat 100%* spoke about autochthonous values and culture in such a manner that the program is (still today) one of the few on Romanian television (public and commercial) that displays confidence and positivity. As such, the program celebrates, proclaims and pushes for the localization (or indigenization) of entertainment television as the 'solution for Romania' in democratizing times. In conclusion, I argue that the producers of this program have managed to demonstrate that a program such as *Garantat 100%* can and does succeed—not only by speaking to specific audience needs, but also by ideologically swimming against the current.

NOTES

1. *Garantat 100%*, June 30, 2001.
2. Idem.
3. Norman Fairclough, *Media Discourse* (London: Blackwell, 1995); Teun A. van Dijk, "The Interdisciplinary Study of News as Discourse," in *A Handbook of Qualitative Methodologies for Mass Communication Research*, ed. Klaus Bruhn Jensen and Nicholas W. Jankowski, 108–120 (London: Routledge, 1999).
4. Michel Foucault, *The History of Sexuality: An Introduction*, vol. 1 (New York: Vintage Books, 1990).
5. Norman Fairclough, *Discourse and Social Change* (Cambridge: Polity Press, 2004).

To be Romanian in Post-Communist Romania 155

6. Fairclough, *Media Discourse*; van Dijk, "News as Discourse."
7. I gathered personal observations in the 2000–2002 time frame, when I worked as reporter and editor for *TVR Cluj*.
8. *Garantat 100%* received the 2002 UNITER (Uniunea Teatrală din România/ The Theater Union of Romania) Prize for Best Entertainment Show in Romanian Television, the 2002 CNA (Consiliul Național al Audiovizualului/ National Council of Audiovisual) Prize for Best Local Television Program, as well as the APTR (Asociația Profesioniștilor de Televiziune din România/ The Association of Television Professionals in Romania) Prize for Best Cultural Program and Best Magazine Program between 2003 and 2006. For all these awards, it competed with many other public and commercial television programs. See "Cătălin Ștefănescu," TVR, , http://www.tvr.ro/prezentator.php?id=279 (accessed June 15, 2011).
9. Also see "TedxBucharest: Cătălin Ștefănescu," TED, http://tedxtalks.ted.com/video/TEDxBucharest-Catalin-Stefanesc (accessed July 5, 2011).
10. Mihai Coman, *Mass Media în România Post-Comunistă* (Iași: Polirom, 2003).
11. The most recent development is the Senate's rejection of a proposal by a National Liberal Party member for the "Law of the Journalist" in March 2011. See Mediafax, "Legea jurnalismului depusă de Ghișe, respinsă de Comisii din Senat," *Mediafax*, March 22, 2011, http://www.mediafax.ro/cultura-media/legea-jurnalismului-depusa-de-ghise-respinsa-de-comisii-din-senat-8085629 (accessed June 14, 2011).
12. *TVR* has several offshoot national channels, *TVR1*, *TVR2*, *TVR3*, *TVR Info*, *TVR Cultural*, and the internationally broadcast *TVR i*. It also has five regional stations, which broadcast locally and sometimes contribute content for the nation-wide channels—*TVR Cluj*, *TVR Timișoara*, *TVR Craiova*, *TVR Iași*, and *TVR Târgu-Mureș*.
13. Alina Mungiu-Pippidi, "From State to Public Service: The Failed Reform of State Television in Central Eastern Europe," in *Reinventing Media: Media Policy Reform in East-Central Europe*, ed. Miklós Sükösd and Péter Bajomi-Lázár, 31–62 (Budapest: Central European University Press, 2003).
14. Henry Carey, "From Big Lies to Small Lies: State Mass Media Dominance in Post-Communist Romania," *East European Politics and Societies* 10 (1996): 44.
15. Petre Berteanu, "Romanian Nationalism and Political Communication: Greater Romania Party [Partidul România Mare], a Case-Study" in *Moral, Legal and Political Values in Romanian Culture: Romanian Philosophical Studies IV*, ed. Mihaela Czobor-Lupp and J. Stefan Lupp, 161–176 (Washington, D.C.: The Council for Research in Values and Philosophy, 2002); Cosmina Tănăsoiu, "Intellectuals and Post-Communist Politics in Romania: An Analysis of Public Discourse, 1990–2000," *East European Politics and Societies* 22 (2008), 80–113.
16. Rogers Brubaker, "In the Name of the Nation: Reflections on Nationalism and Patriotism," *Citizenship Studies* 8 (2004): 115–127.
17. Idem, 120.
18. Berteanu, "Romanian Nationalism"; Tănăsoiu, "Intellectuals."
19. In translation, the Greater Romania Party.
20. Tănăsoiu, "Intellectuals," 100.
21. *Garantat 100%*, June 30, 2001.
22. Romania joined NATO in 2004 and the EU in 2007.
23. "Cine a rezistat peste un deceniu la TV," Click!, http://www.click.ro/actualitate/bucuresti/rezistat-deceniu-TV-FOTO_0_1104489613.html (accessed June 15, 2011).
24. *Garantat 100%*, January 13, 2001.

156 *Adina Schneeweis*

25. Throughout the analyzed season, the program revolved around the moderator, from his entrance on the set, to applause of two dozens spectators, to his opening speeches, to his interviews with popular figures, crowned at the close of each episode with the *Garantat 100%* medal. Ţambal music (a type of dulcimer) played live by musician Darie Iordache peppered the conversation. The set colors—furniture and décor—were casual, dominated by bright yellows and blues. Four cameras caught close-ups with the host and his guest, the music artist and audience members, as well as wider shots to establish a relaxed, comfortable mood.

26. "Garantat 100%," Port.ro, ,] http://port.ro/garantat_100/pls/fi/films.film_page?i_perf_id=10664744&i_topic_id=1 (accessed June 15, 2011).

27. Idem.

28. To name a few, on *TVR1*, *Surprize! Surprize!* (*Surprises! Surprises!*, a show that surprises individuals with things they wish for, such as seeing estranged family members) and *Iartă-mă* (*Forgive Me*, a program for families and individuals that attempt to resolve emotional issues); on the commercial station *Antena 1*, *Din Dragoste* (*Because of Love*, with struggling couples asking for forgiveness) and *Academia Vedetelor* (*Star Academy*, a singing reality TV show).

29. In translation, *Impact*, a program similarly structured, with short films about exceptional Romanians, but without on-set guests. It often included translated foreign documentaries about non-Romanian topics. *Impact* never rose above the audience ratings of the other competing commercial stations *Pro TV* or *Antena 1* at the time of its broadcast.

30. *The News of This Saturday* (a *Saturday Night Live*-type program, with heavy emphasis on skits).

31. See Isabela Ieţcu, "Argumentation, Dialogue and Conflicting Moral Economies in Post-1989 Romania: An Argument against the Trade Union Movement," *Discourse & Society* 17 (2006), 627–650.

32. Foucault, *History of Sexuality*.

33. Diane Macdonell, *Theories of Discourse: An Introduction* (Oxford: Basil Blackwell, 1986); Richard Terdiman, *Discourse / Counter-Discourse: The Theory and Practice of Symbolic Resistance in Nineteenth-Century France* (Ithaca, NY: Cornell University Press, 1985); van Dijk, "The Interdisciplinary Study."

34. See footnote 8.

35. André de Peretti, Jean-André Legrand and Jean Boniface, *Tehnici de comunicare* (*Communication Techniques*), trans. Gabriela Sandu (Iaşi: Polirom, 2001).

36. *Garantat 100%*, January 27, 2001.

37. Idem, March 3, 2001.

38. Idem, March 31, 2001.

39. Idem, June 9, 2001, when Andreea Marin (now Marin Bănică), a television presenter and Romanian celebrity, was the guest.

40. Idem, June 23, 2001, when Romanian actor, folk musician, theater director and radio director Florian Pittiş was the guest.

41. Idem, June 30, 2001.

42. Ion Biberi, *Arta de a scrie şi de a vorbi in public* (*The Art to Write and Speak in Public*) (Bucureşti: Editura Enciclopedică, 1972), 75, 115.

43. The themes of 'the Romanian' and of the 'solution for Romania' most directly contribute to this discourse, yet all the identified topics supply evidence of *Romanianism*. See Table 8.1 and the previous section.

44. Over two-thirds of his opening texts start from Ştefănescu's experience (78.26%), whereas in a third of his texts he invokes acquaintances' stories (34.78%).

To be Romanian in Post-Communist Romania   157

45. *Garantat 100%*, January 20, 2001.
46. Idem, March 17, 2001.
47. Idem.
48. *Garantat 100%*, February 3, 2001.
49. Ibidem, March 17, 2001.
50. Idem, April 7, 2001.
51. See Igor Primoratz, "Patriotism," *Stanford Encyclopedia of Philosophy*, Spring 2010, http://www.science.uva.nl/~seop/archives/spr2010/entries/patriotism/ (accessed July 1, 2011).
52. *Garantat 100%*, March 24, 2001.
53. Idem.
54. Idem, March 17, 2001.
55. Idem, March 24, 2001.
56. Idem, March 24, 2001
57. Idem, January 27, 2001.
58. Idem, March 24, 2001.
59. Idem, February 3, 2001.
60. Idem, February 24, 2001.
61. Idem, January 20, 2001; emphasis added.
62. Idem, May 5, 2001.
63. Idem, February 3, 2001.
64. Idem, February 24, 2001.
65. Idem, May 5, 2001.
66. Idem, June 30, 2001.
67. Allusions to a Romanian lazier work ethic than the western examples public discourses praise and seek to emulate feature in several episodes; see *Garantat 100%*, April 28, 2001; Idem, May 5, 2001; Idem, June 2, 2001.

REFERENCES

Bandura, Albert. 1977. *Social Learning Theory*. Englewood Cliffs, NJ: Prentice-Hall.

Berteanu, Petre. 2002. "Romanian Nationalism and Political Communication: Greater Romania Party [Partidul România Mare], a Case-Study." In *Moral, Legal and Political Values in Romanian Culture. Romanian Philosophical Studies IV*, edited by Mihaela Czobor-Lupp and J. Stefan Lupp, 161–176. Washington, D.C.: The Council for Research in Values and Philosophy.

Biberi, Ion. 1972. *Arta de a scrie și de a vorbi in public (The Art to Write and Speak in Public)*. București: Editura Enciclopedică.

Brubaker, Rogers. 2004. "In the Name of the Nation: Reflections on Nationalism and Patriotism." *Citizenship Studies* 8: 115–127.

Carey, Henry. 1996. "From Big Lies to Small Lies: State Mass Media Dominance in Post-Communist Romania." *East European Politics and Societies* 10: 16–45.

Click!. "Cine a rezistat peste un deceniu la TV." http://www.click.ro/actualitate/bucuresti/rezistat-deceniu-TV-FOTO_0_1104489613.html. (Accessed June 15, 2011).

Coman, Mihai. 2003. *Mass Media în România Post-Comunistă*. Iași: Polirom.

de Peretti, André, Jean-André Legrand and Jean Boniface. 2001. *Tehnici de comunicare (Communication Techniques)*. Translated by Gabriela Sandu. Iași: Polirom.

Fairclough, Norman. 1995. *Media Discourse*. London: Blackwell.

Fairclough, Norman. 2004. *Discourse and Social Change*. Cambridge: Polity Press.

158 Adina Schneeweis

Foucault, Michel. 1990. *The History of Sexuality: An Introduction, Vol. 1.* New York: Vintage Books.

Gerbner, George, Larry Gross, Michael Morgan and Nancy Signorielli. 1986. "Living with Television: The Dynamics of the Cultivation Process." In *Perspectives on Media Effects*, edited by Jennings Bryant and Dolf Zillmann, 17–40. Hillsdale, NJ: Lawrence Erlbaum.

Iețcu, Isabela. 2006. "Argumentation, Dialogue and Conflicting Moral Economies in Post-1989 Romania: An Argument against the Trade Union Movement." *Discourse & Society* 17: 627–650.

Macdonell, Diane. 1986. *Theories of Discourse: An Introduction.* Oxford: Basil Blackwell.

Mediafax. 2011. "Legea jurnalismului depusă de Ghișe, respinsă de Comisii din Senat." *Mediafax*, March 22, 2011. http://www.mediafax.ro/cultura-media/legea-jurnalismului-depusa-de-ghise-respinsa-de-comisii-din-senat-8085629. (Accessed June 14, 2011).

Mungiu-Pippidi, Alina. 2003. "From State to Public Service: The Failed Reform of State Television in Central Eastern Europe." In *Reinventing Media: Media Policy Reform in East-Central Europe*, edited by Miklós Sükösd and Péter Bajomi-Lázár, 31–62. Budapest: Central European University Press.

Paler, Octavian. *Vremea întrebărilor.* Bucharest: Albatros, 1995.

Port.ro. "Garantat 100%." http://port.ro/garantat_100/pls/fi/films.film_page?i_perf_id=10664744&i_topic_id=1. (Accessed June 15, 2011).

Primoratz, Igor. 2010. "Patriotism." *Stanford Encyclopedia of Philosophy*, Spring 2010. http://www.science.uva.nl/~seop/archives/spr2010/entries/patriotism/. (Accessed July 1, 2011).

Tănăsoiu, Cosmina. 2008. "Intellectuals and Post-Communist Politics in Romania: An Analysis of Public Discourse, 1990–2000." *East European Politics and Societies* 22: 80–113.

TED. 2010. "TedxBucharest: Cătălin Ștefănescu." http://tedxtalks.ted.com/video/TEDxBucharest-Catalin-Stefanesc. (Accessed July 5, 2011).

Terdiman, Richard. 1985. *Discourse / Counter-Discourse: The Theory and Practice of Symbolic Resistance in Nineteenth-Century France.* Ithaca, NY: Cornell University Press, 1985.

van Dijk, Teun A. "The Interdisciplinary Study of News as Discourse." In *A Handbook of Qualitative Methodologies for Mass Communication Research*, edited by Klaus Bruhn Jensen and Nicholas W. Jankowski, 108–120. London: Routledge, 1999.

TVR. "Cătălin Ștefănescu." http://www.tvr.ro/prezentator.php?id=279. (Accessed June 15, 2011).

9 Post-Transitional Continuity and Change
Polish Broadcasting Flow and American TV Series

Sylwia Szostak

A typical weekday evening in an average household in Southwest Poland. A married couple in their early 40s are awaiting the evening showing of one of their favorite series, *M jak Miłość* (*L for Love*, TVP, 2000–). When 7:30 pm approaches, the wife is reminded that all the tasks still to be done need to be finished very quickly as in 40 minutes the episode will begin, marking the end of their working day. The husband, busy working in his garage, urges his wife: "Let me know when it starts" (Halawa 2006, 54). The broadcast time of the series is treated as a stable point, a ritual, around which other activities are structured, marking the shift into leisure time. This account, found in Mateusz Halawa's 2005 field research of the viewing habits of Polish audiences, reveals the essential features symptomatic of viewing habits in Poland, such as a heavy reliance on the broadcasting flow and the importance of the broadcaster as "the intermediary between the audience and the television text," which is not challenged by alternative modes of watching television (Green 2005, 280).

Contemporary Western media scholars may move away from studying traditional modes of watching television in favor of approaches emphasizing the model of convergence, where the broadcast stream is no longer the primary site for the experience of television, as it is disintegrated by the changes in content distribution that enable viewers to watch television on computer screens and mobile phones. For Poland, however, the more traditional approach remains predominant as the "living room only viewer" is still very much the essential concept for the discussion of television (Lotz 2007, 243). In 2009 an average Polish viewer consumed as many as 240 minutes of television (supplied by the broadcasting flow) each day, placing second to U.S. viewers, who watched 280 minutes per person per day (Gazeta Prawna 2010). While in 2010 the exposure to the broadcasting flow in Poland grew to 245 minutes per day (Wirtualne Media 2011b), watching television online was reported by only 21% of respondents (Centrum Badania Opinii Społecznej 2010). The broadcasting flow was not threatened by DVR devices either, which allow the users to record linear television and

160 *Sylwia Szostak*

then play back—*time-shift*—this content whenever or however they please (Carlson 2006, 102). Only 7.3% of Polish households were equipped with such devices in 2010 (Wirtualne Media 2011a). Roger Silverstone argues about television is no longer "an isolated media technology, [. . .] but one increasingly embedded into a converging culture of technological and media relationships that also involve computing and telecommunications" (Silverstone 1994, xi). In contrast, Polish viewing involves practices that contradict Silverstone's argument. Polish broadcasters have been introducing video-on-demand services, and experimenting with multiplatform content delivery but despite those efforts, *watching* television in Poland still takes place in 'the living room' and involves participation in a national broadcast culture.

As a result, Polish broadcasters are the main gatekeepers of the television experience. While in Poland linear broadcasting flow is the primary way to experience television, broadcast TV is losing prominence in television studies in this age of technological, economic and cultural convergence. In this shifting media culture "flow can thus seem like a relic of television's past, a descriptor that no longer captures the [. . .] complexity of what television has become" (Kackman et al. 2011, 1). Anglo-American academics may think that flow is dead but it is alive and well in Poland.

Polish viewers' reliance on broadcasting flow means that in order to see how audiences have been exposed to American TV serialized programming in the course of the transition from the state-controlled broadcasting to the free market paradigm, the broadcasting flow delivered by the terrestrial broadcasters is the place to look. I have chosen to concentrate on shows of American origin for two reasons. First, this type of programming, virtually absent in the pre-1989 era, began to gradually dominate the Polish broadcasting landscape in the 1990s. In Poland, the influx of foreign cultural imports has had its impact on the domestic conditions of scheduling, leading to the development of new practices—as it has in other countries before. What is more, as the Polish market matured, the content of Polish TV shows has been increasingly dictated by visual aesthetics, narrative conventions and storylines found in American shows. In this article, I demonstrate how broadcasters in a post-communist television system such as Poland incorporate American TV series in their industrial practice of scheduling. I address the organization of what Williams calls "an evening's viewing" (Williams 1974, 93). This day-part has a particular significance in Poland: this is where continuities from pre-1989 broadcasting are most visible. *Familiarity* and *innovation* are crucial concepts to understanding Polish scheduling practices. For the public broadcaster TVP1, providing schedules that conform to its tradition of broadcasting, and thus provide a viewing experience that is *familiar* to the viewers, is a significant, if not crucial, broadcasting objective. Polsat, a commercial broadcaster, on the other hand, consistently provides a different viewing experience by exercising innovative scheduling strategies. These binary scheduling practices, driven by *familiarity* and *innovation*, continue through 2011, at the time this article was written.

Primetime schedules "are the most carefully tailored to domestic viewer preferences, due to the economic importance of prime-time advertising revenues" (Havens 2007, 229). As a result, Havens suggests primetime schedules are the site of negotiation between both home-grown and non-domestic scheduling practices. The investigation of the primetime schedules of terrestrial broadcasters offers an opportunity for an overview of the ways in which American serialized programming has been used over the years to "create expectation, to foster audience habits, [and] to build up the channel's image" (Rizza 1994, 10). The case of TVP1 shows how familiarity proved more important than innovation. In comparison, the case of the commercial broadcaster, Polsat, which is free of pre-established scheduling practices, proves how the ability to experiment with programming strategies led to establishing a particular channel image.

CONTINUITY OR CHANGE?

The first channel of the public broadcaster TVP has been operating the longest in Poland, since 1952. For more than 30 years *Telewizja Polska* (TVP) functioned as a state-controlled broadcaster, whose output—often politicized and iconoclastic—was not only censored but also controlled directly by governing communist officials. The socio-political transformation that followed the collapse of the Soviet Union freed Polish television from the Soviet paradigm. Poland's Broadcasting Act, which set up the legal framework for the regulation of the newly introduced dual pluralistic model of media typical for Western countries, where both public and private media coexist, was passed on December 29, 1992, after three years of discussion. Yet, it took another five years for the licensing process to come to an end, creating a stable television environment in which the three major terrestrial broadcasters—TVP now a public service broadcaster, and its two commercial competitors Polsat and TVN, began operating.

TVP not only transformed into a national broadcaster but also began to play "a double role as public service broadcaster, with the advantages of State funding, and also a fully commercial television broadcaster," seeking advertising revenues (Open Society Institute, 2005, 1103). Under the Broadcasting Act public television may obtain income not only from license fees, penalties for late payment or non-payment of license fees, sponsorship, the sale of rights to programs but also advertising. The multichannel environment conditions that gradually emerged after the end of the licensing period, combined with the inability of TVP to sustain its functioning exclusively from license fees collection, forced TVP into fierce competition with its commercial counterparts for advertising revenue to ensure its survival. The drive to maximize advertising is particularly visible within primetime:

162 *Sylwia Szostak*

in December 1997 the first channel of TVP started artificially dividing the main news edition at 7:30 pm into different segments to increase the amount of advertising that may be broadcast, and has continued to do so ever since. The slot between 7 and 8 pm is divided as follows: a children's program—ads—news—ads—sports news—ads—weather forecast—ads—evening program forecast—ads (Open Society Institute, 2005, 1108). This illustrates that TVP1, despite being a public service broadcaster, competes for advertising revenue with its commercial counterparts, including Polsat.

The processes toward the creation of a stable dual television market brought about a shift in the function of TVP1: from state-controlled broadcaster to public service. This profound modification clearly forces the now almost 60-year history of TVP1 into a simple dichotomy, namely *pre-* and *post-*1989. The transformation in the media environment that came about as a result of the events of 1989 could then suggest a complete detachment from the 'tradition' of broadcasting from the pre-1989 period—marking a new era in Polish broadcasting (Paterson 1990, 30). My research, however, reveals that Polish broadcasting after 1989 is, in many respects, dependent on its past. This suggests that the transformation in the audiovisual sector, profound as it was, allowed for some practices from the pre-1989 broadcasting to survive, one of the evident examples being the primetime scheduling practices.

FRIDAY Sept 18	SATURDAY Sept 19	SUNDAY Sept 20	MONDAY Sept 21	TUESDAY Sept 22	WEDNESDAY Sept 23	THURSDAY Sept 24
7pm Wieczorynka – evening cartoon	**7pm** Wieczorynka – evening cartoon	**7pm** Wieczorynka – evening cartoon	**7pm** Wieczorynka – evening cartoon	**7pm** Wieczorynka – evening cartoon	**7pm** Wieczorynka – evening cartoon	**7pm** Wieczorynka – evening cartoon
7.30pm *Wiadomości* – news	**7.30pm** *Wiadomości* – news	**7.30pm** *Wiadomości* – news	**7.30pm** *Wiadomości* – news	**7.30pm** *Wiadomości* – news	**7.30pm** *Wiadomości* – news	**7.30pm** *Wiadomości* – news
8.10pm *Łatwa Forsa* (*Easy* *Money*) – U.S. feature	**8.05pm** *Pod* *Ostrzałem* (*Under Fire*) – U.S. feature	**8pm** *Matki, Żony* *Kochanki* (*Mothers,* *Wives,* *Lovers*) – domestic series	**8.10pm** *Gliniarz z* *Dżungli* (*The Sentinel*) – U.S. series	**8.10pm** *J.A.G.* – U.S. series	**8.10pm** *W sidłach* *miłości* (*Addicted to his* *Love*) – U.S. feature	**8.10pm** *Pan i pani* *Smith* (*Mr and Mrs* *Smith*) – U.S. series
9.50pm *W Centrum* *Uwagi* – evening magazine	**10.15pm** *MdM po* *Godzinach* – entertainment show	**9pm** *Program* *Rozrywkowy* – entertainment show	**9pm** *Zagraj w* *reklamę Vena* '99 – game show	**9pm** *W Centrum* *Uwagi* – evening magazine	**9.45pm** *W Centrum* *Uwagi* – evening magazine	**9pm** *W Centrum* *Uwagi* – evening magazine
10.05pm *MdM* – entertain- ment show		**9.20pm** *Decyzja* *należy do* *Ciebie* – evening magazine	**9.15pm** Teatr Telewizji – *Późne Kwiaty* – TV Theatre	**9.25pm** *Czas na* *Dokument* – documentary series	**10.05pm** *Kronika* *Kryminalna* – evening magazine	**9.20pm** *Życie Moje* – evening magazine
		10.05pm *Opinie* – evening magazine	**10.15pm** *W Centrum* *Uwagi* – evening magazine	**10.20pm** *Ktokolwiek* *Widział,* *Ktokolwiek* *Wie* – evening magazine		**9.50pm** *Automania* – entertainment show

Figure 9.1 TVP1 primetime schedule, September 18–24, 1998 (*Tele Tydzień*, 1998).

Post-Transitional Continuity and Change   163

In 1998, only a few months after the end of the licensing period, when the television market emerged in the form in which it remains today, TVP1 already had a well-established architecture for the primetime and thus a stable slot for entertainment programming, such as American TV series. Figure 9.1 shows a week's primetime schedule for TVP1 for September 18–24, 1998.

That week American serialized programming (highlighted in Figure 9.1) appeared three times in the slot following the main news edition at 7:30 pm, which, along with the evening cartoon, were two fixed points marking the transition into the evening's block of programming. This layout of primetime was symptomatic of the whole year's programming output, where American TV series had a fixed point in the schedules. American scripted series such as *Early Edition* (CBS, 1996–2000), *The Big Easy* (USA, 1996–97), *Nash Bridges* (CBS, 1996–2001), *Mr. and Mrs. Smith* (CBS, 1996), *Lace* (ABC, 1984) and *The Sentinel* (UPN, 1996–99) appeared throughout the year in the same slot after the evening news edition. This slot occupied by American series was not created as a result of the free market restructuring but had been a well-established one for entertainment programming, feature films and TV series alike—a tradition that goes as far back as 1960. This tradition is connected with the architecture of primetime that TVP1 has been adhering to ever since stable scheduling practices were established in the mid-1960s. The schedule structure of the first channel of the public broadcaster TVP remained faithful to the same basic practices that were used in the years of its pre-1989 monopoly.

When we look at the pre-1989 broadcasting past of TVP1, historical continuities in primetime scheduling practices become clear. Traditionally, the earlier part of this period on what was then the state broadcaster was thought of as a slot devoted to children's programming. This tradition goes as far back as 1962 when the first children's programming was broadcast as part of the programming slot known as *Dobranoc* (the word *dobranoc* means "goodnight") on Monday, October 1 as a five-minute program at 8 pm. *Dobranoc*, later called *Wieczorynka* (from the word *wieczór*, meaning "evening"), has moved in the schedule throughout the years: at the end of the 1960s it moved to 7:20 pm as a ten-minute program, then in the late 1970s a stable slot was established at 7 pm where it has remained up to 2011 when this article was written.

In a similar vein, the evening news program has been an equally essential element of primetime on TVP1. The tradition of news broadcasting in Poland goes as far back as 1956, when *Wiadomości Dnia* (*The News of the Day*) began to broadcast, which then changed its name to *Dziennik TV* (*TV Daily*) (Godzic 2005, 21). In 1985 the communist broadcasting authorities changed the name from *Dziennik TV* to *Dziennik Telewizyjny* (*Television Daily*), in order to eliminate the letter 'v' in the word 'TV' from the title as to disassociate the news edition from the victory sign that Solidarity leader Lech Walesa was known for giving (Godzic 2005, 11–15).

164 Sylwia Szostak

The role of the main news edition in the pre-1989 era was key to the whole broadcasting stream. It regulated the schedule: marking the end of daytime, mainly educational programming directed at school kids and youth, symbolizing the beginning of the 'main' broadcasting part—aimed at adult audiences—which consisted of first-run, non-educational programming, being the 'evening's main attraction' (Godzic 2005, 13–14).

This historical paradigm of primetime, with its stable positioning of evening cartoon and news, placed all entertainment programming aimed at adult audiences in the slot following *Dziennink Telewizyjny*. And so films and TV series as early as the 1960s began to be placed after 8 pm. In 1965 *Dr. Kildare* (NBC, 1961–1966) and *Stawka Większa Niż Życie (More Than Life at Stake)*, a Polish domestic TV series, were broadcast in that slot, just to provide few of many examples (*Radio i Telewizja* 1965). In the 1980s the tradition was still dominant and as a result imported TV series such as *Shogun* (NBC, 1980) and *Escrava Isaura* (*Isaura the Slave Girl*, Rede Globo, 1976–1977) were also placed in the slots following the evening news edition.

The profound transformation processes in the early 1990s, such as the transition into a public service broadcaster, the emergence of a commercial sector and finally the end of the licensing period in 1997, created potential for a deep change in the broadcasting practice. Yet TVP1 continued its traditional practice of scheduling children's television at 7 pm every evening followed by the main news edition at 7:30 pm. *Dziennink Telewizyjny* disappeared from the schedule on November 18, 1989, which was a symbolic end of the Soviet, highly politicized style of news broadcasting. Yet, it was immediately replaced by *Wiadomości* (*News*)—a news program for a democratic Poland. Since the slot for the evening news edition remained the same, entertainment programming (feature films and TV series) assumed their traditional slot after 8 pm. Even the time marking the beginning of the evening's entertainment slot has a historical legacy, as the evening block in the pre-1989 era always started soon after 8 pm, rarely at 8 pm sharp.

This primetime architecture became so strongly rooted in the broadcasting tradition of TVP that when the broadcaster became obliged to cater to Polish viewers living abroad, it decided to export not only Polish programming, but also the Polish experience of primetime. Poland's Broadcasting Act bestows upon TVP, as part of its public mission, an obligation to produce and transmit "national and regional program services [. . .] for reception abroad in the Polish language" (Broadcasting Act, article 21, 1992). In order to ensure that people of Polish descent and Poles living abroad have access to such programming, the Act guarantees the existence of a satellite channel—TV Polonia, as part of the public service broadcaster *Telewizja Polska—Spółka Akcyjna* (*Polish Television—Joint-Stock Company*)—broadcasting to Europe, and to Polish communities in the U.S, where the channel is also available as a video-on-demand service. Primetime on TV Polonia is constructed in an analogous way to the broadcasting

Post-Transitional Continuity and Change   165

service provided by TVP1, so that Polish viewers in Europe (at least in the countries within the same time zone) share the same evening experience as viewers at home, with the exception that the evening cartoon is broadcast 10, sometimes 15 minutes later and is called *Dobranocka* instead of *Wieczorynka*, as it is called on TVP1. *Dobranocka* opens primetime on TV Polonia at 7:10, sometimes 7:15 pm and is then followed by *Wiadomości* and entertainment programming at 8:10 pm, which, due to the channel's obligation to "transmit program services in the Polish language," consists of Polish films, series and other entertainment (Broadcasting Act, article 25, 1992). Watching *Dobranocka* and *Wiadomości* in real time is impossible for viewers outside of Europe, who live in different time zones. However, in order to provide Polish viewers in America with the same traditional Polish experience of primetime as can be enjoyed in Poland, TV Polonia broadcasts reruns of the evening cartoon for children at 1:15 am (CET) and calls them *Dobranocka za Oceanem* (*Dobranocka Overseas*), followed by a rerun of the main edition of the news *Wiadomości* at 1:30 am (CET). The reruns allow viewers in America (at least those living on the East Coast) to experience primetime as if they were watching it in Poland—children's cartoons, followed by news at 7:30 pm local time.

The example of TV Polonia and its attempts to recreate for viewers abroad the conditions of watching television as they remember it from their home country proves how significant it is not only to broadcast programming with which viewers are familiar but also to broadcast it in the very same context, namely at 7 and 7:30 pm respectively. Similarly, the case of TVP1, whose profound reconfiguration from a state broadcaster to a public one did not lead to significant changes in primetime construction, shows that scheduling relies not only on providing a certain type of programming but also on providing it in a framework that does not force viewers to abandon their established routines—habits of watching particular programs at particular times. This places this broadcasting practice among other temporal patterns of social life.

Eviatar Zerubavel contends that "the world in which we live is a fairly structured place," where our immediate environments are based on a certain degree of "orderliness" (Zerubavel 1981, 1). The fundamental parameter of this orderliness is time and so "most of our routine daily activities are scheduled in a fairly rigid manner for particular times of the day and for particular days of the week" (Zerubavel 1981, 7). In modern social life many events, activities and situations are routinely fixed at pre-arranged, often standard points in time. We very often eat not necessarily when we are hungry but during designated eating periods such as 'lunchtime.' We go to bed when it gets 'late,' not necessarily when we feel tired (Zerubavel 1981, 7). Television, argues Silverstone, has "colonised these basic levels of social reality" (Silverstone 1994, 4) and qualifies as what Zerubavel recognizes as *"sociotemporal order,* which regulates the structure and dynamics of social life" (Zerubavel 1981, 2).

166 *Sylwia Szostak*

As Zerubavel convincingly demonstrates, many of the rhythms that govern social life are purely conventional. Any socio-temporal order is "a socially constructed artefact which rests upon rather arbitrary social conventions," which reveals the artificial nature of social scheduling (Zerubavel 1981, xii). The fixed notions of what constitutes 'the proper time' for an activity is arbitrary and standard temporal locations of many activities in our lives may be located differently in other cultures (Zerubavel 1981, 9). In Poland the 7:30 pm news edition clearly marked the beginning of programming targeting adult audiences and was a customary time to put children to bed. The fact that it was precisely 7:30 pm and not 8:30 pm that marked bedtime for children, for example was nothing but an arbitrary custom—a routine—not necessitated by nature, rather, a matter of social convention alone, as are so many other patterns pertaining to when we do things, how often, how long, and in what order. In this sense the primetime of TVP1 is based on a purely arbitrary social convention. Because *Wiadmomości* and *Dobranocka* have continued to be broadcast in the same context since the 1970s, this has allowed "viewers to form routines of watching based on repetition" (Carlson 2006, 100). What emerged as a social, arbitrary convention, in Poland and other countries of the Soviet bloc, developed into a regulation of the family's life, especially of children, through TV schedules and was standardized throughout the Soviet empire. As a result, the context of primetime for Polish society has come to be perceived as "given, inevitable, and unalterable" (Zerubavel 1981, 42).

Paterson argues that the attachment to historical tradition in the schedule benefits both the broadcaster and viewer: "it allows a predictability or resource deployment within television organizations, and it makes particular schedule points easy to remember for audiences" (Paterson 1990, 38). Nora Rizza seems to agree, saying that once "viewing habits—linked to particular time-slots—[are] settled, it is thought to be suicidal to betray those expectations' (Rizza 1994, 15). TVP decided not to betray viewers' expectations, and despite the profound transformation brought about by the events of the year 1989 decided not to break the well-established tradition of broadcasting from the pre-1989 era and to stay faithful to the architecture of primetime with which viewers were familiar.

The case of TVP1 supports Paterson's claim that "The key to television schedules is still repetition and continuity" (Paterson 1990, 35). For TVP1 that continuity goes as far back as the 1960s and has obviously had a deterrent effect on the possibility of innovation. Placing different children's programming every night of the week along with the news in the lead-in period to central primetime has been continually preventing TVP1 from experimenting with scheduling practices with regards to this particular day-part, which have not changed much from the pre-1989 era. TVP1 with its attachment to the broadcasting tradition did not have enough room in the schedules to use American TV series resourcefully in the creation of broadcasting flow or to experiment with American scheduling practices.

As a result, American series have not been incorporated in innovative or resourceful ways. Their employment was determined by the historical paradigm; and the shift from state broadcasting to a free market model did not introduce any profound changes to the way this type of programming was scheduled. American serialized programming filled slots historically devoted to entertainment.

In this respect, for TVP1, the process of scheduling is more complicated than for that of its commercial competitors. TVP was bound by its broadcasting tradition; but the commercial channels that began operating in the 1990s did not have to deal with an existing historical paradigm. This lack of tradition became a "vacuum to be filled," which granted commercial broadcasters more freedom in the creation of "recognizable schedules and audience stability" (Rizza 1994, 15).

INNOVATION

Nora Rizza suggests that the less a broadcaster is rooted in tradition, the easier it is for them to adapt in the area of programming and scheduling (Rizza 1994, 16). This freedom is visible when looking at the schedules of Polsat, which, launched in 1992 and then licensed to broadcast in 1994, was not bound by any broadcasting tradition and had to build its entire schedule from scratch. Polsat therefore had more flexibility in structuring its output and, as a result, was able to set itself apart from the public service broadcaster, challenging, and ultimately breaking, TVP's monopoly of the broadcasting industry. American series were used in a number of ways to support and help the schedule of Polsat—ways entirely different from the strategies of TVP1—to provide a different viewing experience based on "high-quality entertainment: cult shows and foreign blockbuster movies" (Polsat). Figure 9.2 shows a late afternoon until late evening schedule for a week in the fall of 1998.

The analysis of one week's broadcasting output reveals programming strategies that were symptomatic of Polsat's programming in 1998. The lack of viewer routines to be respected allowed Polsat to employ the strategy of responding to TVP1's 7 pm slot with radically different program content— a strategy known as counterprogramming. While TVP1 broadcast children programming followed by news at 7:30 pm, Polsat identified audience segments whose needs were not being served by TVP1 in those slots and programmed to appeal to these by launching an entertainment format— American TV series (highlighted in Figure 9.2). By placing series such as *Lois & Clark: The New Adventures of Superman* (ABC, 1993–97) and *Renegade* (USA, 1992–97) in the 7 pm slot, Polsat aimed to direct the flow away from its competition (Eastman, Tyler, Head and Klein 1985, 13).

As "most viewers stay with a program from start to finish," scheduling an episode of *Lois & Clark* or *Renegade* at 7 pm—each an hour's duration

168   Sylwia Szostak

FRIDAY Sept 18	SATURDAY Sept 19	SUNDAY Sept 20	MONDAY Sept 21	TUESDAY Sept 22	WEDNESDAY Sept 23	THURSDAY Sept 24
5.45pm *Świat według Bundych (Married with children)* – U.S. series	**5.15pm** *Pacific Blue* – U.S. series	**4.45pm** *Miłość od pierwszego wejrzenia* – entertainment show	**5.45pm** *Świat według Bundych (Married with children)* – U.S. series	**5.45pm** *Świat według Bundych (Married with children)* – U.S. series	**5.45pm** *Świat według Bundych (Married with children)* – U.S. series	**5.45pm** *Świat według Bundych (Married with children)* – U.S. series
6.15pm *Pomoc Domowa (The Nanny)* – U.S. series	**6.10pm** *Xena (Xena: Warrior Princess)* – U.S. series	**5.20pm** *Jezioro Marzeń (Dawson's Creek)* – U.S. series	**6.15pm** *Pomoc Domowa (The Nanny)* – U.S. series	**6.15pm** *Pomoc Domowa (The Nanny)* – U.S. series	**6.15pm** *Pomoc Domowa (The Nanny)* – U.S. series	**6.15pm** *Pomoc Domowa (The Nanny)* – U.S. series
6.45pm *Informacje* – news	**7.05pm** *Disco Polo* – music promgram	**6.15pm** *Herkules (Hercules: The Legendary Journeys)* – U.S. series	**6.45pm** *Informacje* – news	**6.45pm** *Informacje* – news	**6.45pm** *Informacje* – news	**6.45pm** *Informacje* – news
7pm *Renegat (Renegade)* – U.S. series	**8pm** *Idź na całość* – game show	**7.05pm** *Idź na całość* – game show	**7pm** *Renegat (Renegade)* – U.S. series	**7.05pm** *Powrót Supermana (Lois & Clark: The New Adventures of Superman)* – U.S. series	**7.05pm** *Renegat (Renegade)* – U.S. series	**7.05pm** *Powrót Supermana (Lois & Clark: The New Adventures of Superman)* – U.S. series
8pm *Baza Pensacola (Pensacola: Wings of Gold)* – U.S. series	**8.50pm** Lotto	**8.10pm** *Strażnik Teksasu (Walker, Texas Ranger)* – U.S. series	**8pm** *One West Waikiki* – U.S. series	**8pm** *13 Posterunek* – domestic series	**8pm** *Był sobie złodziej (Once a thief)* – U.S. series	**8pm** *Coctail* – U.S. feature
8.50pm Lotto	**9pm** *Nocny Patrol (Baywatch Nights)* – U.S. series	**8.50pm** Lotto	**8.50pm** Lotto	**8.30pm** *Wiecej Czadu (Pump Up the volume)* – U.S. feature	**8.50pm** Lotto	**9.55pm** *Przybysz (The Visitor)* – U.S. series
9pm *Nikita (Femme Nikita)* – U.S. series	**10pm** *Snajper (Sniaper)* – U.S. feature	**9pm** *Tak zwany bohater (Some Kind of Hero)* – U.S. feature	**9pm** *Quest* – U.S. feature	**10.25pm** *Telewizyjne Biuro Śledzcze* – evening magazine	**9pm** *Ostry Dyżur (ER)* – U.S. series	
9.55pm *Posterunek Brooklyn (Brooklyn South)* – U.S. series					**9.55pm** *Ludzie Tajfuna (Typhon's People)* – U.S. series	

Figure 9.2   Polsat primetime schedule, September 18–24, 1998 (*Tele Tydzień*, 1998).

(including commercials)—caused them to run past the starting and stopping points for programs on TVP1 and prevented an audience from switching to TVP1 at 7:30 pm—a crossover point when *Wieczorynka* (evening cartoon) ended and *Wiadomości* (news) began (Eastman, Head and Klein 1985, 412). This strategy of bridging was similarly employed with the 8 pm slot, where Polsat scheduled its series 10 minutes before TVP1 did. James

Post-Transitional Continuity and Change 169

Tiedge observes that where a series has no competition beginning at the same time it "should be extremely likely to inherit the audience from the preceding program [within the same channel], since its [audience's] only other choices are to join a program already in progress on another network or turn off the set" (Tiedge and Ksobiech 1986, 61). By placing *One West Waikiki* (CBS, 1994–96) on Mondays and its domestically produced *13 Posterunek* (*Precinct 13*, Polsat/Canal+, 1997–1998) on Tuesdays at 8 pm, against respectively *The Sentinel* and *J.A.G.* at 8:10 pm on TVP1, Polsat was likely to lose very little of its audience to TVP1 as viewers would have to tune to the news edition already in progress or watch commercials waiting for a series to begin at 8:10 pm.

Besides using American series to compete with TVP1 on an hour-to-hour basis by using the strategy of counterprogramming, Polsat employed this type of programming to create synergy on two levels: horizontally, by broadcasting every day of the week, and vertically, by scheduling back-to-back within an evening's viewing. Those scheduling strategies were designed to maintain two types of audience flow, on a daily and weekly basis: flow from one program to another within the same day-part (in this case prime-time) and flow across the weekdays, from one day to the next. TVP1 never employed either of those strategies in its broadcasting practice, therefore the way Polsat incorporated American TV series was unprecedented within the Polish broadcasting environment and should be considered innovative.

Polsat experimented with the scheduling practice known as stripping programs, that is, "scheduling them Monday through Friday at the same time each day" (Eastman, Tyler, Head and Klein 1985, 11). This strategy is ideal for habit formation as it generates more viewer loyalty than a series of five different shows each week. Viewers know where to find a particular program and thus it is easier to form routines of watching around a stripped program. Polsat used this practice of stripping in scheduling *Married with Children* (FOX, 1987–97) at 5:45 pm and *The Nanny* (CBS, 1993–99) at 6:15 pm, Monday through Friday. By placing two stripped shows at the beginning of a late afternoon block of programming that would stretch into primetime, Polsat employed one of the most commonly used scheduling strategies—namely the lead-in placement strategy, which relies on the strength of the preceding program to boost the ratings of the program following it.

Another use of American TV series that demonstrated scheduling innovation and utilized genre more flexibly was scheduling TV series back-to-back. Polsat created synergy between programs belonging to the same broadcasting sequence. Shows were selected not on the basis of their thematic similarities but rather on that of genre homogeneity, creating a single block consisting of serialized, mostly American programming. Those blocks were long and could consist of up to seven programs. Such was the case with Polsat's Friday slot in 1998 when from 4:45 pm up until 11 pm, viewers were able to watch serialized programming with only two short breaks, which were devoted to a news edition at 6:45 pm and

170   *Sylwia Szostak*

a national lottery draw at 8:50 pm. Offering several adjacent programs of highly similar type or content is called block programming. The basic idea underlying this strategy is what Owen and Wildman call the principle of 'adjacency,' which suggests that "viewers are more likely to watch a program if they have watched the previous program or intend to watch the succeeding one on the same channel" (Owen and Wildman 1992, 54). Viewers "may be more likely to stay around for an immediately following program if it is of the same type" (Tiedge and Ksobiech 1986, 60). By beginning the afternoon block with a stripped programming that had strong habit formation power, Polsat used strong lead-ins to blocks of programming, where consistency in program genre/type across the block of programs was positively related to audience inheritance, thus promoting effective flow.

Susan Eastman, in her investigation of the American broadcasting environment, claims that "each station seeks a unique, positive image separating it from its competitors and giving the audience reasons to seek it out' (Eastman, Tyler, Head and Klein 1985, 188). In most markets, however, "finding the right counterprogramming formula is not quite so easy" (Eastman, Tyler, Head and Klein 1985, 91). Both comments are well suited to describe the Polish broadcasting context as well. Polsat, in order to offer its viewers a strong alternative to the types of shows available on other channels in the market and to maximize its audience potential and inevitably draw some viewers away from its competitors, employed the strategy of counterprogramming with specific programs, using American scheduling strategies and also developing a stronger overall program line-up than either competitor. What allowed Polsat to differentiate itself from its competition in terms of audience appeal and create a distinct overall channel design was the lack of a broadcasting tradition, which would have a deterrent effect on the programming strategies. Rizza claims that if a network does not have a broadcasting tradition, "it is impossible to give it one; the network will then have to make up for this lack by intensifying its efforts to define and communicate its identity" (Rizza 1994, 14). Polsat convinced its audience that the channel is really different from its competitors by developing a program-identified image—as an entertainment channel—and communicated this identity through both the type of programs broadcast and the way those were scheduled.

CONCLUSION

Looking at the scheduling practices of the two main players in the Polish broadcasting market, TVP1 and Polsat, at a time when the post-communist Polish television system was just taking shape, allows us to see how scheduling as an industrial practice developed in Poland and to establish what the roots of the scheduling strategies of Polish broadcasters are.

Post-Transitional Continuity and Change   171

A broadcaster can significantly affect its share of the available audience through "the proper use of scheduling strategies" (Adams 1997, 839). While TVP1 was bound by its tradition of broadcasting, Polsat, free of similar restrictions, possessed the resources to develop scheduling as "a specialized craft to stay current in the emerging climate of commercial competition, where efficient continuity strategies were needed in order to deliver heads to advertisers" (Ytreberg 2002, 286). In order to compete with TVP1, its biggest competitor in the market, to draw away its audience and then retain them by encouraging within-channel flow, Polsat began employing American programming strategies and imported American series to execute them.

In the atmosphere of competition, where TVP1 and Polsat equally compete over viewership and advertising revenue, both broadcasters have managed to secure a stable position in the market. Both channels of TVP have been consistently seizing the biggest audience share of 4+ demographics in an all-day perspective. In 2010 TVP1 captured 19.6% of the viewership, Polsat placed third with 13.7%, after the second channel of the public broadcaster (Wirtualne Media 2011c). When we look closely at primetime, referred to as peak time (6 pm–11pm) in Polish statistics, among 4+ demographics, the audience share of TVP1 is on average 20.6% in 2010, which is again a significantly larger share of the audience than Polsat at 14.6%. In peak time among 16–49 demographics Polsat and TVP1 go practically head-to-head, at an average of 16.9% and 16.6% respectively, in the first half of 2011. Polsat is ahead of TVP1 only among 16–49 demographic in urban areas whose population is over 100,000 residents, where in the period of January till May 2011, Polsat seized 14.2% of the audience (on average) leaving TVP1 slightly behind at 13% (TVN S.A, 2011). Viewership statistics illustrate that TVP1 is a more popular channel than Polsat, even in primetime. Polsat, however, manages to attract larger audiences in primetime among young city dwellers. Despite the fact that statistics stand testament to TVP's dominance over the Polish broadcasting industry, Polsat—the first national private terrestrial broadcaster, over the course of its 20-year existence, managed to secure itself a stable position alongside the public service one, which in the highly competitive market should be considered a huge achievement. This illustrates that the strategy of TVP1 to provide a familiar viewing experience and that of Polsat to counterprogram on the level of program type and their schedule, are both successful.

Because of this established success, as the market matures, the programming architecture of primetime on both TVP1 and Polsat remains the same. For TVP1, the general design of broadcasting that emerged in the pre-1989 era still remains the dominant paradigm and the conservational measures, which preserve certain types of established programming, such as *Wieczorynka* and *Wiadomości*, still prove more important than the commercial need to introduce a stronger lead-in to its primetime schedule. Similarly, Polsat remains faithful to its programming strategy established in the early

172 Sylwia Szostak

stages of the development of the dual Polish television market and it still employs American scheduling practices, such as daily stripping, block programming and counterprogramming.

In recent years, there has been a strong tendency to rely on Polish programming in primetime. This reveals what we already know about developing television markets: they go from heavy importation in their early years to domestic production as they mature. This trend, however, has not as of 2011 contributed to any profound changes in the way primetime is designed, in terms of the scheduling grid. The very same scheduling strategies are used on both channels, yet they are executed through a combination of American and Polish programming, with a growing number of domestic shows. Polish series are appearing in the slots previously occupied by American ones, thus primetime becomes predominantly 'domestic,' yet leaving the scheduling architecture, on both TVP1 and Polsat, virtually unaffected. Timothy Havens claims that scheduling is "both dynamic and always-already hybrid in today's world, and even the most powerful television markets are not immune from imported scheduling practices" (Havens, 2007, 235). As we have seen, the case of TVP1 and its traditional scheduling practices that retain their domestic character contradict Havens' position. The primetime scheduling grid of TVP1 has been 'immune' to foreign practices for more than 20 years now and is likely to remain domestic in its origin.

The schedules of Polsat and TVP1 contain "the distillation of the past history of a channel, of a national broadcasting as a whole, and of the particular habits of national life" (Ellis 2000, 26). The domestic Polish scheduling patterns of TVP1 and Polsat's employment of American programming strategies reveal that the concepts that have been at the center of the debate over the post-communist transition in the domain of politics, among others, namely of continuity and change, are also essential for the discussion of Polish broadcasting. The Polish experience might be distinctive in some ways but the observations made here may also correspond to other broadcasters from the region, as all Central and Eastern European nations went through, to a varying degree, similar processes of TV market restructuring.

REFERENCES

Adams, William J. 1997. "Scheduling Practices Based on Audience flow: What are the Effects on New Program Success? *Journalism and Mass Communication Quarterly* 74: 839–858.

Broadcasting Act. 1992. http//www.krrit.gov.pl/bip/eng/Documents/BroadcastingAct/tabid/374/language/pl-PL/Default.aspx. (Accessed August 10, 2010).

Carlson, Matt. 2006. "Tapping into TiVo: Digital Video Recorders and the Transition from Schedules to Surveillance in Television." *New Media & Society* 8: 97–115.

Post-Transitional Continuity and Change   173

Centrum Badania Opinii Społecznej. 2010. "Komunikat z badań: Korzystanie z komputerów i Internetu." ("Market Research: The Use of Computers and the Internet"). http://eregion.wzp.pl/var/cms_files/obszary_wykresy/si/2011/korzystanie_z_komputerow_i_Internetu_CBOS.pdf. (Accessed October 10, 2010).

Ellis, John. 2000. "Scheduling: The Last Creative Act in Television?" *Media, Culture & Society* 22: 25–38.

Eastman, Susan Tyler, Sydney W. Head and Lewis Klein, eds. 1985. *Broadcast/ Cable programming.* Belmont: Wadsworth Publishing Company.

Gazeta Prawna. 2010. "Polacy są mistrzami w oglądaniu telewizji." ("Polish viewers are Champions at Watching Television"). http://www.gazetaprawna.pl/wiadomosci/artykuly/474995,polacy_sa_mistrzami_w_ogladaniu_telewizji.html. (Accessed December 20, 2010).

Godzic, Wiesław, ed. 2005. *30 najważniejszych programów TV w Polsce.* (*30 Most Important TV Programs in Poland*). Warszawa: Wydawnictwo Trio TVN S.A.

Green, Joshua. 2005. "Network Acts of Translation: Young people, American Teen Dramas, and Australian Television 1992–2004." Ph.D. Diss., Queensland University of Technology.

Halawa, Mateusz. 2006. *Życie codzienne z telewizorem.* (*Daily Life with a TV Set*). Warszawa: TVN.S.A.

Havens, Timothy. 2007. "The Hybrid Grid: Globalization, Cultural Power and Hungarian Television Schedules." *Media, Culture & Society* 29: 219–239.

Kackman, Michael, Marnie Binfield, Matthew Thomas Payne, Allison Perlman and Bryan Sebok. 2011. *Flow TV: Television in the Age of Media Convergence.* New York: Routledge.

Lotz, Amanda D. 2007. *The Television Will be Revolutionized.* New York: New York University Press.

Owen, Bruce M. and Steven S. Wildman. 1992. *Video Economics.* Cambridge: Harvard University Press.

Open Society Institute. 2005. "Television across Europe: Regulation, Policy and Independence." http://www.soros.org/initiatives/media/articles_publications/publications/eurotv_20051011/voltwo_20051011.pdf. (Accessed June 20, 2011).

Paterson, Richard. 1990. "A Suitable Schedule for the Family." In *Understanding television*, edited by Andrew Goodwin and Garry Whannel, 30–41. London: Routledge.

Polsat. http://www.polsat.pl/O_Nas,2860/Historia,2863/index.html. (Accessed June 25, 2011).

Radio i Telewizja. 1965. (*Radio and TV*) 1–52.

Rizza, Nora. 1994. "Putting Programmes Together." *Réseaux* 2: 7–35.

Silverstone, Roger. 1994. *Television and Everyday Life.* London: Routledge.

Tele Tydzień. 1998. September 18–24.

Tiedge, James T. and Kenneth J. Ksobiech. 1986. "The 'Lead-in' Strategy for Prime-time TV: Does it Increase the Audience?" *Journal of Communication* 36: 51–63.

TVN S.A. 2011. "Miesięczne udziały w oglądalności." "Monthly audience viewership breakdown." http://www.tvn.pl/grupatvn/investor/27/news. (Accessed June 26, 2011).

Williams, Raymond. 1974. *Television: Technology and Cultural Form.* London: Fontana/Collins.

Wirtualne Media. 2011a. "Nielsen Audience Measurement będzie mierzyć PVR." ("Nielsen Audience Measurement will Assess PVR"). http://www.wirtualnemedia.pl/artykul/nielsen-audience-measurement-bedzie-mierzyc-pvr. (Accessed January 15, 2011).

174 *Sylwia Szostak*

Wirtualne Media. 2011b. "Polacy w 2010 spędzili więcej czasu przed telewizorem." ("In 2010 Poles Spent More Time in Front of the TV"). http://www.wirtualnemedia.pl/artykul/polacy-w-2010-spedzili-wiecej-czasu-przed-telewizorem. (Accessed January 5, 2011).

Wirtualne Media. 2011c. "W 2010 największe telewizje straciły widzów, najmniej TVN." ("In 2010 the Biggest Broadcasters Lost Viewers, TVN the Least"). http://www.wirtualnemedia.pl/artykul/w-2010-najwieksze-telewizje-stracily-widzow-najmniej-tvn. (Accessed June 25, 2011).

Ytreberg, Espen. 2002. "Continuity in Environments: The Evolution of Basic Practices and Dilemmas in Nordic Television Scheduling." *European Journal of Communication* 17: 283–304.

Zerubavel, Eviatar. 1981. *Hidden Rhythms: Schedules and Calendars in Social Life*. Chicago: Chicago University Press.

Part III
Television and National Identity on Europe's Edges

10 Big Brothers and Little Brothers
National Identity in Recent Romanian Adaptations of Global Television Formats

Alice Bardan

"Remember the Writers Guild strike in '88? That was the year that gave rise to reality TV."

(Tabloid TV pioneer Peter Brennan quoted in Raphael 2006, 129)

BIG BROTHER IN POST-SOCIALIST COUNTRIES

In a review of the most recent research on *Big Brother*, Liesbet van Zoonen and Minna Aslama (2006) note that audience studies of the famous reality show format found that the viewers' fascination emerges from the interest in simulated everyday occurrences in the Big Brother house as well as from guessing and assessing the 'authentic' versus the 'artificial' behavior of the participants. In contrast to cultural approaches that discussed *Big Brother* as a format belonging to the category of documentary and reality television, the critics invested in audience studies placed it in the genre of soap opera. As with soap operas, they claimed, the show's major appeal was due to audience investments in issues of authenticity and the self (91).

Annette Hill's surveys and interviews in the UK, for instance, found that the main interest and pleasure in the show had its origin in the process of distinguishing between 'the authentic' and 'the performed.' When asked what aspect of *Big Brother* they liked most, the majority of British respondents said that what they enjoyed was not the voyeurism it involves, but the mere fact of watching people live without modern comforts. This, Hill suggests, can be related to the fascination of observing how real people react in a manufactured situation when the lack of contact with the outside world forces contestants to interact and inevitably engage in conflict with each other (2002, 333). Questions of authenticity also seemed to attract German viewers.

Notwithstanding the theoretical value of such research, the majority of such studies focus primarily on countries such as Germany and England, which are both developed, individualized societies in which "the obsession with authenticity and the self builds on and is replicated in other media genres" (van Zoonen and Aslama 2006, 92). By contrast, in underdeveloped societies with stronger communal structures, the leading factors of impact accounting for the success of *Big Brother* were found to be different

178 *Alice Bardan*

(van Zoonen and Aslama 2006: 93). For instance, while *Big Brother Pan-Africa* and *Big Brother South Africa* were primarily discussed in terms of nation- or continent-building or read as an attempt at promoting cross-national tolerance, *Big Brother Middle East* (cancelled soon after its creation) was analyzed with respect to the debates it created concerning the clash between conservative Islamists and the young generations showing preference for Western desires.

While there are numerous publications on the show's popularity all over the world, conspicuously lacking from the literature on the subject are analyses of the show's appeal to Eastern European audiences. The study of reality television in Eastern Europe presents, as Aniko Imre (2011) rightly emphasizes, unique ethical, methodological, and disciplinary challenges. This is not only due to the relative obscurity of local national languages and traditions, but also to the fact that Eastern European critics tend to distance themselves from associations with forms of commercial television, which are almost always dismissed for lowering cultural standards (Imre 2011, 5).

So what happens when a reality show such as *Big Brother* is adapted for audiences in Eastern European countries that experienced totalitarian regimes and became overexposed to artifice, isolated, as they were, from the rest of the world? Moreover, are reality television shows received in the same way in these countries, given the fact that after 1989 they underwent similar transformations? Does the culturally situated audience in the post-socialist region employ the same strategies to appropriate and rearticulate the pre-packaged global formats of reality television, which Adina Popescu (2006) calls "entertainment prêt-a porter"? In other words, was the adaptation of the *Big Brother* format received similarly in countries with similar historical trajectories, such as Romania and Bulgaria? What distinguished the adaptations of this show in these countries? What are the viewers' attitudes in post-socialist countries about the value of privacy in reality television and how do these attitudes affect viewers' willingness to accept some of these programs' 'grand narrative' about surveillance and privacy in contemporary societies? By tracing examples of the processes of appropriating and adapting reality television in Romania, I will demonstrate how the indigenization of international programs is thoroughly embedded into a national discourse repertoire and the local media economy.

After a brief overview of the format's adaptation in Eastern Europe, I will focus on the reception of the Romanian version of the *Big Brother* format, whose failure I contrast to the Bulgarian version's fate.

When *Big Brother*, and Endemol product, was adopted with nationally specific variations in diverse television territories after its initial broadcast in the Netherlands (1999), these specificities included the reactions of the broadcasters involved to content that could be considered offensive or challenging to the norms expected of television in different countries. Thus, while some of the contestants of the first British series easily stripped off their clothes and even covered themselves with paint in order to make an

Big Brothers and Little Brothers   179

imprint of their bodies on the walls, the American contestants talked a lot about sex but did not take their clothes off. In Holland, they proved to be even more uninhibited than in Britain.

Of the Eastern European countries, Poland was the first to create its own version of *Big Brother* in March 2001. Despite criticisms of the show's low cultural value, *Wielki Brat* (*Big Brother*) attracted four million regular viewers, and six million viewers for the final episode (Raicheva-Stover 2006, 12). The sexual content on the show also generated a fierce debate in the strongly Catholic country, prompting several Polish film directors to write an open letter condemning the show's negative effects on its viewers.

Seven months later, a slightly adjusted format of the show was introduced in Russia as *Za Steklom* (*Behind the Glass*), also the country's first reality show. In this highly successful adaptation, three men and three women had to live together for 34 days in a one-room apartment in a hotel facing Moscow's Red Square. One-way mirrors allowed pedestrians to see into the bedroom, living rooms and bathrooms while security guards protected the glass. When Endemol threatened to initiate legal actions against *Za Steklom* on grounds that it was not licensed through them, the makers of the show insisted that the idea for such a program came to them after reading Yevgeny Zamyatin's futuristic novel *We* many years earlier. In this book, which also inspired George Orwell to write *Nineteen Eighty-Four,* people lived in glass houses where everything could be seen by everyone else (O'Flynn 2001). The show's producer stated that he conceived *Za Steklom* as an experiment to see how people would interact without television. Yet the success of the show came from its highly explicit sexual material, not from any engaging conversations: given the choice between beer and books, the young contestants went for the beer.

The former Yugoslav republics had their own version of a show similar in structure to the Big Brother franchise, *To Sam Ja* (*That's Me*). Although when it started out in 2004, this show was filmed in Macedonia with a Macedonian cast, by the third season its strategy changed and the ratings immediately increased. The newly advertised "first Balkan reality show" brought members from all six nations of the former Yugoslavia to live together as a model of post-conflict harmony. The show was framed as an effort to negotiate symbolically the ongoing ethnic, religious and regional tensions. Although the participants spoke five languages in the house (and no subtitling or dubbing was featured), the (officially defunct) Serbo-Croatian language became dominant, which attracted criticism for reproducing the linguistic hegemony of the former Yugoslavia (Volcic and Andrejevic 2009, 11). As Volcic and Andrejevic suggest, ironically, in this case "history repeated itself, first as tragedy and then as prime-time entertainment" (2009, 13). *To Sam Ja* was carried by the satellite channel MKTV SAT, and thus accessible to viewers of Yugoslav origin living across Europe, the U.S., Canada and Australia. The evening installment of *To Sam Ja* showcased

180 Alice Bardan

feedback from this international audience, displaying excerpts from telephone and text messages.

In the fall of 2006, TV Pink brought to Bosnian audiences the Serbian version of *Big Brother, Veliki brat,* whose ratings surpassed all expectations. This version also featured a multi-ethnic cast of characters, including a young man from Sarajevo, who competed for a prize of 100,000 Euros. *Veliki brat*'s first season aired simultaneously on B92 and RTV Pink's subsidiaries in Montenegro and Bosnia-Herzegovina. The airing of the show on B92 was surprising to many: this was a TV station famous for its critique of the Milosevic regime, and a trusted venue for independent journalism with a public service orientation in Serbia. To justify the decision to produce *Big Brother,* B92's director commented that if reality TV is our reality—that is, if all TV stations in the world broadcast reality shows, and if *Big Brother* remains a leader in programming formats, then B92 should aim to produce the best of the best reality TV shows (Hozic 2008, 156). The diary room in *Veliki brat* is called '*ispovedaonica,*' which means 'confessional' in Serbian. The main difference between the interviews in this room and in other versions of *Big Brother* is the way the Big Brother's voice is rendered. Unlike in most other versions, in this one the producers' voices are processed to give the illusion that the Brother always speaks in the same robotic way.

In Bulgaria, *Big Brother* was introduced as the country's first reality show in the fall of 2004, and immediately became the biggest media event in the country. The second season was even more successful than the first one, with 5% higher ratings. It 'changed everything' overnight, reviving the inert television market in Bulgaria and generating national discussions on taboo subjects such as bisexuality and homosexuality (Raicheva-Stover, 2006). The show featured a colorful combination of participants, whose personalities clashed. An Orthodox monk was selected in the casting process, but was prevented from participating by the church. In only three months, the show not only transformed Bulgarians' understanding of how contemporary television is made and how to maximize advertisement revenue but also gave new insights on the TV viewer's agency. According to Alexander Boytchev (2005), *Big Brother* Bulgaria demonstrated the enormous potential gain that could be made out of SMS voting. In addition, the show's website advertised a special e-card that allowed those who purchased it to watch what happened in the house at all times. In addition, those who paid more could get news updates on their cell phones and listen to what was going on in the house via a special 'spyline' (Raicheva-Stover 2006). Although the big prize was double that offered in the Romanian version of the show (about 100,000 EUR), it ended up gaining six million Euros in advertising revenues for Nova TV, the broadcaster.

In the Czech Republic, commercial stations were reluctant to bring reality TV shows to their public, as investment in this type of entertainment was considered too risky and expensive in an environment with an allegedly conservative audience. Such concerns, which were publicly expressed

Big Brothers and Little Brothers 181

at least up until 2003, were dismissed in 2005, when TV Prima launched a version similar to *Big Brother*, *VyVolení* (*The Chosen Ones*). Only two weeks later, TV Nova, the Czech Republic's leading commercial broadcaster (backed by its multinational owner CME), started broadcasting *Velký Bratr*, the licensed version of the same reality show, as a direct response to its competitor. However, it was the "fake Big Brother" from TV Prima that attracted the highest audience, eventually managing to force the franchised version off primetime (Štětka 8). *Velký Bratr* is especially remembered for the controversy it created when one of its contestants, Filip Trojovsky, admitted to having acted in gay porn films (under the name Tommy Hansen), even though he denied being gay. When Filip was voted immediately out of the house as a punishment for his past actions, the show's ratings dropped significantly. As a result, he was voted back in the house, and the voting was changed from 'evict' to 'save contestant.' Filip started a heterosexual relationship in the house, and managed to stay until the show's finale in December 2005.

As in many other Eastern European countries, the Czech version of *Big Brother* led to numerous criticisms and debates on both sides of the political spectrum regarding the role of privacy and the display of nudity on TV. On several occasions, the Czech Broadcasting Council fined TV Prima for breaking the Broadcasting Act (mainly due to inappropriate content aired before 10 pm); but its decisions were later revoked by the court to which the cases were brought (Štětka 9). Significantly, however, the two shows opened the door for the adaptation of other global reality television formats, which have permeated the Eastern European market in the past several years.

BIG BROTHER: AN UNSUCCESSFUL FORMAT FOR ROMANIA

> "It may have duped the Germans, the Italians, the Danes, the Finns and Brits. But it just couldn't fool us Romanians." (Comment on *Big Brother* Romania posted by "Monitoxous," April 27, 2004, 17:14; author's translation)[1]

The first of the two Romanian series of *Big Brother*, *Fratele cel Mare*, was broadcast on Prima TV in 2003, and lasted 113 days, from March 16 to July 6, 2003. Despite the big buzz created by aggressive television and billboard advertising, the show did not attract a large audience as its producers had anticipated. Romanian audiences proved to be too skeptical of the show and ultimately too distrustful of the selection procedures. The fiasco happened at all levels. Within two months of its first airing, the National Audiovisual Council rebuked the *Big Brother* franchise for being an Orwellian nightmare that had come true. Accusing the producers of violating the human rights of its live-in cast by filming them incessantly, even

182   *Alice Bardan*

in the bathroom, the Council ordered producers to give contestants some means to escape the cameras and to "respect human dignity, the rights of participants, and family values" (quoted in Nadler 22). This contrasted sharply with the Bulgarian case, for instance, where *Big Brother* was condoned by officials and where the chief secretary of the Interior Ministry visited the house, subsequently praising its high-tech equipment.

The first season's failure with the audience was an unexpected shock for the Romanian producers. Nobody could really explain why this happened, but the blame fell either on the lack of sex on the show or on the fact that the participants were not attractive enough. Most of them were too shy and reluctant to undress in front of the cameras or engage in personal physical relations. Since the house where they lived was packed with video cameras and microphones, the female contestants showered with their bathing suits on, and one even brought a cape from home to cover themselves when they were taking a shower. The newspapers took this as a sign of inhibition, and started comparing *Big Brother Romania* with its Western versions, where the participants had no qualms about engaging in sexual adventures.

For the 2004 edition, the second and last, the producers changed the selection criteria and cast younger, better-looking and bolder contestants. They also raised the stakes of the show by increasing the final prize to $75,000. As predicted, some participants who were very much aware of the producers' concerns started walking around the house naked, were less conscious of their gestures and did not shy away from having sex. Romania's broadcasting authority, The National Audiovisual Regulatory Agency (known as CNA), felt obliged to take note. Sharply criticizing the show, CNA stated that its fly-on-the-wall format would compromise the dignity of the participants in the long term. CNA president Radu Filip declared that by offering a large amount of money to participants so that they would undress and have sex, the show promoted a form of prostitution in disguise. Some members of the parliament and of the Orthodox Church also expressed their outrage. CNA ordered an interruption of the program for 10 minutes and imposed the most severe sanctions against a broadcaster in Romania to date. During those 10 minutes, Prima TV had to show the CNA decision on screen, indicating that by broadcasting pornographic content, the show had infringed certain provisions of the Audiovisual Act (No. 504/2002) (Stoican 2004, 30).

Romanian newspapers seized the moment to capitalize on what happened. Some speculated that the participants were merely looking to have sex to increase ratings, and there was a general distrust regarding the voting process. On popular internet portals and discussion lists, viewers expressed their suspicions that their votes would not count, since Prima TV producers allegedly made the selections themselves. Writing for *Curierul National*, Simona Tudorache (2004) wondered:

Big Brothers and Little Brothers 183

We don't know if what happened on *Big Brother* was paid by the male participant, and we don't know what 'bonus' they will get for this [. . .] Rejected by 'Aly,' the 'little sister' opted, eventually, for another 'little brother' [. . .] Andrea admitted many times that she has sex for money. Daniel is a barman and in the house he plays a sort of 'neighborhood Don Juan.' Serban Huidu's [the host of a popular fake news show on Prima TV] presence in the *Big Brother* studio, who was specifically brought to deal with the CAN fines, made it all seem that it was a big fake, a made-up show to increase audience ratings.

In another article suggestively titled "The Double Trap," Florin Antonescu (2004) warned that both ordinary viewers and the media merely fell into the trap set by the show's producers and provided free advertising for the show. Such comments illustrate how in Romania, the controversy surrounding the show was not merely sparked by questions surrounding the contestants' authenticity but also by widespread cynicism at the time toward institutional selection processes as well as a deep distrust in Romanians' ability to produce adapted shows which would maintain the quality of their Western counterparts.

Colin Sparks (2007) has noted that contrary to public perception, shows such as *Big Brother* often end up being expensive. Indeed, as in the Bulgarian case, Prima TV spent around $2 million each season for one of the most aggressive campaigns to promote a Romanian television show. This money was ultimately recuperated from advertisement revenue, but it represented only a quarter of the profit made by *Big Brother Bulgaria*. Although its producers cited the enormous success of *Big Brother* all over the world and created a huge horizon of expectations, *Big Brother Romania* did not manage even for one week to withstand competition from its biggest rivals for television ratings, Pro TV, Antena 1 and Romania 1.

The irony was that when faced with a choice between the grand finale of the show on July 2003 and a 1973 Indian box-office hit showing on Antena 1 at the same time, Romanians chose the latter (18% versus 12% in ratings for the finale). They did so because the screening of *Yaadon ki Baaraat* (*Procession of Memories*, Nasir Hussain), starring Raj Kapoor and Salman Khan, brought back powerful images associated with communism. For Romanians, watching this film offered a chance to nostalgically recuperate some pleasant associations with their communist youth, when Hindi cinema was popular, as well as to recall memories of specific film-viewing contexts during communism and the dispositions attached to those contexts. As Bradeanu and Thomas (2006) astutely note, in present-day Romania such traces from the past "coexist with and feed a new cosmopolitanism, based largely within popular mass culture" (144). Whereas in the past the cultural elite mocked Hindi cinema's success with the public, "today there is a growing awareness that Romanians have become consumers of a new

184   *Alice Bardan*

transnational popular culture in which fusion, quotation, irony, parody and hybridisation are all the rage" (2006, 144).[2]

On the surface, the reason for the Romanian preference for an old Indian film over the *Big Brother* finale may be that the people were nostalgic for communist-era experiences. However, this 'nostalgia' has to be understood as eliciting and evoking a wide range of affective memories. In this case, affective memories may involve not necessarily the plot of the Hindi film, but how going to the cinema to see the film's special screening around Christmas time meant that one risked having the apartment broken into by gangs who stole nothing but the (pork) delicacies painstakingly prepared by families. Since food was hard to find at the time, gangs coordinated their operations with the screenings for the successful Indian films, when people "dared" to leave their houses and headed for the unheated theaters (Bradeanu and Thomas 2006, 142). [3]

Daniela Zeca-Buzura, who has studied the scant online forum discussions on *Big Brother* Romania, notes that approximately 78% of the participants addressed the format's poor fit with the Romanian public (2007, 119). This illustrates the extent to which Romanians were preoccupied with the image that they project for themselves and for others. While the concern with CNA's fines and interdictions faded quickly, it subsequently made room for a larger discussion on 'the freedom of self-expression' and 'cyberdemocracy.' Out of the 1,000 messages posted on various internet fora in connection with *Big Brother*, 58% debated the evolution of Romanian mentalities and the question of public morality, 22% talked about the money at stake and the making of celebrities, 17% were impressed by the participants' courage to be on the show and decided they would have enjoyed doing so themselves and, significantly, only a remaining 6% were interested in the candidates' profiles and the intrigues in the house (Zeca-Buzura 2007, 120).

The sex on the show, which seemed strategically calculated to increase ratings, did not impress Romanians, unlike in the case of so many other franchised editions. One forumite, 'Jonny Bravo,' for instance, decried that the show lacked the necessary tension conducive to interesting sex scenes, and therefore labeled the show "boring and obscene." For him, it was only when *Big Brother* Romania showed the female participant taking a shower that his interest was piqued, as he wondered if her body would be revealed.

One forumite in particular, 'Alinus,' seemed to synthesize the general tendency of Romanian viewers to blame their own allegedly "weak" national character. Speaking of the Romanian participants' inclination to wallow in self-pity and disappointed that this "flaw" was rewarded by the voters, 'Alinus' bemoaned: "This is relevant to our spirit. [. . .] remember 'Mioritza'? or Ana from 'Mesteru Manole'? We always praise the weakest ones [. . .] make them our heroes."[4] In other words, he rejected what he read as a presumably "Romanian" vulnerability in the participants, a character trait that for him conflicted with neoliberal ideas of self-improvement and competitiveness.

Big Brothers and Little Brothers   185

'Alinus' referenced two of the best-known pieces of Romanian folklore, endlessly recycled in works of 'high' national literature and widely discussed under communism. The pastoral ballad "Miorița" ("The Little Ewe") is about an enchanted ewe who tells her Moldavian shepherd that the shepherds from other regions are plotting to murder him. The shepherd replies that were this to happen, she should bury his body and tell the rest of the sheep that he married a princess and had a wonderful wedding. "Mesterul Manole" ("Master Builder Manole") is about a mason who dreamt that in order to build the most beautiful monastery, he had to wall in someone much beloved by him and his masons. Manole and his team decided to immure the first wife who came in the morning to bring them food. By chance, Manole's own pregnant wife ended up being the victim whom they had to sacrifice.

What 'Alinus' signals as a national flaw according to which 'ritual death' is valorized and artistic will is pitted against hostile cosmic forces and passionate self-sacrifice should not, however, be read as a representative of Romanian tendencies. It should be pointed out that the legend of immuring was not a key feature of a national culture but a story recycled transnationally by Greek, Bulgarian and Hungarian cultures among others (Neubauer 2007, 275). As John Neubauer has shown, one can identify common historical mechanisms that operated within literatures in the East-Central European region. Moreover, the motif of immurement can also be taken as a metaphor for the nationalist mobilization of folk poetry. Neubauer elucidates: "Writers have time and again extracted from texts such as the immured wife national metaphysical features, thereby 'immuring' in the fabric of the national edifice something that is supposed to distinguish it from others." Yet such edifices of fiction (a castle in the Hungarian version, a bridge in the Greek one, a fortress in the Albanian one, a monastery in the Romanian one)—"were built on grounds crisscrossed by a European, even worldwide, rhizome of folk poetry, as they were not conceived originally as national symbols" (Neubauer 2007, 275).

From this perspective, the reception of *Big Brother* Romania should take into consideration a transnational perspective within the national perceptions, or, in this case, misperceptions. In countries such as Japan, *Survivor*, one of the world's most popular shows, was unpopular with the audience because it was perceived as a program that does not sit well with local beliefs and habits. The stress on individual success achieved at the expense of others was seen in contradiction to the values emphasized in Japanese culture (Iwabuchi 2004, 25). Similarly, the marketing of *The Simpsons* in Asia focused on Lisa's intelligence rather than on Bart's disrespectful attitude towards his parents, which would not have been well received by Asian viewers (Ferrari 2009, 20).

In Romania, however, the participants' vulnerability in *Big Brother*, their inability to use individualistic tactics to succeed in the 'competition' was read by the young viewers as a weak national characteristic difficult to

186   *Alice Bardan*

change. To be sure, as many critics have emphasized, cultural identification can exist both within and across nation states, and this can be different from and is often in direct conflict with what might be called the 'national culture' or cultural identity (Moran 2008, 461; Kolar-Panov 2005, 69). Much has been made, for instance, of crowing a Black woman born in the Dominican Republic Miss Italy in 1996, despite the fact that some of the judges argued that she could not represent the concept of Italian beauty because she had "nothing to do with Italy or with Sophia Lauren's naughtiness." There has also been a lot of discussion around the fact that Eastern European Roma, who are usually seen as unable and unwilling to assimilate to the national project, ended up as representative of their countries in the *Eurovision* contests and were mobilized by corporate agents of globalization and Europeanization as objects of token exchange between the Roma, the respective country and the European Union. [5] As Anikó Imre insightfully notes, "the distinction between Roma identities and 'proper' Eastern and Central identities is the discursive and institutionalized product of Eurocentric nationalisms, contingent on the perpetual performance of its own legitimation" (2009, 128).

The Romanian Roma were not sent as representatives of the country to *Eurovision*, but recent reality television shows have capitalized on the discursive distinction between 'proper' Romanian identities and Roma identities. In recent years, shows such as *The Adventures of Vijelie Family* (broadcast on Prima TV in 2005), *Clejanii (The Clejani Family* Kanal D, between 2009–2011) and *Dragostea de la Clejani (Love in Clejani*, which aired on Prima TV in 2006 and 2011), have capitalized on the discursive distinction between 'proper' Romanian identities and Roma identities. In *Satra*, for instance, which most closely resembles Fox's *The Simple Life* with Nicole Richie and Paris Hilton, Romanian celebrities are sent to live for 24 hours with a Gypsy family. The show stages an especially interesting confrontation between rich people who claim to be excited about 'the Gypsy way of life' and various (poor) Roma families that host them. The show asks the contestants to live among Roma people who have "old traditions, an exotic culture, with a-typical rules and regulations and a lifestyle difficult for outsiders to understand."[6] They have to eat, work, sleep and earn money exactly as a Roma family does. In the end, the 'survivors' of a world 'so different than ours' tell the world 'what they have learned.' The Romanian Roma are presented by *Satra* as a (historically constructed) fantastic other, no longer the nomadic or parasitical street traders—as they were viewed under communism—but rather as biologically different people who happen to have a 'work ethic' which needs to be 'discovered.' While the celebrities display their genuine interest in learning about the Gypsy and their 'authentic' culture and about the specificities of their work, the Roma incessantly fight to 'prove themselves' and 'their way of life.' One by one, the guests emphasize their open attitude towards the Roma but inevitably end up berating them for who they are. For instance, Claudia

Patrascanu, a Romanian singer who declared that she was afraid that her dark features might mislead the Roma into thinking that she was (God forbid) one of them (Cismaru 2009), was especially outraged by the way in which the Roma men treat their women: "They subjugate them and make them submissive. Their women do everything in the house and their lazy men merely give them orders" (quoted in Cismaru 2009).

If, as some argue, the voyeuristic game of watching reality television is to find evidence of 'the truth' in the performative environment, to find 'the real' in what is performed, what emerges in the reception of the Romanian adaptations of global formats is a profound distrust of authenticity. Thus, the majority of reality TV programs are disavowed by Romanians not only because they are poor imitations of Western models but also because they cause national shame. The female contestants who appeared on local real-love TV shows were lambasted by their audiences for their contrived artificiality. The women's romantic preference for foreign contestants seemed to underscore the emasculation of Romanian men. In *Rita's Choice* a Welsh wealthy banker is the final winner, and in *The Diamond Ring* some of the millionaires for whom women have to endure humiliating tasks in order to be chosen are either Italian or from the Middle East. Last but not least, I argue that while watching *The Osbournes* poses few problems for Romanians, the reception of Ozzy's substitute, a Romanian Gypsy singer, is problematic because he is perceived as a 'fake nonconformist.' Derek Kompare suggests that the appeal of shows such as *The Osbournes* is due to the format's established normative parameters of genre and family, which ultimately underscore how everybody loves one another even though they fight all the time. I argue that it is precisely these normative parameters that do not work in the Romanian version. The unpopularity of the show exposes how unprepared Romanian audiences are to accept that, despite their unconventional lifestyle, the Gypsy family is just as 'normal' as the rest of Romanian families.

One of the most striking aspects of recent tendencies on Romanian television is how national redefinitions have been articulated around female subjectivity and notions of the feminine. Romania's new television format, *Miss Fata de la țară* (*Miss Country Girl*), produced by Media Factory and first broadcast on Prima TV in September 2010, is an illustrative example in this respect.

For a long time, Romanians' insecurity about their ability to produce authentic formats was publicly expressed by the representatives of various production studios. In 2007, a headline in the daily *Adevarul* bemoaned that "The Local TV Production Studios Live in The Shadow of International Formats," that is, merely copying foreign formats that have demonstrated guaranteed success with the audience. The article lists various directors of television production studios who deplore, each in their own way, the "cheap" quality of formats imported from aboard, whose Romanian adaptation does not meet "Western" standards. One of the main

Figure 10.1 Miss Country Girl promo.

problems leading to this, they point out, is the lack of trained specialists with permanent contracts. "We are still a long way from resembling the British or the French models, where production studios have a complex personnel structure, which contributes to the realization of various stages in the creation of a show," Marius Toader commented in an interview

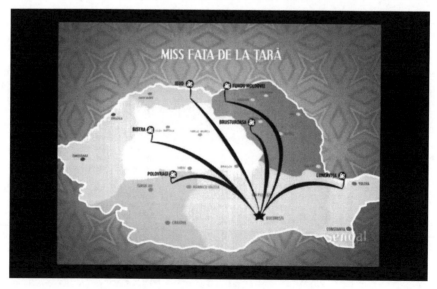

Figure 10.2 Map of Romania in Miss Country Girl.

Figure 10.3 Miss Country Girl contest.

(qouted in Preda 2007). Toader founded one of the first independent production studios in Romania, Media Factory, in 2002. Acting as creative director and co-owner, Toader launched *Miss Country Girl*, which won in the category 'best reality show' at the APTR (The Association of Romanian Television Professionals) gala. In an effort to sell Romanian formats abroad, he collaborated with Tim Crescenti, president at Small World IFT (International Format Television). As a result of this collaboration, *Miss Country Girl* was launched at the 2011 NATPE (National Association of Television Program Executives) market and conference. Before launching Small World, Crescenti was Vice President of International Production for Fox World, where he covered the worldwide rollout of Fox's expanding roster of international formats, including *Joe Millionaire*, *Simple Life* and *My Big Fat Obnoxious Fiancé*. He also served as Vice President of International Formats for Sony Pictures Television International, and cultivated a global reputation for finding the most unique and entertaining television properties around the world.

Thanks to Crescenti and Toader's advertising strategies, Viasat Broadcasting (owned by Swedish Media Conglomerate Modern Times Group) bought the *Miss Country Girl* format and the rights to distribute it in the following territories: Sweden, Denmark, Norway, Estonia, Letonia, Lithuania, Bulgaria, Slovenia, Czech Republic and Ghana. Tim Crescenti has recently declared that he is close to announcing a transaction for the production of *Miss Country Girl* in the U.S. and that the format has also been sold to Ukraine, Russia and France (bought by Endemol France). Ukraine will be the first country where the Romanian format will enter production for one of the

190 *Alice Bardan*

country's most important TV channels, 1+1. Another format developed by Media Factory and Small World IFT, *Dracula Tour Challenge*, was "inspired by Dracula's Myth" and selected as a finalist for the MIP Formats Talent Pitch contest.[7] According to Toader, the intention behind *Dracula Tour Challenge* was to bring several foreign couples to Romania to discover Dracula. The format was supposed to have several stages in which the couples would be taken to places linked with the Dracula myth, such as Bran, Poienari and Hunedoara. At the end of each stage, one couple would be eliminated. The last couple standing would discover Dracula's secrets and receive a present. Intended for distribution outside Romania, the format competed with other ones from Spain, Germany and France, but was not selected as winner. However, a similar version of the format is advertised by Crescenti as *Bite This: The Real Vampire Adventures*. His website offers a trailer that promises a format that "will push teams of contestants to their limits as they fight to stay alive in the home of a vampire legend. Teams compete in challenges designed to test their limits of fear, strength, memory and knowledge in the most iconic Transylvania locations."[8]

Miss Country Girl is about "finding beauty in the most unlikely places," a pretext used by producers to reintroduce notions of authenticity about Romanian culture. The celebrities who search for authentic Romanian beauties in the most remote regions of the country take the opportunity to showcase the country's 'forgotten' treasures—whether they are related to landscape, customs, or folk traditions and food. For example, when the show goes to Dorina Colnita's house in Fundu Bargaului, a small village in Bistrița County, the young woman puts on display for viewers the folk regional costumes she has inherited from her grandparents, rather than the beautiful dresses that her mother, who works in Germany, sent her.[9] Spreading old folk blouses on her bed, Dorina enthusiastically speaks about the delicacy of their embroidery, praising the cultural traditions in her village and conveying her pride to be part of these traditions. "Even though people mock us that we are from the countryside," Dorina explains as she single-handedly brings two horses under her command, "we are hard workers and we are proud of who we are." Her comments served as springboard for passionate expressions of national pride on YouTube, in which Romanians stressed how beautiful their women and country are. By contrast, *I'm a Country Boy* did not generate similar feelings of enthusiasm. Although it was advertised with tag lines such as "from farm boys to Fabios," it soon became clear that the village boys did not have the same skills as the women.[10] While women, for instance, demonstrated that they can be quite adept at dancing wildly to Shakira songs, most men proved clumsy in dance competitions.

THE COLD WAR'S OBSCENE BIG BROTHER

In an article in *Variety* from June 2003, suggestively titled "Romania: 'Big Brother' is too Orwellian, watchdog sez," John Nadler, a foreign correspondent for the magazine decried: "Reality TV stalwart 'Big Brother' is déjà vu for Romanian regulators still reeling from 40 years of totalitarianism" (22). Such associations between "Big Brother," surveillance, and Eastern Europe are well known and still very much alive 20 years after the dismantling of the Soviet Union and the end of the Cold War. Communist Romania's symbolic space on the European map as a repository of darkness and repression and as a country ruled by a cold-blooded dictator has particularly captured the Western imagination. While other communist-led countries in Eastern Europe had witnessed acts of popular resistance and revolt, Cold War Romania always seemed to be in the grip of absolute control, frozen in time by its passive acquiescence to a form of authoritarianism which ruthlessly intruded into the private realm and the intimate rapports among the citizens. There seemed to be no escape from the all-knowing, obscene "Big Brother," as if at all times, hidden cameras or microphones would register the citizen's every move. Romania, in other words, always figured as the closest to the original Big Brother, the famous enigmatic dictator of Oceania in George Orwell's novel *Nineteen Eighty-Four*.

To be sure, this analogy wasn't necessarily too far-fetched: in communist Romania, mass communication channels were continuously subjected to extremely strict surveillance. For many years, Romanian Television broadcasting was reduced to two hours a day, and for those working in the field, censorship was pervasive. Rumors have it that Elena Ceausescu, dictator Nicolae Ceausescu's wife, was accused of having had the Securitate plant hidden cameras in the bedrooms of high Romanian officials to later watch them as they made love (Roger and Raceanu 1994, 39). Mircea Raceanu, coauthor of *Romania versus the United States: Diplomacy of the Absurd, 1985–1989*, states that a close photographer friend of his was once ordered by the Securitate to develop a clandestine film showing Valentin, Elena and Nicolae's own son, making love to a female friend in his apartment. The Securitate would have never dared to place a hidden camera in Valentin's apartment without the explicit instruction of either Elena or Nicolae, the author points out (39). Most likely, the film was developed for Elena's private entertainment.

Of course, there is a long history of state surveillance—from baroque listening devices through the mail censorship of the notorious "black chambers" in 18th-century Europe, to the secret agents of 19th-century police and today's video monitoring of public space.[11] Yet the recent hype around films such as *The Lives of Others* (Florian Henkel von Donnersmarck's 2006 film) powerfully reveals the Western public's enduring fascination with state paranoia behind the secret police surveillance in Eastern Europe.

NEOLIBERALISM AND THE OBSCENE, CAPITALIST BIG BROTHER

The current proliferation of television formats predicated on day-to-day surveillance, such as in *Big Brother*, seems to have restored the public image of the much-maligned Big Brother. As Mark Andrejevic (2002)

192   *Alice Bardan*

rightly points out, the commercial, capitalist version of Big Brother does not stir the same feelings of revulsion as its predecessor did for the Cold War generation (252). His gaze is no longer associated with the threat of mass homogeneity, but with "the promise of a paradoxical mass individuation" (267). Andrejevic analyzes how the rise of surveillance-based reality television has emerged in the U.S. and Western Europe at a particular time when the online economy began to draw on surveillance methods as a form of economic exploitation, training viewers and consumers for their role in an "interactive" economy. For today's media-saturated generation, the commodification of private lives for mass consumption does not seem too threatening. The architects of the online economy, Andrejevic underscores, rationalize consumer labor and rely on surveillance methods "not only as a means for anticipating and customizing consumer demand, but [also] for adding value to products and creating new ones" (2002, 253).

For critics such as John Freeman (2007), a reality television show such as *Big Brother* is, ironically, one of the most public and overt means of "staging the obscene," a word whose etymology goes back to "off scene," out of sight (7). In this case, the obscenity is linked to the show's ability to exist and thrive on revealing for mass audiences the banalities of life that were hitherto kept safe from view, "the sleeping, snoring bodies, interspersed with 3 a.m. conversations, out-pausing Pinter and taking the nothing happens twice of Beckett's *Godot* to the dread endpoint where nothing happens nightly" (8).

To be sure, the specific associations between Big Brother, surveillance and Cold War Romania or Eastern Europe often seem to occlude a much less popular story. Commentators tend to ignore the fact that the beginnings of reality television are also thoroughly intertwined with state paranoia in the U.S., specifically during the McCarthy era. Moreover, as I further show, the genre has played a crucial part as a strategy to control labor unrest in the late 1980s.

Laurie Ouellette and Susan Murray (2009) have recently noted that much of what we call popular reality TV can be traced to existing quiz formats from the late 1950s and staged pranks pioneered by *Candid Camera* (1953–67), makeovers and charity games, celebrations of ordinary people in unusual or unusually contrived situations and amateur talent contests (4). However, Fred Nadis (2010) reminds us that the *Candid Camera* format initially began on radio, much earlier, as *Candid Microphone* (on June 28, 1947), a program initiated by Allen Funt as a "comic inversion of the HUAC hearings" (13), at the beginning of television's household dominance and in response to Cold War fears of national security. In those days, Funt recalls, the public was fascinated by the idea that recording equipment was so small that it could be hidden, and the same recording technology that was used in the entertainment industries of film and television was used for espionage and surveillance.

Candid Microphone gained currency in an environment where vigilant citizens were encouraged by government propaganda to observe, record

Big Brothers and Little Brothers   193

and report any suspicions of "un-American" activity. As the first program to be aired on the new ABC network and a prototype for reality TV programming, it launched a new era of television broadcasting and helped to reshape the entertainment industry. This was the time when, in response to the expansion of government surveillance that signaled the beginning of the Cold War, George Orwell published *Nineteen Eighty-Four* in 1949. It also coincided with an age of loyalty oaths, fears of communist infiltration and organized crime, when the concept of Neighborhood Watch generated feelings of paranoia and suspicion (Clisssold 2004, 38). Only one year before the creation of *Candid Microphone*, the Truman administration established the national security state apparatus, which included an expanded FBI that could run background checks on employees, the formation of the CIA and of the National Security Council (Nadis 2010, 13). In addition, shows such as *Candid Microphone* and *Candid Camera* emerged at a time when communications research aided by new postwar funding began to examine how people handled the unexpected and amidst concerns about conformity and totalitarianism (Nadis 2010, 17).

Notwithstanding criticism for being unethical, offensive and voyeuristically exploitative, Funt explicitly emphasized his desire to expose "conformity and weakness in the face of authority" (Nadis 2010, 18). At the same time, however, he deliberately sought to depict situations in which individuals were called upon to act heroically, validating American ideals of perseverance, ingenuity and grace (Clissold 2004, 40). As such, he was "turning average Americans—those who were minding their own business (self-surveillance) and discretely minding their neighbors' (civic duty)—into celebrated and heroic social actors" (Clissold 2004, 41). By reversing the traditional power dynamic associated with hidden surveillance, *Candid Camera* granted the individuals the right to decide whether the captured materials of their candid exchanges could be aired or not. Surprisingly, however, 99% of all the 'victims' signed the release in exchange for a small fee ($50 at the time). As Bradley Clissold (2004) rightly underscores, such releases effectively converted the act of invasive surveillance into a commodity exchange, a business transaction that anticipated late-capitalist practices of information collection and the abuse of corporate "marketing" (42) in today's neoliberal culture.

On the one hand, especially in the U.S., reality TV programs promote a rationale of self-improvement that rarely resists the wider features of neoliberal culture. Offering a culture of judgment, reality TV promotes a type of aggression that resonates with other forms of communication in the neoliberal workplace (Couldry 2010, 81). Shows such as *Big Brother*, Nick Couldry points out, are premised upon ideas of compulsory teamwork and team conformity, even as they promote competition between individuals. Participants are forced to socialize and dissent from "required gregariousness" is not tolerated. "Since the norm of teamwork cannot be challenged, its falsity (in this light) cannot be challenged," Couldry astutely notes (78).

194   *Alice Bardan*

SHIFTING ECONOMIC PRACTICES, REALITY TV PROGRAMMING EXPANSION AND LABOR UNREST

It is important to emphasize that the popularity of reality TV has increased over the years due to a real need on both the producers' and broadcasters' part to respond to the changing economics of contemporary television (Sparks 2007). In the U.S., the genre emerged as a fiscal strategy in the late 1980s, as a response to the economic restructuring of U.S. television. Furnishing the need for cheaper programming, it ultimately led to a wider industry move towards using non-union, freelance production crews. As Chad Raphael (2009) points out, after the changes in federal tax laws in the mid-1980s, producers were no longer able to deduct 6.7 percent of the cost of their production from their federal tax bills and lost up to $100,000 per episode for half-hour shows and up to 300,000 for hour-long dramas. In addition to increasing costs driven up by "above the line" costs (such as talent, scriptwriting, music composition or location costs), the first wave of reality TV programming expansion can be traced back to the 22-week writers' strike in the U.S. in 1988 (Raphael 2009, 129), when the genre proved to be an integral part of network strategies to control labor unrest.

The second wave was propelled in the U.S. by the success of the game shows *Who Wants to be a Millionaire* and *Survivor* in 2000, which happened at the same time as actors and writers threatened another strike in 2001. In order to prepare for upcoming tensions with the writers, the networks increased the demand for the creation of reality TV series, which could fill in hours on the network schedule. Reality TV programs then cut costs by adopting low-end production values, such as handheld cameras and the use of available lightning. The return of conflicts between labor and management in Hollywood, including the 2007–08 Writers Guild of America strike, further aided the resurgence of reality programming, a third wave so to speak.

Reality TV programming has attracted network investors and producers because of its ability to sell abroad, which until now has been done by using two methods. The first method follows the traditional way in which U.S. programming has been marketed through the licensing of shows to foreign broadcasters. The second involves the formatting of the shows by selling or licensing a program's concept for local production with local subjects (Raphael 2009, 134). In Europe, the growth of reality TV was sparked by widespread movement to privatize and deregulate broadcasting in the early 1990s and mostly answered the need for European public broadcasters to follow the logic of private channels when competition for audiences and funding started increasing (Raphael 2009, 137).

CONCLUSION

Moran (2008) stresses that local and national audiences invariably prefer to see a program that looks and sounds like one of their own. "They ask that on-screen figures act and sound like them, that situations and places are familiar and recognizable, and that stories told on screen have to do with their" he comments (2008, 462). Similarly, Silvio Waisbord argues that, "when given a choice, audiences prefer domestic and regional content to foreign programs" (2004, 369). Moreover, critics of *Survivor* and *Big Brother* adaptations in countries such as Australia or Finland point out how the producers strove to emphasize the "Australianess" of the house (Turner 2005, 372) or to "flag the Finnishness" through a combination of setting, themes, and cultural practices shared by the contestants (Aslama and Pantti 2007). This notwithstanding, as I hope to have demonstrated, the Romanian case proves that at times the national audience may be particularly critical of the local adaptations of an ("authentic") global format whose quality is better. In other words, Romanians may prefer watching a foreign version of *Big Brother*, *The Bachelorette* and *The Osbournes* rather than local adaptations of these shows, and express their preference for *The Jersey Shore*, which they watch on MTV Romania, over *The Vijelie Family*, whose characters they detest and blame for lowering the cultural quality of Romanian programming.[12] From this perspective, one could interpret the disappointment with which the winner of *Big Brother Romania* was received (as a weak character who complained too much in order to gain the audience's sympathy), as a case of "inverted" banal nationalism. "Banal nationalism," a concept introduced by Michael Billing, refers to the way in which the nation is recreated in the everyday context of popular culture through the use of symbols, themes and other unnoticed, everyday practices of representation. Yet the recreation of national symbols does not necessarily lead to positive identifications with the national character. On the contrary, viewers may even project negative national stereotypes over the everyday cultural contexts created by television shows.

To be sure, recent shows such as *Miss Country Girl* and *Country Boy* were used as an excuse for "performing the nation," and reinforced stereotypical expectations of gender performance. Instead of limousines, the young women contestants made their appearances on horse-driven carts. While the girls had to cook traditional food, feed the house animals and prove themselves in sewing or milking cow contests, the boys had to drive the tractor and plow the earth.[13] Judging from the audience's responses on blogs and on YouTube, the new formats no doubt succeeded in reigniting nationalist attachments. The women's beauty and the careful emphasis on the splendor of natural landscape served to mobilize affective investments in the country's "authenticity," allegedly forgotten but rediscovered thanks to these shows. At the same time, however, the new formats revealed how hard it is to sustain images of authenticity in the age of (media) globalization. For instance, Maria Chindris, the contestant from Ieud, Maramures, rolled her eyes with a knowing smile as she was "elegantly" milking the cow for the sake of the show and struggled to keep her 'traditional' headscarf from sliding off her head. Later on, without the traditional costume, she skillfully danced in a mini black dress.[14] Madalina Furdui, a contestant

196 *Alice Bardan*

from Bistra, was less preoccupied with cooking traditional food than with her very busy gym schedule. In her "remote village" house, she proudly showed the producers her fancy treadmill and articulated her clear goals for her future and a strict daily timetable. In other words, the shows foreground the tension between expectations to conform to national traditions and young Romanians' investment in cultural globalization and neoliberal ideas of responsibility and self-making.

NOTES

1. This comment was retrieved from: http://forum.softpedia.com/lofiversion/index.php/t25798.html.
2. See also Dwyer and Uricaru (2009).
3. Other examples include the absurd coordination of taking showers during the weekly run of *Dallas* on National Television in the early 1980s: only when one's neighbors were not using water would the low-pressure liquid reach the top-floor flats of Bucharest tower-blocks (Bradeanu and Thomas 2006, 142).
4. This comment is available at: *http://forum.gsmhosting.com/vbb/archive/t-92456.html*. Accessed August 8, 2003.
5. For more on see chapter "Euro-Visions: Musical Play and Ethnic Entertainment in the New Europe" (Imre 2009, 95–128).
6. These comments are taken from the advertisement for the show available at http://port.ro/satra/pls/fi/films.film_page?i_perf_id=7068358&i_where=1&i_where_tv=1 Accessed August 10, 2009.
7. This contest is used as a platform for pitching original concepts of never-before seen non-scripted entertainment formats. The 2011 selection process video can be watched on YouTube at http://www.youtube.com/watch?v=84mH1t7ikl. Accessed May 1, 2011.
8. The trailer is available at http://www.smallworldift.com/format_item.php?pageid=real_vampire_adventures. Accessed May 1, 2011.
9. A segment of the show is available on YouTube at http://www.youtube.com/watch?v=KcssqlQCvgw&feature=related. Accessed April 1, 2011.
10. A description of the show can be watched at http://www.smallworldift.com/format_item.php?pageid=country_boy. Accessed April 1, 2011.
11. See, in this respect, Thomas Y. Levin, Ursula Frohne and Peter Weibel (eds.), *CTRL [SPACE]: Rhetorics of Surveillance from Bentham to Big Brother* (Cambridge, MA: MIT Press, 2002).
12. For examples of how much viewers detest the show see http://forum.softpedia.com/index.php?showtopic=76707&st=54. Accessed May 1, 2008.
13. An example of such contests is available on YouTube at http://www.youtube.com/watch?v=XgXnxrFV2qQ&feature=related. Accessed Sept. 30, 2010.
14. See, for instance, this video on YouTube: http://www.youtube.com/watch?v=phAkR31wlDk. Accessed Sept. 30, 2010.

REFERENCES

Andrejevic, Mark. 2002. "The Kinder, Gentler Gaze of Big Brother: Reality TV in the Era of Digital Capitalism." *New Media and Society* 4 (2): 251–270.

Big Brothers and Little Brothers 197

Antonescu, Florin. 2004. "Capcana Dubla." (The Double Trap). *Curierul National*, March 23. http://www.curierulnational.ro/Opinii/2004–03–23/Capcana+dubla

Aslama, Minna and Pantti, Mervi. 2007. *Flagging Finnishness: Reproducing National Identity in Reality Television. Television & New Media* 8(1): 46–67.

Boytchev, Alexander. 2005. "The Big Brother of Changes on the Bulgarian TV Market." *Media Online*, January 26. http://www.mediaonline.ba/en/?ID=346.

Bradeanu, Adina and Rosie Thomas. 2006. "Indian Summer, Romanian Winter: A 'Procession of Memories' in Post-communist Romania." *South Asian Popular Culture* 4(2) (October): 141–146.

Cismaru. Monica. 2009. "O 'Şatră' de vedete." ("A 'Gypsy Camp' made of Super-Stars"). *Evenimentul Zilei*, June 21. http://www.evz.ro/detalii/stiri/o-satra-de-vedete-855783.html.

Clissold, Bradley D. 2004. "Candid Camera and the Origins of Reality TV: Contextualizing a Historical Precedent." In *Understanding Reality Television*, edited by Su Holmes and Deborah Jermyn, 33–53. London: Routledge.

Couldry, Nick. 2010. *Why Voice Matters: Culture and Politics after Neoliberalism*. Thousand Oaks: Sage .

Dasgupta, Sudeep. 2007. "Whiter Culture? Globalization, Media and the Promises of Cultural Studies." In *Constellations of the Transnational: Modernity, Culture, Critique*, edited by Sudeep Dasgupta. Amsterdam: Rodopi.

Dwyer, Tessa and Ioana Uricaru. 2009. "Slashings and Subtitles: Romanian Media Piracy, Censorship, and Translation." *Velvet Light Trap* 63 (Spring): 45–57.

Freeman, John. 2007. "Making the Obscene Seen. Performance, Research and the Autoethnographical Drift." *Journal of Dramatic Theory and Criticism* 21(2): 7–20.

Hill, Annette. 2002. "Big Brother: The Real Audience." *Television and New Media* 3(3): 323–340.

Hozic, Aida A. 2008. "Democratizing Media, Welcoming Big Brother: Media in Bosnia and Herzegovina." In *Finding the Right Place on the Map: Central and Eastern European Media Change in a Global Perspective*, edited by Karol Jakubowicz and Miklós Sükösd, 145–164. Chicago: Intellect Books.

Imre, Anikó. 2009. *Identity Games: Globalization and the Transformation of Media Cultures in the New Europe*. London: MIT.

Imre, Anikó. 2011. "Love to Hate: National Celebrity and Racial Intimacy on Reality TV in the New Europe." *Television and New Media* 20(10): 1–28.

Iwabuchi, Koichi. 2004. "Feeling Glocal. Japan in the Global Television Format Business." In *Television Across Asia: Television Industries, Program Formats and Globalisation*, edited by Albert Moran and Michael Keane, 12–35. London: Routledge.

Kolar-Panov, Dona. 2005. "Television and Cultural Cooperation in Southeastern Europe." In *The Emerging Creative Industries in Southeastern Europe*, edited by Nada Svob Dokic, 67–81. Zagreb: Institute for International Relations. http://www.culturelink.org/publics/joint/cultid07/Svob-Djokic_Creative_Industries.pdf.

Kirk, Roger and Mircea Răceanu. 1994. *Romania versus the United States: Diplomacy of the Absurd, 1985–1989*. New York: St. Martin's Press.

Moran, Albert. 2008. "Makeover on the Move: Global Television and Programme Formats." *Continuum* 22(4): 459–469.

Murray, Susan and Quallette, Laurie. (Eds). 2008. *Reality TV: Remaking Television Culture*. New York, NY: NYU Press.

Nadis, Fred. 2010. "Citizen Funt: Surveillance as Cold War Entertainment." In *The Tube Has Spoken: Reality TV and History*, edited by Taddeo Julie Anne and Ken Dvorak, 11–26. Lexington, KY: University Press of Kentucky.

198 *Alice Bardan*

Nadler, John. 2003. "Romania: *Big Brother* is too Orwellian, Watchdog Sez." *Variety* 391(3): (June 2–8): 22.

Neubauer, John. 2007. "Introduction: Folkore and National Awakening." In *History of the Literary Cultures of East-Central Europe: Junctures and Disjunctures in the 19th and 20th Centuries, Vol. 3*, edited by Marcel Cornis-Pope and John Neubauer, 269–284. Amsterdam and Philadelphia: John Benjamins Publishing Company.

O'Flynn, Kevin. 2001. "Country Enthralled by *Behind the Glass.*" *The St. Petersburg Times*, 721 (88), (November 13). http://www.sptimes.ru/index. php?action_id=2&story_id=5892.

Popescu, Adina. 2006. "Divertisment *pret-a-porter.*" *Dilema Veche* 134(18), (August 2): http://www.dilemaveche.ro/sectiune/mass-comedia/articol/ divertisment-ipret-porteri.

Preda, Raluca. 2007. "Casele de productie tv autohtone trăiesc la umbra străinătăţii." ("Our Local TV Production Studios Live in the Shadow of International Formats"). *Adevarul*, November 21. http://www.adevarul.ro/financiar/ media/Casele-productie-autohtone-traiesc-strainatatii_0_35397029.html.

Raicheva-Stover, Maria. 2006. "You'll See, You'll Watch: The Success of *Big Brother* in Postcommunist Bulgaria." Paper submitted to the International Division of the Broadcast Education Association Conference in Las Vegas, April 27–29. *http://www.cwsp.bg/upload/docs/Big_brother_for_web.pdf.*

Raphael, Chad. 2009. "The Political Economic Origins of Reality TV." In *Reality TV: Remaking Television Culture*, edited by Susan Murray and Laurie Ouellette, 123–140. New York and London: New York University Press.

Roger, Kirk and Racenau, Mircea. 1994. *Romania versus the United States: Diplomacy of the Absurd, 1985–1989.* Washington, D.C.: Palgrave Macmillan.

Sparks, Colin. 2007. "Reality TV: The Big Brother Phenomenon." *International Socialism: A Quarterly Journal of Socialist Theory* 114 (April 9). *http://www. isj.org.uk/index.php4?id=314=114#114sparks4.*

Štětka, Václav. 2010. "Globalization, Reality TV and Cultural Inclusion: The Case of the 2005 Czech Search for a Superstar." *Eastbound.* http://eastbound.eu/ site_media/pdf/EB2010_Stetka.pdf.

Stoican, Mariana. 2004. "Romania: Controversy over the *Big Brother* Show." *IRIS Legal Observations of the European Audiovisual Observatory* 6(15): 30. http:// merlin.obs.coe.int/iris/2004/6/article30.en.html.

Tudorache, Simona. 2004. "Sex la Big Brother." ("Sex on Big Brother"). *Curierul National*, March 24. *http://www.curierulnational.ro/Eveniment/2004–03–24/ Sex+la+Big+Brother.* (Accessed July 25, 2011).

Turner, Graeme. 2005. "Cultural Identity, Soap Narrative, and Reality TV." *Television and New Media* 6(4): 415–422.

Volcic, Zala and Mark Andrejevic. 2009. "*That's Me*: Nationalism and Identity on Balkan Reality TV." *Canadian Journal of Communication* 34: 7–24.

Waisbord, Silvio. 2004. "McTV: Understanding the Global Popularity of Television Formats." *Television and New Media* 5(2): 359–383.

van Zoonen, Liesbet and Minna Aslama. 2006. "Understanding Big Brother: An Analysis of Current Research." *Javnost–the Public* 13(2): 85–96.

Zeca- Buzura, Daniela. 2007. *Totul la vedere : televiziunea dupa Big Brother.* Bucharest, Romania: Polirom.

11 The Way We Applauded

How Popular Culture Stimulates
Collective Memory of the Socialist Past
in Czechoslovakia—The Case of the
Television Serial *Vyprávěj* and its Viewers

*Irena Carpentier Reifová, Kateřina
Gillárová and Radim Hladík*

Popular television has some distinct privileges in representing the past. As Irwin-Zarecka asserts, it frames collective memory in at least two important ways: exposure, since "for many people, television offers the main, if not the only information they have about a great number of historical events"; and claims to historical accuracy, as "television presents us with reality-based drama, docudrama and document where the strength of writing, visuals, and faithfulness to detail all combine" (Irwin-Zarecka 1994, 155–156). These mnemonic capacities of television make it a worthwhile object of study in countries like the Czech Republic, which arguably still try to come to terms with their state socialist legacy.

For the analysis of how television programming intervenes in the formation of post-socialist identities, we are going to look at parallels between different forms of remembering the past. We do not strive to put forward any particular "genre of memory" (e.g., amnesia, nostalgia, displacement, collective guilt) nor any specific social enclave (former dissidents, intellectuals or alternative culture practitioners). Our main goal is to examine how memory (interrupted by the politics of a thick line after 1989) is secured by the "semiotic power of people" (Fiske 1987, 236) and how practices of reading popular culture are involved in this process. We are interested in the ways which ordinary people use to regain the sense of continuity by fostering different genres of memory and in the ways the mnemonic function of popular television can stimulate this process.

POST-SOCIALISM AND MEMORY STUDIES

As the prefix "post" suggests, state socialism still survives in Central and Eastern Europe, at least to the extent that we continue to designate it as a post-socialist space. The region remains alive in personal and collective, private and public, dominant and marginalized narratives of the past. The continuing relevance of the past in the present constitutes the essence of collective memory (Halbwachs 1992) that transforms landscapes and mediascapes into countless places of memory (Nora 1989). Cultural and collective memory ensure, for better or worse, that the new identities emerging from the turmoil of fundamental socio-political transformations not only adhere to novel practices and institutions but also take root in the imaginary of the past.

The burgeoning discipline of memory studies has, to a considerable extent, managed to empower narratives of the state socialist past that lack the sanction of scholarly historiography and yet remain formative of both social bonds and animosities among social groups and nations. However, memory studies so far have not arrived at a consensual account of the principles of commemoration, remembering and forgetting that help post-socialist Europe make sense of the state-socialist experience. As the coiner of the term "collective memory" Maurice Halbwachs (Halbwachs 1992) predicted, the very multiplicity of groups in which individual members of society participate seems to preclude a unitary formation of memory. Gil Eyal suggests, however, that more is at stake than simply the dispersed ways in which we think collective memory operates. In his words:

> The sense of a crisis of memory, and the diagnosis of too much or too little memory, are generated not by the universal nature of human memory but by a historically specific *will to memory*, a constellation of discourses and practices within which memory is entrusted with a certain goal and function, and is invested, routinely, as an institutional matter, with certain hopes and fears as to what it can do. It is always against this goal that memory is measured and found wanting. (Eyal 2004, 6–7)

In light of these remarks, we find it advisable to refrain from sweeping statements on the workings of memory in the post-socialist context that diagnose it one-sidedly in terms of trauma, nostalgia, amnesia or in another pathological or functional variety of remembrance. Instead, we prefer to assume from the outset that collective memory consists of a wide repertoire of practices and discourses whose variants may be conducive to different results of remembering and forgetting. Specifically, we will give an equal consideration to the two main concepts that are most commonly summoned in order to describe the bearing of the state-socialist past on the post-socialist present: nostalgia and (cultural) trauma. Although these concepts tend to be mutually exclusionary—with nostalgia making the past an object of longing, while trauma conceiving of it as a haunting image—we conducted a qualitative research of television audiences that suggests their discursive coexistence.

The Way We Applauded 201

POST-SOCIALIST MEMORY AND NOSTALGIA

In the Czech Republic as well as in many other post-socialist countries recollections of the socialist era have been on the agenda since the early 1990s, when the first measures of transitional justice—such as restitutions of nationalized property or the disqualification of former elites from the state administration—were discussed and implemented (see e.g. Teitel 2000, Přibáň 2002). With the inevitable unavailability of proper historiographical accounts, collective memories dominate the representation of the past and have been constitutive of the Czech political arena (Eyal 2003).

To date, the most complex account of the diverse "registers" of collective memory on which Czech social actors draw in order to construe their positive self-image has been presented by French sociologist Françoise Mayer. In her work, *Češi a jejich komunismus* (*Czechs and Their Communism*; Mayer 2009), she shows that among Czechs there are in fact a number of distinct renditions of the past, which can be traced to particular social groups. She documents the quick shift of official memory from the concept of national "integration" to "decommunization." However, official memory fails to be decisively hegemonic. Other competing discourses of remembrance include the narrative of "betrayal" among the members of the former ruling Communist Party, while the "memory for identity" dominates among the supporters of the CP's post-socialist successor. The political prisoners of the Stalinist era tend to remember the past in terms of "resistance," whereas the later dissidents of the Normalization era (1969–89) prefer its legalistic condemnation. Distinct registers of memory can also be identified among intellectuals and historians. Mayer, however, chooses to leave out one register from her analysis. The blind spot of her treatise is in fact quite significant and consists of the vast and ever-growing archive of popular and media culture, which she only mentions in passing, with a disdain for the presumed triviality of the products of the cultural industry: "The enthusiastic reception [of mass culture artifacts that represent the state-socialist past] can probably be best explained by the fact that they offer a nonpolitical view of history and thus return the past to all those people 'without a story'" (Mayer 2009, 258).

Such assumptions imply that the texts of popular culture cannot sustain the critical work of memory; and thus the recollections of the past by such means only generate an uncritical remembrance of a nostalgic type. The nostalgic discourses usually refer to the socialist past either directly (better to say indexically) by recycling individual tokens of an authentic socialist culture or indirectly (symbolically) by producing new representations of the past. To put it simply, nostalgic discourses either *present* the preserved parts of the past (e.g. pop singers or actors who became popular in socialist times as epitomes of the era) or they *represent* "them" (e.g. contemporary feature films going back to the days of socialism) (Dominková 2008).

202   *Irena Carpentier Reifová, Kateřina Gillárová and Radim Hladík*

Nostalgia, "a longing for a home that no longer exists or has never existed, [. . .] a sentiment of loss and displacement" (Boym 2001, xiii), has over the course of modernity acquired temporal as well as spatial sense. It now often counts among threatening emotions of post-modern Western life and many times it has been theorized as such. Fredric Jameson, for instance, sees *nostalgia films* as emblematic of the period of late capitalism, which erodes a sense of history: "The nostalgia film was never a matter of some old-fashioned 'representation' of historical content, but instead approached the 'past' through stylistic connotation, conveying 'pastness' by the glossy qualities of the image" (Jameson 1991, 19). Linda Hutcheon (1998), however, suggests post-modern irony as an antidote to the arresting effects of nostalgia. Jameson, in actuality, also recognizes that there is a utopian impulse operating even in nostalgic artifacts (Jameson 1990, 229). The problem with nostalgia lies in its renunciation of history, which according to Jameson amounts to giving up the only way to actually pursue the utopian impulse. This inbuilt subversion in the nostalgic longing of the very means for realizing a utopian goal constitutes the defining aporia of nostalgia. Svetlana Boym attempts to address this duality by distinguishing conservative "restorative nostalgia" from a more critical "reflective nostalgia," which is able to connect "historical and individual time, with the irrevocability of the past" (Boym 2001, 49).

Some post-socialist discourses mediating between the past and the present, of which popular culture genres create a considerable part, were demarcated and explicated by cultural scholars as post-socialist nostalgia (Enns 2007, Boyer 2006, Volčič 2007, Reifova 2009). Post-socialist nostalgia cannot be fully subsumed under postmodern nostalgia as it is experienced in the West. Although post-socialist nostalgia started to grow in the environment influenced by a convergence of post-socialism and postmodernism, it also resonates with a modernist vision of history, of which state socialism was probably the last big project (Ray 1997). The specificity of post-socialist nostalgia stems from the fact that it strives for an integration of memory divided by the social rupture in 1989 (more precisely, futile but compulsive attempts to attain integration) in the sense of including the "forbidden" past in a larger historical continuity. Post-socialist nostalgia is a memory-compensating nostalgia; it helps to restore the memory that was disintegrated by the break between the socialist and neoliberal capitalist systems. In response to Mayer's judgment discussed above, it can be said to be a vindication of the status of stories that have been forgotten in many official and some scholarly records. Hence, the compensation of memory in post-socialist Czechoslovakia via the mnemonic function of popular culture is partly of an anti-hegemonic nature.

The official, dominant discourses of economics and politics in the 1990s, inaugurated by the state authorities, political representatives or judiciary, were firmly grounded in the logics of disjunction, divorce from the socialist past. Most social subsystems were built anew to be totally different from the

The Way We Applauded 203

past, as in privatization in the economical sphere or lustration in elite human resources. The past was defined as something that should be replaced with a better present—and if not fully erased, then only because the capacity to remember the old faults increases the chance that they will not be repeated in the future. The past was simply defined by the dominant discourses as a loose end, which should have stayed loose, not as an object to which society should reconnect. The logics of disjunction became hegemonic in the early transformational years of the 1990s. Michael D. Kennedy argues that the idea of a profound historical rupture lies at the core of "transition culture." He remarks with regards to the treatment of the past: "Transition's tradition tends to draw more on capitalist experience from across the world than it does on any nation's socialist past. Socialism is something to be escaped, repressed, and destroyed" (Kennedy 2002, 13). The societal turnover from state socialism to capitalism settled conditions for a new anti-hegemonic struggle—one that is about gaining less restricted access to the past; about nurturing collective memory which would embrace a broader repertoire than just an uncompromising denouncement of the past. That is why we think that the first attempts to compensate for displaced memory took place in the demiworld of popular culture, below the radar of transition's proponents, and not in more highly valued elite cultural areas. Popular culture remains one of the principal sites where consumers can experience (nostalgic) links to the socialist past without having to face public reproach.

POST-SOCIALIST MEMORY AND CULTURAL TRAUMA

Apart from nostalgia, the concept that many other scholars find fruitful in explaining how post-socialist societies relate to their own pasts is the one of cultural trauma—in spite of its bad reputation as a culturalist buzzword. According to Jeffrey Alexander, "cultural trauma occurs when members of a collectivity feel they have been subjected to a horrendous event that leaves indelible marks upon their group consciousness, marking their memories forever and changing their future identity in fundamental and irrevocable ways" (Alexander 2004, 1). Many skeptical queries have appeared in connection with this definition. Is trauma an event or rather the way it is remembered? (Eyerman 2004, 62; Caruth 1995, 4). Can trauma be cultural at all? Can it be collective in the sense of having a new quality going beyond a summary of individual traumas? (Joas 2005, 372). Should non-violent events be also included into the category? (Kansteiner 2004, 206). And then there is a group of thinkers who feel that taking the concept of trauma not only beyond the borders of medicine and psychoanalysis, where it originated, but also mainly outside of the discourse on Holocaust, is a sacrilege and causes inflation of the concept's value.

While working with the concept of cultural trauma it is important to stay away from simplifications such as confusing cultural trauma with "an

204 *Irena Carpentier Reifová, Kateřina Gillárová and Radim Hladík*

aggregate of individual traumata" (Carpentier 2007, 251, see also Kansteiner 2004, 209). It is clear that cultural trauma is not a summary of disconnected, personal reminiscences about approximately the same period. It must have an added quality of collectivity—shared clusters of meanings associated with the particular traumatizing event. But it should also be said that symptoms of cultural trauma are only accessible via individual stories and personal voices. The memories of individual survivors are an inevitable source of data, which of course have to be further selected and processed. General demonization of all uses of the personal in cultural trauma research thus makes little sense.

In spite of all the discontents, it seems that some sort of collective shock (Sztompka 2000, 457), shattering or paralysis is generally accepted as at least a partial element of cultural trauma. Radical social changes (together with many other events, which can be of natural or social origins, momentary eruptions or long-term processes, violent massacres or discursive pressures) such as the turnovers of social systems in Central and Eastern Europe, meet this condition. We find it inspiring to look for indices of cultural trauma in the viewers recollections provoked by the retrospective television serial. If the trauma is supposed to be cultural it must penetrate the general public and television-induced remembering provides an insight into exactly this layer of memory.

What is exceptionally troublesome about post-socialist cultural trauma is that it cannot be easily located in one single site. Piotr Sztompka reduces this question to the social and economic insecurities of newly established capitalism: "The event greeted with greatest enthusiasm by most people, has resulted, for some time and for some groups, in traumatic experience known as the pains of transition (e.g. unemployment, status degradation, impoverishment, rise of crime)" (Sztompka 2000, 458). We think that there are at least three types of "conducive conditions" (Smelser 1962, 22) for post-socialist cultural trauma. First, there are the new instabilities mentioned in Sztompka's quote above. Second, trauma could also be activated by the occurrence of embarrassing or anxious life situations in totalitarian socialism. And third, a mere disruption in the continuity of everyday, personal lives and the workings of social institutions could also constitute trauma. It is most likely that it is not an "either/or" case, but that all these processes run alongside one another and compose post-socialist cultural trauma together. It is not only a sequential (Sztompka 2000, 453), but also a multilayered phenomenon.

The collapse of state socialism inspires us to see this kind of cultural trauma more as a dislocation (temporary lapse of determining power of structure) than as Alexander's 'horrendous event' with clearly devastating consequences. Dislocation, a concept introduced by Ernesto Laclau (who rephrased Gramsci's 'organic crisis'), explains mainly a discursive divide between 'before' and 'after' the traumatic event. Dislocation refers to the rupture in the order of the things as it was fixed by the now shattered discourse.

The Way We Applauded 205

In his reading of Laclau, Torfing understands dislocation as "a destabilization of a discourse that results from the emergence of events which cannot be domesticated, symbolized or integrated within the discourse in question" (1999, 301). Technical and methodological bias embedded in the dislocation approach avoids evaluative insights into the difference between the "before" and "after" and enables us to see ambiguities of dislocations. Looking at the dislocatory dimension of cultural trauma (if it has one) helps to see that "dislocatory events on the one hand threaten identities, on the other hand they are foundations on which new identities are constituted" (Laclau 1990, 39). From this perspective it cannot be overlooked that dislocation may have destructive as well as productive aspects (Critchley and Marchart 2004, 207).[1] As far as some segments of the post-socialist cultural trauma can be seen as a dislocation, we are interested precisely in the tension between its destructive and productive side. The popular urge for the restoration of memory (not the least by use of popular culture, including television) falls into the productive category. For many years television was condemned for being "presentist," having a bias for immediacy and thus nullifying history. Only was recently television exculpated from this kind of sinning. According to Mimi White, "history, duration and memory are as central to any theoretical understanding of television's discursive operations as liveness and concomitant ideas of presence, immediacy, and so forth" (White 1999). We would like to argue (and take advantage of the fact) that television not only makes history an important part of its programming, but is also indispensable in stimulating (and thus cocreating) collective memory. It provides "the food for memory" and its bias towards personalization, narrativization and iconicity makes the process of memory creation accessible to diverse groups of viewers. We can also say that the higher the cultural diversity is in the input of the collective memory, the more beneficial it is.

TELEVISION AS A MNEMONIC MEDIUM

In order to explore the adequacy of concepts of nostalgia and cultural trauma to representations of the state-socialist past in post-socialist popular culture, we completed a study of a successful retrospective television program. The guiding principle of the analysis was not a search for one-way media effects but instead a focus on the viewers' use of media contents for making meaning of the past. With this purpose, we examine how the retrospective television serial *Vyprávěj* (*Tell Me How It Was*; Czech Television, 2009–10) facilitates recollection and thinking about the socialist past. The research took the form of focus groups in which the viewers talked about their use of *Vyprávěj* as a mnemonic device that helps them to deal with the cleavage between the socialist past and the capitalist present. The visual sociology approach informed the study (Banks 2007): we used the TV serial partly as audiovisual elicitation from the research participants

206 *Irena Carpentier Reifová, Kateřina Gillárová and Radim Hladík*

within the focus groups.[2] This technique—among others—should be an effective tool to generate the feelings associated with certain contexts, and provide data enriched with the abstract layer of emotions.

Vyprávěj is a hybrid comedy-docudrama serial. It presents the story of an ordinary family whose fictive everyday life is intertwined with real political events and their consequences. The show was produced by the public broadcaster Česká televize (Czech Television) as a program commemorating the 20th anniversary of the fall of the state socialist regime in 1989. The narrative is packaged in four seasons. The first two seasons (covering the periods 1964–75 and 1975–85) have already aired, while the seasons covering the periods 1985–95 and 1995–2005 are forthcoming.[4] Among the serial's defining characteristics are the shifts between the enacted plot and the documentary parts and the heavy dependence of its visual aspect on pedantic fidelity to the period's lifestyle. The average rating of the serial per episode in 2009 was 1.3 million viewers. It is an above-average result even in primetime and qualifies *Vyprávěj* as a great favorite with viewers.[5] It was extremely popular with female viewers (women constituted up to two thirds of the spectatorship) and also achieved good results with the young audience in the age segment of 25–34.

The audience research took place in May 2010 in Prague, the Czech Republic. We organized eight focus groups chosen from viewers who had independently written to Czech Television about the serial. The population of the study thus consists of respondents who cared to express their appreciations of the serial, complaints regarding supposed inaccuracies, questions, etc., to The Audience Center of Czech Television. On our request, the Center sent an email to addresses in its database describing the concerns of our research and eliciting participation in the qualitative audience survey.

The final sample thus represented active viewers, fans who apparently like to share their opinion with the producers as well as with scholars. There were 42 respondents in total, of which 23 were female and 19 male. The groups were controlled for age and organized into two clusters: the first one consisted of young people who do not have any personal adult experience with socialism; the second included the participants who do have personal adult experience with socialist everyday life; and two of the groups were mixed with regards to the age of the respondents.[6]

We conceived of the processes of memory reproduction through the serial *Vyprávěj* as a constant activity of comparing the retro-signifiers (signifiers that signal the particular text as being of the past) with the stock of knowledge that the audiences have available to them. In this respect, Pierre Sorlin speaks of "historical capital," which the audience needs to possess in order to understand a particular narrative as a representation of the past (Sorlin 2000, 37). In our case, it may be more appropriate to refer to this stock of knowledge as "memory capital." Kansteiner's scrutiny of the processes of collective memory highlights two different positions: "memory makers" and "memory consumers" (Kansteiner 2002, 180). In this context the

The Way We Applauded   207

revision of his typology suggests itself: on the one hand, we have memory producers, but on the other hand, there are memory *prosumers* (productive consumers), who use their stock of knowledge in encounters with the mass media representations that they consume. The memory prosumers of *Vyprávěj* used retro-signifiers in two ways: retro-signifier as a *trigger* and retro-signifier as a *reality indicator*.

The first role refers to the situation when the retro-signifier generated reconnection with one's personal memories from the state-socialist past. In this case the participants liberated themselves from the narrative of the series and started to narrate their own stories. This "aberration" in reading (Eco 1979, 141) took basically two forms. The first form stimulated subjective memories that were connected relatively closely to one's private stock of knowledge and thus were not shared with other participants. The second form engaged the viewers with collective memories, by which we mean more encompassing stories shared by all participants.

In their second role, the retro-signifiers functioned as *indicators of true or false* elements in the series. In this case, the participants remained committed to the text and confronted it with their stock of knowledge. In a sort of interpretational conflict,[7] the participants proclaimed the serial to be a truthful representation of reality if it corresponded to their stock of knowledge and a misrepresentation if it contradicted their knowledge. Typically, this occurred with factual types of information. However, there was a subgenre of the text that was excluded from this principle: the documentary section. The serial consists of two types of text: the predominantly fictional section (the story of the family) and the minor documentary one. The participants perceived this latter text as inherently true. According to them, the documentary perfected the representation of the past, making it appear "the way it was." The inclusion of period footage was accepted as a general factual framework—the "historical capital" in which the viewers had a share—of the fictional plot, which in turn was the point of personal identification with the audiovisual text; the part of the serial that allowed the viewers to re-experience, relive their own past. Compared to the fictional plot, which was perceived as a dynamic and open text, the documentary section figured in the focus group as a static element, a given content that is not to be discussed. One participant, for example, commented on the screening of documentary clips from the serial in the following way:

> MFG 8 [commenting on the documentary section]: Such was the general opinion, or whatever was valid. Whereas the family, which was there, it lived its own life and, overall, it was as if it was not aware of the period, it was not aware of politics. So it was kind of a great contrast and it was a kind of refreshing moment in the serial.

Besides the two roles of retro-signifiers, we also identified their organization into four basic categories. The scale proceeds from the physical and

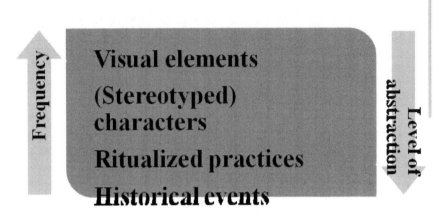

Figure 11.1

concrete signifiers that tend to appear with higher frequency to the most abstract ones that exhibit lower frequency. All of these categories can function in both of the aforementioned ways. The categories can be labelled in this order:

The first term embodies all of the visual elements that showed up in the series and served as indexical traces (Rosen 2001) of the state socialist past. The objects of daily use such as clothing, design, furniture and appliances were the most frequent case. The other ones, which were specific to the time period, belonged to the category of "socialist symbols," e.g. a pioneer scarf or a bouquet of red carnations. An image of the latter in a clip inspired one participant to make a comment in the course of which he obviously relied on the collective memory of others in the group:

> MFG 1: Those terrible red carnations, right?! Nowadays, I probably do not know anyone who would like carnations. And besides, the oath of the pioneers, you said it perfectly. I myself had to recite at the People's Committee of Prague 10, I remember that very well.

While the first category of retro-signifiers functioned both as a narrative trigger, i.e. a signal for association of personal memories, and as a reality indicator, the other three categories were biased toward the function of the narrative trigger and motivated the participants to tell the stories about their own past. With increasing levels of abstraction, they were less likely to be subjected to a challenge or a critique within the group of discussants.

The second category centered on certain characters, particularly on their stereotyped features.[8] In comparison with other categories, this type

Figure 11.2 The scene from the second sample used in the focus groups. Jarka reads her poem at the International Women's Day meeting to glorify socialist womanhood.

of retro-signifier was somewhat more often used as a generator of personal narratives. Thus, for instance, the character of a shop floor party official in the serial inspired this recollection of a real world person:

> MFG 2: A shady character. It reminds me of my boss at that time. [. . .] He spelled "fish" with "y", but he was a manager and a Member of Parliament, right?! So it was very difficult to work with him, difficult to work with him, for real, and he was also very dangerous.

The third category covers ritualized practices such as queuing or marching in a Labor Day parade. These retro-signifiers were quite often coupled with objects that were symbolic of socialism. Thus this more abstract category of retro-signifiers combined with the rather concrete category of the visual elements. A female discussant recalled a scene from the series in which people line up in front of a store as an instance of this category:

> MFG 1: For example, the fridge. Personally, I have never had to queue for a fridge but I know exactly that this is what our parents used to tell us, the way in which one had to queue for bananas, so one also had to queue for those fridges.

Historical events represented the highest level of retro-signifiers. This fourth category is underrepresented in the serial in comparison with the two previous narrative-triggering categories. August 1968, the month of the occupation of Czechoslovakia by five of the Warsaw Pact armies, which

210 *Irena Carpentier Reifová, Kateřina Gillárová and Radim Hladík*

Figure 11.3 The scene from the third sample used in the focus groups. The Dvořák family and their friends listen with astonishment to the radio announcement about the self-burning act of the student Jan Palach in 1969.

put an end to the reformist movement known as the Prague Spring, is an example of such a retro-signifier that was included in the televised text and triggered remembrance on the part of the viewers.

> MFG 3: When I used to go to school, my dad once checked out my notes from the civics class, it was in the seventh grade, and it caught his attention, so he read them, and there it was briefly described, what it was, that it happened.

Each category of retro-signifiers has its specific language. Also, it was articulated in a manner differentiating them from one another. We highlighted the expressive formulations and were able to group them into three modes of enunciation:

1. nostalgia
2. morality
3. experience/expertise

The first mode, nostalgia, attempts to describe the case of memories that were reproduced through emotional means of expression and mostly by using first-person singular or plural. This discourse was characteristic of the usage of retro-signifiers as a mnemonic trigger and encompassed all of the categories of retro-signifiers.

> MFG 1: Hearing [the song] "Bratříček" reminds me of Karel Kryl. I recall, when we were at the weekend house, our parents opened a bottle

The Way We Applauded 211

of wine and we listened to the tapes, that one was noisy, God knows how many times it had been copied, so this is something that is deeply ingrained in me. It even evokes nice feelings in me because it was simply nice. Weekends with the family, this comes to my mind.

The next mode is close to expressions of "nostalgia," at least in the sense that in both of these modes the participants assume the role of the narrator. However, in the "morality" mode, unlike in the mode of "nostalgia," the narratives of the discussants called forth collective and shared memories rather than private ones. The more abstract categories of retro-signifiers were employed in this mode of discourse. Also, the typical means of expression in this case was the third person in either singular or plural.

> MFG 1: It worked so that everybody was pushed into joining the party, and so those who didn't want to join, they had to face sanctions such as: "What about your boy—he wants to go to college." Like the kids couldn't get into a school and such. So under this regime people had to constantly think about whether to sign up and keep their mouth shut and let the kids study or not to sign up, keep their pride, but the kids, right, garbage men and such. It worked, the pressure was probably normal in those times; it was exerted onto people who had not joined the party yet.

When the retro-signifiers functioned as a reality indicator and thus were confronted with a person's stock of knowledge, the participants tended to take on the role of critic or expert. Whereas in the two previous cases (of nostalgia and morality) the participants took over the narrator role from the text, in this third case, they would move away from the text and position themselves on its outside. In addition, the "morality" and "nostalgia" modes were more connected to emotional means of expression, whereas the mode of "experience/expertise" was shaped by factual and evaluative vocabulary. The mode was thus identified by the usage of verbs that express value judgments and are conjugated in the first person singular.

> MFG 1: That was completely wrong, I think, it was the biggest mistake that I have noticed in it, and it had to do with the Nuselský Bridge and those R-1 trains, the construction of the subway, the R-1 trains, and the underground tram [. . .] Firstly, that was simply set in a wrong time, I think, the dramaturgy failed with this one, I think that there was a difference of three years when compared to the facts, and secondly, I think that it was—I do understand that they wanted to make it attractive for the viewers, but they overdid it.

No doubt, these three modes of enunciation were interconnected. For example, if the participants used retro-signifiers as triggers and took on the roles of a nostalgic or a moralist, they tended to present their subjective memories as objective ones—they would speak of "the way it was."

212 Irena Carpentier Reifová, Kateřina Gillárová and Radim Hladík

MFG 3: [. . .] all the women were celebrating and all the men were drinking like fish, everything was subordinated to MDŽ celebration.

When faced with other participants' narratives and memories with contrary claims, they would defend their own truth and take recourse in the enunciative position of an expert or an experienced witness. However, as the discussion progressed, the memories that were originally perceived as taken for granted and objective became more relative and subjective in their rendition.

M1/M2 FG 2:

M2: I was born in 1963, my mom got married sometime in 1960, and she had the stiletto boots, the synthetic leather ones, she had those stiletto boots.

M1: But later, certainly later.

M2: Certainly before I was born. Because she had those when she was frequenting dance lessons with dad.

M1: Because I have photos . . .

M1/M2 FG3:

M1: And another thing that bothered me personally, there was a girl who wore the same skirt I've bought in a shop recently, a dotted one. So I told to myself . . .

M2: But the fashion is repeating!

M1: I know but I told to myself it was not possible.

M2: Besides, eighties are in . . .

The "experience/expertise" mode was activated when older participants defined themselves as such to the younger viewers who did not have an authentic experience with communist times. Even though the older participants considered the serial to be an important didactic tool, they still had a tendency to emphasize the incapacity of the youngsters to read the serial "the right way." Thanks to their lived experience, they would perceive themselves as the rightful experts of textual interpretation.

MFG 8: After all, if I had experienced something, I therefore have a source of knowledge in what I had seen, like, it didn't concern the regime directly. For example, the corrupted deeds that you couldn't see, those can't be included in a family TV series. Then one family would be a target of every wrongdoing and that wouldn't be credible. And, precisely, the documentary footage, it provides a framework, it follows a certain topic, so that they [the young ones] simply realize in what ways the regime was unlawful. Why the times are better today and so on.

On the other hand, the younger participants would sometimes counter similar claims based on their experience with claims based on expertise.

The Way We Applauded 213

Their expertise did not derive from authenticity; instead, they would refer to external authorities. Significantly, however, they would not appeal to the authority of historiography. While the senior participants supported their arguments by using narratives of their subjective or collective memories, the junior ones used the style of speech reminiscent of mass media. The phrase "I think," often accompanied by the clause "my close relatives said," were the typical means of expression in this instance.

M1/M2 FG 8:

M1: I think that even the party membership had to be based on a voluntary principle because you can't have a party in which you force the people to participate in the power [. . .].

M2: But that isn't true. Well, I think that you have some distorted information [laugh] or actually some distorted ideas. So.

M1: Why do you think that it was different, or do you . . .

M2: Well, I know it from my own experience. And from the stories of my close relatives.

"Nostalgic" and "moralist" roles were more readily accepted by the cluster of older participants. Relegating communist ideology to the background opened up a way for them to recount their childhood and teenage lives. In contrast to other television programs in which the political regime is foregrounded, the *Vyprávěj* serial allowed them to experience the pleasure of reconnecting with the past. They were not forced, either by the textual composition of the serial, or by the administrators of the focus group, to defend the positive emotions that they attached to childhoods spent in the state socialist period—a period typically presented as inherently bad in normative, post-socialist representations.

MFG 8: It affects me more than the politics. The politics, the documentary, it is very distant. And it can't even be named properly, not even understood, let alone captured somehow, so why should I care. I'm interested in what affects me, in the things that I have to deal with, and there it was in the story.

To sum up, in our research we found out that the retro-signifiers—ranging from physical objects through characters and ritualized practices to events—offered by the television serial *Vyprávěj* did not function simply as clues to a historical time; rather, they were used by audiences as mnemonic devices for generating their own subjective or shared memories. The remembrance thus stimulated occurred in different modes, which were expressed by the roles of a nostalgic, a moralist, or a (lay) expert. The more abstract the retro-signifiers were, the less likely they were to be used as reality indicators and the more likely they were to be seen as taken-for-granted aspects of the past. The mode of experience/expertise was typical for the

214　*Irena Carpentier Reifová, Kateřina Gillárová and Radim Hladík*

young participants' rhetoric. It was also utilized by the senior participants to establish themselves as more knowledgeable in front of younger viewers. However, it is important to underscore the tentative status of our observations regarding a possible generation gap. The database at our disposal included only a limited number of younger viewers. The latter provide the producers of the serial with significantly less feedback. This could be either due to the younger cohorts' lesser interest in watching the serial, or to their reluctance to share their opinions and fandom.

INDICES OF TRAUMATIZED MEMORY

A considerable part of the respondents' comments reflected an experience of cultural trauma. This category encompasses comments which relate to new social insecurities brought about by capitalist society, but mainly to disruption of biographical/institutional continuity (dislocation) and feelings of embarrassment/stress about life in totalitarian socialism. The most relevant parts of the comments were those untangling the coping strategies that people use to reconcile themselves with the embarrassing or unsettling flashbacks and incorporate these recollections back into the memory.

The respondents hinted at three separate reasons for keeping the collective memory active in the sense of overcoming the rupture between the present day and the socialist past. They can be summarized as: 1) preventive continuity, 2) historiographic continuity, 3) everyday continuity. Preventive continuity is the least controversial form of the memory-compensating approach and as such it has been part of the post-socialist mentality since the beginning of the 1990s. It recognizes the relevance of uninterrupted memory as prevention against the return of totalitarian socialism.

> MFG1: To me, it is really important that these days shall not come back, I mean the communists who ruled here . . .

Preventive continuity is close to historiographic continuity, although the latter refrains from making moral judgments and objectifies the period of socialism as an inseparable stage of history.

> MFG4: It is important for the young generation because it is becoming part of history. So they should know, because it is a piece of our history.

The most refined and nuanced meanings were included in the respondents' comments about the continuity of everyday life. They felt that the socio-political rupture between the past and the present had been overly generalized to the extent that it also affected the integrity of everyday life.

The respondents indicated a two-way nexus between seemingly detached periods of the past and the present in the sphere of the everyday: in some respects, the past was not so different from the present, and in others the present is even permeated with the past. Very often, respondents voiced their opinion that everyday actors in totalitarian socialism took their living conditions for granted as a given social environment, very much like contemporary people understand their social realities nowadays.

> MFG4: The last 20 years brought enough information about all the bad things that happened. To do justice, it should also be said that people were living their normal lives in those days too. Brutality, prosecution, penalization, these things impacted on one part of population. The majority of the people tried to conduct their normal lives even in those days. Under communism, we did not live in the trees; marching under the red flags wasn't our daily bread. Normal human affairs were also on the agenda, such as television shows.
> MFG5: I was happy to be a pioneer.[9] I took it for granted.
> Moderator about S2: How would you feel if it were you, participating in the International Women's day celebration?
> MFG3: Mhm, I'm not sure, maybe we wouldn't think it to be anything special or even be able to see that it was totally [. . .] crazy.

Another connection between the past and the present is seen in the transference of some habits (assumed to be socialist deformations) into the capitalist system.

Figure 11.4 The scene from the first video sample used in the focus groups. Comrade Karpíšek (left) recruits Mr. Dvořák (right) to become a member of the Communist Party.

MFG4 [about S1]: Comrade Karpíšek is exactly the young career-oriented person who was told: "stick with us and you will be well off." They taught him what to say, what words one should use. It is absolutely normal today in any sales company. If you go for a sales person position, they teach you the ways in which to move and speak. Absolutely normal today . . .

A rich source of data indicating cultural trauma were the comments in which respondents rehearsed their feelings of embarrassment or anxiety during totalitarian socialism. Alternatively, they interiorized the feelings of the serial protagonists.

Moderator: Did you consider the scene picturing the bus trip to Austria to be funny?
MFG2: Not at all, I was really sympathetic with the characters, so that the custom officers would not find any illegal stuff.
MFG2: I feel strange about crossing borders to this day. Today, one doesn't even have to present a passport and yet I still feel fear and get goosebumps.

A concept that gets referenced often in scholarly reflection on the aftermath of state socialism is the *guilt* over collaboration or silent agreement with the CP rule. The entire 1990s discourse on decommunization, to a great extent, dealt with a redistribution of the guilt for "the widespread injustice of the communist regime, imprisoning people for stating publicly their political views opposing the policies of the Communist Party and the regime in general" (Marada 2007, 91). Guilty feelings (as well as shame, flagellation, metaphoric schizophrenia and embarrassment) were indeed present in our respondents' comments, although not in a straightforward form. Guilty feeling presupposes the existence of a perpetrator—partial or full acceptance of such a role and a stigma left on the cultural memory. In Czech post-socialist culture the position of a perpetrator—the symbolic figure guilty of and responsible for the crimes of totalitarian socialism—was never fully determined. Who is to be blamed? The CP top executives? All members of the Communist Party? The entire silent majority? As far as the position of a perpetrator is a no man's and everybody's land, it is open to being assumed (or imposed upon) by a wide range of actors. The process of consenting to the role of perpetrator may, indeed, include or induce cultural trauma—Bernhard Giesen coined the concept of "trauma of perpetrators" to refer to a similar development in post-Nazi Germany (Giesen 2004, 115). However, our data disclose a more complex structure of guilty feelings in the traumatic memories of socialism than is usually assumed. We found symptoms of guilty feelings fidgeting with a role of perpetrator in an unusually delicate way. Uncertainty permeating the identity on the

The Way We Applauded   217

move between roles of a victim and a perpetrator can be demonstrated by comparing the two following quotes:

> MFG7 [about S1]: My father was forced to enter the Communist Party. They came to talk to him about his daughter (it was me) having good school results and if it would not suit her to go to the high school? So after this, kind of, blackmail and persuasion he had to agree to become a party member.

> MFG3 [about watching the episode capturing the Labor Day parade with her 9-year-old daughter]: [. . .] and I tell her, go sit and watch, look at Husák,[10] look at the way we applauded him.

In the first statement the discussant clearly sees her father as a victim. By contrast, the logic of the second statement is based on a deeply embedded duality. The respondent seems insecure about who exactly should be an object of the gaze: the communist President Husák or those who applauded him? Who should be tightly observed: the communist apparatchik or "us," the obedient, anonymous mass? Where is the borderline between perpetrators and mere victims in the film scene? The comment reflects people's potential collaboration and shows that the position of a perpetrator resists being bound to the top communist officials. Consequently, the identity of the respondent as an ordinary person, who applauded when told to do so, moves on the victim–perpetrator scale and hardly ever rests in peace. In this case the respondent compulsively invites her daughter to pay attention to the conforming behavior of the older generation. It can be interpreted as an act of masochism and flagellation, as if it could undo the shame. In the above sketched comparison, cultural trauma of an ordinary man is visible as a permanent ambivalence and oscillation. It points to the never-ending stumbling from guilt to suffering and back; to the discontent following from not having one overarching narrative which would safely redeem the ordinary people as innocent victims.

CONCLUSION

As we argued in the introduction, the post-socialist collective memory of the state-socialist past does not lend itself easily to one principle. The statements of the participants in the focus groups reinforce our notion of the complexity of remembrance. In virtually all the cases, the kind of remembrance that was stimulated by viewing and discussing clips from the *Vyprávěj* television serial reminds us of a memory prosumption process that appears to be more of a patchwork of personal needs and textual offerings rather than a single mnemonic practice.

218   *Irena Carpentier Reifová, Kateřina Gillárová and Radim Hladík*

Nostalgic renditions of the past were commonly observed. Their manifestations were often explicit, as when the older discussants acknowledged a sense of longing for the past, although they would clearly define the desired past in terms of childhood and memories of the family and avoid the political context. The existing theories of nostalgia seem to be correct in the sense that nostalgic remembrance did not seem to engage a deeper sense of historicity of either state socialism or private capitalism, nor did it inspire an appeal to change history's course. The nostalgia did appear "reflective," but less in a sense attached to it by Svetlana Boym, i.e. a type of nostalgia "more concerned with historical and individual time, with the irrevocability of the past and human finitude" (Boym 2001, 49). The viewers quite simply exhibited awareness of the nostalgic sentiment in their recollections by spelling out the bygone nature of the past in question; so perhaps we could speak more precisely of a case of "reflected" nostalgia. Furthermore, the analysis of relevant statements supports the claim that nostalgia adheres to commodified kitsch and stereotypes, as they tend to be elicited by the less abstract retro-signifiers.

Nostalgic discourse itself does point to aspects of the past over which our discussants express a sense of loss. We deem the ado about the post-socialist nostalgia to stem from the (disrupted) continuity of collective memory and (eroded) integrity of everyday life. In this light, nostalgia is just one of the secondary reactions to a primary distress: it is as though an excess of official memory and historiography (Hladík 2009) results in the "lack" of everyday memory. The moralizing mode of discourse appears to be an intermediary position, a moment of reflection on nostalgia as well as a precursor to the dilemma of assigning guilt in traumatized remembrance. If some scholars see the post-socialist popular culture of remembrance as a space for people "without a story," we tend to see it as a space of many stories, private and collective ones, for which the narrators seek a forum. Their trauma is truly cultural—not traceable to an essential event, not stimulated by experienced horrors, not even reducible to economic distress—in that it stems from the impossibility of seamlessly integrating the past with the present by means of acceptable narratives. To the extent that serials such as *Vyprávěj* bear witness to these unrecognized stories, they have a therapeutic element and perhaps even political ramifications. However, there seems to be no prescription for a proper type of remembrance, no easy exit out of post-socialism.

Our research has confirmed the relevance of popular television in the formation of collective memory and showed that the medium's mnemonic dimension has a particular role to play in the context of a post-socialist country like the Czech Republic. We followed the discourse of viewers of the television serial of mixed genres, and found that the way in which they articulate singular forms of remembrance, such as its traumatized or nostalgic type, turns them into complex negotiations of the meaning of the state-socialist past.

The Way We Applauded   219

NOTES

1. By "tokens of an authentic socialist culture" we refer to material objects or immaterial images that were produced or used in the past and preserved to the present day not only in official archives and museums but also by informal ways of storage in people's households, etc. This can be clothing, furniture, do-it-yourself objects or television shows produced before 1989. Indexical signs of the past hardly stand by themselves; they are usually parts of bigger wholes of symbolic nature. It can be e.g. the case of a particular authentic object preserved from the past and used as a prop in the film. The typical example can be original labels of cans, bottles and other grocery products used in the film *Goodbye, Lenin!* (Germany 2003). "The appeal of the index" in creating an effect of historicity in visual representation is emphasized by Philip Rosen (2001, 127). He puts forward a distinction between "preservationist" and "restaurationist" positions, where the first one encompasses attempts to show the past through authentic, unmodified objects (in spite of their natural wear and imperfections) while the second one strives to aestheticize them by renovation (Rosen 2001, 52).

2. We are far from suggesting that all cultural traumas are dislocations or that dislocation is an underlying pattern in all segments of a particular cultural trauma. E.g. in case of natural disasters like tsunamis or earthquakes the discursive dislocatory function of the traumatic event is not so strong. Similarly, some other cultural traumas, e.g. the radical social changes (like the rule and collapse of state socialism in Central and Eastern Europe), may be showing signs of discursive dislocation only in some of their segments whereas other segments are non-discursive in their substance (real casualities, human suffering, material damage . . .).

3. We facilitated the focus group debates by screening three video samples.

    Sample 1 (S1) was taken from the episode one, *Od začátku—1964* (*From the Beginning—Year 1964*). In this part, father Josef Dvořák is approached by the deputy of a factory council of the CP, Comrade Karpíšek, who hands him an application for Communist Party membership. The father looks very sheepish and does not want his colleagues to spot the scene. Karpíšek subtly threatens him that a potential refusal may have an impact on his children's educational opportunities in the future.

    Sample 2 (S2) was taken from the episode 21, *MDŽ—1973* (*International Women's Day—Year 1973*). In this part, there is an International Women's Day celebration at the father's workplace. He participates in it (after a separation from his wife, Jana Dvořáková) with his new girlfriend, Jarka. It turns out that Jarka (unlike Josef Dvořák and especially his mother, who also comes along) is an ardent supporter of the Communist Party line. As a surprise, she reads aloud a poem she personally wrote to celebrate socialist womanhood.

    Sample 3 (S3) was taken from episode eight, *Velká očekávání—1969* (*Grand Expectations—Year 1969*). In this part, there is a documentary footage used to recall the atmosphere of the Prague Spring in 1968 before and after the invasion of the Warsaw Pact military forces into Czechoslovakia. The feature film continues with the father's birthday party (prepared by his wife, Jana) which is interrupted by a radio announcement informing that Jan Palach, a university student from Prague, burned himself in protest on the main square in Prague as a living torch.

4. The first season aired from to August 31, 2009 to February 22, 2010 and had 26 episodes. The second season aired from September 9, 2010 to December 17, 2010 and had 16 episodes.

220 *Irena Carpentier Reifová, Kateřina Gillárová and Radim Hladík*

5. The average share of the serial *Vyprávěj* was 32.38% of viewers. In 2010 CT1 (the channel which aired the show) had 18.74% of viewers as the total average share in primetime (Source: http://www.ato.cz/vysledky/rocni-data/share/15)
6. More details on the composition and organization of the focus groups are available from the authors upon request.
7. Philip Rosen dubs this process the Everett's Game. The inspiration for the term was a letter of complaint written to a film studio by a certain Mr. Everett, who wished to point out a historical inaccuracy that he had noticed in a movie. The rule of the Everett's Game requires "that every detail of the film be gotten 'right' or else he [Mr. Everett] can assert a victory, consisting in a claim of knowledge of the detail superior to that of the film" (Rosen 2001, 156).
8. For a useful overview of the problem of "historical character" in film and an appropriate typology, see the work of William Guynn. (Guynn 2006, 97ff.)
9. The Pioneer Organization of Socialist Youth Union (PO SSM) was a communist youth organization in 1970–89.
10. Gustáv Husák was the President of Czechoslovak Socialist Republic from 1975 until 1989.

REFERENCES

Alexander, Jeffrey C., Ron Eyerman, Bernhard Giesen, Neil J. Smelser and Piotr Sztompka. 2004. *Cultural Trauma and Collective Identity.* Berkley: University of California Press.

Banks, Marcus. 2007. *Using Visual Data in Qualitative Research.* London: Sage.

Boyer, Dominic. 2006. "Ostalgie and the Politics of the Future in Eastern Germany." *Public Culture* 18: 361–381.

Boym, Svetlana. 2001. *The Future of Nostalgia.* New York: Basic Books.

Carpentier, Nico, ed. 2007. *Culture, Trauma and Conflict: Cultural Studies Perspectives on War.* Cambridge: Cambridge Scholars Publishing.

Caruth, Cathy. 1995. *Trauma: Explorations in Memory.* Baltimore: John Hopkins University Press.

Critchley, Simon and Oliver Marchart. 2004. *Laclau: The Critical Reader.* London: Routledge.

Dominková, Petra. 2008. "We Have Democracy, Don't We?" In *Past for the Eyes,* edited by Péter Apor and Oksana Sarkisova, 215–243. Budapest: CEU Press.

Eco, Umberto. 1979. *A Theory of Semiotics.* Bloomington, IN: Indiana University Press.

Enns, Anthony. 2007. "The Politics of Ostalgie: Post-socialist Nostalgia in Recent German Film." *Screen* 48(4): 475–491.

Eyal, Gil. 2003. *The Origins of Postcommunist Elites: From Prague Spring to the Breakup of Czechoslovakia.* Minneapolis, MN: University of Minnesota Press.

Eyal, Gil. 2004. "Identity and Trauma: Two Forms of the Will to Memory." *History and Memory* 16, (1) (Spring/Summer): 5–36.

Fiske, John. 1997. *Television Culture.* London: Routledge.

Guynn, William. 2006. *Writing History in Film.* London and New York: Routledge.

Halbwachs, Maurice. 1950. *La Mémoire Collective.* 1st ed. Paris: Presses universitaires de France.

Halbwachs, Maurice. 1992. *On Collective Memory.* Chicago and London: University Of Chicago Press.

Hladík, Radim. 2009. "Between Resentment and Forgiveness: Public Histories in Czech and South African Transitions." *Teorie vědy* (*Theory of Science*) 31(2): 113–137.

The Way We Applauded   221

Hutcheon, Linda. 1998. "Irony, Nostalgia, and the Postmodern." http://www.library.utoronto.ca/utel/criticism/hutchinp.html.

Irwin-Zarecka, Iwona. 1994. *Frames of Remembrance: The Dynamics of Collective Memory.* New Brunswick, NJ: Transaction Publishers.

Jameson, Fredric. 1990. *Signatures of the Visible.* New York: Routledge.

Jameson, Fredric. 1991. *Postmodernism, Or, the Cultural Logic of Late Capitalism.* Durham: Duke University Press.

Joas, Hans. 2005. "Cultural Trauma? On the Most Recent Turn in Jeffrey Alexander's Cultural Sociology." Review of *Cutural Trauma and Collective Identity*, by Jeffrey C. Alexander. *European Journal of Social Theory* 8(3): 365–374.

Kansteiner, Wulf. 2002. "Finding Meaning in Memory: A Methodological Critique of Collective Memory Studies." *History and Theory* 41(2): 179–197.

Kansteiner, Wulf. 2004. "Genealogy of a Category Mistake: A Critical Intellectual History of the Cultural Trauma Metaphor." *Rethinking History* 8(2): 193–221.

Kennedy, Michael D. 2002. *Cultural Formations of Postcommunism: Emancipation, Transition, Nation and War.* Minneapolis, MN: University of Minnesota Press.

Laclau, Ernesto. 1990. *New Reflections on the Revolution of our Time.* London: Verso

Marada, Radim. 2007. "Paměť, trauma, generace" ("Memory, Trauma, Generation"). *Sociální Studia (Social Studies)*, 1–2: 79–95.

Mayer, Françoise. 2009. *Češi a jejich komunismus: Paměť a politická identita (The Czechs and their Communism: Memory and Political Identity).* 1st ed. Praha: Argo.

Nora, Pierre. 1989. "Between Memory and History: Les Lieux de Mémoire." *Representations* (26): 7–24.

Přibáň, Jiří. 2002. *Dissidents of Law: On the 1989 Velvet Revolutions, Legitimations, Fictions of Legality and Contemporary Version of the Social Contract.* Aldershot: Ashgate.

Ray, Larry. 1997. "Post-communism: Postmodernity or Modernity Revisited?" *British Journal of Sociology* 48 (4): 543–560.

Reifová, Irena. 2009. "Rerunning and 'Rewatching' Socialist TV Drama Serials: Post-Socialist Czech Television Audiences between Commodification and Reclaiming the Past". *Critical Studies in Television* 4(2): 53–71.

Rosen, Philip. 2001. *Change Mummified: Cinema, Historicity, Theory.* Minneapolis, MN and London: University of Minnesota Press.

Smelser, Neil J. 1962. *The Theory of Collective Behavior.* New York: Free Press of Glencoe.

Sorlin, Pierre. 2000. "How to Look at an 'Historical' Film." In *The Historical Film: History and Memory in Media*, ed. Marcia Landy, 25–49. Piscataway: Rutgers University Press.

Sztompka, Piotr. 2000. "Cultural Trauma: The Other Face of Social Change." *European Journal of Social Theory* 3(4): 449–466.

Teitel, Ruti G. 2000. *Transitional Justice.* Oxford: Oxford University Press.

Torfing, Jacob. 1999. *New Theories of Discourse.* Oxford: Blackwell.

Volčič, Zala. 2007. "Yugonostalgia: Cultural Memory and Media in the Former Yugoslavia." *Critical Studies in Media Communication* 24(2): 21–38.

White, Mimi. 1999. "Television Liveness: History, Banality, Attractions." *Spectator* 20(1): 37–56.

12 Coy Utopia
Politics in the First Hungarian TV Soap

Ferenc Hammer

> One of the enduring formative features of soap opera, as well as a major source of its pleasures, has been its reliance on the creation and slow consolidation of a unified, fictional community, a community whose rules and logic form an ordered normative system to which all characters—despite their differences and antagonisms—are ultimately subjected. In this sense, the traditional soap community can be seen as a metaphor for (the ideal of) modern society. (Ang and Stratton 1995, 122)

Increasing globalization in world television in the 1980s brought not only such genre-setting television series, soap operas and shows as *Miami Vice*, *Dallas* or *M.A.S.H.* (Smith 1998) and the first stream of international scholarly reflections on these products (Ang 1985; Katz and Liebes 1993) but also an array of genuinely developed formats and adaptations that contributed to the contours of national media cultures around the world (Allen 1995; Curran and Park 2000). Television in the Eastern Bloc from the very beginning had developed a deeply ambivalent attitude to spreading international (mostly Eastern) television formats. While Western media had been largely treated by officialdom as mere instruments of the political leadership in capitalist constitutional democracies, the fame and prestige associated with certain Western media outlets had been utilized frequently for a range of political purposes. For instance, Hungarian party leader János Kádár gave long interviews to Western papers, such as *Le Monde* in 1982, which portrayed him as an increasingly independent voice in Eastern Bloc politics (Schreiber 2008) or to *Time* magazine presenting him as a seasoned political orchestrator of the Hungarian thaw ("An Interview" 1986). When in the mid-1980s Hungarian Television decided to produce a soap opera focusing on the lives of everyday people in a realist genre format, the BBC's *EastEnders* had been utilized successfully as a model that legitimized the producers' decision (Vadas 1989).

INTRODUCTION: *SZOMSZÉDOK*—FORMAT, GENRE, TEXT, PRODUCTION, RECEPTION

Neighbors (Szomszédok), the first Hungarian TV soap, ran between February 1987 and December 1999, producing altogether 331 30-minute episodes. The biweekly program was broadcast on Thursdays in prime-time on Hungary's state (later, public service) television channel. After its termination, the whole series was aired twice again in the 2000s, and in the course of these years in the eyes of the increasingly nostalgic audience the program's narrative increasingly diverted from a purportedly realist narrative and representation into a poetical status comprised of nostalgia, retro and perhaps camp with particular attention to the Ancient Regime before 1989. After a quick assessment of the position of *Szomszédok* in the context of changing cultural politics in the late 1980s in Hungary and in a global context of television transformation, I discuss in this chapter the treatment of politics in *Szomszédok* in four somewhat overlapping layers. First, I assess the politics represented by narratives in *Szomszédok* that reflect the whirling events of the late 1980s resulting in the domino collapse of communist regimes in Europe. This analysis highlights the way *Szomszédok* functioned as a very peculiar political news outlet. Second, I pursue an analysis of the discussion of basic concepts, institutions, players and processes of constitutional democracy appearing (increasingly in 1988–90) in *Szomszédok* narratives. Third, through the analysis of prevailing identities, roles and performances of major *Szomszédok* characters, I present the contours of the main modes of citizenship appearing in the soap, particularly the way the program discusses social justice. And finally, I present an outline of the dominant way the communist past was viewed and discussed in conversations and events in *Szomszédok*.[1]

The plot of *Szomszédok* covers principally the lives of three families all living on the first floor of 10-story building at 8 Lantos Street in the newly built (1985) Gazdagrét housing project. The members of the Takács, Mágenheim and Vágási families represent professions such as beautician, EMT paramedic, shop assistant, taxi driver, elementary school teacher and printer. Some two dozen more or less important figures also appear regularly in the soap, some of them representing caricatures like the entrepreneur (Gábor), the old-fashioned teacher (Báthory), the forestry engineer Szelényi or the aging single artist (Sümeghy, and also Etus). László Czető Bernát, the first producer of the program, described the initial intention of the project:

> We had to invent characters whose life the whole Hungarian population could relate to. There had to be young, old and middle generation figures, also workers, intellectuals, and possibly those having some sort of ties with the countryside. (Vadas 1989, 9)

The production team had received (with the help of the communist government) four apartments on the same floor, three of them assigned as shooting locations for the three families, and the fourth as a technical space for the production crew. The production was fully funded by Hungarian Television's Drama Department. The majority of *Szomszédok* episodes was broadcast before the appearance of national commercial channels (1997) in

224   *Ferenc Hammer*

a channel-scarce television structure where the soap had no serious competition in primetime, a fact that brought it considerable audience attention in the late 1980s and the 1990s.

According Ádám Horváth, the program's director, *Szomszédok* was meant to represent a sort of community of good neighbors, in which most of the hardships presented by the hostile, alien world of Hungary in the 1980–90s could be tackled with attention, understanding, patience and tolerance, values that made *Szomszédok* a utopian social fiction in the rapidly transforming, economically troubled and occasionally politically-conflicted decade of the previous century (Sztankay 2006). Horváth saw a clear pedagogical role for the program. He argued (in 1989) that positive attraction from the audience towards the protagonists of the soap could make these characters positive examples for society:

> I do profess that these people [in *Szomszédok*] act according to extremely high moral standards, they behave decently, and even when they quarrel they transcend to a certain purity. This country lacks these things. The moral decline of the country has been catastrophic in the past 20 years. (Vadas 1989, 141)

Horváth has asserted that central characters in *Szomszédok* constantly passed tests offering occasionally seducing immoral rewards (Vadas 1989, 136), but these characters in most cases had no other choice than resisting the temptation. Referring to Dr. Mágenheim's, the married EMT paramedic's developing affair with a young architect woman, Horváth unambiguously stated that the emotional adventure may have jeopardized the integrity of the physician, a decision that was subsequently echoed by a wave of letters from the concerned audience objecting to Mágenheim's womanizing (Vadas 1989, 136). Quite interestingly, when the sociological accuracy of the social realist genre clashed with the pedagogical function, Horváth chose the latter with no hesitation. Addressing whether the program had ever considered mirroring the life of the actual lower middle class living in the Gazdagrét block estate neighborhood, he put it bluntly:

> No. Initially there had been no neighbors at all [around the four apartments serving as a production sites for the program], the new dwellers came only after we had arrived to Gazdagrét. But we did not wish to pursue a block estate saga, the problems of these neighborhoods do not interest me. I care little about the "block estate psyche," because it is a special, separate world, and if we focused on this environment, we would evidently exclude those from the prospective audience of the program not living in the block estate world. (Vadas 1989, 138)

The utopian world of *Szomszédok* was guaranteed by never allowing any serious conflict among members of the three central families. This modest middle-class social utopia, which turned out to be the signature feature of *Szomszédok*, was supported by a strange mix of classicist populism, in which even minor characters spoke professionally trained polished Hungarian, never using expressions that characterizes residents in the housing blocks, and never even smoking (Tucsni 2011). In our view, it is crucial to highlight the explicit production intention concerning the community-centered harmony in the program, saving subsequent analyses from discovering somewhat tautologically utopian harmony in a production that was meant to be deliberately harmonious. It is perhaps more compelling to highlight the aesthetic and political costs and consequences of the utopian diegesis in the course of the extraordinarily swift collapse of the communist order in Europe. *Szomszédok* presents eloquently the element of change in Hungary's media history at the end of the 20th century. As a biweekly serial it covered communist Hungary's last three years and the first nine years of the emerging democracy. Since the program was the first TV soap of its kind in Hungary, following the production's experimenting with various designs of allocation of the work regarding character and plot development among various scriptwriters, the production team had to make significant changes in the production process, and the product itself embodied certain professional compromises, mainly having to do with the increasingly antiquated character of the visual design of the soap, dominated by talking head and direct address shots, and also with the often strikingly pedagogical tone of the program. By the late 1990s the utopian peace of the Gazdagrét housing block neighborhood had started losing its credibility among viewers, who had become more attentive to reality programs. The didactic tone of the program resulted in particularly negative responses among professional reviews, and increasingly among the audience, which is reflected by the falling rates of the program after 1997. Most likely, the whole idea in the 1980s (not only in Hungary but also in other countries in the region) that a primetime social realist soap that covers the life of average people in a country would attract a significant audience segment from all social groups had just become an antiquated notion in the channel-rich era of the late 1990s. Early producer László Czető Bernát's somewhat sour comment reflects something of the general attitude regarding the fate of *Szomszédok*:

> My idea was that with choosing *EastEnders* as a professional standard of quality, we could do a quality television series in Hungary. We hadn't made it. That's all. People in every country get the television serial that they deserve. (Vadas 1989, 17)

The production was characterized by an obvious paradox. On the one hand, the choice of a lower-middle-class setting on the outskirts of Budapest and characters who looked at politics and the world outside with suspicion, disdain and a touch of learned helplessness, created a soap opera

226 *Ferenc Hammer*

world that represented the lives of the working classes. On the other hand, according to director Ádám Horváth, the characters had to be extraordinarily good, and from time to time exemplary. They had to make decisions in concrete moral dilemmas facing the narrower community, that is, family members and neighbors at Lantos Street, and they also had to show the path to society at large, represented by the biweekly 600,000–800,000 viewers, for example whether or not to go to vote next weekend, or choose material success over moral integrity (Antalóczy 2001). This double standard resulted in regularly erratic plot developments. For example in part 181, broadcast March 31, 1994 on the eve of national elections, in most of the 15 scenes, characters in *Szomszédok* presented something sad, awful, unfortunate, conflictual or depressing; a consistent dominant tone in the soap[2] meant to guarantee social realism in the narrative.

> Scene 3: Kenéz, the hardliner old guard communist complains to Feri Vágási about the dire realities of his life as a retired printer.

> Scenc 4: Employees in the beauty shop fight with their boss.

> Scene 5: Ádám Mágenheim and Mr. Takács meet in the hallway, tell each other how their cars were vandalized, decide to organize a local neighborhood watch initiative but find they don't know how to do that.

> Scene 7: Mrs. Takács (Lenke) dismisses the young party activist, refusing to give him her party endorsing slip, asserting that each political promise has to be discounted by 50% to take it as real, and also that one should not pay attention to what parties tell about each other.

> Scene 8: Lenke and Sümeghy agree that all the political campaign promises about pensioners' support are lies. Lenke admits that she mixes up parties all the time, because she cannot differentiate them by their acronyms. Lenke concludes: "I'm a bit fed up with politics." Sümeghy agrees, and adds that he is not scared to let everyone know it.

> Scene 9: It turns out that Juli Mágenheim wants to be an actress, but her father's advice is that it would be economically more rewarding if she was trained to be homeless or as a beggar.

> Scene 10: Virág complains to Etus that he wouldn't change living in Budapest for living in Naples or Rio—particularly if he were left alone to do that (the practicing head physician laryngologist, sociologically an elite position, does not specify the hardships he has to bear from the alien outside world).

Scene 11: The conflict in the beauty parlour continues. The core of the conflict is the lack of money.

Scene 12: Virág and Etus, the single artists, visit the Csontváry exhibit at the National Gallery, a major art event displaying the collected works of one of Hungary's most acclaimed modernist artists. Etus, concluding her passionate art guide monologue, turns to Virág: "[Csontváry's art] helps protect me from all that is ugly, disgusting and harmful."

Scene 13: Jutka Vágási meets with her mother, who doesn't want to see a private doctor because of the price of the service.

Scene 14: Alma finds out that her partner, Szelényi, is cheating on her. They break up.

After this ordeal of social hardships, human conflicts, hopeless situations, in the concluding 15th scene Feri Vágási, Kutya and Sümeghy diligently prepare flyers to put on cars' windshields, in an effort to attract volunteers for the neighborhood watch initiative. This invigorating experience of neighborly caring and solidarity serves as an introduction to Lenke's optimistic anticipation of a high turnout and a landslide support of one or another party (assuming that viewers have already forgotten that the very same character in her previous scene dismissed an activist, despised empty campaign promises and declared that she was fed up with politics). Lenke's forecast then is followed by the characters' direct-address pledge to the viewing audience, urging them passionately to go vote on Sunday. In Kutya's words: "People, go vote, because the future depends on you!"

CULTURAL POLITICS, POLITICAL CHANGE AND MEDIA POPULISM

The changing cultural-political context around the production, the text itself and reception of *Szomszédok* is key to the understanding of this markedly transitional cultural product connecting Hungary's clearly authoritarian media epoch of the mid-1980s with the era of the dual electronic media system of the 1990s characterized by the coexistence of public service and market-driven media. The popular culture of the second part of the 1980s in Hungary, regardless to the thrust of liberalization, was still connected to the "classic" cultural policy of communist Hungary. Though such Soviet-styled products as propaganda production films of the 1950s or the wildly popular pop contests of the 1960s were present only in historical documentaries or retro collections in the 1980s, popular entertainment, particularly performed by high-access media such

228   *Ferenc Hammer*

as television or radio, was still the most closely observed and policed area of cultural policy in Hungary in the second part of the 1980s. The basic structure of cultural governance in the Kádár regime (1956–89) classifying cultural products either as prohibited, tolerated or promoted, could be observed in the field of popular entertainment too. Horror, porn or products in any printed or electronic format critically addressing communist countries (such as the whole Bond series) were assigned to the prohibited category until about 1988. The most obvious promoted forms of popular entertainment could be found in television and radio, resulting in actors and media figures appearing in these formats becoming instant celebrities among the audience, which was largely isolated from genuine Western radio and television. In more marginal cultural spaces, such as cultural centers, clubs, art galleries, bars or even in private apartments, a range of more autonomous forms of entertainment emerged, as a parallel popular public sphere had in the late 1950s (Hammer 2009), such as jazz concerts, music clubs, punk gigs, commercial discos, or performances of non-conformist artists, all comprising the cultural sphere, tolerated more or less unwillingly by the cultural governance, a fact that naturally entailed also that these often rather mundane locations were closely observed by the state security (Szőnyei 2005).

Popular entertainment as a means of seducing the minds and hearts of the populace, particularly the young, was an important consideration in cultural politics and governing the media in the 1960–80s. This principally state-funded and -operated cultural industry aimed to fight Western influence, such as starting a pop music program with up-to-date Western tune lists on the Hungarian radio in 1965 to compete with the influence of Western stations, most particularly Radio Free Europe, Voice of America or Radio Luxemburg. The functioning of this cultural policy sphere was often surprisingly heterogeneous. It could easily happen in the 1960s that while the party-funded youth magazine published the lyrics and the chords of the latest Animals or Beatles hit, in the same week the party's newspaper would warn against dangers of West-aping in a grumpy editorial. An increasingly obvious pattern in the development of new media entertainment formats was the adaptation of Western formats that could be observed in such cultural products as rock operas in the theaters, obtaining a Western look, taste and orientation by teenagers, all in the 1970s, or when pop groups in the 1980s identified their work with such globalizing labels as disco, rock, country western or punk. The share of Hungarian Television in this overall cultural adaptation process was quite obvious with such experiments as introducing video clips, television quiz shows or a television soap opera in 1987.

When producers in Hungarian Television's Drama Department started discussing the possibility of a long-term television series of a social realist format, through personal connections, British television drama traditions were chosen as a model at large. The period of design planning and

Coy Utopia   229

implementation of the program already witnessed important changes in Hungarian media culture. While in 1986 the state information machinery performed classic Cold War disinformation propaganda when it announced blunt lies about the supposedly harmless consequences of the explosion in Chernobyl, a good two years later, a photo was circulated in the world press showing Hungarian party leader Károly Grósz posing with Mickey Mouse in Disneyland. In the course of this turbulent period of cultural-political transformation in and outside of Hungarian Television, the nature of cultural governance in the particular sphere of the electronic media turned out to be crucial regarding the shape and fate of *Szomszédok*. If historians in the distant future wish to locate the censor's office in the monumental headquarters of Magyar Televízió, they will be surprised to find no such location in the spacious building that served as the stock exchange before World War II. The key to cultural governance in the communist period was the lack of an explicit normative system such as an index of forbidden practices. Censorship largely functioned as an implicit system of cultural socialization in which actors in the cultural field observed (or sometimes did not) the rules known by everyone, but that was seen as a whole by nobody. In this implicit system of norms and expectations influential individuals served as "brokers" and "translators" in case of controversies, with the first among them György Aczél, the head of cultural matters in the party through the main period of the Kádár regime. When Ádám Horváth, already a renowned television and opera director, took over the executive producer's role in the production of *Szomszédok*, no further cultural political inquiry was necessary about the possible directions of the program, because his reputation as a man of classical humanistic values as well as a reliable fellow traveller of communist cultural politics guaranteed that as long as he oversaw the program, it would not divert from an expected path acceptable for a reformist cultural policy in the latter part of the 1980s. This assumption turned out to be accurate and secured a stable format for the program; but this format also sealed the fate of the program by the 1990s, which were dominated by infotainment and reality genres.

SZOMSZÉDOK AS A CHRONICLE OF POLITICAL CHANGES AND EVENTS

Ádám Mágenheim: [In Romania] it is still more difficult to be a Hungarian than here. She did not dare take her child to the hospital, because "she is just a Hungarian" [. . .]

Júlia Szikszay, Mágenheim's wife: People living together hate each other, only because one of them is Hungarian, the other of German descent, and the third is Romanian. It must be a Central-European magic spell [. . .]

230   Ferenc Hammer

> Ádám Mágenheim: America? Come on. They've got the Negro question. Here we've got unemployment, party wars, anti-Semitism. (*Szomszédok*, 75)

Every main character served as an impersonator of a particular set of complaints, concerns and fears in the series. Ádám Mágenheim, for instance, represented the critical ethos of an intellectual; and therefore the home of the Mágenheims on an average Thursday turned into a study circle about contemporary political issues. The appearance of events and processes of the larger political and social arena in *Szomszédok* was the result of an explicit production intention, that is, the soap was made to interrogate contemporary social realities. The second reason for the regular treatment of events and issues in *Szomszédok* echoing contemporary media themes stemmed from the peculiar structural design of the soap's narrative. Obviously, one cannot design an exciting long-term plot that mobilizes all the characters in equal intensity in a narrative. Thus, in *Szomszédok* producers had to choose between narrative consistency and complexity, ensuring robust and surprising strings of events, versus the thorough and extensive representation of the members of the three families and their acquaintances. The production didn't hesitate to favor the latter. Therefore, since long-term plots were virtually non-existent in the soap, characters, such as family members in their apartment, and particularly passers-by in the hallway of 8 Lantos Street, had virtually no other topics to discuss than contemporary news events.

Taking into consideration the narrative paradox associated with political agency that sought to combine in a credible way "grassroots" helplessness with idealized community-minded stewardship, the soap's paradoxical relationship with contemporary stormy political events (particularly in the late 1980s) is not too surprising. In an interview Horváth stressed that *Szomszédok* generally tried to avoid explicit political statements, and in 1988, silence or speech about political events were clear-cut political statements (Sztankai 2006). Major political events often go virtually unnoticed in the course of 1987 and 1988 in *Szomszédok*, probably as a result of the self-restraint of the producers, perhaps also, not too surprisingly, since television was the most closely watched media outlet during communism.[3] Nevertheless, as Tucsni (2011) points out in his analysis of thematic and narrative treatments of regime change in *Szomszédok*, as positive opinions regarding the contemporary changes were represented by central (that is, positive) characters in *Szomszédok*, the "hidden curriculum" of the series was the endorsement of the democratic political changes in the late 1980s.

National independence from Soviet influence was perhaps the most undisputed political value that *Szomszédok* characters shared. In the 82nd episode, broadcast in July 1990, just after the last Soviet soldier left Hungary, Mr. Takács, the patriarch-like taxi driver, notes that the removal of Soviet memorials from public spaces is probably a good idea, but "one

Coy Utopia   231

of them should be kept to make everyone remember that they were here" (*Szomszédok*, 82). A good seven years later on the eve of Hungary's accession to NATO, Sümeghy, after being fooled by a friend to believe that the Russians are back, argues that the NATO accession for Hungary must be a good thing if Russia objects to it (*Szomszédok*, 260). With regards to endorsing or supporting one or another social and political organization, the series performed a range of positions from explicit rejection, through neutral treatment or denial, to enthusiastic support (including presenting bank account numbers for supporters). Actual political parties were hardly mentioned in the soap. One of the few occasions when someone criticized the government came after the 1990 democratic elections, when the old shoe repairman complained that he could survive heavy years of communism earlier, but could not bear the economic hardships caused by the last, reformist communist government and had to close his shop: "The government's last trick was to outplay the renegade private entrepreneurs" (*Szomszédok*, 79). Rather interestingly, while the narratives of the soap employ a distancing from the government, the state receives an explicitly favorable understanding and almost warm treatment in the soap. When, at the end of episode 70, the main characters wish for something for the community (meaning the country), Mr. Böhm, the guardian of classical culture and community values in the Lantos Street community, says a Latin phrase, *salus rei publicae suprema lex esto*, meaning the supreme law should be the well-being of the state (republic). After the elections, two main characters argue about the government's hard job and how many people had to start their work in bankruptcy with little popular trust.

Organizations with less direct political ties, however, received extensive and unanimous support, such as when the teachers in Jutka Vágási's school discussed the advantages of the newly established independent trade unions (*Szomszédok*, 76), when Dr. Mágenheim discussed with his colleagues what the Chamber of Physicians could offer them (*Szomszédok*, 52) or when Alma Takács praised the Fehér Gyűrű Egyesület (White Ring Association), an independent association supporting crime victims (*Szomszédok*, 75). The serial clearly supported and promoted grassroots initiatives, as long as they did not threaten the community with disintegration, such as skinheads, the Satanist subculture or racist hooligans (*Szomszédok*, 147, 99, 298, respectively). The dwellers of 8 Lantos Street created a small community center for gatherings and for reading in the basement of the house, they collectively subscribed to newspapers and, when a traffic blockade was organized by taxi drivers in 1990 in Hungary to protest against increased gasoline prices, Mr. Takács, a taxi driver himself, joined the demonstrators (*Szomszédok*, 92). When discussing with students whether politics should be allowed in the high school classroom, Juli Mágenheim asserted that afternoon sports classes for the students would be more useful instead (*Szomszédok*, 73). The most obvious case of open support for a joint community effort came when Father László, a (real) Catholic priest

232 *Ferenc Hammer*

in the Gazdagrét neighborhood, launched a joint effort to build a church, and the process of gathering donations and planning the opening ceremony was integrated thoroughly within the *Szomszédok* narrative, resulting in characters from *Szomszédok* actively participating in the consecration ceremony of the church; conversely, the actual process of church building was fully incorporated into the soap's plot, including a case, perhaps not too frequent in television history, when a real cardinal (László Paskai) consecrated a church shown in a primetime soap. After finishing the classical music program of the ceremony, organized partly by the Lantos Street neighbors, Mr. Böhm, the main organizer, concluded: "The same thing should be accomplished in Parliament too. Everyone plays a different phrase, but the harmony is still beautiful and useful" (*Szomszédok*, 84).

SZOMSZÉDOK AS EDUCATION IN DEMOCRACY

> Do you know what the European Union is? Do you have any idea about NATO accession? The newspapers are full or articles written for insider experts, but I understand not a single word of them.—Kutya (*Szomszédok*, 260)

As illustrated by previous examples, the producers of *Szomszédok* consciously encouraged political participation, particularly in the form of parliamentary elections. This strategy included scenes wherein sympathetic key characters argued about the importance of voting, and several times, one or another character turned to an older family member or colleague asking if she could explain the basics of the electoral system. Preceding the first democratic elections in 1990, the event became a constant topic on *Szomszédok*.[4] Hável, the middle-aged teacher in the school where Jutka Vágási was teaching, was chosen to perform the role of the cynical, disinterested individual who claims that after many years of forced participation, he was just happy to be disinterested in politics, and as expected, his community joined forces to convince him of the merits of political participation. A young trade union activist colleague argued:

> In a normal democracy people vote for parties. Consequently, parties and candidates should be examined by the people. You just have to be happy that this time you can really choose from meaningful options. Unlike in the past.

His old colleague, Báthory, representing the classical teacher figure trained before communist times, joined his colleague:

> Hável. Today and tomorrow you go and get prepared. Your young and enthusiastic colleague has called on you, you get informed, and you

Coy Utopia 233

develop your opinion, and take the fate of the country into your hands. (*Szomszédok*, 76)

Though certain characters, such as Ádám Mágenheim or István Takács—performed by acclaimed theater and film actors János Kulka and Ferenc Zenthe—impersonated credible and likeable figures encounters and situations, when the narrative of the soap addressed political agitation as the dialogue above demonstrates, the scenes seemed more like a didactic high school drama. What this didactic frame suggests is that the natural status of the citizen is one that lacks knowledge, information and opinion on public issues—a set of shortcomings that could only be tackled with diligent teaching by more experienced fellow-citizens and the media. This attitude was expressed by Sümeghy's passionate exclamation on the eve of the NATO referendum:

I'll go to the Parliament Library and will keep reading until I have an understanding of these many new things. After all, I have the right to know what things mean. (*Szomszédok*, 260)

Preceding the 1989 four-question national referendum on fundamental political questions of regime change and the subsequent elections in 1990, Mr. Böhm, the manager of the technical-administrative issues of the building (elected by the community) made displays of political parties' and politicians' statements on important political issues clipped from newspapers, all intended to help the Lantos Street citizens make sound political decisions. The vision of the citizen as naturally innocent and ignorant assumes that politics itself is an artificial thing that one needs to be trained to understand, and generally a thing that is foreign to the way most people live. As suggested above, this implicitly anti-political stance was paired with the explicit intention of the producers to mobilize the populace. This dual and conflicted requirement often served as a frame for fairly absurd and unrealistic scenes, such as the following one, at the breakfast table of the Takács family. This little scene, in some instances flirting with true Dadaistic qualities, was probably intended to combine such elements as real-life popular anxiety regarding growing crime rates, lack of public knowledge regarding procedures and functions of elections—and perhaps the elite's perception of that lack of knowledge— a pinch of wicked, populist irony against slogans of political mobilization, and an aphoristic, "message between the lines" strategy, suggesting a wider relevance for the moral of the given comment. These occasionally very different narrative claims produced a sometimes rather confusing dialogue that is halfway between a comedy sketch and a dadaist performance:

Lenke: The doors are locked, the bike storage room is locked, and still there are thefts. I hear nothing but thefts are everywhere, how did things get this way?

234 *Ferenc Hammer*

Takács: Where voter turnout was high, the public administration will blame the criminals. Where the voting turnout was low, people can only blame themselves if their bike was stolen later. Because if you didn't vote, they stole your bike. That's all.

Alma: We'll see a number of elections before the bikes are safe.

Szelényi: The building's lock is so poor that it can be opened even with a simple knife. The bike storage lock can be opened with a pin.

Takács: I know a solution. For a certain period let's suspend voting and let's use the money we save this way for buying good locks. Or, let's take away the knives from everyone.

Lenke: I don't give away my pins. Thank you for the breakfast. (*Szomszédok*, 90)

While, as suggested above, the state, the ever-struggling government, and the parliament receive sympathy in the narrative, parties (mentioned always in plural) represent everything negative about politics. It is fair to say that basically all the main characters express disdain regarding parties and party politics. Gábor Gábor, the beauty parlor owner, blusters in episode 92: "Incompetent individuals' pointless debate is not democracy, but stupidity." Kutya and Sümeghy, in one of their many discussions about politics, conclude in episode 260: "[. . .] this is not even politics. Parties are just about fighting for power. [. . .] They are only interested in power and not in the well-being of everybody." The main reason behind this unanimous dislike of parties is probably quite simple: producers and writers either did not grasp or deliberately rejected the idea of debate and conflict in politics. Conflicts in the lives of *Szomszédok* characters could be always worked through with good intentions and rationality, and those who did not conform to this requirement were portrayed as driven by various wicked motivations, all unknown in the political utopia of 8 Lantos Street.

MODES OF CITIZENSHIP IN *SZOMSZÉDOK*

Feri Vágási: I'm afraid that in the coming months I'll have to work overtime a lot. The season of high politics has just started.

Jutka Vágási: Even more than before? You couldn't hear about anything else in the past months than politics.

Feri: In the next two days there will be a party congress. The party may split, things will turn upside down, then we'll have the election period, election, should I continue?

Jutka: I'm only interested in when they will finally take a look at how people could live in security, and perhaps a bit better too. What I can see around is that everybody is nervous, and there is no money. Prices are going up. Would things ever improve?

Coy Utopia 235

Feri: I think lots of workers, teachers and farmers ask the same thing in the evenings and they don't know the answer either. Let's clean up this here and off to sleep. I'll do the dishes, you go and have a rest. Go ahead. (*Szomszédok*, 64)

I assess the range of citizen virtues, features and norms featured in *Szomszédok* within a simple construction of citizenship, based on rights, identities and attitudes regarding others. Again, the production generally struggled with a pair of conflicting expectations regarding the portrayal of political agency. The intended social realism included the dominant vision of the everyman as unmotivated and vulnerable regarding larger issues of society and the polity, a social poetics that is often difficult to reconcile with the explicit democratizing agenda of *Szomszédok*. Fundamental individual rights received a somewhat materialistic account. In a scene when Mr. Takács takes a couple of Hungarian expatriates from a Western country on a sightseeing tour around Budapest, the couple's comments represent a naïve outsider's textbook attitude toward democracy in Hungary, which is shown to have little to do with "our" reality:

Woman: But now you can travel freely, can't you? You can keep foreign currency in the bank. There is freedom of expression. All these are good things, aren't they?
Takács: Oh yes. Those with foreign currency can surely travel. But for the majority, like us, this is not really an option. Everyone can talk, we can say whatever we want, but the great changes are still to come. Perhaps our grandchildren will enjoy the benefits of these changes. (*Szomszédok*, 81)

Gábor Gábor, struggling with a stubborn back ache, asserts with a painful grimace on his face:

Freedom, democracy. Where there is not health, there is no freedom. I could launch a party based on this idea. We wouldn't be a small party—unfortunately. (*Szomszédok*, 75)

Freedom of the press as a newly acquired fundamental right in the late 1980s gained a somewhat paradoxical representation in the soap. Generally, media, press and freedom of speech issues appeared quite often in each family's life, but the work of Feri Vágási, the program's "working class hero" at the printing company provided a natural habitat for free speech issues. Ironically, the fact that a few years before the regime change, when public life had been invigorated by publications and discussions about previously forbidden or silenced facts and events, was often presented in the soap as a source of difficulties. When new publications such as encyclopedias and lexicons were printed, Feri Vágási complained

236   *Ferenc Hammer*

that lexicon entries of political relevance had to be continuously revised, due to changing political realities.

When dozens of new newspapers and magazines were launched in the late 1980s, this transformation was portrayed in scenes as when a journalist, who lost his job as a result of changes in the press, complained: "I'm the freest journalist now. That's about the freedom of the press" (*Szomszédok*, 79). Similarly, Jutka Vágási confiscated a Nazi comic book, complaining about the negative dimensions of press freedom (*Szomszédok*, 63). Lamenting about sensationalist, muck-raking, fear-mongering media abounds in the serial. In episode 64, members of the Takács family complain about changes in television programming, such as the appearance of foreign language channels or the live broadcast of the Parliament's sessions.

In episode 271, a good seven years after of the regime change, Sümeghy complained: "Democracy is the privilege of rich countries. And we don't belong to them. And it will not change in the course of our lives." Often expressed explicitly, the ideal status of democracy for the producers of the program was one in which politics is peaceful and harmonious and the standard of living is constantly increasing. Since Hungary in the given period (and in most democratic countries most of the time) did not meet this high expectation, the most frequent citizen virtue in *Szomszédok* was silent growling against virtually everything, as epitomized by Feri Vágási's stance on politics:

> I don't say a damn word, I'm the silent majority. Consequently, I'm not afraid of the new gentlemen or of the old comrades. I'm having fun observing the way they kill each other, at least they may serve as a safety valve for all the pressures collected in the past. And things just evolve—in some direction. (*Szomszédok*, 149)

In terms of political agency, the distribution of work between governments and citizens portrayed in *Szomszédok* formed a simple construct, where citizens do their jobs by voting and in return their expectations are fulfilled by politicians. This somewhat childish version of politics, assigning not much role to citizens besides throwing a paper slip into a cardboard box every four years, and the continuous indignant disappointment caused by the ill-performance of such experience of politics that is virtually responsible for everything in people's lives, is a signature element of politics in *Szomszédok*. Lenke eloquently spells out the basics of this view of politics "from below":

> We have gone to vote three times. Now we have got our new government. But it will still be very long before these changes really reach us, when we really start to feel them. And this would be the job of the politicians. (*Szomszédok*, 81)

Coy Utopia 237

Morality and change are often intertwined in *Szomszédok* in such a way that the morality of the main characters gives them perseverance in the face of material and other seductions of changing realities in Hungary. In Tucsni's (2011) account "*Szomszédok* [. . .] meant to express the view that good citizens can cope while with changes while preserving their integrity in the meantime." British productions that served as a model for the soap had developed stances of morality while including issues affecting some of their main characters' lives, such as crime, rape and drug use (all impossible to imagine in the Lantos Street utopia, of course):

> Both *Brookside* and *EastEnders* have a commitment to dealing seriously with social problems and indeed to appeal to viewers who watch these soaps and not *Coronation Street* or *Neighbours* precisely because they attempt to deal with social issues in a positive way. (Geraghty 1995, 69)

Social issues and justice are represented as the province of the weak and the good, in that the central characters never get into trouble because of alcoholism, drugs or crime. However, no one gets rich; rather, their existence is cushioned by the solidarity of the community. Tucsni (2011) has analyzed the food store, Lenke's workplace, as a political space in *Szomszédok*:

> [. . .] all the employees in the food store work in the service of the customers. Profit is not the consideration here, all the employees are victims of the tragic situation that they cannot sell the products as cheaply as they would like to, therefore they cannot offer anything other than sympathy and regret to the customers. The role model is Lenke, who works part time to complement her tiny pension. She is also the one who transmits wisdom to the younger generation. Of course, Lenke, as a role model, possesses all the features beneficial for the customers— helpfulness, diligence, straightforwardness—and shows total contempt towards profit.

Burning social issues, such as racism and long-term unemployment, do appear in the soap, but rarely in a way that would pose a serious dilemma to a main character. Rather, these occurrences just happen to characterize the alien and wicked world surrounding the harmony of the good neighbors. Truly tragic events, such as when a Roma teacher is beaten severely by some hooligans, always happen to others in *Szomszédok* (*Szomszédok*, 298). Quite interestingly, Feri Vágási, the character who previously experienced hardships because he grew up in an orphanage, was perceived by Roma viewers as a Roma character:

> When *Szomszédok* started, we thought that Ferenc Vágási would be Gypsy. I was very happy that a character, even if not of Gypsy

238 *Ferenc Hammer*

origin, but at least of Gypsy looks, will appear. (Bernáth and Messing 1996)

A gay character showed up for a while in *Szomszédok*, as a colleague of Juli in the beauty parlor. His character (Mr. Oli) represented a transition concerning the representation of sexual difference in public life. By today's standards, Mr. Oli, a funny gay man in a pink outfit with a lisp, represents the worst stereotypical representations of homosexuality.

TAKING ACCOUNT OF THE COMMUNIST PAST

I can't be judgemental towards others, I just don't want to do that. It wouldn't be right if we all started judging everyone who had done something [in the past].—Jutka Vágási (*Szomszédok*, 75)

Accounting for the recent communist past was an important element of the politics of *Szomszédok*, because about a quarter of the series was broadcast before the fall of the Berlin Wall, while the rest of the program chronicled Hungary's fresh democratic experience, including making some of the first observations about the communist past. The program leaves no doubt about the nature of the political system that helped produce *Szomszédok*: any outspoken character who turned out to be an important figure in the communist past was endowed with particularly negative traits. The old guard characters were often violent, such as a man who wanted unjustly to sue Mágenheim for medical malpractice (*Szomszédok*, 82) or an angry parent who wanted schoolchildren to learn communist propaganda songs (*Szomszédok*, 40).

One of the most negative characters on the soap was Albert, who never actually appears in the series, but only in conversations of others. Albert is a caricature of the opportunistic turncoat, who, as a high ranking communist apparatchik, quickly joined one of the new democratic parties, and would quite soon regain a similar position. The teaching of *Szomszédok* with regard to the communist past is exceptionally clear: communism always relates to others, such as former bureaucrats, party members, and beneficiaries of the old system, but never to members of the Lantos Street community.

CONCLUSION

The dialogues and the storylines of *Szomszédok* are historical documents of key importance for understanding changing public attitudes towards—and norms of—democratic politics and citizenship. This is so, firstly, because characters in *Szomszédok* represented those living in unspectacular circumstances: struggling lower-middle-class dwellers in a 10-story

Coy Utopia 239

housing block on the outskirts of Budapest. Secondly, "political education" in *Szomszédok* often elucidated pro and con arguments regarding controversial political issues in the course of the transition in the late 1980s. The moral of this political commentary often highlighted contours of a rather radical utopian politics, suggesting a classical Athenian aura for the Gazdagrét block of flats, in which tolerant citizens refrain from forming political opinions unless they listen to all the arguments regarding a political issue. At the same time, such aspects of politics as self-interest, competition or media politics remained consigned to a dubious and reproachful status. The main argument I have pursued throughout in this article with the analysis of layers of politics presented in *Szomszédok* is that the format and tone of the program, strictly controlled by director Horváth and the institutional-professional norms of Hungarian Television—a key broker in Hungarian cultural politics—increasingly lost credibility and popularity by the latter part of the 1990s with the appearance of a full-fledged market-driven television culture.

NOTES

1. The most important source for my analysis is the text of the soap opera itself, which can be accessed online on the site of Hungarian Television. Since the coverage of politics was the main topic of my inquiry, I paid particular attention to episodes that were broadcast in the periods preceeding the 1990, 1994 and 1998 parliamentary elections as well as episodes that were broadcast in the eventful years of 1989–90. Further sources include secondary literature and media criticism of the production. All the translations of quotes from Hungarian literature and dialogues from the program are mine.
2. Sándor (2010) notes this grumpy tone as a *Szomszédok* signature: "This nagging, annoyed, growling, then subsequently lecturing tone has been acquired since then by other Hungarian-made soaps at commercial channels."
3. Not completely paradoxically, in the democratic era, on the eve of the launch of the 1994 election campaign season, Gábor Nahlik, executive of Magyar Televízió, asked the production to present the forthcoming *Szomszédok* plot and scripts to be reviewed (Sztankai 2006).
4. Curiously, maybe as self-imposed campaign silence, in the very episode preceding the first election round, politics or elections were not discussed at all.

REFERENCES

"An Interview with Kádár." 1986. *Time Magazine,* August 11. http://www.time.com/time/magazine/article/0,9171,962001,00.html.
Allen, Robert C., ed. 1995 *To Be Continued . . . Soap operas around the world.* London and New York: Routledge.
Ang, Ien. 1985. *Watching "Dallas": Soap Opera and the Melodramatic Imagination.* London: Methuen.
Ang, Ien and Jon Stratton. 1995. "The End of Civilization as We Knew It: Chances and the Postrealist Soap Opera." In *To Be Continued . . . Soap operas around*

240 Ferenc Hammer

the world, edited by Robert C. Allen. London and New York: Routledge. pp. 122–144.

Antalóczy, Tímea. 2001. "A szappanoperák genezise." *Médiakutató*. http://www.mediakutato.hu/cikk/2001_03_osz/08_szappanoperak_genezise_2/02.html?q =Szomsz%E9dok#Szomsz%E9dok.

Bernáth, Gábor and Vera Messing, Vera. 1998. *"Vágóképként, csak némában"—Romák a magyarországi médiában*. Budapest: Nemzeti és Etnikai Kisebbségi Hivatal.

Böcskei, Balázs. 2010. "Lakótelep, modernitás, Szomszédok-party." *Élet és Irodalom, 12*. March 26. http://www.es.hu/?view=doc;25509.

"Bőhm úr és Taki bácsi a népszavazásról." 2008. *Heti Vilaggazdasag*, February 22. http://hvg.hu/itthon/20080222_szomszedok_taki_bacsi_vagasi_feri.

Curran, James and Myung-Jin Park, eds. 2000. *De-westernizing Media Studies*. New York: Routledge.

Geraghty, Christine. 1995. "Social Issues and Realist Soaps. A Study of British Soaps in the 1980/1990s." In *To Be Continued . . . Soap Operas around the World*, edited by Robert C. Allen. London and New York: Routledge. pp. 66–80.

Hammer, Ferenc. 1995. "Az éjszakai élet mint populáris nyilvánosság a szocializmusban." *Médiakutató* (Winter): 89–107,

Horváth, Ádám, dir. 1987–1999. *Szomszédok*. Budapest: Hungarian Television.

Katz, Elihu and Liebes, Tamar. 1993. *The Export of Meaning: Cross Cultural Readings of "Dallas"*. 2nd ed. Cambridge: Polity Press.

McEachern, Charmaine. 1993. "Time and the Significance of the Rural in a British Soap Opera." *Time and Society* 2(1). pp. 7–28.

Sándor, Erzsi. 2010. "Én vagyok a szomszédom (Szomszédok sorozat, ismétlés 1–331. rész az m1-en, naponta. Rendező Horváth Ádám." *Mozgó Világ Online*. http://mozgovilag.com/?p=1120.

Schreiber, Thomas. 2008. "Az önálló francia 'Ostpolitik' és a 'különutas' Magyarország." *Kitekintő*, January 9. http://m.kitekinto.hu/hatter/2008/01/09/az_onallo_francia_ostpolitik_es_a_kulonutas_magyarorszg.

Smith, Anthony, ed. 1998. *Television—An International History*. Oxford, New York: Oxford University Press.

Szőnyei, Tamás. 2005. *Nyilván tartottak. Titkos szolgák a magyar rock körül 1960–1990*. Budapest: Magyar Narancs & Tihany-Rév Kiadó.

Sztankay, Ádám, 2006 "Szomszédok voltunk," *168 Óra*. http://www.168ora.hu/arte/szomszedok-voltunk-4420.html?&lm=2.

Tucsni, László. 2011. "Szomszédok és a rendszerváltás." Manuscript.

Vadas, Mihály. 1989. *Szomszédok—20 beszélgetés az alkotókkal*. Budapest: Mezőgazdasági Kiadó.

13 Why Must Roma Minorities be Always Seen on the Stage and Never in the Audience?

Children's Opinions Of Reality Roma TV[1]

Annabel Tremlett

THE ROMA MEDIA STAR

The rise of the Roma[2] media star across Europe is said to be a "love to hate" phenomenon, particularly in Central and Eastern Europe where the traditional Roma musical entertainer has been transformed into an "admired, albeit ambiguous, celebrity" (Imre 2011, 2). The *Eurovision Song Contest* (broadcast across Europe and beyond), along with local versions of *Pop Idol* and *Big Brother*, have turned Roma musicians into nationwide celebrities. Furthermore, shows such as Hungary's *Győzike* (2005–10, RTL Klub) and Romania's *Aventurile familiei Vijelie* (*The Adventures of the Vijelie Family*, 2005–present, Prima TV) have linked "Gypsy" with "reality" formats to grab large audience shares in some of the most successful shows for these channels in recent times. Whilst this trend is publicly debated and beginning to analyzed and theorized, there is still one gaping hole in the discourses: who is actually watching these shows? What do the Roma audiences think of such "reality" stars? Whereas we are prepared to discuss and critique the Roma-as-performer, there has been a dearth of literature on Roma as media consumers.

Researching Roma people as consumers may seem inherently wrong at a time when they are also amongst the poorest people in Europe. The rise of the Roma media star has stood in stark contrast to the abject poverty and discrimination suffered by the overwhelming majority of the estimated 12 million people that fall under this umbrella term.[3] On the one hand immensely popular shows such as Hungary's *Győzike* revel in the image of "the Gypsy" as a larger-than-life cultural icon that is fun to watch as he wastes money and dispenses with morality in jaw-dropping examples of hyper-materialism. On the other hand the seemingly blithe, mischievous, eternal Gypsy survivor is counteracted by reports from European institutions and human rights organizations that give a sobering picture of poverty and discrimination. Extreme poverty affects Roma minorities more than any other group, particularly in Central and Eastern Europe (*Eurostat report* 2010), and endemic discrimination has recently grown to sinister proportions with state-sponsored forced evictions of new Roma migrants

242   *Annabel Tremlett*

in Italy and France (Tremlett 2011) and recent violent racist attacks in the Czech Republic and in Hungary (Amnesty International Report 2010).

So what can we do with such incongruous information? Why are Roma both celebrated and despised in such dramatic fashions? These types of questions are beginning to be explored by theorists such as Imre, who argues that the question of Roma people's appearances on reality and other popular formats belies deep radical shifts in the class structures of post-socialist societies and growing inequality that often sees Roma positioned as the underclass (Imre 2006, 2011). Imre's work has led the way for others to take Roma minorities' presence in popular culture seriously, but there is still one glaring omission: what do Roma people themselves think of these shifts? What do they consume, when and how, and what has it got to do with their lives? Why must Roma minorities be always seen on the stage and never in the audience?

The lack of data on ethnic minority TV viewing patterns is lamented elsewhere (Buckingham 2002; Ross 2000). This chapter does not attempt to fill the huge gaps in knowledge on Roma minorities' viewing habits, but does base its discussion on some data that was produced during ethnographic research with Roma and non-Roma children in Hungary 2004–05, at the height of the aforementioned Roma reality TV show *Győzike*. The majority of the children in the research, both Roma and non-Roma, loved the show and it formed part of everyday conversations at school and home. This chapter looks at how the children's reactions to the show might inform future media research on such communities. The importance of empirical studies on television viewing that includes marginal ethnic groups is highlighted, along with the significance of recognizing Roma people as both producers *and* consumers of popular culture. Not only has this the potential to transform entrenched views of Roma people as traditional and marginalized but also to speak to television studies in order to encourage an analytic approach that can help decipher the current cultural and political shifts in an expanding Europe.

THE MUTED ADMIRERS OF ROMA REALITY TV

In February 2005 on a frosty Tuesday afternoon in Central Hungary, I was sitting in a primary school classroom on the suburb of a town as a part of a 15-month ethnographic study. A lot was always going on—as I had noted the day before, "there are so many tiny interactions that take place" I wrote, "I just cannot ever know the whole story" (Tremlett fieldnotes 07.02.05). Nevertheless, despite never being able to know the 'whole story,' that Tuesday afternoon I witnessed some more 'tiny interactions' that, thanks to fieldnotes, over time took on more significance to become a telling point about the status of television viewing in Hungarian society.

Children's Opinions Of Reality Roma TV 243

It was the form tutor's lesson. After some items concerning the forthcoming *Farsang* festival (spring carnival), and a stern telling off for "whoever" had vandalised the boys' toilets, the teacher turned to the previous night's TV. A new show had just been broadcast on the Hungarian commercial channel RTL Klub, the first in a series that, similar to *The Osbournes* show in the U.S., would follow a celebrity family around in their everyday lives. RTL Klub had chosen the family of a Hungarian Roma pop star called "Győzike," who had found fame through fronting the three-person pop group *Romantic* from 1999–2006. The teacher introduced the topic by saying there was this new show that had come from America, and on it you can see when a person wakes up and when they go to pee. She then asked the class who "in the world" would be interested in such a thing, and a couple of boys called out that they thought the show was stupid, and didn't like the pop tunes produced by the star's band *Romantic* in any case.

The teacher then asked the class to say who actually liked the show. Three girls put up their hands, quite bravely, I thought, as I had noted in my fieldnotes that the teacher "sounded quite threatening" (Tremlett fieldnotes 08.02.05). But their answers were muted: one girl said nothing; another muttered about wanting to see the lives of the characters, but then shrugged her shoulders and fell silent; the third girl just blushed and laughed and said she didn't know why she liked it. The form tutor then said she would give her own opinion: when she watches television, she wants to see something cultural, or something informative and interesting. She said watching people wake up, pee, argue, fight and spending money on clothes did not count as informative or interesting: "That's not what I want to watch on television. Tha's not culture!" There ended the class. That early classroom interaction about the show became telling in three ways. First, the teacher framed the show within her own values of what constitutes "good" television. Her appraisal of the meaning of "good" television was grounded in a certain idea of "high" culture and interest, which clearly was not reality formats copied from America. This belied a snobbery of popular culture that, whilst not an uncommon trait amongst conservative figures worldwide, is taking on a particular form and significance in post-socialist countries (Imre and Tremlett 2011).

Second, she did not allow the children any space to actually express their views on the show, embarrassing those who had differing views into silence. The teacher as the all-authoritative voice is not unusual, particularly in Prussian-inspired classroom environments that the pre-1989 Communist Party endorsed and still are typical in Hungary today (Kende and Neményi 2006). Furthermore, refusing the girls' opinions directly mirrored wider society—in the months that followed Győzike's rising popularity, I found it really hard to access the opinions of "real" fans. Even those who I knew who watched and enjoyed it to some degree, would end up belittling the show as "compulsive crap"—an awareness noted by other researchers

244 *Annabel Tremlett*

of "the cultural attitude of derision towards 'reality' television, and indeed television *per se*, as a bad object" (Skeggs et al. 2008, 9). Therefore accessing the children's opinions on the show made the data all the more significant, perhaps enabled by the age of the children, which made them less concerned of formulated adult responses (10–11-years-old), but also by the facts that the interviews were carried out early on in the popularity of the program and embedded in an ethnographic context with myself as a non-authoritative figure, being both foreign and taking a passive position in their school lives (Tremlett 2009a). Third, the teacher so clearly abhorred the show, along with many other prominent public voices, so its subsequent runaway success, above and beyond other reality formats in Hungary, was a mystery. Why this show in particular proved so enduringly popular, and why teacher-types found it so utterly appalling whilst children gleefully devoured each show, were questions that began to hang around my fieldwork.

At the time I wrote the fieldnotes on that cold Tuesday in February, I had no idea how popular *Győzike* was or would become. The weekly 90-minute reality show (aired on Monday nights from 9 pm) promised a series that would contain eight episodes following the family's everyday lives. The show ended up continuing for a further six years and a total of 97 episodes, and has proved to be one of the most popular programs of recent times in Hungary, with figures from the RTL group's Annual Report 2005 showing that the *Győzike* show featured nine times in the top 20 most popular programs in Hungary in 2005, with an audience share average of 46.1% amongst adults 18–49 years of age.[4] This popularity did not decline—in 2009, the average share was up to 50.2 %.[5] At the same time, whilst viewing figures were overwhelming, *Győzike*'s popularity did not equal a positive reception in public discourses in the media or online. Just as the teacher's opinion in the above vignette, cultural critics tended to devalorize the reality format itself as tasteless and the show's protagonists as not worthy of primetime viewing, calling the show an example of "shameful stupidity" (György 2005), "exotic trash" (Horváth 2008), "a Gypsy circus" (Kürti 2008). Moreover, was said to "bring severe disadvantage to the Hungarian Roma" (Daróczi 2006, quoted in Kürti 2008). More extreme views produced by so-called "fans" used the show to vent violently racist feelings towards Gypsy people, with web forums, even from the show's own website, overflowing with comments that—whilst not receiving much resistance from fellow bloggers—would be outrageous to a Western middle-class sensibility and sensitivity towards articulated intolerance (Imre and Tremlett 2011).

So did people watch the show in order just to hate it? Whilst strong discourses always appear more potent and prevalent, those girls who admitted they liked the show went on to watch every episode over the next year, and it was clear that they didn't share the disgust for the show shown either by their teachers, the critics or other so-called 'fans.' The show became a part of everyday conversation, and far from hating it, there was a lot of banter and laughter around antics on the show, and a following of the fashion paraded by the family members and in their home, from the wife Bea's sporty-sexy outfits to the zebra stripes that adorned rugs, bed-linen and even Győzike's pajamas. The possibility of a fan-base not motivated by hatred is also supported by the positions of Győzike and his wife Bea as celebrity endorsers of the channel RTL Klub;[6] Győzike's appearance in the 2010 Top List of Influential People in Hungary;[7] and also in various polls. Győzike and his wife Bea, for example, were voted favorite TV personalities in popular gossip magazine *Hot*'s poll in 2008.[8] Whilst this magazine presumes an adult readership (as does the show's later viewing time of 9 pm), it appears that, along with the children in my research project, there was a wider children's fan-base as well. A survey amongst 1,500 primary school students in Southern Hungary in 2007 showed that when asked whom the children considered as their role model, a third of them answered Győzike.[9]

So what kind of space is left for such viewers to admit, discuss, or even justify their devotion to the show in the face of the increasing racist exclusion of the Roma underclass and the elitist pressure to resist the temptations of commercial television? There is virtually no visible public arena that could explain *Győzike*'s popularity, and no in-depth exploratory ethnographic research available to answer this question. There is a dearth of studies on reality television audiences even in contexts where television ethnography does enjoy some legitimacy, perhaps, as McElroy and Williams suggest, because it redefines traditional notions of the audience, "participatory fan audiences blur the boundaries between television production and consumption" (McElroy and Williams 2011, 191). In the case of such reality shows as *Győzike*, audience studies are fundamental both to understanding broad cultural shifts occurring in post-socialist landscapes and to recognizing other 'ordinary' viewers, such as children, women, lower-class groups and/or Roma minorities as avid participants in Hungary's growing media industry,[10] who often remain undervalued and underresearched.

LISTENING TO THE FANS

Indeed, in ethnographic interviews conducted with children, a rather different picture emerges from 'fan' and 'critical' responses outlined above. Rather than the disgust of previous reactions to the show, the children, from both Roma and non-Roma backgrounds, appeared to embrace the personality of Győzike and his family as fun characters without positioning them as an ethnic 'other.' The interviews were carried out in 2005 as part of a larger research project.[11] This chapter focuses on those interviews with 19 children aged 10–11 years, from a mixture of ethnic backgrounds.[12] The study was conducted in a small school of about 120 pupils on the

Table 13.1 Children's Reactions to the TV Show Győzike

| | Children who claimed to watch the show | Children who reported finding the show 'funny' | Children who likened their family to Győzike's family | Children who didn't liken their family to Győzike's because . . . | |
				Győzike is 'cigány' ['Gypsy']	Győzike is 'different' [not because of being cigány]
Total no. of children (out of 19, 6 Roma, 13 non-Roma)	16	16	11	2	3
Roma (out of 6)	5	5	3	1	1
Non-Roma (out of 13)	11	11	8	1	2
Girls (out of 8)	7	7	7	0	0
Boys (out of 11)	9	9	4	2	3

Children's Opinions Of Reality Roma TV   247

outskirts of a city of about 100,000 people in the Southern Great Plain (*Dél-Alföld*) region of Hungary. The children were from similar local low socio-economic backgrounds, with the school records showing that the majority of children (nearly 60%) came from families who were in need of some government assistance, with roughly a third living below the 'normal' standards of living.[13] Approximately 20% of the school's pupils[14] were from a 'Hungarian Gypsy' (*Magyar cigány*) background,[15] and whilst a few of these families were amongst the poorest attending the school, not all Hungarian Gypsy families were in this category, and there were some non-Gypsy families who were also deemed extremely poor.[16] Out of the 19 children in the fourth grade, six children could be said to be from a Hungarian Gypsy background and 13 from a non-Gypsy background. Such a small sample is not meant to be representative and, indeed, imposing very broad labels such as 'Roma,' 'Hungarian Gypsy' or 'non-Gypsy" onto the children does not do justice to their myriad of identifications. However, here I use the terms with the acknowledgement that wider discourses often refer to a Roma/non-Roma divide in social and cultural practices. Whatever particular 'subgroup' is being discussed, this divide is described as distinct and enduring (Tremlett 2009b). I therefore use these terms to explore whether, in viewing terms, there may be some indications that such a difference is apparent in the way children from Roma minority backgrounds may be viewing TV shows.

In the interviews, the children were asked whether they would liken their families to Győzike's.[17] As Table 13.1 below shows, in response, the majority of them did, whilst there appears to be no obvious Roma/non-Roma divide in this response (11 out of a total of 16 children—three Roma; eight non-Roma). However, there is an evident gender divide, as all girls likened their families to Győzike's (7/7), compared to only four out of nine boys. Out of the five who did not, only two boys said it was because of their difference in ethnic backgrounds. Thus despite all the hype and scorn surrounding Győzike as a *Roma* media star, in these interviews, ethnic identity was only voiced by two out of 16 children, one Roma and one non-Roma. This suggests that children were not verbalizing 'Roma' or 'Gypsy' as the most obvious element of the *Győzike* show. Considering that Győzike's ethnic background appears so prominent in the promotion of and responses to the show, these results prove surprising.

For the children, the main attraction of the program was its ability to make them laugh. As the table above shows, all the children who watched the show reported finding it 'funny,' as also clearly seen in the extracts below:

Extracts 1.i–iii[18]

1.i "We just giggle at it" (Balázs, Roma boy);
1.ii "You can have a good laugh at it!" (Sára, non-Roma girl);
1.iii "There are some really funny things in it." (Kevin, non-Roma boy).

248   *Annabel Tremlett*

The children cited many examples of humorous antics, which seemed mostly to center on the anti-authority narratives: they found Győzike's younger daughter, Virág, especially amusing because of her mischievous behavior. It seems that Virág provided a source of comic, slapstick type of behavior, with a strong sense of waywardness that the children found very appealing, as the following extracts show:

Extract 2: Ferenc (Roma boy)

Ferenc: I often really laugh at the little girl, at Virág. [. . .] Well, because last time there was this part, when . . . when the little girl was playing with some drink, and she held the drink like this . . . (Ferenc mimics holding a drink) and then, and it didn't move, she just fell over backwards! I really like it.

Extract 3: Sophia (non-Roma girl)

Sophia: Virág is always on it really a lot . . . that little girl always does naughty things in it! (laugh) She always tips something over, or really shouts, or cries, there is always a problem with her, or she covers the sofa with something!

The focus in Extracts 2–3 is the delight in Virág's "naughty" behavior. Her mischief—the way she spills drinks, falls over, shouts, messes up the pristine family home. As other researchers of child TV viewers have noted, children enjoy watching programs that break with notions of "good" behaviour. These reactions may also explain the teachers' abhorrence of the show, as Seitler points out, "No wonder many teachers hate popular children's TV, when it is associated with bedlam, rule-breaking, forbidden activities" (Seiter 1999, 5).

However, the glee in deviant behaviour the children display is also symptomatic of a shared culture, in other words the children are displaying a shared knowledge of what is "normal" in terms of behavioral expectations (whether it is what they actually do at home or not) (Seiter 1995, 8). In the case of wider representations of Roma minorities this proves an interesting point. Whilst discourses, both from Romani studies and more broadly, reiterate the marked differences between Roma and non-Roma family life (often referred to as 'the Gypsy way' see Gay y Blasco 1999, 174; Liégeois 1986, 85; Okely 1983, 77; Stewart 1997, 17–94), here Roma and non-Roma children appear to unite in their understanding (and enjoyment) of public transgressions from an understood universal family "norm," along with a shared (child-like) humor in transgressing "acceptable" behavior.

The idea that the children were engaged in some shared understanding of familial identity can be further explored as the children were asked more specific questions about how they related their family to Győzike's. This had the potential to bring up expressions of ethnic difference or affiliation.

Children's Opinions Of Reality Roma TV   249

We may have assumed that Roma children would display a stronger affiliation (or perhaps disassociation) to a celebrity Roma family. However, both Roma and non-Roma children reported both similarities and differences between their own families and Győzike's. Where a divide became more apparent was not, in fact, between ethnic groups, but between gender groups. Girls appeared keen to liken their families to Győzike's, whilst boys tended to emphasize difference (see also Table 13.1 above).

The desire to connect their own families with Győzike's was also apparent in all seven of the girls' interviews who watched the show (both Roma and non-Roma). Two girls saw Győzike's family as a "type" (e.g. funny, argumentative) similar to their own families

Extract 4: Anna (Hungarian Gypsy girl)

Anna: My family is also this kind of humorous type. Sometimes we believe in everything, sometimes nothing at all. Sometimes we are angry, sometimes we are in a good mood.

Extract 5: Sophia (non-Gypsy girl)

Sophia: Well, we can say yes, because Győző's family also fall out a lot. My mum and everyone, they really row a lot. Well maybe not so much, but from time to time.

Whilst the above two extracts are quite vague ("this kind," "sometimes," "well maybe not so much"), other girls saw direct similarities between characters on the show and members of their families. For example, Csilla, a Roma girl, likened her brother to Győzike's younger daughter Virág ("Tomika is just as naughty as little Virág") whilst her dad's busy work life and telephone habits were likened to Győzike's, which prompted her to say "my dad is the same as Győzike." Similar to Csilla, Márta, a non-Gypsy girl, also went through each member of her family to compare and contrast them, for better or worse. She said her father had the same big belly as the lead character Győzike's, and that his hair was a similar color. She said her mum shouts just as much as Győzike's wife Bea, whilst her older brother was as fat and swore as much as the eldest girl in Győzike's family, Evelin. She also said she was as naughty and clumsy as the youngest child Virág. This final similarity was interesting to me, as Márta was one of the best behaved girls in the fourth grade, and I had never seen her fall over, be clumsy or heard her swear:

Extract 6: Márta (non-Roma girl)

Marta: [. . .] because I also often use bad language, and she also uses bad language, and I also often fall over, Virág also often falls over, well she also is often naughty, and I am often naughty, she

250   *Annabel Tremlett*

uses bad language, I also use bad language. So there are a lot of
. . . a lot of similarities between us. Really a lot.

The desire to be connected to the family, (emphasized by Márta's last sentence "Really a lot") even if those connections could be tenuous, vague or not really based in reality, points to the importance the girls placed on affiliation to their TV heroes, something Greenwood and Long have noted derives from the need to belong through "imagined intimacies" (2011, 282). Significantly here, none of the girls used any ethnic or national labels in these expressions of solidarity.

The girls' responses confirm that Győzike's family could very well represent the national family—a possibility the adult responses, both overtly racist and intellectual-liberal, simply could not contemplate and must disavow. The girls may well articulate here the attraction to the show that adults, including their parents, cannot speak aloud, assuming, based on the interviews, that *Győzike* is watched in the context of family viewing. On the other hand, some of the boys were keener to express the differences between Győzike's family and their own. This is where a gender divide became apparent. One non-Roma boy, lamenting on Győzike's failure to discipline his puppy dog, stated that his own family were not '*cigány*' (*Gypsy*) and therefore would never let their own dogs into their home. This was the only negative expression from the children that directly ethnicized Győzike. However, the other boys were not so focused on differentiating Győzike through a definite Roma/non-Roma divide but found other, more class-based strategies of distancing their family's life from their own. Kevin, for example said his family was not like Győzike's because they behave differently:

Extract 7: Kevin (non-Roma boy)

Kevin: We aren't naughty. Well they shout and everything. We normally play cards, watch TV, play on the computer, or we go out cycling.

For Kevin, the difference was expressed in behavior and activities. Kevin's 'us' is not specifically ethnicized, but implies the sense of something better-behaved, quieter and more placid, as opposed to the 'them' of Győzike's family, who are naughty and loud. Balázs (Roma boy) also brought up behavioral differences when he pointed out that his mother was stricter in controlling her children. Győzike's family is here described as more lenient than Balázs'—something he disapproves of:

Extract 8: Balázs (Roma boy)

Balázs: For example Győzike's little girl is very obstinate, and I don't know what . . . she runs wild, and my sister would never do things like that. Never!

Children's Opinions Of Reality Roma TV 251

AT: And it wouldn't be allowed by . . . ?
Balázs: And my mum would never allow it in any case.

The children, whilst delighting in the entertainment afforded by chaotic family scenes, potentially show a gender divide in the degree of difference in their readiness to identify with on-screen characters. The boys could be more concerned with affiliating themselves to this "other" of Győzike, although direct formulations of what this "other" is are not (yet) clearly labeled.

Here it is important to step away from romanticizing children's responses by rendering their imaginations unfettered by politics. As we know from David Buckingham, interpreting children's talk in the course of ethnographic research presents its own special caveats. The influence of the researcher, of the group setting, and the inconsistencies of individual responses create so many contingencies that any meaningful generalization may seem untenable (Buckingham 1991, 1993). But even as we take extreme care not to assume that children's words are windows into their minds, taken collectively, the difference from the "public" responses to the show is striking: the children watch the show primarily as a TV show. The anxieties about shifting national identities, class and racial mixing set off by *Győzike* are so overwhelming that the public responses simply ignore the show's status as a television text that hovers ambiguously between fiction and reality. The children, however, pick up and comment on the most immediate quality and effect of the program: its performative, playful dimension and only indirectly register and even more vaguely articulate ethnic and class comparisons.

One could legitimately speculate that these pre-teen children's memories are not overdetermined by a small nation's social, economic and political transition from state socialism to capitalist neoliberalism. At the same time, of course, the children are not immune to nationalism's racial and gendered reliance on the proper, normative family, as is indicated by the boys' keener awareness of the ethnic or "other" features of Győzike's family. However, in stark contrast to the public discourses on *Győzike*, all the children reveled in the anti-authority narrative whilst, at least for the girls, the notion of the national family is not threatened but rather confirmed. Shouting, "bad" behavior and pot-bellied dads who are always on the phone are recognized rather than disavowed. The middle-class Roma family thus emerges into tangible existence both on and off the television screens. Whilst the children are eager to enjoy the show for its comic plotlines and amusing moments, particularly along a strong identification with Győzike's own daughter, the gender divide emerging between the boys' and girls' responses is an indication of the children's budding sense of the distinct hierarchies and spaces assigned to men and women, and the existence of 'others' within and outside the nation. The girls showed a strong investment in the domestic arena in which the show is anchored, subordinating other social institutions and organizational structures to the family. The boys showed more awareness of their own roles as future

252   *Annabel Tremlett*

citizens who get to set the standards and determine the lines of legitimate difference within the public national arena.

CONCLUSION

In the 1990s, there were concerns from both politicians and academics that 'globalization' would mean a loss of local cultures of media broadcasting. In fact, these concerns were unfounded. The failure of attempts at pan-European television and the localization strategies of international broadcasters such as MTV actually highlight the audience's preference for *local* programming and *domestic* content (Esser 2009, 24). In a similar fashion, whilst global formats of shows have been reproduced in many different countries, the striking element is the way such formats are localized to suit a national context. Aslama and Pantti conclude in their analysis of Finnish reality TV that the media have two essential functions: firstly to construct and maintain a nationally bounded audience; and secondly to make a profit (2007, 63–64). Their main argument is that national values and intertextual references sell on the domestic front. Reality programs, with their inclusion of local participants and celebrity presenters or judges, are primed for such an environment.

In the case of Hungary's *Győzike* show, this argument becomes more complex. How can a representative from the most despised and deprived minority front one of the most popular programs of all time? Imre (2011) argues that *Győzike* represents a new type of "racialized celebrity" in post-socialist countries that relates to specific political and cultural shifts in the region:

> These factors include the primacy of national belonging over neoliberal ideas of individual self-making and responsibilization, and the threatened class status of intellectuals, who continue to perform a central normative function in national cultures (Imre 2011, 22).

Such factors have produced deep anxieties about nationhood and nationalism, with celebrities such as Győzike representing an emerging, racially mixed economic middle-class that "has long been a missing element in Soviet-controlled, allegedly egalitarian societies" (Imre 2011, 22–23). The possibility that a Gypsy family can represent the Hungarian national family provokes a crisis in identity that points to the "unreconstructed state of whiteness" that post-socialist countries are now struggling to come to terms with (Böröcz 2001, quoted in Imre 2011, 23).

The danger is that we can too easily explain away the high viewing figures for *Győzike* as down to the audience taking macabre delight in watching something they despise. Of course, the possibility that many viewers watch the show to reinforce their own sense of 'good' moral values would explain the Hungarian teacher's hostile views in the opening anecdote, and chimes with other studies of reality TV audiences (Ang 1985; Seiter 1999; Skeggs et al. 2008).

Yet the children I spent day after day with didn't seem to despise the show, but loved it. Children from differing ethnic backgrounds loved the flamboyance, the materialistic extravagance, the way the family interacted in a loud, jubilant manner. As the interviews showed, this was not about them judging a Roma family for their ethnic peculiarities, but an embracing of a sense of transgressive family behavior that was refreshingly put on public display without the usual reprimands of not living up to the ideal national family.

Listening to "ordinary" audience opinions of reality TV has not been a priority of academics and critics of these shows, particularly in Central and Eastern Europe. Whilst particular care should always be taken in "the process of extrapolation from ethnographic examples" (Morley 2006, 108), this chapter has shown that ethnographic research has the potential to illuminate important differences between current public deficit discourses on recent reality formats, and local practices of those who potentially enjoy such formats. The political landscape is shown as ever-present in reactions to such formats. Just as Skeggs et al. see the making of class through "moral extension" on UK reality TV (2007), so here we have seen how ideas of Roma ethnic identities can be debated and renegotiated through the production and consumption of a reality show in Hungary.

At the same time, with an expanding European Union, there is a political surge to talk more broadly about Roma minorities.[19] *Győzike* is an example of one show amongst an emerging trend of Roma "celebrities" who are often portrayed as excessive, moneyed and larger than life (Imre 2006, 2009, 2011). Take a moment, then, to try to reconcile these images with a rather more sobering description of Roma from the EU Commission:

> Particular attention is to be paid to the most vulnerable groups, those suffering from multiple discrimination and those at high risk of exclusion. Among these are ethnic minorities and clearly identifiable as some of the most marginalized groups are many Romani communities (*EU Commission Report* 2011, 13).

How can we reconcile the flash happy free figures of primetime TV with terms such as "multiple discrimination," "exclusion," "marginalized"? In one medium the Gypsy is a dynamic, consumer-enthralled social player, in the other they are poor victims suffering from imposed exclusion. This chapter calls for a recognition of the incongruence of such representations, and aims to entice other academics into researching and thinking across and not within such frameworks.

NOTES

1. I am grateful to Anikó Imre for earlier collaborations which helped contextualize my ethnographic research in the broader political and cultural sphere. Thanks also to the editors who gave helpful suggestions for this chapter.

254 Annabel Tremlett

2. I take the view that self-identification of ethnic grouping is important. Nevertheless, in order to talk about wider discourses of people and practices associated with Gypsies, travellers, Roma, Romanies and other groups, I will use the term 'Roma' in recognition of its predominant (if at times contested) use as an umbrella term in public forums.
3. "The social situation of the Roma and their improved access to the labour market in the EU" European Parliament's study 2008, http://www.europarl. europa.eu/sides/getDoc.do?pubRef=-//EP//NONSGML+TA+P6-TA-2009–0117+0+DOC+PDF+V0//EN (accessed July 27 2011).
4. RTL Group "Annual Report 2005," http://www.rtlgroup.com/www/assets/ file_asset/AR2005_RTLGroup_COMPLETE.pdf (accessed July, 27, 2011).
5. "Szenzáció! Győzike lekörözte a *Barátokat*" ("Sensation! Győzike runs circles around *Between Friends*"), http://www.est.hu/cikk/47650/szenzacio_gyozike_lekorozte_a_baratokat/ro409 (Accessed August 4, 2011).
6. As would be obvious for any viewers of RTL Klub, Győzike and his family are not just confined to their own reality program, but are ubiquitous across the channel's programming. Győzike and his wife Bea are regulars on RTL Klub's talk shows, quiz shows and other reality program, from dancing on the Hungarian version of *Strictly Come Dancing* to sharing their culinary expertise on *Come Dine With Me*. They are thus deployed as the 'celebrity endorsers' of RTL Klub itself, the most popular TV channel in Hungary. As celebrity endorsers, their status depends on them being credible, attractive, congruent with the product and engaging in activities that can enhance it (Seno and Lukas 2005).
7. Győzike's appeared in the 2010 Top List of Influential People in Hungary (Topista Emberek, Arcok, published by Figyelő and United Publisher) in which he is amongst the nine most influential people in the media industry, http://www.rtlgroup.com/www/htm/home_news.aspx?ID=CFAE45CBB47 0453F8277F36359FD700.3 (Accessed March 28, 2011)
8. "Hot Top 100 Sztár: A száz legfontosabb magyar híresség" ("Top Hot 100 Stars: The 100 most important Hungarian celebrities"), (2008/1), Budapest: Euromedia BT.
9. "Hmmm . . . Győzike a példaképe minden harmadik somogyi általános iskolásnak", ("Hmmm . . . Győzike is the role model for every third primary school pupil in Somogy county") February 9, 2007. http://www.mtv.hu/ modernkepmesek/cikk.php?id=183025 (Accessed October 4, 2010).
10. Hungary has one of Central Europe's most highly developed and quickly evolving TV markets (see *Television Across Europe*, 2005: 247).
11. The research project included 15 months of ethnographic research. Only a small part of that research is represented in this chapter. For results and discussion of the whole project see Tremlett 2008.
12. In accordance with ethical guidelines, all names of places and people have been changed. All data was collected in Hungarian without the use of interpreters. The translations here are my own. Although there is not enough space to discuss it in more detail here, the issue of researching in a second language (and a second culture) is considered very important in any claims of understanding the fieldwork context (see Borchgrevink 2003, Tremlett 2009a).
13. Data taken from school records. Overall, 32% of the pupils (39/123) from the primary school were considered poor, whilst 57% (70/123) were receiving government-funded school meals and 51% (63/123) of families received upbringing benefits.
14. Even though the collection of ethnic data is banned in Hungary under the Data Protection Act 1993, the school did record ethnic data in relation to poverty.

Children's Opinions Of Reality Roma TV   255

15. There are said to be three main Roma groups in Hungary who are mainly identified by the languages they speak, although there are no reliable statistics: Hungarian Gypsies who speak Hungarian only (*magyar cigányok* or *Romungro*) approximately 65–75% of the Roma population; Vlach Roma who speak a Romani language, Lovari, that is rooted in Sanskrit (*oláh cigányok*), 20–30%; and Beás or Romanian Roma (*beások* or *román cigányok*), 5–10%, who speak a Romani language, Beás, that derives from an archaic form of Romanian (from Immigration and Refugee Board of Canada 1998, or for more information on language, see Matras 2002). However, as sociologist Péter Szuhay points out, "Of course, one should not assume these three groups must always constitute the basis for any classification, but there is no denying that the various groups do usually place themselves in one of these three main groups. At the same time, Roma placing themselves in one of the main groups do not necessarily accept all other Roma placing themselves in the same main group" (Szuhay 2005, 237)

16. The pupils who attended József Attila primary school during my fieldwork were from similar low socio-economic backgrounds, and from my everyday experience at the school and from visiting children's homes I did not feel that material inequality was huge between children, although the Roma families did seem overrepresented in the poorest families. The school kept records on each child to determine the level of disadvantage of the child's background. Figures from these school records (created by a child welfare expert) showed that overall, 32% of the pupils (39/123) from the primary school were considered poor, whilst 57% (70/123) were receiving government-funded school meals and 51% (63/123) of families received 'child-rearing' benefits. Whilst there was not individual statistics on each child, there was not a consistent parallel between the number of Roma children and those deemed poor in the various categories—for example in the fourth grade, (6/19) of the children were from a Roma background, whilst 45% were considered materially poor, 75% were on funded school meals; and 60% received child-rearing benefits.

17. Throughout these interviews, no direct questions were asked about the children's ethnic or national identities, as the methodology aimed at seeing if, when, where and how these identities came up in talk about everyday lives, rather than forcing a specific response. However, in the semi-structured questionnaire, some questions were pre-prepared on television programs known to be popular amongst the children, including *Megasztár* (a version of the UK's *Pop Idol*), *Barátok közt* (*Between Friends*, a daily Hungarian soap opera) and *Győzike*. Questions about Győzike also allowed a chance to see whether and how children aligned themselves and their families with this Roma celebrity, although his ethnic status was not commented upon by the researcher herself, unless the subject was brought up first by the child.

18. Interviews were carried out in Hungarian, the researcher's second language, without the use of translators (Tremlett 2009a). The transcription of the interviews was carried out by the researcher alongside paid Hungarian speakers (non-linguists) who transcribed the interviews *verbatim*. The transcription chosen is focused on accessibility and readability.

19. A European strategy for Roma minorities was adopted by the European Parliament on January 31, 2008 (document RC-B6–0050/2008, http://www.europarl.europa.eu/sides/getDoc.do?type=TA&reference=P6-TA-2008–0035&language=EN (accessed July 27, 2011), and in May 2011 the European Commission put forward a European Framework for National Roma Integration Strategies which calls on EU countries to set goals concerning the education, employment, health and housing of their Roma minorities (see EC webpages for up to date information, http://eceuropa.eu).

256 Annabel Tremlett

REFERENCES

Amnesty International Report. 2010. *Attacks against Roma in Hungary. Time to investigate racial motivation.* London: Amnesty International Publications. http://www.amnesty.org/en/library/asset/EUR27/001/2010/en/7ee79730-e23f-4f20-834a-deb8deb23464/eur270012010en.pdf. (Accessed August 4, 2011).

Ang, Ien. 1985. *Watching Dallas: Soap opera and the Melodramatic Imagination.* London: Routledge.

Aslama, Minna and Mervi Pantti. 2007. "Flagging Finnishness: Reproducing National Identity in Reality Television." *Television & New Media* 8(1): 49–67.

Barrer, Peter. 2010. "National Hysteria: The First Year of Reality TV in Slovakia." *Journal of European Popular Culture* 1(1): 7–23.

Bernáth, Gábor and Vera Messing. 2002. "The Neglected Public. On the Media Consumption of the Hungarian Roma." In *The Gypsies/The Roma in Hungarian Society* edited by Ernő Kállai, 107–125. Budapest: Regio.

Bindel, Julie. 2011. "The Big Fat Truth about Gypsy Life." *The Guardian*, February 25. http://www.guardian.co.uk/lifeandstyle/2011/feb/25/truth-about-gypsy-traveller-life-women. (Accessed March 15, 2011)

Borchgrevink, Axel. 2003. "Silencing language: Of Anthropologists and Interpreters." *Ethnography* 4(1): 95–121.

Buckingham, David. 1991. "What are Words Worth? Interpreting Children's Talk about Television." *Cultural Studies* 5: 228–245.

Buckingham, David. 1993. *Children Talking Television: The Making of Television Literacy.* London: Falmer Press.

Buckingham, David. 2011. *Children and Media.* London: UNESCO, 2002. http://www.european-mediaculture.de/fileadmin/bibliothek/english/buckingham_childrenmedia/buckingham_childrenmedia.pdf. (Accessed March 31, 2011)

Clark, Colin. 2004. "'Severity has Often Enraged but Never Subdued a Gipsy': The History and Making of European Romani Stereotypes." In *The Role of Romanies*, edited by Nicholas Saul and Susan Tebbutt, 226–246. Liverpool: Liverpool University Press.

Clark-Ibáñez, Marisol. 2004. "Framing the Social work with Photo-elicitation Interviews." *American Behavioral Scientist* 47: 1507–1527.

Corner, John. 2002. "Performing the Real: Documentary Diversions." *Television & New Media* 3: 255–269.

Danchev, Alexi. 2008. "Problems of Cultural Integration in Transition Societies—Case Study of Bulgaria." *Annals of Computational Economics* 1(36): 87–101. http://feaa.ucv.ro/AUCSSE/0036v1-005.pdf. (Accessed March 31, 2011).

Epstein, Iris, Bonnie Stevens, Patricia McKeever and Sylvain Baruchel. 2006. "Photo Elicitation Interview (PEI): Using Photos to Elicit Children's Perspectives." *International Journal of Qualitative Methods* 5(3): 1–9.

Esser, Andrea. 2009. "Trends in Television Programming: Commercialization, Transnationalization, Convergence." In *Media in an Enlarged Europe*, edited by Alec Charles, 23–36. London: Intellect books.

European Union (EU) Commission Report. 2011. "Improving the Tools for the Social Inclusion and Non-discrimination of Roma in the EU." http://ec.europa.eu/social/main.jsp?catId=423&langId=en&pubId=613&type=2&furtherPubs=yes. (Accessed March 15, 2011).

Eurostat Report. 2010. "Combating Poverty and social exclusion. A statistical portrait of the European Union 2010." http://epp.eurostat.ec.europa.eu/cache/ITY_OFFPUB/KS-EP-09-001/EN/KS-EP-09-001-EN.PDF. (Accessed July 3, 2011).

Frost, Vicky. 2011. "Channel 4's Big Fat Gypsy Ratings Winner." *The Guardian*, February 7. http://www.guardian.co.uk/media/2011/feb/07/big-fat-gypsy-weddings. (Accessed March 15, 2011).

Children's Opinions Of Reality Roma TV   257

Gay y Blasco, Paloma. 1999. *Gypsies in Madrid: Sex, Gender and the Performance of Identity*. Oxford: Berg.

Greenwood, Dara N. and Christopher R. Long. 2011. "Attachment, Belongingness Needs, and Relationship Status Predict Imagined Intimacy with Media Figures." *Communication Research* 38(2): 287–297.

György, Péter. 2005. "Ablak a világra" ("A Window to the World"). *Élet es Irodalom (Life and Literature)* 49(41), (October 14). http://www.es.hu/gyorgy_peter;ablak_a_vilagra;2005–10–16.html. (Accessed August 4, 2011).

Hill, Annette. 2002. "Big Brother: The Real Audience." *Television & New Media* 3: 323–340.

Hill, Annette. 2005. *Reality TV: Audiences and Popular Factual Television*. Oxon: Routledge.

Horváth, Aladár. 2008. "International Roma Day: Aladár Horváth on Reality TV in Hungary." Interview by Danielle Tyree for *Cafe Babel* online magazine, April 7. http://www.cafebabel.co.uk/article/3115/international-roma-day-aladar-horvath-on-reality-t.html. (Accessed August 4, 2011).

Immigration and Refugee Board of Canada. 1998. "Roma in Hungary." http://www.unhcr.org/refworld/docid/3ae6a823c.html. (Accessed August 4, 2011).

Imre, Anikó. 2005. "Whiteness in Post-socialist Eastern Europe: The Time of the Gypsies, the End of Race." In *Postcolonial Whiteness: A Critical Reader on Race and Empire*, edited by Alfred J. Lopez, 79–102. Albany: State University of New York Press.

Imre, Anikó. 2006. "Play in the Ghetto: Global Entertainment and the European 'Roma Problem'." *Third Text* 20(6): 659–670.

Imre, Anikó. 2009. *Identity Games: Globalization and the Transformation of Media Cultures in the New Europe*. Cambridge: MIT Press.

Imre, Anikó. (2011). "Love to Hate: National Celebrity and Racial Intimacy on Reality TV in the New Europe." *Television & New Media* 20(10):1–28.

Imre, Anikó and Annabel Tremlett. (2011). "Reality TV Without Class: The Post-socialist Anti-Celebrity Docusoap." In *Real Class: Ordinary People and Reality Television across National Spaces*, edited by Helen Wood and Beverly Skeggs, . London: British Film Institute.

Joanou, Jamie P. 2009. "The Bad and the Ugly: Ethical Concerns in Participatory Photographic Methods with Children Living and Working on the Streets of Lima, Peru." *Visual Studies* 24(3): 214–223.

Kende, Anna and Maria Neményi. 2006. "Selection in Education: The Case of Roma Children in Hungary." *Equal Opportunities International* 25(7): 506–522.

Kürti, László. 2008. "Media Wars: Cultural Dialogue and Conflict in Hungarian Popular Broadcasting." SUSDIV paper from the *Fondazione Eni Enrico Mattei* Series Index, January 8. http://www.susdiv.org/uploadfiles/SD2008–008.pdf. (Accessed October 4, 2010).

Levinson, Martin P. 2007. "Literacy in English Gypsy Communities: Cultural Capital Manifested as Negative Assets." *American Educational Research Journal* 44(1): 5–39.

Liégeois, Jean Paul. 1986. *Gypsies: An illustrated history*. London: Al Saqi Books.

Matras, Yaron. 2002. *Romani: A Linguistic Introduction*. Cambridge: Cambridge University Press.

McElroy, Ruth and Rebecca Williams. 2011. "Remembering Ourselves, Viewing the Others: Historical Reality Television and Celebrity in the Small Nation." *Television & New Media* 12(2): 187–206.

Miller, Carol. 2009. *Lola's Luck: My Life Among the California Gypsies*. California: Gemmamedia.

Morley, David. 2006. "Unanswered Questions in Audience Research." *The Communication Review* 9(2): 101–121.

258   *Annabel Tremlett*

Okely, Judith. 1983. *The Traveller-Gypsies*. Cambridge: Cambridge University Press.

Ross, Karen. 2000. "In Whose image? TV Criticism and Black Minority Viewers." In *Ethnic Minorities and the Media*, edited by Simon Cottle, 133–148. Buckingham: Open University Press.

Seiter, Ellen. 1999. *Television and New Media Audiences*. Wotton-under-Edge: Clarendon Press.

Seiter, Ellen. 1995. *Sold Separately: Children and Parents in Consumer Culture*. Piscataway: Rutgers University Press.

Seno, Diana, and Bryan A. Lukas. 2005. "The Equity Effect of Product Endorsement by Celebrities." *European Journal of Marketing* 41(1/2): 121–134.

Skeggs, Beverly, Helen Wood and Nancy Thumin. 2007. "Making Class through Moral Extension on Reality TV." http://www.sprak.umu.se/digitalAssets/29/29326_workshop_intimacy_ahorarkop.pdf. (Accessed October 4, 2010).

Skeggs, Beverly, Nancy Thumin and Helen Wood. 2008. "'Oh goodness, I am watching reality TV': How Methods Make Class in Audience Research." *European Journal of Cultural Studies* 11(1): 5–24.

Stewart, Michael. 1997. *The Time of the Gypsies*. Oxford: Westview Press.

Szuhay, Péter. 2005. "The Self-Definitions of Roma Ethnic Groups and their Perceptions of Other Roma Groups." In *Roma of Hungary*, edited by István Kemény, 237–246. New York: Columbia University Press.

Television Across Europe 2005, Open Society Institute Monitoring Report, http://www.soros.org/initiatives/media/articles_publications/publications/eurotv_20051011/summary_20051011.pdf. (Accessed March 19 2012).

Tremlett, Annabel. 2008. "Representations of Roma; Public Discourses and Local Practices." Ph.D. diss, King's College London.

Tremlett, Annabel. 2009a. "Claims of 'Knowing' in Ethnography: Realising Anti-Essentialism through a Critical Reflection on Language Acquisition in Fieldwork." *Lost (and Found) in Translation. The Graduate Journal of Social Science* (GJSS), special issue, (December): 63–85. http://www.gjss.org/index.php?/Vol-6-Issue-3-December-2009-Lost-and-found-in-Translation.html. (Accessed August 4, 2011)

Tremlett, Annabel. 2009b. "Bringing Hybridity to Heterogeneity: Roma and the Question of 'Difference' in Romani Studies." *Romani Studies* 19(2): 147–168.

Tremlett, Annabel. 2011. "Trying to Solve a European Problem: A Comprehensive Strategy for Roma Minorities." *Open Democracy E-Zine*, January 11. http://www.opendemocracy.net/annabel-tremlett/trying-to-solve-european-problem-comprehensive-strategy-for-roma-minorities. (Accessed August 4, 2011).

Willems. Wim. 1997. *In Search of the True Gypsy: From Enlightenment to Final Solution*. London: Frank Cass.

14 Racing for the Audience
National Identity, Public TV and the Roma in Post-Socialist Slovenia

Ksenija Vidmar-Horvat

INTRODUCTION

The chapter explores the role of national public television in the construction of Slovenian national identity in post-socialism. In particular, it addresses the implication of public broadcasting in the processes of ethnic renationalization and the homogenization of collective identity after the collapse of Yugoslavia and, related to this, its politics of representation of the Roma minority. Since the breakup of Yugoslavia in 1991, the Roma have been pushed to the margins of national society where, as a collective subject, they occupy the position of the permanent stranger (Kuhar 2006, Petković 2002, Vidmar-Horvat et al. 2008). The estrangement of the Roma from the national territory has taken many shapes, most of them expressed in derogatory racist rhetoric but also demands for actual expulsions and the destruction of Roma settlements (Erjavec et al. 2000, Vidmar-Horvat et al. 2008, Vidmar-Horvat 2009). In this analysis, the focus is as much on the overt as on the symbolic violence and "polite," "non-racist" forms of racism (van Dijk 1993, Downing and Husband 2005, Fiske 1996, Hall 1990) in which Roma are made into aliens of the national community. My argument is that non-explicit racism, or "inferential racism," as Stuart Hall calls it, especially demands our critical attention because, as far as the Roma in Slovenia are concerned, it is usually articulated with "good intentions"—allegedly to help the Roma in adjusting to the majority society. In order to demonstrate the joint labor of racist and "non-racist" racism, I take under scrutiny public TV Slovenia. The intent of the analysis is to show, with the help of the selected case study of the infotainment program *Pyramid*, how in the ideological landscape of the national television, rude forms of racism against the Roma have been publicly deemed as improper, while polite Romophobia continues to function as the politically acceptable terrain on which the dominant ethnic community of Slovenes is being constructed. As the analysis of the particular program also reveals, gender plays a visible role in negotiating the racism that is seen by television as acceptable to the public.

The chapter analyzes the live broadcast of *Pyramid* on November 2006, which has been associated with one of the major national scandals of post-

260 Ksenija Vidmar-Horvat

socialist Slovenia as regards the Roma and their symbolic lynching by the media. The scandal is treated as a media event in the sense elaborated by Fiske (1996), that is as a production site of the (hyper)reality which both refers to an actual event and creates it through its discursive presence (Fiske 1996, 2). Translated to our case, this would mean an investigation of the actual affair triggered during and after the broadcast of the show; and the discursive, visual and verbal means by which the affair came into (media) being. Following Fiske's argument, because media events are increasingly becoming the only events through which reality is made present to us, representations do not only reflect the social world, but in fact organize it. Investigation of the *Pyramid* affair in this sense sheds light on the making of the post-socialist social order and allows us to inspect, through the eruption of the public debate that accompanied the media affair, the unfolding of relations of race and ethnicity in post-Yugoslav Slovenia.

As Fiske also notes, the discursive manufacturing of the media event never occurs in isolation from other, contributing discursive realities (Fiske 1996, 3). To illuminate the scandal from the broader perspective, the first part of the paper therefore provides a brief insight into the general media atmosphere in which, since the early 1990s, the Roma have been isolated as the "problematic minority." Next, the media politics of the depiction of the Roma in transition society is brought in line with the institutional contexts of the national TVS and the role it performed in the transition from a Yugoslav multinational and multicultural to a monocultural model of imagining the national community. The discussion in this part touches on the crisis of cultural legitimacy which TVS has been facing since the change of government in 2004 to show how two separate realms of public culture—one associated with the negative image of the Roma, the other with that of the public broadcaster—together through a media event created a shared national drama. Third, the analysis focuses on the broadcast itself. By using discursive and visual methods of reading the program, I point to the importance of studying the conflict in the studio also as a conflict of gender and sexuality, thus, as already mentioned, rendering visible the assistance of gender in making some forms of racism more tolerable than others. Considering this last result of the analysis, in the concluding part of the chapter, the interrelatedness between political contexts of the Slovenian transitional democracy, present-day racism and its institutional, media face is addressed through the lens of gender.

THE ROMA IN POST-SOCIALIST SLOVENIA

It should be acknowledged that there are considerable differences regarding the legal and socio-economic situation of the Roma among individual European countries (Will 2001, Klopčič 2002, 2007). However, until the present day, the Roma have been "united" by the shared fate of being collectively discriminated against, legally prosecuted and economically traumatized across Europe, old and new. According to Vera Klopčič, in the past as well as in the present, the Roma in every country of their residence have most certainly been "the disadvantaged group, a subject to discrimination and exclusion" (Klopčič 2002, 2–3). In Central and Eastern Europe, the situation has worsened with the collapse of socialism. This clearly holds true in the case of post-Yugoslav Slovenia where it would hardly be an overstatement to argue that, as a group, the Roma are the most neglected victims of transition. With the move to market economy and the consequent closure of many state-run enterprises, and with the Roma most often being the first to be laid off, the rate of unemployment among the Roma in post-socialist Slovenia has rapidly increased. This rate of unemployment is partly related to the employers' negative attitudes towards the Roma; the main reason, however, is their low education level. Permanent structural unemployment and illiteracy, but also other effects of socio-economic deprivation, such as bad housing conditions, dependence on state support, poor hygiene etc., have become interpreted as a Romani "way of life." Consequently, when encountering the image of the Roma in public, the dominant narrative that frames the Romani collective subject refers to notions of conflict, crisis, and problems. The "obviousness" of this kind of representation has been normalized to the point that the Roma communities and their individual members have been, without much tension in reproducing the World War II terminology, subsumed under the head label of the "Roma problem" (Vidmar-Horvat et al. 2008).

Hegemonic media depictions of the Roma of Slovenia have contributed to this "problem" by providing a limited set of signifiers when describing the Roma. The privileged markers of Roma identity have been usually borrowed from terrains of deviance, crime and violence (Erjavec et al. 2000, Kuhar 2006, Vidmar-Horvat 2006). Furthermore, media and populist political discourse have searched for the origins of this pathology in biology: in the most openly racist language, deviance has been explained by blood (Vidmar-Horvat 2006). However, biological racism has been assisted by other bodily inscriptions: for example, the Roma have been referred to as "brown" or "dark-skinned' subjects with "curly hair" (Erjavec et al. 2000). The current editor of the Romani program on public radio thus testified to her "luck" to be more light-skinned that her fellow Roma and thus pass as being an immigrant from the Balkans. "In Slovenia, it is easier to be the 'čefur' [derogatory term for immigrants from ex-Yugoslavia] than a Gypsy," she says (*Žurnal* 2008, 12). In the early days of the transition, the "*čefurs*" were seen as the major threat to the processes of revitalizing the "authentic" cultural fiber of ethnic Slovenes. Lately, as it is demonstrated with the above quote, the role of the other has been passed onto the Roma. After the end of the ideology of the purification of Slovene identity from the Balkan influence, the Roma have been pushed to occupy the prime place in making a racial distinction between "us" and "them" and, in turn, provide the symbolic material for drawing actual boundaries of membership and (non-)belonging.

262 Ksenija Vidmar-Horvat

In short, the identity ascribed to the Roma has borrowed from culturally visible sites of what in fact are structurally imposed disadvantages. This negative politics of representing the Roma as the problem serves well the nationalist discourse which in post-socialist public culture, as I show below, has been involved in the construction of Slovene national identity as culturally superior and "free" of tensions involving ethnicity, race and other social markers of the collective subject.

NATIONALISM AND PUBLIC TELEVISION
IN POST-SOCIALIST SLOVENIA

To understand the role of Slovene public television in the production of the stigmatized image of the Roma, it is necessary to turn to both its structurally general as well as culturally specific involvement in the "nationalizing mission." Public television has been a chief nation-producing machine (Borcila 2004). National mass media, Volčič writes, "provide rhetorical space for nationalistic discourse, and with that, for the creation and re-construction of identities" (Volčič 2005, 288); in the age of electronic media, television stands at the vanguard of these processes. Observed from a historical perspective, however, Slovenian public television has played a rather ambiguous role in the nationalization of collective identity. In Tito's Yugoslavia, TVS was an important agent in furthering Slovenian national consciousness, as the first in 1968 to launch the news in Slovene, disobediently; yet, it was the last to recognize the full political implications of the late 1980s emancipatory struggle for national independence in the contexts of a post-socialist and multicultural European society. As Volčič notes, from the late 1980s and early 1990s, TVS systematically labored to nationalize its programming while hoping to reproduce its viewers as Slovenes. This was done by means of reproducing a primordial view of the nation's "essence"; and shown in the concern for bringing to light "Slovenian national cultural values, traditions and cultural heritage" (Volčič 2005, 296).

The quest was a media echo of the spread of a broader populist ideology of de-Balkanization. Struggling against the memory of being an ex-Yugoslav state, soon after the break-up of the federal state, Slovene populist nationalist political parties and intellectuals embraced the rhetoric of national revitalization by means of purifying Slovene cultural identity of the Balkan "other." Later, with the processes of joining the EU, the notion of de-Balkanization unfolded simultaneously with claiming European identity. Whereas the two discourses and their accompanying ideologies are sometimes hard to isolate, as regards TVS, the important side effect of this shared effort has been a narrow understanding of the role of public service in the democratization of public culture and the pluralization of national audiences.

Instead of embarking on a democratic media politics of (national) identity challenged by new processes of a ethno-cultural pluralization of

Racing for the Audience 263

the public, the public broadcaster turned to the role of a cultural outlet of exclusionary national homogenization and ethno-nationalization of its audience. In 2004, the situation at TVS worsened. The right-wing SDS, which won the national election, began a massive project of "balancing the media." In public, media balance was presented as opening the media space to the right-wing political agenda and political parties which, it was argued, under the previous rule of transitional post-communist elites, had suffered a long period of censorship and uneven representation in the news. As concerns the public broadcaster, the move to equilibrate the ideological landscape of the country was followed by the Law on TVS. The implementation of the law in 2005 first resulted in the removal of all key editors, and in a dramatic change in program politics that followed soon after. The "balance," as critics pointed out, was presented in the form of the promotion of the ideology of "nationalist fundamentalism." For the viewers, this meant the consumption of home-made documentary and entertainment programs of questionable value (Splichal and Hvala 2005). Several quality shows were cancelled while in the primetime slots, a new culture of low-brow, light entertainment was introduced.

THE REDEEMING PYRAMID

Ironically, as it turned out, the post-2005 editorial turn to balanced, "patriotic" broadcasting has significantly exhausted the loyalty of public television viewers; instead, they switched to commercial television. POP TV as the main competitor recorded the increase in audience in both news and entertainment programs.

The declining ratings soon became an ongoing source of frustration for the leadership and arguably stand as a chief cause behind the decision to introduce the new program *Pyramid* in the programming. Two facts support the claim. First, the show was placed in the programming on Tuesdays at 9 pm. This was the time slot when POP TV aired the highly popular, quality investigative magazine show *Verified!* (*Preverjeno!*). TVS aimed at the POP TV's audience by serving them an alternative in entertainment programming on its channel. Namely, *Pyramid*, originally licensed to the Croatian company Castor Multimedia, is a mimicry genre of a public forum in which different public figures discuss various issues in the nation's current social and political life. It is a mimicry because it is designed *qua* entertainment: it depends on the viewers who, via telephone voting, select the winner of the debate, which means that the guests discuss serious issues in the manner of a racing game. With a strange twist in understanding the role of public television, therefore, TVS decided to defeat serious programs offered by commercial TV in the primetime with the infotainment formula. Second, TVS selected as the host of the program Erika Žnidaršič, who at the time was a rising journalist star at POP TV. By bringing Žnidaršič to

264   *Ksenija Vidmar-Horvat*

the show, TVS used the media reputation of the presenter that was already created by commercial TV; this suggests a hope to bring with Žnidaršič her fans and, consequently, enlarge its own audience.

The media noticed the implied battle for the viewers by monitoring the ratings of the two shows. However, to the disbelief of many, already in the second week of the race, two national dailies published the figures which showed that *Pyramid* stayed behind *Preverjeno!* (Matejčič 2006). Then, a real-time event, occurring in the same month that the decline in ratings was made public, helped to overturn public TV's (mis)fortune. Namely, earlier that month, in Ambrus, a small community in south-central Slovenia, a rallying crowd of ethnic Slovenian villagers demanded the expulsion of the Roma Strojan family from their nearby settlement; in the view of the villagers, because of their criminal records and acts of daily terror, the adult Strojans presented an ongoing threat to the well-being of the community and their families. TVS followed the events with daily, sometimes also hourly news, as the drama, together with the expatriated Roma family, being refused the right to settle elsewhere, traveled around the country. On November 28, public television offered a temporary home to the Strojans in its *Pyramid* studio—not to discuss their trauma, but to engage them as the audience of the primetime info-entertaining program.

With the live broadcast of the show with the Strojans, TVS decided, in the words of the editor in chief, to contribute to the public's greater awareness of the problem which erupted with the Ambrus affair; but to tame a potentially "overheated debate," ("Statement" 2006) in their own words, the editors removed the topic from the discussion, offered members of the Strojan family to sit in the audience and invited a Roma representative, Zoran Grm, to appear on stage in their stead. Grm was accompanied in the studio with a young celebrity actress, Tina Gorenjak, and Zmago Jelinčič, the leader of the Slovenian Nationalist Party, SNS, also widely known for his Romaphobic speeches as a Member of Parliament. On that Tuesday night, the guests of the show were to discuss four topics: the right of the MP to immunity; the right to abortion (questioned earlier that month by the Minister of Family, Work and Social Affairs); the sexual conduct of youth in present-day Slovenia (triggered by an incident in a disco club); and the citizenship oath being debated at the time in Parliament. The Strojans, together with some Roma from other communities, observed the debate from the benches in the auditorium.

THE SCANDAL

In all four discussions, the standard stigma about Roma was reiterated. Already with the first topic, the right to immunity claim, Jelinčič seized upon the debate to single out the Roma as the group which should be scrutinized collectively for what, in the MP's view, constituted their undeserving

Racing for the Audience 265

place in the nation with respect to its legal and moral order. The point of departure for this first round of remarks was his opponent who, sentenced for illegal arms possession, held a criminal record. Built around statements like "the whole of Slovenia is under the influence of the Gypsies, who do nothing but damage"[1] or "we, Slovenians, are all good, diligent, laborious and honest whereas one could not say the same for the Gypsies," the MP demonstrated his well-trained Romophobic speech. Interestingly enough, this was done in complete omission of the fact that in their private histories, both male protagonists have encountered the repressive apparatus (hence, arguably, the selection of the topic and the guests), but whereas Grm actually served 26 months in prison, 12 times (!), Jelinčič used the right to immunity—for instance, to avoid prosecution for illegal use of weapon, drunk driving and driving an illegally parked car with blocked wheels—and thus has remained safely protected from *and* by the state.

The second topic of the discussion, which addressed youth sexual behavior, provided yet another ground for Jelinčič upon which to construct the Roma as the deviant other whose otherness was racially determined. The occasion that triggered public concern was an event in a disco club earlier that month, when a young girl got heavily drunk and was later sexually assaulted. However, while the event initiating the debate obviously concerned an ethnic Slovenian girl, the *Pyramid* debate soon became a public forum on family and sexual order in Roma homes, with Jelinčič staging himself as the savior of the nation's moral order. Asked about his own view on the question of sexual liberties among young people, Grm advocated openly the view that the young should "enjoy themselves"; without foreseeing the consequences of his naive openness, he admitted that his daughter "comes and leaves the home as she pleases." The advocacy of lax family rule triggered laughter in the audience; but when it was met with the MP's response later in the show, "that's why there are so many of you," it was no longer a laughing matter. On the contrary, considering not only recently articulated phobia about the decline of the "genetic stock" of ethnic Slovenians due to low birth rate, but also the discourse about "dark-skinned" Romani inhabitants growing in numbers (Erjavec et al. 2000, 22), Jelinčič may have struck a chord in tune with a broader expressions of Romophobia.

The next topic concerned the appropriateness of the new oath and its lengthy text. Jelinčič defended the oath as a vehicle of national glorification. Moreover, in his view, the long text was not only a proper container for the dissemination of "national pride"; the requirement that job applicants should speak the complicated text of initiation aloud in Slovene also, in his view, was a proper instrument of judging the worthiness of the applicant. When he asked whether "some" (pointing to the Roma in the audience) would be able to read the oath in Slovene at all, Jelinčič not only constructed the Roma as illiterate, but also made them appear undeserving of citizenship due to their poor grammar ("It should be said 'with foxes—not with foxis!'" Jelinčič at one point corrected Grm.) Objecting

266   *Ksenija Vidmar-Horvat*

to what, in his view, were overly liberal gestures of the new, independent state in the early 1990s, when citizenship "could be purchased for a price of a five-kilogram bag of potatoes," Jelinčič ignored the long history of Roma belonging to the Slovenian nation as well as the fact that, due to obligatory army service, Roma males, as Grm reminded him, took part both in the armed forces of Tito's Yugoslavia and in the Slovenian war for independence.

The overt Romophobic discourse articulated through the on-screen performance of the right-wing nationalist speaker mapped Slovenian national identity around the dichotomies of cultural difference and group identity. Jelinčič posited the Roma as homogeneously deviant and, with their sexual and family order, threatening to the moral fiber of the dominant ethnic group. His overtly racist speech split the audience along the irreconcilable lines of "us" versus "them." The viewers in the ethnic Slovenian homes were marked as no less collectively cohesive as the Roma on the other side of the divide, yet, in contrast to the latter, the former were also posited as culturally distant and normatively superior.

BELONGING, CITIZENSHIP AND GENDER

During the live broadcast, which lasted 50 minutes, and much to the delight of hostess Erika Žnidaršič, the telephones were "going wild." Public TVS got the attention which it so desired. By allowing Jelinčič to speak openly of the "Gypsies" and, in light of the events in Ambrus, of their threatening presence in the nation of the Slovenes, it opened up the space for the creation of its own media event. In the days to follow, the euphoria gave way to frustration and grief. Instead of celebrating the success, the leadership had to face accusations that, in its pursuit of high audience ratings, the public broadcaster gave in to racism and Romophobia. It turned out that, instead of avoiding the "overheated circumstances" that had paralyzed the country, the broadcast of *Pyramid* initiated its own national crisis.

It should be noted, though, that the ideological effect of racial othering was not the sole accomplishment of the Romaphobic guest. Indeed, watching the program several years later, what strikes one as a crucial yet largely overlooked aspect of the show is how the public at the time of the scandal tended to ignore the two female figures in the studio, while singling out the Romophobic MP and the Roma representative he victimized. Yet the gender composition of the infamous *Pyramid* calls for critical attention. In fact, it will be argued next that the spectacle of gender and sexuality, distributed in opposing pairs between the two men on the one hand, and the actress and the hostess of the program on the other hand, sheds light on how the creators of the show imagined the national community of its viewers before the drama in the studio ever began. The gender selection of the show's participants suggests that the televised image

Racing for the Audience   267

of the ethnic Slovene group's superiority was won not only through the force of the confrontational rhetoric of the MP. With their visual (bodily) choreography, the two women in the studio were employed precisely to contribute to the racial fashioning of the dominant imagined community and the conditions by which the boundaries of its national(ized) body were defined and confirmed.

At first glance, the presence of the two women in the studio appeared a refuge for the viewer, traumatized by the MP's show. As a participant in the TV forum, a well-known actress and frequent tabloid media star, Tina Gorenjak, played a role of the chief contestant to insult Jelinčič. Her frequent responses to the rude arguments and Romophobic expressions of her opponent structurally placed her in opposition and on the side of the "tolerant citizen." Moreover, raising firm protest against racist remarks, Gorenjak assumed the position of the multicultural citizen, a citizen who not only tolerates difference but recognizes it as a valuable feature of democracy. "We should not generalize," she argued against Jelinčič and his view on Roma's criminality. "I think that we could put it equally with respect to Slovenians that they are all the same—yet we are different." Moreover, she continued, "I think that we should understand that both of us, as well as these Roma here, [are] citizens of Slovenia, who have their rights [. . .]." This was voiced in sharp contrast to Jelinčič's expression of overt racism. As Richard Dyer (1997) argues, the operation of racism, which works in tandem with discourses on crime when the deprivileged are concerned, involves contrasting individual and group criminality. Whites' deviance is constructed as the expression of their individual diversity, which is tolerable if not acceptable: "White people in their whiteness [. . .] are imagined as individual and/or endlessly diverse, complex and changing" (Dyer 1997, 12). For non-whites, on the other hand, crime and deviance are always used as staples of group identity. In this regard, Jelinčič situated himself as an individual in the community that is, despite (or because of) his supposedly idiosyncratic criminal record, devoid of group pathology whereas, in accordance with Dyer's argument, the Roma collectively appeared as a crime-prone group through the figure of Zoran Grm.

Gorenjak, by pointing to individuality and diversity *within* groups, contested the simplified racism of Jelinčič. However, in the discussion on the text of the citizenship oath, which expanded the debate on citizenship to immigrants, she agreed with Jelinčič that rights come with duties: "I think that these people [immigrants] who obtain Slovenian citizenship, that they should be aware of what, as we stated before, are their rights and above all their duties!" The statement implied that new citizens needed to be taught the lessons of citizenship and that this should take place prior to assuming full membership and gaining acceptance by the host community.

The argumentation is both patronizing and subjugating. Duties of citizenship of course mean active participation in the social, political and cultural life of the national community. Yuval-Davis (1997) has argued that

268   Ksenija Vidmar-Horvat

"citizenship rights without obligations also construct people as passive and dependent" (92). Yet, before demanding that immigrants, and in our case, the Roma, embrace citizenship as both rights and duties, one should ask about structural conditions that enable one to fully participate in the community of citizens. Plainly, the principle of the universality of duties may work only in so far as the basic human and citizenship rights are universally assured; without this condition being fulfilled, the subjugated who lacks the means of observing the citizen's duties is destined to be criminalized by those who experience no such lack.

More to the point, the discourse of duties is based on the repression of the fact of the societal making of both "good" and "bad" citizens; repression is the key element in legitimating the exclusion that uses the argument of group criminality. It is important to note how women from the dominant ethnic group are regularly imbued with a prime role in the reproduction of the two categories of citizens. Svašek (2006) has pointed out how, after the collapse of communist regimes in Eastern Europe women celebrities have assumed an especially visible place in giving lessons of citizenship by which to differentiate between the good and bad members of the national community. Discussing the events in Ambrus, a Slovenian beauty contestant performed this role in an exemplary fashion. "If the laws are to be observed only by the ethnic community of Slovenes," Miss 2006 Hawaiian Tropic said in a public statement, "soon our young and beautiful state will become a gathering place of criminals, dropouts and other law-evading people, whose ethnicity is not Slovenian" (quoted in Miheljak, *Dnevnik*, 2006, 5). Returning to Gorenjak, her argument may not have been as explicit in depicting the threat of the ethnic other to the community of ethnically Slovene citizens; the drawing of boundaries between the ethnic "us," who automatically belong to the group of the dutiful by the virtue of ethnicity, and the "other" who, by the same virtue (or, rather, because of it), has no such fortune, nonetheless employed the same logic.

The theme of the threatening other resurfaced when addressing abortion rights. The heated debate actually began when Erika Žnidaršič, pointing to Grm, speculated aloud, "You, Roma are known to have lots of children." To be honest, with her statement, Žnidaršič subtly suggested that the Roma could be the key to solving the low fertility rate of the nation and, in this sense, placed herself in opposition to Jelinčič's argument as discussed above ("That's why there are that many of you [the Roma]"). However, the noble gesture notwithstanding, the invitation to the Roma to contribute to the nation's natality map is a prime case of covert racism. The projection of large Roma families onto the popular screens of imagining the the nation's reproduction and casting them as potential saviors of the nation is predicated on a disavowal of the fact that the Roma in Slovenia have *already* contributed to the nation's growth. When a bit later the Roma were also kindly compared to immigrants who, in the words of Žnidaršič, too, have "been known for their high fertility rate," the effect of estrangement from

Racing for the Audience 269

the national belonging was reinforced. Finally, when calling Grm and his Roma community "citizens of the world" and, in a separate discussion, interrogating Grm about his community's "relationship to the Slovenian state," Žnidaršič reiterated, in a "tolerant" manner, the racist exclusionary politics of imagining the nation and its other: a vision of the nation split along the lines of two separate entities, the host community and the outsider, where the Roma are moved to the realm of the other whose place on the map of national belonging is, *together with* the more recent immigration, yet to be negotiated.

MASCULINE VS. FEMININE PERFORMANCE OF NATIONALITY

The discussion presented so far demands a turn towards a closer inspection of the relationship between aggressive and polite racism as regards the Roma in Slovenia, and their joint ideological effect, through the lens of gender. Post-colonial feminist theory has made us aware of the interrelatedness between nationalism and gender and the role of the dominant ethnic group of women in the reproduction of social relations of power. Because women are seen as biological, cultural and symbolic reproducers of the nation (Yuval-Davis 1997), in modern Western patriarchal societies, family order and motherhood stand at the center of the reproduction of power, which always also includes privileges of ethnicity, class and race. The deployment of gender is omnipresent in the field of women's reproductive rights, especially as regards minority women. At the same time, the instrumentalization of gender (and sexuality) can also be observed as it orders the symbolic map of racism. As symbolic mothers of the nation, women play a central role in delineating spaces of national belonging but, due to the prescribed tasks of nurture and compassion, their involvement in racist ideologies is often disguised in mantles of tolerance and "understanding." In contrast, as warriors and bearers of the law, fathers represent the repressive and militant, non-compromising politics of belonging. Derived from this, brute and aggressive racism is represented as masculine, and gentle and tolerant, "inferential" racism stands as its feminine counterpart.

How was this feminine mode of racism evident in the *Pyramid* studio? Both female figures in the studio have been subject to publicity, mainly as icons of mainstream society and its celebrity culture. In addition, both have been frequent guests of tabloid media, targets of interest for both their sexual attractiveness and professional success. However, in contrast to Žnidaršič who has had a history of training in journalism and thus has had credits to host studio debates, such as *Pyramid*, Gorenjak has had no record of acquired professional skills to tackle hot social and political issues such as the citizenship oath and/or the sexual manners of the young—beside the skills of an ordinary citizen—her acting career and the tabloid career of the "party girl" notwithstanding. In fact, the latter "quality" exposed by the

270 *Ksenija Vidmar-Horvat*

gossip press may rather make her an improper candidate for the debate on the morals and manners of middle-class girls. However, it was the former quality, namely being a well-known actress, and, related to her celebrity profession, being generous to the media with her sexual appeal, which better matched the program design in which serious issues are played out as matters of entertainment. This warrants a reconsideration of Gorenjak's role of the tolerant citizen and, in addition to focusing on her discursive participation in the television forum, demands attention to the visual spectacle of the show in which the effect of her "tolerance" was produced.

Throughout the debate, the actress and the camera were involved in a visual interplay of mutual sexual attraction (repeated focus on the actress's cleavage and bare-footed legs by the camera, frequent direct and inviting eye contact with the camera lenses by the actress). Through this exchange of the looks, television made Gorenjak available to the (sexual) fantasies of the (implied male) audience. In the studio, however, the display of sexuality had a different symbolic target. In its visual-sexual layout, *Pyramid* reiterated the family scene with quarrelling sons and disciplining mothers. Not only Gorenjak but also Žnidaršič reprimanded Jelinčič for his *enfant terrible* behavior. On several occasions, Žnidaršič asked Jelinčič to be seated and, at one point, crossing her hands on the chest in the manner of an upset mother, she uttered in a most severe tone that, unless he stopped his stampede of insults she herself would not say another word—which, in turn, triggered a new wave of laughter on stage and in the audience.

In contrast, when addressing Grm, the two women avoided challenging his views openly—even when, for example, Grm's argument on the sexual upbringing of children, contained in the statement that "We have to enjoy things while still young" sharply contradicted the bourgeois code of the actress-mother advocating strictness, which, in her view, should be accompanied by "of course with love and understanding." Instead, the two women acted as his protectors, raising for him and the audience a symbolic defense wall against the verbal attacks of the violent white male. The differential address to the two males made Jelinčič and Grm symbolically into two kinds of sons, one in need of a (parental) lesson and one in need of (maternal) protection. The latter act of "tolerance" and understanding relegated Grm to the position of pre- or non-subject, an individual who has not reached a full social and political maturity to be able to speak for himself. Consequently, he also could not (yet) proceed to assume the future role of the father and therefore, to apply Freud's explanation of the working of the family romance between mothers and sons, could not make her mother sexually available to him.

This was not the case with the other "son" on the show. At one point in the debate, Jelinčič asked Gorenjak whether she wore silk underwear (a reference to the Minister of Family, who proposed abortion be payable and whose next step, in the MP's view, was likely to forbid women from

Racing for the Audience 271

wearing silk underwear). Gorenjak replied with coquettish amusement, "I frequently wear none, just in case." Later on, Gorenjak and Jelinčič also found themselves in a friendly exchange of compliments regarding their respective (in both cases younger than themselves) romantic partners. Being assigned to the position of a male subject not able to provide for the national family, Grm was excluded from both debates.

CONCLUSION

Whiteness, Dyer writes, "has been enormously, often terrifyingly effective in unifying coalitions of disparate groups of people. It has generally been much more successful than class in uniting people across cultural differences and against their best interests" (Dyer 1997, 19). To this, critical feminists add that we need to recognize how "white femininity constitutes the locus through which borders of race, gender, sexuality, and nationality are guarded and secured" (Shome 2001, 323; see also Banet-Weiser 1999, Minh-ha 1989, Yuval-Davis 1997). How can this post-colonial theoretical legacy be incorporated into studying mass media in post-socialism? Is it even possible to conceptualize the studio debate of the particular *Pyramid* show as a case of "racial coalition" between the whites on the show (and at home), built by either means of tolerance or violence around the exclusion of the other, the Roma in the studio, and in the country? Is it proper at all to employ the notion of whiteness in the culture with no colonial experience and whose collective identity rests on pillars of ethnicity rather than race? Should the *Pyramid* program not be treated as a case of ethnocentric nationalism, rather than of racism?

In my analysis, I investigated the notorious *Pyramid* show and its televisual structuring of the relationship between gender and the national subject through the contrasting representation of the Roma, and their combined placement in the construction of visual and verbal sites of national identification. Moreover, a theoretical challenge of this paper has been to address the question of how gender has been instrumental in the reproduction of racism in post-socialism. This, in my view, is an important aspect, given that in post-socialist feminist and gender studies (Gal and Kligman 2000, Wilford and Miller 1998), questions of race have been rather overlooked. Moreover, the post-colonial perspective informs us that whereas the "privilege" of reproducing the nation is used to keep women in the place of sexual subordination, by virtue of their structural positioning, white women are nonetheless "privileged and oppressive vis-à-vis non-white people" (Dyer 1997, 30). As the case of *Pyramid* shows, white women may not only be involved in the polite modes making racial subjects, they also can be quite "motherly" in the way mothers and fathers of underprivileged groups are being cast onto the national screens of the patriarchally imagined community as a racial other.

272 Ksenija Vidmar-Horvat

In order to understand processes of ethnic homogenization and attempts at exclusionary renationalization in post-socialist societies of Europe, I will thus conclude by arguing that the notions of race and whiteness need to be incorporated in critical post-socialist theory as its vital concepts. Critical investigation of polite, tolerant, even tolerable racism is crucial to understanding new articulations in which citizenship, belonging and membership are negotiated in the post-socialist world. Postcolonial theory has paved the way in illuminating the shift from crude biological to non-racist cultural racism, which defines the present-day discourse of national belonging. From the perspective of a post-socialist society, it is imperative to also include in this consideration the role of gender, and, given the legacies of socialist feminism, which emphasize the liberation of women from the confines of family and motherhood, ask about the role of white women in the construction of "non-whites" by means of placing them on the side of the other of the national family in post-socialism.

Anticipating further crises of national media, and their quest to take part in the race for commercialization and tabloidization of their contents, it is quite likely that post-socialist viewers are about to see more of this kind of racing with women.

NOTES

1. All the quotes are taken from the *Pyramid*, aired on 28 November 2006, author's copy. The show has since been removed from the TVS video archives.

REFERENCES

Banet-Weiser, Sarah. 1999. *The Most Beautiful Girl in the World: Beauty Pageants and National Identity*. Berkeley, CA: University of California Press.
Borcila, Andaluza. 2004. "How I Found Eastern Europe: Televisual Geography, Travel Sites, and Museum Installations." In *Over the Wall/After the Fall: Post-Communist Cultures through an East–West Gaze*, edited by Sibelan Forrester, Magdalena Zaborowska and Elena Gapova, 42–64, Bloomington and Indianapolis: Indiana University Press.
Brizani, Enisa. 2008. "Intervju" ["Interview"], *Žurnal*, 5.4.: 12.
Downing, John and Charles Husband. 2005. *Representing 'Race': Racism, Ethnicities and Media*. London: Sage.
Dyer, Richard. 1997. *White*. London: Routledge.
Erjavec, Karmen, Sandra Hrvatin Bašić and Bojana Kelbl. 2000. *We About the Roma: Discriminatory Discourse in the Media in Slovenia*. Ljubljana: Peace Institute.
Fiske, John. 1996. *Media Matters: Race and Gender in U.S. Politics*. Minneapolis, MN: University of Minnesota.
Gal, Susan and Gail Kligman. 2000. *The Politics of Gender After Socialism: A Comparative Historical Essay*. Princeton: Princeton University Press.
Hall, Stuart. 1990. "The Whites of Their Eyes: Racist Ideologies and the Media." In *The Media Reader*, edited by Manuel Alvarado and John Thompson, 8–23. London: British Film Institute.

Racing for the Audience 273

Klopčič, Vera. 2002. *Evropa, Slovenija in Romi (Europe, Slovenia and the Roma)*. Ljubljana: Inštitut za narodnostna vprašanja.

Klopičič, Vera. 2007. *Položaj Romov v Sloveniji (Situation of Roma in Slovenia)*. Ljubljana: Inštitut za narodnostna vprašanja.

Kuhar, Roman. 2006. "Media for Citizens." In*Media for Citizens*, edited by Petković, Brankica, Bašić-Hrvatin, Sandra, Kučić, Lenart J., Jurančič, Iztok, Prpič, Marko, Kuhar, Roman,123–172. Ljubljana: Peace Institute.

Matejčič, Katarina. 2006. "*Preverjeno!* povozilo *Piramido*" [*"Preverjeno!* Run Over the *Pyramid.*" http://www.finance.si/167656/Preverjeno-povozilo-Piramido.9.11. 2006.

Miheljak, Vlado. 2006. "I Feel Slovenia." *Dnevnik*, 15.11. 2006: 5.

Minh-ha, Trinh T. 1989. *Woman, Native, Other: Writing Postcoloniality and Feminism*. Bloomington and Indianapolis: Indiana University Press.Petković, Brankica. 2002. "Romi v Sloveniji—Tujci za vedno?" ("Roma in Slovenia– Foreigners for Ever?"). *Poročilo skupine za spremljanje nestrpnosti (Intolerance Monitor Report)*, Ljubljana: Mirovni inštitut.

Shome, Raka. 2001. "White Femininity and the Discourse of the Nation: Re/Membering Princess Diana." *Feminist Media Studies* 1(3): 323–342.

Splichal, Slavko and Ivan Hvala. 2005. *For Public Television*. Ljubljana: Občanski forum.

"Statement on the *Pyramid* by the TVS Management." http://www.rtvslo.si/slovenija/vodstvo-tv-slovenija-o-piramidi/63615; 29.11.2006.

Svašek, Maruša, ed. 2006. Postsocialism: *Politics and Emotions in Central and Eastern Europe*. New York and Oxford: Berghan Books.

Van Dijk, Teun A. 1993. *Elite Discourse and Racism*. London: Sage.

Vidmar-Horvat, Ksenija. 2005. "Evropa na televiziji." In *Za javno Radiotelevizijo Slovenije* ["Europe on Television."In *For Public Television]*,, edited by Slavko Splichal and Ivan Hvala, 44–49. Ljubljana: Občanski forum.

Vidmar-Horvat, Ksenija. 2006 "Strah pred multikulturalizmom: Primer bršljinske zgodbe." ["Fearing Multiculturalism: The Case of the Bršljin Story."] *Teorija in praksa* 43(3–4): 567–585.

Vidmar-Horvat, Ksenija, Miro Samardžija and Julija Sardelić. 2008. "Balancing the Roma Voice: The Ambrus Drama and Media Construction of Intercultural Dialogue in Slovenia." *In The Future of Intercultural Dialogue in Europe : Views From the In-between*, edited by Ksenija Vidmar-Horvat, 153–171. Ljubljana: Faculty of Arts Publishing.Vidmar-Horvat, Ksenija. 2009."Romani Women, Motherhood and National Identity in Media Discourse in Slovenia : The Case of 'Mamma Jelka'." In *Media Landscapes in Transition : Changes in Media Systems, Popular Culture and Rhetoric of Post-Communist Era*, edited by Škerlep, Andrej, Jontes, Dejan, Tomanić Trivundža, Ilija, Turnšek, Maja, 167–180. Ljubljana: Slovene Communication Association.

Volčič, Zala. 2005. "'The Machine that Creates Slovenians': The Role of Slovenian Public Broadcasting in Re-Affirming and Re-Inventing the Slovenian National Identity." *National Identities*, 7(3), 287–308.

Yuval-Davis, Nira. 1997. *Gender and Nation*. London: Sage.

Will, Guy, ed. 2001. *Between Past and Future: The Roma of Central and Eastern Europe*. University of Hertfordshire Press.

Wilford, Rick and Robert L. Miller. 1998. *Women, Ethnicity and Nationalism: The Politics of Transition*. London: Routledge.

Contributors

Alice Bardan holds a Ph.D from the University of Southern California, Los Angeles. She has taught writing and film courses at the University of Southern California, California State University, Fullerton, and at Boston University's Los Angeles Internship Program. Her articles have appeared in the edited collections *Transnational Feminism in Film and Media* (Palgrave 2007), *Branding Post-Communist Nations* (Routledge 2012), and in the peer-edited journals *New Cinemas: Journal of Contemporary Film (2008)*, *Flow* (2010) and *Popular Communication* (2012). She has forthcoming essays in *Popular Television in Central and Eastern Europe: Entertaining a New Europe* (Routledge 2012), *Not Necessarily the News? News Parody and Political Satire Around the Globe* (Routledge 2012), *Transnational European Cinemas (LIT 2012)* and *Italian Migration and International Cinema* (Cambridge Scholars Publishing 2012).

Evelyn Bottando is a Ph.D. candidate in communication studies at the University of Iowa. Her research interests include media globalization, political economy of media and new media. She is currently completing research on a project examining the response of the French government to Google's efforts to digitize French libraries. Her work has been presented at numerous national and international conferences, including the National Communication Association and the International Communication Association.

Ferenc Hammer, Ph.D., is an Assistant Professor at ELTE University's Institute for Art Theory and Media Studies (Budapest) and publishes in the fields of media studies and material culture.

Radim Hladík is a postdoctoral researcher in the Institute of Philosophy at the Academy of Sciences of the Czech Republic in Prague. In his dissertation he focused on the conjunctures of media and memory studies with regard to media representations of the socialist past. In 2009–10 he was a Fulbright scholar at Columbia University in the City of New York.

276 Contributors

Kateřina Gillárová is a PhD. student and instructor in Sociology at Charles University in Prague. She received her M.A. in Media Studies from the Institute of Communication Studies and Journalism at Charles University in Prague. Her Ph.D. project focuses on teenage group communication in the context of contemporary network society. She also works in marketing research, where her main interest lies in ethnographic research.

Katja Kochanowski is a Ph.D. fellow at Martin-Luther-Universität Halle-Wittenberg, Germany, where she studies television use among working-class families in the former German Democratic Republic. She has published research on East German television in a recent monograph and two edited anthologies.

Sabina Mihelj is Senior Lecturer in Media, Communication and Culture in the Department of Social Sciences at Loughborough University, UK. She is the author of *Media Nations: Communicating Belonging and Exclusion in the Modern World* (2011), co-editor of *Central and Eastern European Media in Comparative Perspective: Politics, Economy, Culture* (2012, with J. Downey) and has published a wide range of journal articles and book chapters on media and nationalism, religion and the new media, cosmopolitanism, European communication, comparative media research and Cold War culture.

Dana Mustata is an assistant professor in the Department Journalism Studies and Media at Groningen University, The Netherlands. Her research looks at constructions of agency within Romanian television before and after 1989 and investigates the modernizing, subversive or conservative performances of the medium in the arena of political power. It argues for television as a historically contingent medium, stepping away from discourses conceiving of television as being inherently modernizing. Concomitantly, she is a researcher on the European projects "Video Active: Creating Access to Europe's Television Heritage" and "EUScreen: Providing Access to Audiovisual Heritage"; and a member of the European Television History Network.

Dorota Ostrowska's research interests are in interdisciplinary approaches to film production, film industry and film culture; French cinema and criticism; the history of television in Europe; Eastern European cinema and visual culture. She is a lecturer of film and media studies at Birbeck College, University of London. She is the author of *Reading the French New Wave: Critics, Writers and Art Cinema in France* (2008) and coeditor of *European Cinemas in the TV Age* (2007).

Irena Carpentier Reifová is a lecturer and researcher at Charles University in Prague, Faculty of Social Sciences; Department of Media Studies. She teaches courses on critical media theories, cultural studies and media audiences. Her major scholarly interests are in television and popular culture with a focus on Czechoslovak and Czech serial television fiction. She was an editor of the journal *Media Studies* and sat on editorial board of the film studies journal *Iluminace* until 2010.

Adina Schneeweis is an Assistant Professor of journalism and media studies in the Department of Communication and Journalism at Oakland University. Her research is on contemporary and politicized constructions of (Gypsy/Roma) race and ethnicity, positioned at the intersection of international mass communication, cultural studies, and postcolonial studies. Her work has been published in the *International Communication Gazette, Journal of Visual Literacy, Intercultural Communication Studies, Ecquid Novi* and *Journalism & Mass Communication Quarterly*. A native of Romania, Schneeweis was a documentary writer, reporter, editor, and producer, creating 53 documentaries for a national public television station.

Sylwia Szostak is a Ph.D. candidate in the University of Nottingham's Department of Culture, Film and Media. Her research examines the impact of international media flows on Polish television in the post-Soviet era, with particular attention to the influence of American fiction television. Her work has also appeared in the *Journal of European Television History and Culture*.

Matthew S. Thatcher is an Assistant Professor of Communication Studies at Arkansas State University. His research interests include health communication and computer-mediated communication. He has professional experience in the health-related industry and has published and presented papers in a variety of national and regional publications and conferences.

Annabel Tremlett is a Senior Lecturer at the University of Portsmouth, UK. Her research interests include looking at the way minority groups are represented in European contexts, both in public discourses and local practices. She is an ethnographer with particular experience of working with Roma minorities in Hungary including over six years of in-depth experience in community projects and 15 months of ethnographic fieldwork. She has published in a variety of journals and books on researching marginalised minorities, from the use of visual representations to the politics of popular culture.

Sascha Trültzsch is an Assistant Researcher in the Department of Communication Studies at the University of Salzburg, Austria. His research on East German television has appeared in numerous edited anthologies.

278 *Contributors*

His recent monograph was published by VS Verlag, Wiesbaden. He is also coeditor of the anthology *Popular Culture and Fiction in Four Decades of East German Television* (2009).

Ksenija Vidmar-Horvat is a Professor at the Department of Sociology, Faculty of Arts, University of Ljubljana, Slovenia. Her research interests are in the sociology of culture, global media, Europe, gender, postsocialism and cultural diversity. Her most recent publications include "The Globalization of Gender: *Ally McBeal* in Post-Socialist Slovenia" (*European Journal of Cultural Studies*, 2005: 2); reprinted in Charlotte Brundson, and Lynn Spigel (eds.), *Feminist Television Criticism* (2007); with Denis Mancević, "Global News, Local Views: Slovene Media Reporting on 9/11" (in Tomasz Pludowski (ed.), *Global Media Reactions to September 11*, , 2007); with Gerard Delanty, "Mitteleuropa and the European Heritage," *European Journal of Social Theory*, 2008, 11 (2); and "Consuming European Identity: The Inconspicuous Side of Consumerism in the EU," *International Journal of Cultural Studies*, 2009, 13 (1).

Reinhold Viehoff is Dean of the Faculty of Philosophy and Professor of Communication at Martin-Luther-Universität Halle-Wittenberg. From 2003–08, he was the speaker for a research project on the history of East German television funded by the German Research Foundation. He is the author of several articles on entertainment and television that have appeared in edited anthologies in both German and English, as well as coauthor of the book *Geschichte im Fernsehen* (2007).

EDITOR BIOGRAPHIES

Timothy Havens is an Associate Professor of Television and Media Studies in the Department of Communication Studies and the Program in African American Studies at the University of Iowa. His research explores the intersections between cultural and economic practices in media globalization, particularly the ways in which racial and ethnic differences shape cultural flows. He is the author of *Black Television Travels: Race, Media, and Globalization* (2010) and *Global Television Marketplace* (2006), and a former Senior Fulbright Scholar to Hungary. His research has also appeared in *Communication, Culture & Critique, Critical Studies in Media Communication, The Journal of Broadcasting & Electronic Media, International Communication Gazette* and *Global Media Journal*; as well as in several anthologies of media globalization and television studies.

Anikó Imre is an Associate Professor in the Critical Studies and Interdivisional Media Arts and Practice Ph.D. Programs in the School of

Cinematic Arts of the University of Southern California. Her research has focused on Eastern European media cultures in relation to globalization and Europeanization. She is the author of *Identity Games: Globalization and the Transformation of Post-Communist Media Cultures* (2009), editor of *East European Cinemas* (Routledge, 2005) and the *Blackwell Companion to East European Cinemas* (2012), and coeditor of *Transnational Feminism in Film and Media* (2007) as well as special issues of the *European Journal of Cultural Studies* on "Media Globalization and Post-Socialist Identities" and of *Feminist Media Studies* on "Transcultural Feminist Mediations." She is coeditor of the Palgrave book series Global Cinemas and is an advisory board member of the journal *Studies in East European Cinema.*

Katalin Lustyik is an Assistant Professor of Media Studies at the School of Communication of Ithaca College, U.S. and a Regional Visiting Fellow at the Institute of European Studies at Cornell University, U.S. Her research and teaching interests include children's media, television studies, media globalization and international communication. Her publications on children's television in Eastern Europe, global youth culture, primetime animation and transnational children's media have appeared in book collections and academic journals. She is currently completing a coauthored book with Dr. Norma Pecora on the business of children's entertainment with Lexington Press. She is the North American Book Reviews Editor of the *International Journal of Media and Cultural Politics* published by Intellect.

Index

A

Adventures of Sir Lancelot, The 17
advertising 28, 118, 123, 127, 129,
    161, 162, 171, 180, 181, 183,
    189
Aczél, György, 107, 229
Aiello, Giorgia 125
Albania 34, 35, 185
allegory 76, 77
Alternatywy 4 65–80
Arion, Anca 55
Aubry, Patrice 125
audience research 17, 52
Audiovisual Media Services Directive.
    See Television Without Frontiers
Australia 130, 137
Austria 18
*Aventurile lui Val Vartej (The Adven-
    tures of the Val Vartej Crew)* 53

B

Bakhtin, Mikhail 66, 69, 70
Bareja, Stanisław 65–80
BBC 16, 20, 21, 51–52, 58, 133
Beatles and Others, The 17
Berlin Wall 57
Bertelsmann 127
Beverly Hills 90210 15
Bewitched 17
Big Brother 241
    Big Brother, Fratele cel Mare 181
"Block of Flats" Genre 65, 76–77
Bonanza 17
Bonfires of Kapela, The 19
Böröcz, József 127
Bosnia and Herzegovina 116
Bratescu, Florin 55
Broadcasting flow, 6, 159
Britain. See United Kingdom (UK)

Brookside 237
Brucan, Silviu 50–51
Bulgaria 15, 16, 21
Burgelman, Jean-Claude 127
Budapest 27, 58, 113, 114, 120, 122,
    155, 158, 220, 225, 226, 235,
    239, 240, 254, 256, 275

C

cabaret 65, 66, 69–73
Cairo International Festival of Televi-
    sion Films 49
Canada 130, 137
Canal Plus 127
Canzonissima 53
carnivalesque 66, 69–70
Cartoon Network 113, 116, 117
Ceausescu, Nicolae 52, 55–56, 57, 59,
    62
censorship 67
Česk Televize (Czech Television) 206
Charles de Gaulle 23
Chello Central Europe 117
children's media, children's television
    105-
Cinema of Moral Disquiet 72
Citizenship 268
CNN 58
Cojocaru, Virgil 52
Cold War 3, 6, 13–15, 20, 21, 25, 26,
    47
collective memory 200
Coman, Mihai 126
Coronation Street 237
Cuba, 89–91, 93–95, 98
cultural memory 5
Czech Republic 116, 201-, 242, 132
Czech Television. See Česk Televize
Czechoslovakia 15, 18, 19

282 Index

Czterdziestolatek 69, 75–76

D

Dallas 15, 58–59, 125
David Copperfield 16
democracy 13, 27, 59, 61, 121, 122, 141,
    147, 154, 184, 220, 223, 225,
    232, 234–236, 258, 260, 267
Dennis the Menace 16
deregulation 25
Deutche Welle 58
Die Lieben Mitmenschen
Dietl, Jaroslav 19
Dimitriu, Stefan 55
Dislocation (by Laclau) 204–5
Disney 17, 113, 116, 117, 121, 122,
    138, 229
Disneyland 17
distribution 45, 159, 190, 216, 236,
Dobranocka 165, 166
Dumitrescu, Carmen 55
Duna TV (Hungary) 128, 136–137
Dynasty 15
Dziennink Telewizyjny 164

E

East Germany (See German Demo-
    cratic Republic) 9, 19, 21–23,
    28, 34, 81, 86–88, 91, 94, 96,
    99, 106
EastEnders 222, 225
edutainment 5, 30–33, 35, 37, 39, 41,
    43, 45, 46
Ellis, John 48, 53, 61, 62
Else De Bens 21
Elsner, Monika 50
Endemol 178, 179, 189
entertainment 13–21, 23–25, 27,
    29–35, 37, 39, 40, 41, 43–45,
    51, 68, 71, 81, 82, 84, 85,
    92, 101, 107, 111, 116, 119,
    121, 141–145, 147, 154, 155,
    163–165, 167, 170, 178–180,
    191–193, 196, 197, 227, 228,
    251, 257, 263, 270, 278, 279
E.R 15
Esti Mese ("Evening Tale") 109
ethnographic interview 245;
    ethnographic research 252
European Broadcasting Union (EBU)
    58
European Union (EU) 232,
    EU Enlargement 127; EU Commis-
    sion 252

Eurovision 241

F

family series 81, 82, 83, 86, 99
Federal Republic of Germany 18, 21,
    23, 24
Fedorowicz, Jacek 71
Fiske, John 260
Flenley, Paul 47
Folk culture 31, 32, 37, 39
Forsyth Saga 16, 23
France 21, 23, 24

G

Garantat 100% 141–158
Gdańsk 67, 73
genre 19, 53, 56, 65–66, 69, 134–135
Gender 25, 25, 39. 195, 247, 249–251,
    257, 259, 260, 266, 269,
    271–273, 278
German Democratic Republic 15, 18,
    19, 21
Germany 130–131, 133–135
Gheorghiu-Dej, Gheorghe 50
Gillard, Frank 51
globalization 9, 103, 121, 122, 173,
    186, 195–198, 222, 252, 257,
    275, 278, 279
Gorale 40, 41
Gruza, Jerzy 71
Győzike 241
Gypsy (see Roma) 186, 187, 197,
    237, 238, 241, 244, 246,
    247–250, 252, 253, 256–258,
    261, 277

H

Habsburg Empire 36
Hallstein Doctrine 85, 87, 91
high culture 38, 39, 44, 243
historical drama series 31
historiographic continuity 214
Hall, Stuart 259
Hollywood 136
Honecker, Erich 18
Hong Kong 130
Horváth, Ádám 224, 226
Hospital on the Edge of Town 19
Hot Wind 19
Hungarian National Radio and Televi-
    sion Commission (ORTT) 106,
Hungarian Television (MTV) 106,
    109–112, 222, 228, 239, 128,
    133, 136–137

Index 283

Hungary 16, 21, 105–119, 222-, 242, 123–140

I

Iliescu, Ion 61
Intervision 107, 132
Ionita, Bujor 52
Ireland 21
Italy 21, 23–24, 130, 132, 133–135

J

Jabukowicz, Karol 126–127
Jameson, Fredric 202
Janosik 32, 37–44, 46
Japan 24
Jetix Europe 113
Jumbo 17

K

Kádár, János 222, 228
Kees Brants 21
Kieślowski, Krzysztof 71
Kruschev, Nikita 16
kuruc 38, 43, 44

L

Latey, M.B. 51
Latin American 130, 133
Lazar, Diana 60
Lazarov, Valeriu 49
Leonid Brezhnev 18, 20
Lévi-Strauss, Claude 5
Liberty Global 116
Lord John Reith 21
Lubelski, Tadeusz 71

M

Mai aveti o intrebare? (Do You Still Have a Question?) 49
Małżeństwo doskonałe 71–72
Mayer, Francoise 201
Media imperialism 124–128
Media Law of 1996 (in Hungary), 109
Media policy 32, 121, 127, 155, 158
MEDIA Programme 126
Mickey Mouse 113, 229
Mickey Mouse Club .17
Mickiewicz, Ellen P. 64
Minimax 114–116
miniseries 19
Miś 72
Miss Fata de la ţară (Miss Country Girl)
Mleczko, Andrzej 73

mnemonic devices 200, 213
Moldova 116
Monte Carlo International Television Festival 49
Montenegro 116
MTV (Music Television) 252
Muller, Thomas 50
musicals 49
national identity 4, 24
nationality 269

N

NATO 66, 85, 153–155, 230–233, 272
NBC 20
Neighbors (Szomszedok) 222
neoliberal 252
neoimperialism 127
news 13, 14, 18, 34, 40, 44, 45, 49, 50, 56, 57, 58, 61, 68, 71, 81, 85, 105, 107, 109, 115, 116, 121, 123, 142, 143, 146, 147, 151, 154–156, 158, 162–169, 173, 180, 182, 183, 223, 228, 230, 231–233, 236, 254, 262–264, 275, 278
Nickelodeon 114
Noam, Eli 47
Norway 21
nostalgia (see also cultural memory) 9, 32, 78, 109, 112, 154, 184, 199–203, 211, 205, 210, 211, 218, 220, 221, 223

O

Omul din umbra la soare (The Shadow Man in the Sun) 49
Omul si Camera (The Man and the Camera) 49
Organisation Internationale de Radiodiff usion et de Télévision (OIRT) 57, 58
Orwell, George 179, 191, 193
Osbournes, The 243
Ottoman Empire 36
Our Small Town 19

P

patriotism 141–145, 147, 149, 151, 154, 155, 157, 158
Passendorfer, Jerzy 38
Paulu, Burton 47
Pauwels, Caroline 127
Petrut, Catinca Ralea 52
Peyton Place 16

284   *Index*

Płoński, Jan 65, 72–73
Poland 116
Poland 15, 17, 18, 21, 65–80
political commentary 239
political education 239
Poltel 66
Polsat 160–162, 167–173
Pomarańczowa Alternatywa (Orange Alternative) 66, 69, 70, 74–75
POP TV (Slovenia) 263
Popescu, Dumitru 55
popular television 9, 11, 14, 19, 25, 26, 101, 112, 199, 218, 175
Portugal 21
postcolonial theory 272
post-socialist collective memory 200, 217
post-socialist nostalgia 202, 218
Prague International Television Festival 49
Prague Spring 210
preventive continuity 214
Preverjeno! (Verified!) 163, 264, 273
Prima TV 145, 146, 181, 181–183, 186, 187, 241
private television, 21–23, 25, 135–137
propaganda 56, 68, 69, 70, 75
ProsiebenSat1 127
Pub of 13 Chairs, The 19
public service television, 21–23, 25, 135–137
Pyramid 259

Q
quiz show 60

R
racism 267
Radio Free Europe 56, 228
Radio Luxemburg 228
Reagan, Ronald 13, 25
reality television 241
Reflector 53, 54–56, 57
Reuters, Thomson 58
Robingo 60
Robin Hood 33, 40
Rodzina Leśniewskich 69
Roma (Gypsy) 4–5, 237, 241–257
   Gypsy 241–257, 259; Romaphobia 265
Romania 16, 116, 47–64, 229
Romanian Revolution 143
Romanienko, Lisiunia 75
RTL-Klub (RTL Group) 109–112, 241, 243, 128
Rybiński, Maciej 65, 72–73

S
satellite 15, 25, 32, 34, 45, 58, 64, 87, 107, 116, 122, 125, 139, 164, 179
Satra 186, 196, 197
scheduling 54–56, 126
   scholarship 9, 47, 48, 62
Seara televiziunii fi nlandeze (The evening of Finnish Television) 53
secret police 67
Serbia 16, 17–18,
Seventeen Moments of Spring 19
Shein, Hagi 127
sitcom 31, 112, 114
Skempton, A.S.W. 52
Slovakia 116
Slovenia 33, 34, 36, 46, 58, 113, 116, 189, 259–262, 264–269, 272, 273, 278
Soap opera 15, 31, 66, 112, 143, 146, 177, 222, 225, 228, 239, 240, 255, 256
Solidarity (Polish Trade Union) 65, 66, 67, 69, 73, 74, 75, 77
Soviet Union 15, 16, 18, 21
Spangenberg, Peter M. 50
Sputnik 34
Stark, Alexandru 55
state socialism 121, 199, 202, 203, 204, 216, 218, 219, 251
surveillance 30, 67, 172, 178, 191–193, 196, 197
Stalin, Josef
Stefanescu, Catalin 141, 145, 155, 158
Szczepański, Maciej 75

T
talk show 59–60
taste 9, 15, 21, 23, 24, 35, 56, 71, 228, 244
Telecinemateca 53
Teleenciclopedia 53
Teleschool 54
Television Without Frontiers Directive 123–124, 129, 133, 137–138
television
   imports 14–17, 20, 24, 28, 30, 111, 123–125, 128–137, 160
   policy 13, 24, 26, 32, 34, 47, 68, 69, 88, 91, 96, 98, 105, 120, 121, 124, 126, 127, 139, 155, 158, 173, 227–229
   history 13–15, 20, 25–29, 31, 32, 37, 39, 41–43, 46, 48, 56, 57,

Index   285

61, 62, 64, 67, 68, 74, 78–80, 83, 96, 120, 121, 124, 150, 154, 156, 158, 162, 172, 179, 191, 197, 198, 201, 202, 205, 214, 218, 220, 221, 225, 232, 230, 256, 257, 266, 269, 276–278
A Tenkes kapitanya 32, 37, 46
Tévé Maci 109, 118
Thatcher, Margaret 25
Theater in the House 19
Theodorescu, Razvan 60
Thirty Adventures of Major Zeman, The 19
Time Warner 113
transition culture 203
trauma, 200;
  cultural trauma 200, 203-, 214
Treffpunkt Flughafen 93
TV Belgrade 16
TV Ljubljana 16
TVP1 (Telewizja Polska) 160–172
TV Polonia 164, 165
TVR1 145, 146, 155, 156
TV Slovenia (TVS) 267
TV2 (ProsiebenSat1) 109–112, 128
Tym, Stanisław 72

U
Ukraine 24
United Kingdom, The (UK) 23, 24,116, 253, 133
utopia 21, 30, 34, 202, 222–225, 227, 229, 231, 233–235, 237, 239

V
Valeriu, Emanuel 60
Varieties Programme 53
Veliki Brat (Big Brother) 180
Viacom 113
Vietnam 94, 95, 98
Violetta Buhl 66, 68
Voice of America 228
Vypravěj (Tell Me How It Was) 205–218

W
Walt Disney Presents Duck Tales 113
Warsaw 65, 68, 74, 76
Westerns 38, 39, 41, 46
West Germany. See Federal Republic of Germany
Wiadomości (News) 163–165, 168, 171, 173
Woman at the Counter, The 19
World Report 57
Writers Guild of America 194

Y
Yugoslavia 16, 19, 21, 23, 24, 267
  Post-Yugoslavia 260
  Youth programming 108

Z
Zanussi, Krzysztof 71
Žnidaršič, Erika 266
Zmiennicy 68
Zorro 17
Zur See 84, 88–90, 93, 99, 100